essential communication

THIRD EDITION

Getting the Most Out of This Book

You are about to explore communication in a variety of situations—online, in person, at home, at work, and during intercultural experiences, to name a few. Along the way, you will have the opportunity to try out communication strategies and see which work best for you.

It's a journey worth taking. As you'll learn here, employers consider good communication skills a must-have for new hires and successful team members. And they aren't the only ones. Listening and supportive communication are among the most desired qualities in friends and romantic partners.

Given that what you learn here can improve your personal life and career success, here are three tips for getting the most from this book.

Don't skip anything.

This isn't your ordinary textbook. For one thing, we have zeroed in on the fundamentals, so this book is shorter than most. For another, chapter elements in the print book look more like magazine stories than traditional texts. So how do you know what is essential and what is extra? In this book, *everything* is essential and nothing is extra. Key words and theories appear in unexpected places, such as question-and-answer features and *Tips & Reminders*. The result is an unconventional experience that feels like pleasure reading but provides the deep-level learning of a traditional text.

Apply concepts to your own life.

As you read, reflect on how you can enhance your communication skills. Self-quizzes in *About You* segments provide insights about your communication strengths and challenges. *Pause to Reflect* and *Putting It All Together* features invite you to apply what you're learning to real-life situations. And throughout the book, we provide handy information in the form of *Tips & Reminders* and *Communication Take-Aways*.

Be receptive to new ideas.

If you are open to trying, this book will help you discuss important topics with other people—even topics that may make you feel uncomfortable. You will learn what to do (and not to do) when talking about race, ethnicity, gender, and politics in order to foster mutual understanding, sincere interest, curiosity, and open-mindedness with your conversational partners. You'll also pick up some tips for making friends with people from a diverse array of cultures and backgrounds.

The bottom line is that every element in this book is loaded with essential information that can help you become a better communicator. Let's get started!

Brief Contents

Contents

New to the Third Edition

An essential part of effective communication involves listening to and learning from one another in a world that's quickly changing. The third edition of *Essential Communication* excels in its coverage of diversity, social media, and career success. In this edition you'll find:

- new features on talking about race and gender, avoiding microaggressions, and making friends with diverse groups of people;
- updated coverage about the advantages of social media, the challenges of multimodal communication, and the impact of technology on relationships;
- strategies for establishing an online identity as a job candidate, creating searchable cover letters and résumés, and participating effectively in computer-mediated interviews and team meetings.

This edition builds upon the engaging design and practical advice that have made the first editions of *Essential Communication* so popular. It stands out for its commitment to active learning with real-life examples, self-quizzes, reflection opportunities, and communication checklists to help students think critically about the material and put what they learn to good use.

In addition to new images and visuals, here's a look at what's new in this edition:

Chapter 1, The Importance of Communication, includes updated examples and a new "Communication and Social Media" feature that describes both the appealing qualities of social media and its potential pitfalls.

Chapter 2, The Self, Perception, and Communication, presents an updated feature on gender and communication, including cisgender and transgender experiences and the implications of gender stereotypes in the workplace. The chapter also includes a revised segment on emotional intelligence.

Chapter 3, Culture and Communication, includes a new learning objective section on "Talking About Race" and a significantly revised segment on communicating about disabilities.

Chapter 4, Language, now covers microaggressions and how to avoid and respond to them. It includes a discussion of confirmation bias—people's tendency to seek out and believe information that's consistent with their beliefs and discredit information that isn't.

Chapter 5, Listening, presents new coverage of multimodal communication and strategies for being an effective listener in today's high-tech environment.

Chapter 6, Nonverbal Communication, includes new features on expectancy violation theory, cultural influences on nonverbal communication, the beauty premium, and nonverbal cues in social media.

Chapter 7, Communicating in Interpersonal Relationships, offers expanded coverage of metacommunication, online communication, and tips for avoiding relationship-damaging communication patterns.

Chapter 8, Communicating with Friends and Family, includes a new feature on making friends with diverse groups of people and coverage of the intergroup contact hypothesis, which reflects that such diverse friendships can diminish prejudice. The chapter also presents updated communication strategies for being a good friend.

Chapter 9, Communicating with Romantic Partners, now explores how mediated communication affects relationship development. The chapter introduces strategies for transitioning from an online dating relationship to meeting in person, and coverage of catfishing and butler lies as forms of deception related to online communication.

Chapter 10, Communication to Land a Job, helps job candidates better appreciate how they can market their communication skills, including how to make the most of online job searches and create résumés that are amenable to online applicant tracking systems. The chapter also includes updated coverage on participating in virtual job interviews.

Chapter 11, Communication in the Workplace, includes new strategies for getting all team members involved and experts' advice on participating effectively in computer-mediated team meetings.

Chapter 12, Preparing Speeches, provides enhanced coverage of the impact of toxic polarization and filter bubbles as well as updated examples, explanations, and visuals to coordinate with the sample speeches in the appendices.

Chapter 13, Presenting Speeches, includes expanded coverage of video conferencing and presenting in virtual settings to align with students' lived experience during the COVID-19 pandemic. In addition, the section on visual aids has been reorganized, with inclusion of new examples and new visuals.

Chapter 14, Speaking to Inform and Persuade, includes expanded coverage of the overlap between informative and persuasive speaking, as well as new examples and clarifications coordinated to the sample speeches in the appendices.

Appendices A and B provide new sample speeches to give students good examples of effective informative and persuasive speeches. The new informative speech is titled, "The Quirky Sex Lives of Ocean Creatures," and the new persuasive speech is titled, "Child Slavery in the Chocolate Industry."

Digital and Instructor Resources

Oxford Insight Courseware

Essential Communication, Third Edition is powered by Oxford Insight. Oxford Insight delivers the trusted and student-focused content of *Essential Communication* within powerful, data-driven courseware designed to optimize student success. Developed with a foundation in learning science, Insight enables instructors to deliver a personalized and engaging learning experience that empowers students by actively engaging them with assigned reading. This adaptivity, paired with real-time actionable data about student performance, helps instructors ensure that each student is best supported along their unique learning path. Features of Oxford Insight include:

- **A dynamically personalized learning experience for each student, based on their own learning needs.** Oxford Insight delivers adaptive practice sessions that function much like a human tutor for students. The content and focus of these sessions is based on student interaction with formative assessment that they encounter as they work through course content.
- **Improved reading retention with chapter content broken down into smaller "chunks" of content that are centered on specific Learning Objectives and accompanied by Formative Assessment activities.** As students progress through chapter reading, they are periodically required to answer formative questions, allowing the platform to collect information along the way and adapt a personalized plan to help improve their learning. The practice plan is followed by a summative quiz to demonstrate learning, turning students from passive readers to engaged problem solvers.
- **A clear, customizable, query-based Learning Dashboard that displays powerful and actionable, real-time data on student performance.** With the query-based Learning Dashboard, instructors can quickly answer questions like:
  - » Which students are having difficulties?
  - » Which objectives are my students having difficulties with?
  - » How often are my students visiting the course?
- **Developed with a learning-science-based course design methodology.** Powered by Acrobatiq by VitalSource, a leading provider of adaptive learning solutions, Oxford Insight builds on years of research at Carnegie Mellon's Open Learning Initiative that was aimed at discovering how best to optimize online learning for both students and instructors.

Additional Digital Resources

The full suite of digital resources that accompanies *Essential Communication*, Third Edition is available to instructors in two ways: via OUP's nationally hosted platform, Oxford Learning Cloud, or in your own LMS, via Oxford Learning Link Direct. Either delivery method includes the full e-book along with interactive activities and assessments to effectively track student progress.

With *Essential Communication*, professors and students get multimedia assignments designed to help students apply what they are learning based on the book's unique pedagogy. Activities in each chapter are carefully matched to suit each learning objective and may include:

- Flashcards to help students master new vocabulary
- Multiple-choice questions to assess students' knowledge and ability to understand and apply information
- *Pause to Reflect* prompts to inspire students to think critically about their own communication
- Interactive versions of the book's *About You* self-assessments to give students immediate feedback on their communication skills and behaviors
- List of collated video links, referenced in *The Essential Guide to Teaching Communication*, to better facilitate class discussions and activities; may be easily imported into an instructors' Learning Management System

Additional Instructor Resources

The Essential Guide to Teaching Communication

The Essential Guide to Teaching Communication by Athena du Pré will get new teachers up and running instantly. The *Essential Guide* also provides experienced educators with a library of new ideas to try out. It contains a full syllabus (including a reading schedule, assignments, grading rubrics, sample work, and more) as well as chapter lesson plans suitable for in-person, hybrid, online, and face-to-face courses. Instructor resources for each chapter include experiential learning activities, lecture notes, videos, discussions guides, journal topics, and public speaking prompts—all organized by learning objective and accompanied by ready-to-use handouts and corresponding PowerPoint slides. The *Essential Guide* for the third edition also includes strategies and tips for using Oxford Insight Courseware in the course. Lesson plans include integrated teaching tips and screen shots of the lecture slides so instructors can choose the elements they like.

PowerPoint Slides

Fully accessible slides correspond to elements of *The Essential Guide to Teaching Communication*, making it easy to prepare for class and post online modules.

Test Bank

The comprehensive Test Bank offers approximately 75 class-tested exam questions per chapter in multiple-choice and short-answer formats. It is available in several formats:

- Word documents
- An importable package for major learning management systems including Blackboard, Canvas, Brightspace/D2L, and Moodle
- Respondus format (for use in the Respondus testing application)

Contact your Oxford University Press representative or call (800) 280-0280 for more information on accessing these resources. You can also visit Oxford Learning Link at https://learninglink.oup.com to request access.

Acknowledgments

While the authors' names appear on the cover, this book is the product of many peoples' ideas and efforts.

We are grateful to the many colleagues whose feedback shaped the final product:

Jenna Abetz, College of Charleston
Rosemarie Alexander-Isett, University of Alaska Southeast
Roger M. Ballard, Tarleton University
Lisa Barrick, Southeast Kentucky Community and Technical College
Amy Bryant, Nashville State Community College
Kay Butler Barefoot, College of the Albemarle
Cheryl Casey, Champlain College
Paula Cohen, The Ohio State University Mansfield
Diane Ferrero-Paluzzi, Iona College
Karley A. Goen, Tarleton State University
Stephanie Greene, Germanna Community College
Debra Harper-LeBlanc, Lone Star College System
Tracey Holley, Tarleton State University
Valerie Jensen, Central Arizona College
Luis Lopez-Preciado, Lasell College
Alexandra MacMurdo Reiter, Georgia Highlands College
Douglas J. Marshall, Southern University at New Orleans
Tom McLaren, UNM Gallup
Laurie Metcalf, Blinn College
Laura Morrison, College of the Albemarle
Rebecca Mullane, Moraine Park Technical College
Travice Baldwin Obas, Georgia Highlands College
John Parrish, Tarrant County College
Clarissa Pierceall, Paradise Valley Community College
Brandi Quesenberry, Virginia Polytechnic Institute and State University
Charles Roberts, East Tennessee State University
Casey J. Rudkin, Kenai Peninsula College
Hannah Shinault, Virginia Polytechnic Institute and State University
Candice Simmons, University of San Diego
Susan Carol Stinson, Virginia Polytechnic Institute and State University
Steve Stuglin, Georgia Highlands College
Oluwatunmise Esther Tesunbi, Montgomery College
Dewey Wayne Ware, University of West Florida
Jennifer Williams, Mesa Community College
Archie Wortham, Northeast Lakeview College
Cora Ellen Young, East Tennessee State University

We are lucky to have worked with a fabulous team of professionals at Oxford University Press. Thank you to our executive editor, Steve Helba, for providing encouragement, support, and expert guidance at every step. Senior development editor Lisa Sussman is an author's dream come true. Her hard work and generous spirit make our words more meaningful, the content clearer, and the experience better for us and for our readers. Associate editor Alyssa Quinones is attentive, organized, and always quick to help. Thanks also to senior media editor Michael Quilligan for creating brilliant online resources. Our gratitude goes out as well to senior production editor Melissa Yanuzzi whose careful eye and wisdom are invaluable, copyeditor James Fraleigh, and to our talented designer Michele Laseau and incomparable marketing manager Tony Mathias.

On the home front, we thank our partners and families for giving us the time and support needed to create this book.

essential communication

THIRD EDITION

Ronald B. Adler
Santa Barbara City College
George Rodman
Brooklyn College, City University of New York
Athena du Pré
University of West Florida

New York Oxford
OXFORD UNIVERSITY PRESS

Oxford University Press is a department of the University of Oxford.
It furthers the University's objective of excellence in research, scholarship,
and education by publishing worldwide. Oxford is a registered trade mark
of Oxford University Press in the UK and certain other countries.

Published in the United States of America by Oxford University Press
198 Madison Avenue, New York, NY 10016, United States of America.

For titles covered by Section 112 of the US Higher Education Opportunity Act, please visit www.oup.com/us/he for the latest information about pricing and alternate formats.

Library of Congress Cataloging-in-Publication Data

Names: Adler, Ronald B. (Ronald Brian), 1946- author. | Rodman, George R.,
1948- author. | DuPré, Athena, author.
Title: Essential communication / Ronald B. Adler, George Rodman, Athena du
Pre.
Description: Third edition. | New York : Oxford University Press, [2021] |
Includes bibliographical references.
Identifiers: LCCN 2021027834 (print) | LCCN 2021027835 (ebook) | ISBN
9780197544310 (paperback) | ISBN 9780197544358 (epub)
Subjects: LCSH: Communication. | Interpersonal communication.
Classification: LCC P90 .A313 2021 (print) | LCC P90 (ebook) | DDC
302.2—dc23
LC record available at https://lccn.loc.gov/2021027834
LC ebook record available at https://lccn.loc.gov/2021027835

Printed by Quad/Graphics, Inc., Mexico

THE IMPORTANCE OF
Communication

1

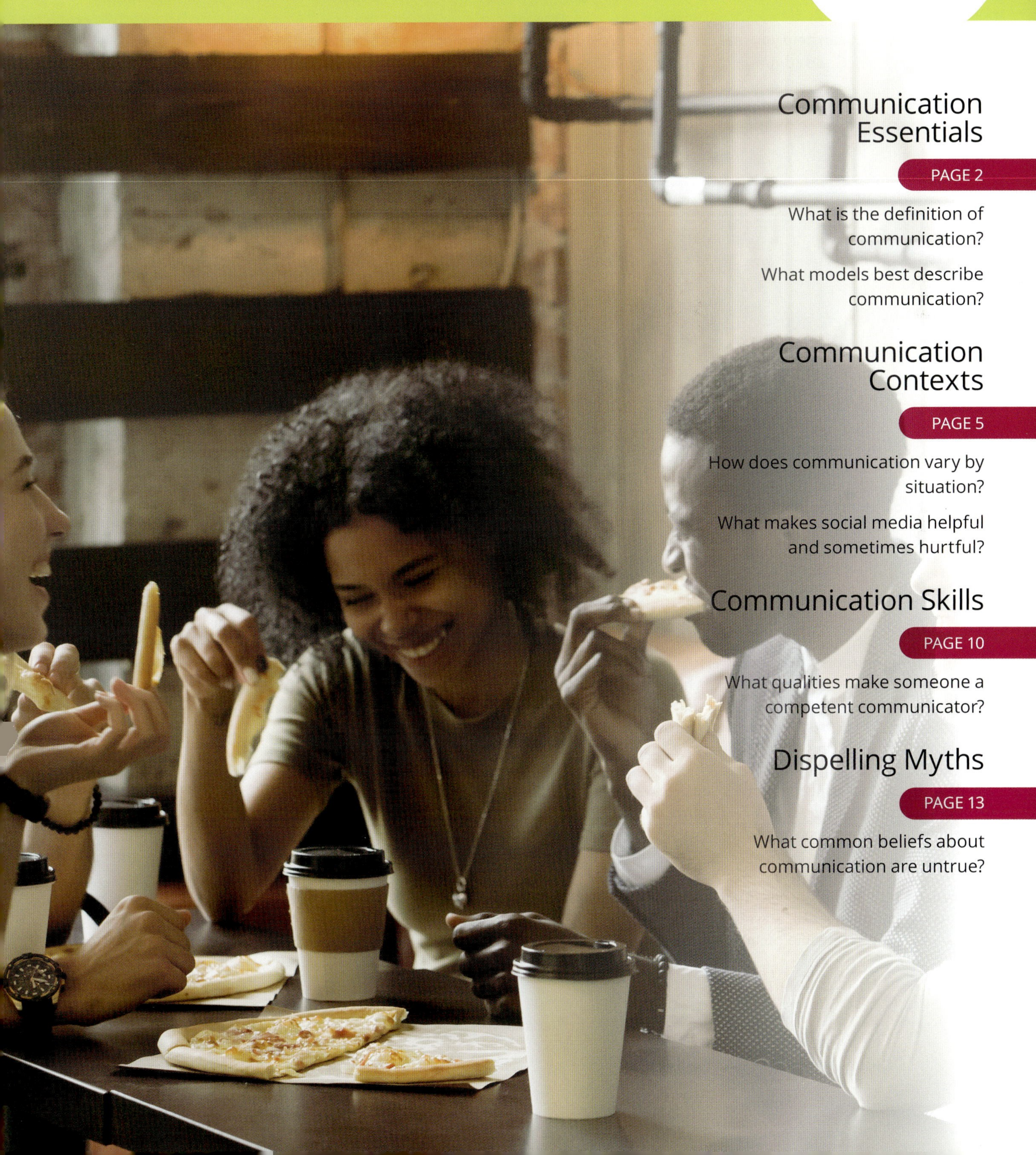

Communication Defined

LEARNING OBJECTIVE 1.1: **Define communication and explain its essential characteristics.**

Imagine skills that can help you make friends, improve relationships, impress the boss, and change the world. Good communication can't guarantee these, but it can certainly help.

Skillful communication can be a powerful force in both your personal and professional lives.[1,2,3,4] It's no wonder that the legendary business leader Warren Buffett once told a college student: "The best way you can improve yourself is to learn to communicate better. Your results in life will be magnified."[5]

As we'll use the term, **communication** is *the process of creating meaning through symbolic interaction*. This definition highlights four important points.

Communication is symbolic.

Symbols represent things, people, ideas, and events in ways that make communication possible. Symbols are arbitrary in that they are based on shared interpretations of what they represent, rather than an inherent link to the entities or ideas themselves. What you are reading now is called a *book* in English, a *libro* in Spanish, and a *knyga* in Lithuanian. Any term will work if the people with whom you communicate use it in the same way.

Communication is a process.

People often think about communication in terms of discrete, individual acts. They might say, "I told them the news" or "We had a talk." But even what seems to be an isolated communication experience is part of a larger process. Imagine that a friend says you look "fabulous." Your interpretation of that will depend on a range of factors: What have others said about your appearance in the past? How do you feel about the way you look? Is your friend prone to sarcasm? As this example shows, communication is embedded in contextual cues such as history, perceptions, relationships, and situations. Appreciating these contextual cues is essential to being a good communicator.

Communication is irreversible.

John E. Gardner once said that "life is art without an eraser." The same can be said of communication. At times, you have probably wished you could take back words you've said or actions you've taken. But once it's out there, you typically can't unsend or unreceive a message. This is especially true online, where a careless comment, photo, or video can haunt you forever. It's always wise to think before you speak, write, or post a message.

Communication is relational.

Communication isn't something people do *to* others. Rather, it is relational—something they do *with* others. As psychologist Kenneth Gergen points out, "one cannot be 'attractive' without others who are attracted, a 'leader' without others willing to follow, or a 'loving person' without others to affirm with appreciation."[6] If a communication episode is disappointing, it doesn't usually make sense to blame just one person. It's usually better to ask, "How did *we* handle this situation, and what can *we* do to make it better?"

Models of Communication

LEARNING OBJECTIVE 1.2: Compare and contrast linear and transactional models of communication.

One way to explore communication in more depth is to look at models that describe what happens when two or more people interact. Communication researchers have identified two main models: linear and transactional.

Linear Model

Theorists once viewed messages as something that one person sends to another.[7] Their **linear communication model** suggested that communication is similar to a tennis match. **Senders encode** messages that they send to **receivers**, who **decode** the messages by assigning meaning. In other words, communicators take turns being either a sender or a receiver. While the linear model is overly simplistic, three aspects of it are helpful.

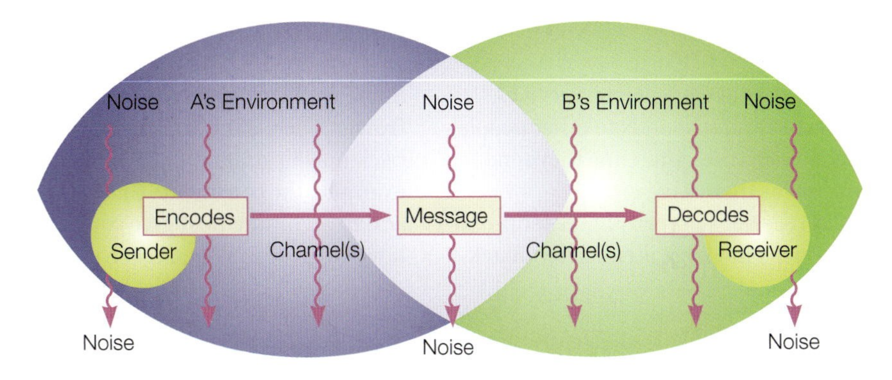

FIGURE 1.1 Linear Communication Model

First, the linear model includes the notion of a communication **channel**—the method by which a message is conveyed between people. You've probably noticed that you use different words in person than you do via a phone call or direct message. Channels influence not only how people communicate but *what* they communicate.

The linear model also includes the concept of noise. The way communication scholars use the term, **noise** includes not only sounds, but any factor that interferes with effective communication. Three types of noise can disrupt communication:

- *External noise* includes factors outside of a person that are distracting or make hearing difficult. For instance, you might be distracted by a noisy lawnmower or the vibration of a phone in your pocket.
- *Physiological noise* involves biological factors that interfere with communication. It's difficult to listen well if you are tired, sick, or hungry.
- *Psychological noise* refers to thoughts and feelings that distort or disrupt communication. If you believe someone dislikes you, you may perceive everything that person says in a negative way.

Finally, the linear model (Figure 1.1) shows that communication occurs in an **environment** that includes both current circumstances and the personal and cultural experiences each person brings to the encounter. Every communicator occupies a somewhat different environment. For example, if someone brings up immigration reform, your reaction may depend on how long your family has lived in this country, what you know about the topic, and whether or not you enjoy talking about politics. If participants' shared environment is small, communication may be challenging. However, there is always some overlap in people's goals and experiences, and it can be rewarding to communicate with people whose perspectives are different than your own. Chapter 3 discusses intercultural communication, and throughout this book we offer ways to bridge the gaps that separate each of us to varying degrees.

Transactional Model

In contrast to the linear view, the **transactional communication model** depicts a process in which people send and receive messages simultaneously. For example, if you tell your mom her new haircut looks "sick," her facial expression might tell you immediately that she is offended, even though you meant it as a compliment. Or perhaps someone yawns while you are telling a story. Even though you are a "sender" in these episodes, at the same time you are also a "receiver" who is aware of other people's reactions. Some types of mass communication flow in a one-way manner, but most personal communication involves a simultaneous exchange between two or more people.[8] Figure 1.2 shows how the roles of sender and receiver that seemed separate in the linear model are redefined as those of "communicators"

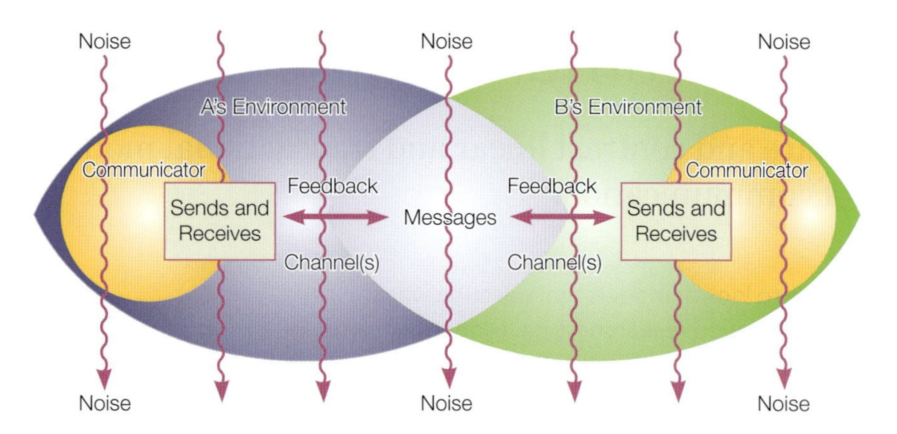

FIGURE 1.2 Transactional Communication Model

to reflect that each person receives, decodes, and responds to other people's behavior at the same time they send messages themselves.

A receiver's perceivable response to a sender's message is called **feedback**. Some feedback is nonverbal—smiles, frowns, eye rolling, and so on. Feedback may be oral or written, too. For example, the comments that viewers add to an online post give you an idea how the post has been received. Even messages once considered one-way communication, such as advertisements and news stories, now include options for influential feedback. For example, Nivea skin care cancelled an advertising campaign with the tagline "White Is Purity" after White supremacists praised it on social media and others condemned the slogan as racist.[9]

Another difference between the linear and transactional models is that the latter includes messages that aren't deliberately encoded. Your facial expressions, gestures, postures, and vocal tones may offer information to others even when you are unaware of them. For this reason, the transactional model replaces the term *encodes* with the broader term *responds* to include both intentional and unintentional actions.[10] ●

PAUSE TO REFLECT *How "Noisy" Is Your Communication?*

1 Pause for a moment to consider what is influencing you. Write down at least three examples of external noise that are present. (Remember that noise includes more than sounds.) ______

2 What types of physiological noise are you experiencing right now? ______

3 Think of a recent conversation. Write down not what you said, but what you were thinking. Did psychological noise interfere with your ability to listen well? ______

Communication Contexts

LEARNING OBJECTIVE 1.3: Distinguish between communication in a variety of contexts.

You probably don't behave the same way with your manager as with your best friend, and you're likely to say different things in a work group than with your family. This section considers eight communication contexts—each with its own characteristics, advantages, and challenges.

Intrapersonal Communication

Intrapersonal communication is "communicating with oneself."[11] It involves the voice in your head that replays conversations, rehearses what you might say to others, and so on. Intrapersonal communication affects almost every type of interaction. The way you handle a conversation with a friend depends on the intrapersonal communication that precedes or accompanies what you say ("I'm making a fool of myself" or "She likes me!").

Dyadic Communication

Social scientists use the term **dyadic communication** to describe two-person interaction. Dyadic communication can occur when people talk in person or via electronic means (a text, a DM, a phone call). Some people assume that dyadic communication is identical to interpersonal communication, but that's not always true.

Interpersonal Communication

Communication qualifies as **interpersonal** when the people involved are part of close relationships in which they treat each other as unique individuals. This helps to explain why dyadic communication isn't always interpersonal. You probably communicate one on one with many people (e.g., new acquaintances, strangers, salespeople) with whom you are not in a close relationship. And interpersonal communication can involve several people at a time, as when you engage in conversation with a group of close friends. Chapters 7 through 9 explore interpersonal communication in detail.

Small Group Communication

In **small group communication**, every person can participate actively with other members. Your family is a group. So are an athletic team, several students working on a project, and a team of colleagues in different locations who work together online. In a group, the majority of members can exert pressure (either consciously or unconsciously) on those in the minority. Such pressure can lead members to take risks they wouldn't otherwise take. On the positive side, groups can be effective at generating creative solutions since there are more people from whom to draw ideas. Groups are so important that Chapter 11 focuses extensively on them.

Organizational Communication

Larger, more permanent collections of people engage in **organizational communication** when they collectively work to achieve goals. Organizations come in many forms: business (such as

a corporation), nonprofit (such as an aid organization), political (a government or political action group), health (a hospital or doctor's office), and recreational (a YMCA or sports league). In organizations, members occupy specific roles (such as sales associate, general manager, corporate trainer) that influence who communicates with whom and how. Culture also plays a role. Each organization develops its own culture, which can be useful to consider when you apply for jobs and communicate in the workplace, the focus of Chapters 10 and 11.

Public Communication

Public communication occurs when a group becomes too large for all members to contribute at one time. One or more people are likely to deliver their remarks to the remaining members, who act as an audience. Even when audience members have the chance to post questions and comments (either in person or online), the speakers are still mostly in control of the message. Public speakers usually have a greater chance to plan and structure their remarks than do communicators in smaller settings. For this reason, Chapters 12 through 14 describe the steps you can take to prepare and deliver effective speeches.

Mass Communication

Mass communication consists of messages that are transmitted to large, widespread audiences via electronic and print media such as magazines, television, radio, websites, and blogs. Most mass messages do not involve personal contact between senders and receivers. In fact, many of the messages sent via mass communication channels are developed, or at least financed, by large organizations such as advertisers and movie studios.

Social Media

Even though it's useful to talk about communication contexts separately, they actually evolve and overlap. Nowhere is this more evident than in **social media**—a collection of electronic platforms that allow everyday people to post, view, comment on, and share content electronically. This form of communication didn't exist until about 20 years ago. Since then it has revolutionized the communication reach of everyday people and blurred the lines between mass and personal communication contexts. Here are three qualities that make social media unique:

- *Users generate their own content.* Everyone who uses social media is essentially a publisher. For example, if you want to post something on Instagram, Twitter, or TikTok, you needn't rely on staff writers, editors, designers, videographers, or marketers. It's all up to you.
- *Audience size varies vastly.* A social media message might reach a few friends or millions of people around the world. A YouTube video in which brothers convince their sister of a zombie invasion has been viewed more than 24.6 million times.[12] That's more than the viewership of *American Idol*, *60 Minutes*, and *America's Funniest Home Videos* combined.[13]
- *Public overlaps with personal.* Social media can reach strangers as well as friends. As one observer put it, "you glance at your Twitter feed over that first cup of coffee, and in a few seconds, you find out that your nephew got into med school and Shaquille O'Neal just finished a cardio workout in Phoenix."[14] A person's social media network may include friends, relatives, potential employers, celebrities, and much more. Managing so many "audiences" at one time can be challenging.

Communication and Social Media

LEARNING OBJECTIVE 1.4: List some pros and cons of communicating via social media.

If you reach for the phone before your head leaves the pillow in the morning, you aren't alone. "Even when I'm still half-asleep, I have an impulse to see if I've missed a text, or an email, or even a huge development in the news," says lifestyle writer Annakeara Stinson.[15]

The urge to scan, swipe, like, and post is hard to resist. Two out of three young adults in the United States check their phone first thing every morning, and nearly as many monitor it until they fall asleep at night.[16]

Why do we cradle our communication devices with such devotion? Here we consider three factors that drive our love affair with social media and three ways that it can cause heartache.

Social media is entertaining.

When researchers tracked viewers' eye movements as they scanned social media content, they confirmed what you might already have experienced: posts that involve colorful graphics and video get the most attention.[17] "There is *literally* never a dull moment on social media," attests marketing blogger Kristi Brown, who adds, "I thrive on it and draw energy from it."[18] The pace, colors, and never-ending stream of novel content can be fun and invigorating. This makes social media especially enticing for people who get bored easily.[19]

Social media is . . . social.

It seems obvious from the name, but this fact can't be overstated: online interactions help satisfy people's craving for community. Having a large number of "friends" and "followers" touches the need to belong and be part of a group. Extroverts are more likely than introverts to regularly use social media and to post messages.[20] And a sense of online social support is often highly valued by people going through hard times.[21]

Social media is a means of identity management.

It's a simple fact of human existence, says journalist Courtney Seiter: "We like talking about ourselves."[22] Social media provides an arena in which people are encouraged to focus on themselves (literally, with cameras), talk about their daily experiences, and broadcast their accomplishments. With the option to omit what isn't flattering, users are able to serve as their own publicists. For some, the objective is to find a love interest or connect with family and friends. Others use social media to advance their careers or even attract worldwide attention, fame, and fortune.

All in all, social media is appealing for many of the same reasons that people engage in communication of all types. It can be stimulating, social, and identity enhancing. At the same time, however, our passion for social media can make us vulnerable to its character flaws.

Social media can hijack your time.

One reason it's so hard to sign off from social media is that platform sponsors don't want you to. "There are literally thousands of intelligent people being paid extremely well to figure out how

to get users to never put their phones down," attests Tristan Harris, a technology expert and ethicist.[23] If you aren't careful, artfully designed clickbait (content designed to lure people onto a website) can rob you of valuable hours. Among social media users, more than half say that device time gets in the way of doing homework and paying attention to the people around them.[24]

Social media is distracting.
Focusing on social media gives someone else the ability to shape your thoughts and priorities. That can be okay in small doses but hurtful in extremes. The average person has more than eight social media accounts,[25] and nearly half of teens in the United States say they are on their smartphones "almost constantly."[26]

Productivity expert Jari Roomer challenges the wisdom of that. "You wouldn't let hundreds of people into your house, blasting their requests and opinions at you," he says, "so why would you let them into your mind through a device?"[27] Rather than going to bed and waking up with social media, a healthier alternative may be to reserve some time for your own thoughts—reflecting on the day and planning what you would like to accomplish.

Social media can make you feel bad.
Theodore Roosevelt once warned that "comparison is the thief of joy." Whereas moderate social media use can enhance feelings of identity and belonging, those who rely heavily on social media for validation are likely to experience more stress, less emotional resilience, and more self-criticism than their peers.[28] And the vividness and volume of social media messages can make real-life interactions seem less appealing by comparison. College students who are highly invested in the feedback they receive online are more likely than others to neglect real-life friends and loved ones.[29]

Like any relationship, our bond with social media has pros and cons. "Social media can gnaw at our insecurities and suck us in," says Courtney Seiter, but it also offers an opportunity to communicate with diverse people, share experiences, and learn about ourselves.[30] All in all, love may be blind, but your relationship with social media needn't be. A clear understanding of the pros and cons can help make sure your relationship is a healthy one. •

TIPS & REMINDERS

Tips for Communicating Well on Social Media

Imagine seeing an "I LOVE YOU" message posted by someone else on your sweetheart's Facebook page. That happened to Brittany, who posted the enraged reply: "F--- off b----," only to find out later that the "other woman" was her boyfriend's mother.[31] Ouch! Social media can make and break relationships in a very public way. Here are some tips for communicating effectively in the unique blend of public and private communication that social media offers.

1. **Choose the best medium.**

   Think carefully about which social media option—if any—to use in a given situation. As Brittany's outburst illustrates, it's easy to misunderstand mediated messages and just as easy to post embarrassing ones. And social media can be too distant and impersonal for sensitive discussions such as sharing bad news, apologizing, and managing interpersonal conflict. Anyone who has been dumped via a direct message knows that it only adds insult to injury. Many difficult conversations are better when conducted face to face. Ask yourself how the recipient would prefer to receive a particular message and act accordingly.

2. **Think before you post.**

   Organizations (and many people) monitor social media for messages that mention them. This means that potential employers and others are likely to see what you post about them. Consider the fate of a high school student who tweeted rude remarks about other students while visiting a college she hoped to attend. University decision makers saw her posts and put her on the "no" list. The author of "They Loved Your G.P.A., Then They Saw Your Tweets" encourages people to consider that anything they post is public information.[32]

Short, casual messages have become so common online that it's easy to forget that there's different etiquette for professional communication.

3. **Adapt to the audience.**

   Short, casual messages have become so common online that it's easy to forget that there's different etiquette for professional communication. Beginning an email to your manager or professor with "Hey" or no salutation can come off as disrespectful. Likewise, don't forget to say "please" and "thank you." Social media encompasses a range of audiences and contexts. Consider who will (or might) read each of your messages.

4. **Respect others' need for undivided attention.**

   If you have been texting and emailing since you could walk, it might be hard to believe that some people are insulted when you divide your attention between them and your phone. As one observer put it, "While a quick log-on may seem, to the user, a harmless break, others in the room receive it as a silent dismissal. It announces: 'I'm not interested.'"[33] Chapter 5 includes more about the challenges of listening effectively. Even if you think you can multitask and still listen well, it's important to realize that others may perceive you as being rude.

5. **Keep your cool.**

   If you have ever posted an offensive comment, shot back a nasty reply to a direct message, or forwarded an embarrassing email, you know that it's easier to behave badly when the recipient of your message isn't right in front of you.[34] The tendency to transmit messages without considering their consequences (especially online) is called **disinhibition**. Before you post an ugly message, keep in mind that it can cause pain and damage your reputation long after you have calmed down or changed your mind.

Communication Competence

LEARNING OBJECTIVE 1.5: Describe characteristics of effective communication and competent communicators.

It's easy to recognize good communicators and even easier to spot poor ones. But what exactly makes someone an effective communicator?

Communication competence involves achieving your goals in a manner that, ideally, maintains or enhances the relationship in which it occurs.[35,36] Is it effective communication if you win an argument but damage a valued relationship in the process? Probably not. Here are eight other maxims about communication competence.

There is no "ideal" way to communicate.

Some successful people are serious, whereas others use humor. Some are outgoing and others are quiet. Some people are straightforward, whereas others prefer subtlety. Just as there are many kinds of beautiful music and art, there are many kinds of competent communication.

Competence is situational.

It's a mistake to think that anyone either is or isn't a competent communicator. Individuals are better at communicating in some situations than in others, and competence is always a matter of degree. A person might be quite skillful socializing at a party but less successful talking with professors during office hours. And no matter how good a communicator is, there's always more to learn.

Competence is relational.

Because communication is transactional—something people do *with* others rather than *to* them—behavior that is competent in one context or culture isn't necessarily effective or appropriate in others. For example, your friends might consider it fun to tease each other by trading insults, but the same comments might offend people at work or in the classroom. The challenge can be even greater when people are from different cultures. If you tell someone from the United Kingdom that you packed two pairs of pants, they might look at you funny. They use the word *trousers* to describe what you wear on the outside.[37] To them, *pants* means underwear.

Competence can be learned.

There are numerous ways to build communication competence. You can boost your skills by taking classes such as the one you are in now, trying out new communication strategies, and observing what works well (and not so well) for the people around you.

Competent communicators are flexible.

Many poor communicators are easy to spot by their limited range of responses. Some constantly make jokes. Others always seem to be argumentative. Still others are quiet in almost every situation. Like a piano player who knows only one tune or a chef who can prepare only a few

dishes, these people rely on a small range of responses again and again, whether or not they are successful. By contrast, competent communicators have a wide repertoire from which to draw, and they are able to choose the most appropriate behavior for a given situation.

Competent communicators are empathic.

You have the best chance of developing an effective message when you understand the other person's point of view. And because other people don't always express their thoughts and feelings clearly, the ability to *imagine* how an issue might look to someone else is also important. For instance, imagine that your longtime friend seems angry with you. Is your friend offended by something you have done? Did something upsetting happen earlier in the day? Or perhaps nothing at all is wrong, and you're just being overly sensitive. Researchers have found that analyzing the behavior of others can lead to greater conversational sensitivity.[38] Because listening is such an important element of communicative competence, Chapter 5 is devoted to the topic.

Competent communicators self-monitor.

Self-monitoring involves paying close attention to situational cues and adapting one's behavior accordingly. High self-monitors ask themselves questions such as "What is expected in this situation?" and "What is likely to please (or offend) the people around me?"

High self-monitors are more likely than low self-monitors to develop relationships with many types of people.[39] Being highly adaptive can be carried too far, however. High self-monitors may be inclined to overuse social media, perhaps because they are concerned with how they appear to others.[40] And people may wonder how high self-monitors really feel, since their behavior tends to vary by situation. You'll read more about self-monitoring in Chapter 2.

Competent communicators are committed.

One feature that distinguishes effective communication in almost any context is commitment. People who are emotionally committed to a relationship are more likely than others to talk about difficult subjects and to share personal information about themselves, which can strengthen relationships and contribute to a heightened sense of well-being.[41] ●

ABOUT YOU *What Type of Communicator Are You?*

Answer the questions that follow for insight about your approach as a communicator.

_______ **1.** You are puzzled when a friend says, "The complex houses married and single soldiers and their families."[42] What are you most likely to do?

a. Tune out and hope your friend changes topics soon.
b. Declare, "You're not making any sense."
c. Ask questions to be sure you understand what your friend means.
d. Nod as if you understand, even if you don't.

_______ **2.** You are working frantically to meet a project deadline when your phone rings. It's your roommate, who immediately launches into a long, involved story. What would you probably do?

a. Pretend to listen while you continue to work on your project.
b. Interrupt to say, "I don't have time for this now."
c. Listen for a few minutes and then say, "I'd like to hear more about this, but can I call you back later?"
d. Listen and ask questions so you don't hurt your friend's feelings.

_______ **3.** You are assigned to a task force to consider the parking problem on campus. Which of the following are you most likely to do during task force meetings?

a. Talk in a quiet voice to the person next to you.
b. Express frustration if meetings aren't productive.
c. Ask questions and take notes.
d. Spend most of your time listening quietly.

_______ **4.** Your family is celebrating your brother's high school graduation at dinner. What are you most likely to do at the table?

a. Ask for dessert in a takeout container so you can leave early.
b. Keep your phone handy so you won't miss anything your friends post.
c. Give your undivided attention as your brother talks about his big day.
d. Paste a smile on your face and make the best of the situation, even if you feel bored.

INTERPRETING YOUR RESPONSES | For insight about your communication style, see which of the following best describes your answers. (More than one may apply.)

Distracted Communicator If you answered "a" to two or more questions, you have a tendency to disengage. Perhaps you are shy, introverted, or easily distracted. You needn't change your personality, but you are likely to build stronger relationships if you strive to be more attentive and proactive. Active listening tips in Chapter 5 may be helpful.

Impatient Communicator If you answered "b" to two or more questions, you tend to be a straight-talker who doesn't like delays or ambiguity. Honesty can be a virtue, but be careful not to overdo it. Your tendency to "tell it like it is" may come off as domineering at times. The perception-checking technique in Chapter 2 offers a good way to balance your desire for the truth with concern for other people's feelings.

Tactful Communicator If you answered "c" to two or more questions, you tend to balance assertiveness with good listening skills. Your willingness to actively engage with people is an asset. Use tips throughout the book to enhance your already-strong communication skills.

Accommodator If you answered "d" to two or more questions, you often put others' needs ahead of your own. People probably appreciate your listening skills but wish you would speak up more. Saying what you feel and sharing your ideas can be an asset both personally and professionally. Tips in Chapters 9 and 13 may help you become more assertive and confident without losing your thoughtful consideration for others.

Misconceptions About Communication

LEARNING OBJECTIVE 1.6: **Explain how misconceptions about communication can create problems.**

Having talked about what communication is, we conclude here with some things it is not. Correcting misconceptions is important because following them can get you into trouble. Here we set the record straight on how communication actually functions.

Myth 1: Communication requires complete understanding.

Most people operate on the flawed assumption that the goal of all communication is to maximize understanding between communicators. Although some agreement is necessary, there are some types of communication in which complete comprehension isn't the primary goal.[43] For example, when people in the United States ask "How's it going?" they typically are not interested in the details of how someone is doing. And sometimes people want to be purposely ambiguous, as when they decline unwanted invitations by saying "I can't make it." If the goal was to be perfectly clear, they might say, "I don't really feel like spending time with you."

Myth 2: Communication can solve all problems.

"If I could just communicate better . . ." is the sad refrain of many unhappy people who believe that, if they could express themselves better, their relationships would improve. Although this is sometimes true, it's an exaggeration to say that communication is a guaranteed cure-all.

Myth 3: Communication is good.

In truth, communication is neither good nor bad in itself. Rather, its value comes from the way it is used. Communication can be a tool for expressing warm feelings and useful facts, but under different circumstances the same words and actions can cause pain.

Myth 4: Meanings are in words.

"Meanings are in people, not in words." This axiom is a reminder that people often interpret the same words differently. You may have learned the hard way that words such as "freedom" and "racism" can mean different things to different people. And new words continually emerge. If *periodt* appears at the end of a written comment, some people may think it's a misspelling, whereas others will assume that the writer feels strongly about the topic, as in, "I am staying home periodt." In Chapter 4 you'll read a great deal more about the problems that come from mistakenly assuming that words mean the same thing to everyone.

Myth 5: Communication is simple.

Most people assume that communication is an aptitude that people naturally have—rather like breathing. After all, we've been swapping ideas with one another since early childhood, and some people communicate well without taking a class on the subject. However, it's a mistake to assume that communication comes easily. Communication skills are a lot like athletic ability. Even the most inept of us can learn to be more effective with training and practice, and those who are talented can always become better.

Myth 6: More communication is always better.

Although not communicating enough is a mistake, there are situations when *too much* communication is a problem. Sometimes people "talk a problem to death," going over the same ground again and again. Doing that can be frustrating and unproductive, and it can even make a bad situation worse. One key to successful communication is to share an adequate amount of information in a skillful manner. Exploring ways to do that is one of the major goals of this book.

The Importance of Communication

Communication Is . . .

- Symbolic
- A process
- Irreversible
- Relational

Models of Communication

Linear Communication Model

- A sender encodes ideas and conveys them to a receiver who decodes them.
- Messages are conveyed via channels, either face-to-face or mediated.
- Three types of noise can disrupt communication—external (outside of a person), physiological (biological factors within a person), and psychological (thoughts and feelings).
- Environment includes physical location, personal experiences, cultural backgrounds, and more.

Transactional Communication Model

- People send and receive messages simultaneously.
- Feedback is a receiver's perceptible response to a message.
- Feedback may be intentional or unintentional.

Communication Contexts

- Intrapersonal communication is communication with oneself.
- Dyadic communication involves two persons interacting.
- Interpersonal communication occurs in close relationships.
- In small group communication, every person can participate actively with other group members.
- People engage in organizational communication when they are part of long-term groups that collectively work to achieve goals.
- Public communication occurs when a group is too large for all members to contribute at once, as when an audience listens to a lecture.
- Mass communication consists of messages that are transmitted to large, widespread audiences via electronic and print media.
- Social media involves communication technology that enables everyday people to view, share, and add content.

Social Media . . .

- Is entertaining
- Is social
- Is a means of identity management
- Can hijack your time
- Is distracting
- Can make you feel bad

5 Tips for Using Social Media Well

- Choose the best medium.
- Think before you post.
- Adapt to the audience.
- Respect others' need for undivided attention.
- Keep your cool.

Communication Competence

People use communication to achieve goals in a manner that, ideally, maintains or enhances the relationship in which it occurs.

- There is no "ideal" way to communicate.
- Competence is situational.
- Competence is relational.
- Competence can be learned.
- Competent communicators are flexible.
- Competent communicators are empathic.
- Competent communicators self-monitor.
- Competent communicators are committed.

Myths About Communication

- Communication requires complete understanding.
- Communication can solve all problems.
- Communication is good.
- Meanings are in words.
- Communication is simple.
- More communication is always better.

Show Your Communication Know-How

1.1: Define communication and explain its essential characteristics.

Describe a conversation you have been involved in recently. Explain how the conversation illustrated the four key elements of communication described in "Communication Defined."

KEY TERMS: communication, symbols

1.2: Compare and contrast linear and transactional models of communication.

Describe an episode in which you changed what you were about to say—or decided not to say something—based on someone else's reaction. Which better describes that episode: the linear communication model or the transactional model? Why?

KEY TERMS: linear communication model, senders, encode, receivers, decode, channel, noise, environment, transactional communication model, feedback

1.3: Distinguish between communication in a variety of contexts.

Imagine that you've been offered a great job far away from where you live now. Describe the different ways you might share that news with a close friend, your manager, and your current work group. In what ways would you adapt your message to suit each relationship?

KEY TERMS: intrapersonal communication, dyadic communication, interpersonal communication, small group communication, organizational communication, public communication, mass communication, social media

1.4: List some pros and cons of communicating via social media.

On average, how much time (if any) do you spend on social media in a typical day? What do you find most appealing about social media? Do you ever take social media use to unhealthy or unproductive extremes? If so, how?

KEY TERM: disinhibition

1.5: Describe characteristics of effective communication and competent communicators.

Rate yourself from 1 to 10 in terms of how well your communication reflects each of the following: empathy, self-monitoring, and commitment. Which of these are you good at? Which might you improve and how?

KEY TERMS: communication competence, self-monitoring

1.6: Explain how misconceptions about communication can create problems.

Which misconceptions about communication discussed in this chapter have caused the greatest problems in your life? How can you approach similar situations more constructively in the future?

2 THE SELF, PERCEPTION, AND Communication

The Self-Concept Defined

LEARNING OBJECTIVE 2.1: Explain the self-concept and its relation to self-esteem.

Take a few minutes to list as many of your traits and characteristics as you can. Try to include all the characteristics that describe you.

What makes you *you*? It's one of the deepest questions ever asked. Part of the answer lies in interactions with others. The way you present yourself to the world, and the way people respond to you, help define how you think about yourself.

- *Physical characteristics* (e.g., tall, petite, slim, overweight, dark-skinned, light-skinned, brown hair, curly hair, straight hair, ugly, attractive, etc.)
- *Social traits* (e.g., outgoing, shy, talkative, quiet, funny, serious, generous, selfish, compassionate, callous, etc.)
- *Social roles* (e.g., brother, sister, mother, father, friend, student, teammate, employee, etc.)
- *Defining interests* (e.g., blogger, gamer, musician, actor, athlete, politician, journalist, etc.)
- *Talents* (e.g., intellectual, musical, artistic, dramatic, athletic, etc.)
- *Your belief systems* (e.g., Christian, Jewish, Muslim, Hindu, Mormon, atheist, libertarian, progressive, etc.)

We'll come back to this list as we consider aspects of your identity.

Self-Concept

The items on your list contribute to your **self-concept**, a set of relatively stable perceptions individuals hold about themselves. It includes your conception of what is unique about you and what makes you similar to others. The self-concept is complex. Even a list of 20 or 30 terms would be only a partial description of the factors that describe you.

To be more complete, your list would have to be hundreds—or even thousands—of words long. Of course, not all items would be equally important. For example, you might define yourself primarily by your skills and accomplishments, while others might define themselves primarily by social roles or physical appearance.

Self-Esteem

An important element of the self-concept is **self-esteem**, a personal evaluation of self-worth. For example, if your self-concept includes being athletic or tall, your self-esteem may be shaped by how you feel about these qualities, as in "I'm glad that I am athletic" or "I am embarrassed about being so tall."

There is a powerful link between communication and self-esteem. It's probably no surprise that people who have close, supportive interactions with others are more likely to have high self-esteem.[1,2] And the same principle works in reverse. People with high self-esteem are more likely than others to take a chance on starting new relationships[3] and showing affection to others,[4] which can enhance their feelings of self-esteem even more.

Despite its obvious benefits, self-esteem doesn't guarantee success in personal and professional relationships.[5] People with an exaggerated sense of self-worth may *think* they make a good impression on others, even if they don't. In fact, people with an inflated sense of self-worth may irritate others by coming across as condescending know-it-alls.[6]

Communication and the Self-Concept

LEARNING OBJECTIVE 2.2: **Analyze ways that communication both influences and reflects the self-concept.**

To better understand the relationship between the self-concept and communication, let's consider some specific ways that they influence each other. This section explores four factors that affect and reflect people's sense of self.

Significant Others

In a classic experiment, researchers told teachers that 20 percent of the children in a certain elementary school showed unusual potential for intellectual growth.[7] The names of the 20 percent were drawn randomly. However, eight months later, these unusually "smart" children showed significantly greater intellectual achievement than did the remaining children, who had not been singled out for the teachers' attention. This example highlights some of the ways that self-concept is formed and how it influences people's behavior.

The concept of **reflected appraisal** describes how individuals develop an image of themselves based on the way they think others view them. As people learn to speak and understand language, verbal messages (both positive and negative) contribute to their developing self-concept. This is particularly true when messages are from **significant others**—people whose opinions an individual especially values. In the study just mentioned, the teachers gave the "smart" students more time to answer questions, and they provided more feedback to them than to other students. The children who were singled out did better, not because they were more innately intelligent than their classmates, but because their teachers (significant others) treated them as if they were. Everyone has probably been influenced, for better or worse, by a teacher, coach, close friend, or relative who has left an imprint on how they view themselves.

Mass Media

As you may remember from Chapter 1, communication includes messages that people receive in magazines, movies, the news, television shows, and so on. One of the most obvious impacts of mass media is the way people evaluate their appearance. In the United States, adolescent boys are likely to feel that they are not as slender or as muscular as society expects them to be,[8] and young women frequently exposed to media images are more likely than others to feel that they are overweight and to have eating disorders.[9] By contrast, in cultures in which people are exposed to relatively few Western media images, eating disorders are less common.[10]

Culture

Cultural expectations affect the self-concept in both obvious and subtle ways. As you will read in Chapter 3, most non-Western cultures, including

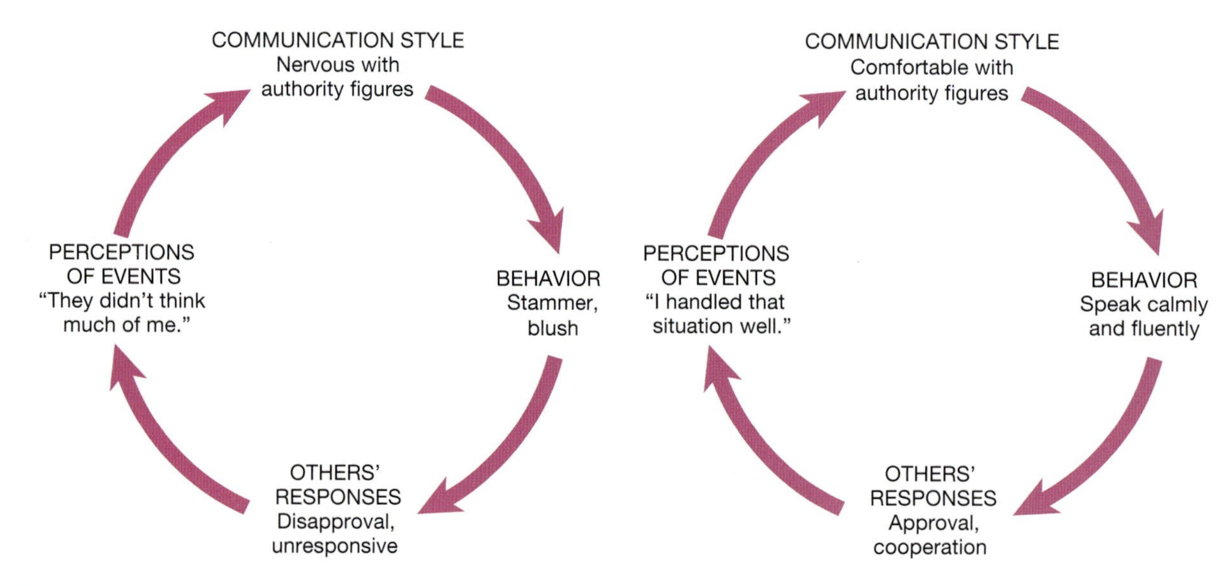

FIGURE 2.1 The Relationship Between the Self-Concept and Behavior

Asian ones, are traditionally considered to be collective. In collectivistic cultures, a person builds identity by belonging to a group. If you have ever worked on a group assignment and been graded on how well the team as a whole performed rather than on your individual contributions, you have experienced collectivism to some extent. In collectivist cultures, feelings of pride and self-worth are likely to be shaped by the behavior of other members of the community.

Expectations

A **self-fulfilling prophecy** occurs when a person's expectation of an outcome and that person's subsequent behavior make the outcome more likely to occur than would otherwise have been the case. One type of self-fulfilling prophecy occurs when your expectations influence your own behavior. For example, if you anticipate having a good (or terrible) time at a party, you might act in ways that make your prediction come true.

Another type of self-fulfilling prophecy occurs when another person's expectations influence your actions.[11] Perhaps an early mentor said you were good (or bad) at sports. You may behave in ways that support that assessment of your abilities, even if you don't realize you are doing so. Of course, self-fulfilling prophecies only go so far. Believing you'll do well in a job interview when you're clearly not prepared or qualified for the position is unrealistic. And individuals may defy expectations, as when a child who is discouraged and belittled grows up to be a confident adult.

All in all, communication is so intertwined with self-concept that it's all but impossible to say which influences the other more. Figure 2.1 illustrates how the self-concept both shapes and is shaped by communication behavior. For example, if you are afraid to speak in front of a crowd, your fear of public speaking may cause you to be especially nervous, which may lead you to be less effective as a speaker, which may cause you to feel even less confident, and so on in a self-defeating cycle.

Breaking a self-defeating cycle can be hard, but one step is to become aware of your thinking and reconsider elements of your self-concept. "Sometimes, we get stuck on an idea we have about ourselves that is left over from when we were younger or less experienced," says Chloe Mason Gray.[12] Gray overcame her fear of public speaking by engaging in self pep talks, practicing, studying great speakers, and pretending to feel confident until she actually was. •

PAUSE TO REFLECT *What Shapes Your Self-Concept?*

1. Think of someone who has had a significant impact on you, for better or worse. Describe how this person has communicated with you and how their messages have influenced your self-concept and self-worth.

2. What cultural expectations have affected your self-concept in terms of being a "good" daughter, son, friend, student, partner, or any of the other roles you play?

3. If you had to predict how well you will do in the rest of your academic career, what would you say? How might you behave to increase the chances of this becoming a self-fulfilling prophecy? On the other hand, what behaviors might prevent your prediction from coming true?

Mistaken Attributions and Communication

LEARNING OBJECTIVE 2.3: Recognize tendencies that lead to distorted perceptions of yourself and others and how those distortions affect communication.

So far, this chapter has covered the way people perceive themselves and others. These perceptions can be highly influential, but they aren't infallible. In fact, humans are prone to perceptual bias.

Some of the biggest problems that interfere with understanding and agreement arise from errors in interpretation, or what psychologists call **attribution**—the process of attaching meaning to behavior. If you assume that someone who is standing on a street corner in rumpled clothing is homeless, you're making an attribution. (Someone else might assume that the same person is a jogger or a construction worker.) Individuals attribute meaning both to their own actions and to the actions of others, but they often use different yardsticks. Here we explore four perceptual errors that can lead to inaccurate attributions, and therefore to troublesome communication.[13] By becoming aware of these errors, you can better guard against them and avoid unnecessary conflicts.

Individuals typically judge themselves more charitably than they judge others.

In an attempt to convince themselves and others that the positive face they show the world is true, people tend to judge themselves in the most generous terms possible. Social scientists have labeled this tendency the **self-serving bias** or **fundamental attribution error**.[14] When *you* suffer a setback, you may find explanations outside yourself ("I got fired because my boss is a jerk."). However, when *others* suffer, you are likely to blame the problem on their personal qualities ("She got fired because she didn't work hard enough."). From a communication standpoint, your harsh opinions of others can lead you to send judgmental messages. At the same time, you may feel defensive when others interpret your behavior less charitably than you do yourself.

People often pay more attention to negative impressions than to positive ones.

Consider a time when you received feedback about your contributions to a team project. Even if 9 out of 10 comments were positive, the negative one probably hit you hardest and stayed with you longest. Scientists speculate that humans' sensitivity to negative information may have a survival advantage. Spotting threatening elements in the environment is sometimes more important than focusing on safe ones.[15] But this tendency can be damaging to your self-concept and your relationships. If a friend says something that hurts your feelings, you may be tempted to focus on that statement rather than the dozens of supportive things your friend has said.

When individuals do perceive positive qualities, they tend to overgeneralize.

When someone impresses you favorably in some way, you are likely to assume they have other positive qualities as well—an attribution error that scholars call a **halo effect**.[16] For example, individuals often suppose that physically attractive people are more intelligent than others, even when they aren't.[17] Of course, the halo effect may dim over time if the person doesn't turn out to be as remarkable as you initially assumed. And sometimes a halo effect emerges over time. Individuals who didn't strike you as physically remarkable at first may become beautiful in your eyes if they turn out to have great personalities.[18]

People gravitate to the familiar.

Individuals tend to judge those who seem similar to them more favorably than those who don't. In one study, participants were more likely to assume that a person profiled on Facebook was likeable if they perceived that they had something in common, such as attending the same university.[19] It pays to remember, however, that people don't always think or behave alike. When there are differences, it's important to show respect. As one blogger puts it, "Expressing your views is supposed to encourage conversation and gain/provide new perspectives . . . not to demean and disprove the beliefs of those to whom you do not agree."[20]

Myths About Gendered Communication

LEARNING OBJECTIVE 2.4: Counteract myths about gendered communication with more accurate information.

Expectations about gender are often communicated the moment people are born—or even before, with the selection of a name, clothing, toys, and nursery décor.

At different times, Paula Stone Williams has experienced the world as a man and as a woman. "The differences are massive," Williams says.[21] Men's clothing is more comfortable and the pockets are larger. But the biggest difference, she says, is how people treat her. "Apparently, since I became a female, I have become stupid," she says wryly. It's not true. But people regularly treat Williams as if she is less capable and less knowledgeable than they did before her gender transition.

Although social ideas about gender are changing, a number of cultural assumptions persist. Here are four common misconceptions and the implications for communication.

Myth 1: *Sex* and *gender* are the same.

In conversation, people tend to use the terms *sex* and *gender* interchangeably. However, they mean different things. **Sex** is a biological category. A person's sex might be classified as male or female based on genitals and other physiological features. (As we will discuss in a moment, male and female are not the only options.) By contrast, **gender** is a socially constructed set of expectations about what it means to be masculine, feminine, and so on.

The term **cisgender** (pronounced *siz-gender*) describes a person whose current gender is the same as the sex attributed to them at birth. For example, a person who was categorized as female at birth and whose identity is female is considered a cis woman. If someone is **transgender** it means that their gender is different from the biological sex attributed to them at birth. Paula Stone Williams says she felt like a girl from a young age, although society viewed her as male until she came out as a transgender woman in 2012.

Myth 2: Communication styles are either masculine or feminine.

Physical attributes and hormone levels make biological sex a more complicated formula than you might think. Everyone's body produces some estrogen and some testosterone, which are sex-related hormones that influence how the body and mind develop.[22] Biologically speaking, no one is entirely masculine or feminine;[23] therefore, it is unrealistic to expect people to observe strict gender differences in the way they communicate.

Myth 3: There is an "opposite" sex.

Conceptualizations of gender have advanced through three main stages over time. The first assumption was that gender is binary. That is, people were considered either male or female. The behaviors associated with being "masculine" or "feminine" were distinct and very often oppositional. This view gave rise to such notions as the "opposite" gender.

The second phase, which gained acceptance near the end of the 20th century,[24] acknowledged that people might also be **androgynous** (combining masculine and feminine traits) or **undifferentiated** (neither masculine nor feminine).

The third phase, emerging now, conceptualizes gender as a multidimensional collection of qualities.[25,26] This view proposes that people are too complex for simplistic labels and that

traditional gender norms can be confining and unproductive.[27,28] From this perspective, the healthiest approach is for people to draw upon a full range of communication skills and strategies.[29]

Myth 4: Gender roles are rooted in biology.

Gender roles that shape communication are learned. For example, people who frequently watch crime shows and sporting events on TV are more likely than others to believe that it's a man's role to be physically strong, socially dominant, and unfeminine.[30] The same pattern is evident in those who regularly play video games with violent content.[31] People who subscribe to such beliefs are likely to consider it acceptable for men to communicate assertively and compete for promotions in the workplace, whereas they may consider it inappropriate for women to display the same behaviors.[32]

Because gender roles are learned, they can change. Some people feel they should. Actor Justin Baldoni, for one, says he's tired of social ideas about masculinity that devalue women and limit his experience of the world. "It is exhausting trying to be 'man enough' for everyone all the time," Baldoni says. He rejects the notions that masculine is the opposite of feminine and that "boys are strong and girls are weak."[33]

Sheryl Sandberg, author of *Lean In*, is another advocate for change. She calls attention to a "broken rung" in the corporate ladder that often keeps qualified women from advancing.[34] In the United States, women earn about 60 percent of all bachelor's and master's degrees, but occupy only 21 percent of executive positions.[35,36] Part of the issue involves the way people think about and talk about gender. A study of 132 companies revealed that women are more likely than men to be labeled "bossy," "intimidating," and "aggressive" when they ask for a raise.[37] With the conviction that words matter, a range of celebrities—including Beyoncé, Condoleezza Rice, Jennifer Garner, Jimmie Johnson, and others—are part of the "Ban Bossy" movement that urges people to stop calling girls and women "bossy" when they display leadership traits.[38]

Changing people's attitudes about gender can be difficult, but it's not impossible. When Paula Stone Williams first came out, her father distanced himself from her. But more recently, he said, "Paula, I don't understand this, but I am willing to try." She reflects, "My father is 93 years old, and he's willing to try. What more could I ask?"[39]

PAUSE TO REFLECT *How Does Gender Influence Your Life?*

1. Do you think people would treat you differently if you were of a different gender? If so, how?

2. A woman may be considered bossy if she communicates assertively. What communication behaviors are considered unsuitable for men?

Emotional IQ and Communication

LEARNING OBJECTIVE 2.5: Explain dimensions of emotional intelligence and practice the technique of perception checking.

When Rafael wasn't given the promotion he wanted, he threw his tablet to the floor and stormed out of the office, yelling, "I quit!" The odds are that Rafael's emotional outburst caused the people around him to be glad he wasn't going to be on their team any longer.

Emotional intelligence (EI) is a person's ability to understand and manage their own emotions and to deal effectively with the emotions of others. The idea was made famous by psychologist Daniel Goleman,[40] who proposes that EI has five dimensions.

Self-Awareness

Understanding your own feelings (self-awareness) can be harder than it sounds. One reason is that emotions are often mixed. When something great happens to your best friend, you might realize that you feel happy but also a little jealous. At other times, like Rafael, your anger might be driven by frustration, disappointment, or embarrassment. Imagine how much better it would have been if Rafael had recognized those emotions, and perhaps even shared them with his colleagues.

Self-Regulation

Blogger Venkatesh Rao says he learned in kindergarten to count to 10 before responding to an emotional issue. To this day, he says, the technique is in his emotional intelligence toolbox because it helps him take stock of his emotions before blurting out something he might regret.[41] Good self-regulators have control over the way they communicate, and they manage their emotions in constructive ways.

Internal Motivation

Internal motivation involves finding the inner strength and determination to accomplish important goals. Consider success as a student. You may assume that people who do well in school are smarter than others, but research shows that a large part of their success arises from their ability to work hard, to persevere when the going gets tough, and to maintain confidence.[42] If pep talks aren't often part of your inner dialogue, you might consider the advice of marriage and family therapist Andrea Brandt, who says, "If your best friend felt stressed about work, what would you say to him or her? Now, try saying that to yourself."[43]

Empathy

Empathy is the willingness and ability to experience things from another person's point of view.[44] Although complete understanding of another person is impossible, if you listen well and make the effort, you can probably get a strong sense of what the world looks like through their eyes. Here are some ways to improve your ability to be empathic:[45]

- Set aside your own opinions and suspend judgment of the other person.
- Listen to better understand what the person is feeling. Remember that they may feel a mixture of emotions—such as joy *and* fear about a new relationship or opportunity.
- Use communication skills such as perception checking (see "Tips & Reminders: 3 Steps to Engage in Perception Checking") to clarify your understanding and listen before you make assumptions.

- Show genuine concern for the other person. Sincere statements such as "I can understand why you are upset" can encourage understanding and open communication.

Social Skills

Social skills involve the ability to communicate effectively with others. Some questions to ask yourself include: *Should I talk or listen right now? Is this a good time to bring up a touchy subject? How much personal information about myself should I share?* Insights throughout this book are designed to help.

Emotional intelligence offers many benefits. Travis Bradberry, who wrote *Emotional Intelligence 2.0*, observes that emotionally intelligent people don't get stressed as easily as others, are better at sharing their feelings, have a larger vocabulary of emotional terms, more easily forgive themselves and others for mistakes, and are less often misunderstood.[46] What's more, organizations led by people with high EI are usually more successful than others, partly because these leaders are self-aware, exercise emotional control, and are good at understanding how employees and customers feel.[47] Keep reading for tips about a process that can help you build empathy and an "About You" quiz on emotional intelligence. ●

TIPS & REMINDERS

3 Steps to Engage in Perception Checking

Perception checking is a communication technique designed to enhance empathy and emotional intelligence. It can help you understand others accurately instead of jumping to conclusions. Because the goal of perception checking is mutual understanding, it's a cooperative approach that minimizes defensiveness and displays respect. Here are the three steps involved.

1. **Describe the behavior you noticed.**

   The first step is to reference a specific behavior, as in, "I noticed that you left the room during my presentation." It's important to avoid jumping to conclusions, making value judgments, or presuming that you know how the other person was feeling. For example, it's not fair to say, "You are so rude" or "I can tell you didn't like my ideas." Such statements are likely to cause defensiveness, and they signal that you have already made up your mind without trying to understand the other person's feelings.

2. **Suggest at least two possible interpretations of the behavior.**

   Presenting two options that may be true opens the way for conversation and makes it explicit that you don't presume to know the other person's motives. For example, you might say, "When you left, I wasn't sure if something important came up or if you were disappointed in my presentation."

3. **Ask for clarification about how to interpret the behavior.**

   This step is simple but important. You might simply ask, "What was going on?" Here are some examples of perception checking that include all three steps:

   "Hey, when you slammed the door [behavior], *I wasn't sure whether you were mad at me* [first interpretation] *or just in a rush* [second interpretation]. *Are we good, or do you want to talk* [request for clarification]*?"*

   "You haven't laughed much in the last couple of days [behavior]. *I wonder whether something's bothering you* [first interpretation] *or whether you're just feeling quiet* [second interpretation]. *What's up?* [request for clarification]"

As you can see, a perception check takes a respectful approach by implying "I know I'm not qualified to understand your feelings without some help." Of course, it can succeed only if your nonverbal behavior reflects the open-mindedness of your words. An accusing tone of voice or a hostile glare will suggest that you have already made up your mind about the other person's intentions no matter what you say.

ABOUT YOU *How Emotionally Intelligent Are You?*

Answer the questions below for insights about how EI influences you as a communicator.

______ **1.** A friend says something that hurts your feelings. What are you most likely to say?

a. "That is so insensitive! I can't believe you just said that."
b. "I feel hurt by what you said."
c. "That makes me feel bad. Tell me why you feel that way."
d. Say nothing. You'll get over it.

______ **2.** It's Monday morning and you feel great. What are you most likely to do?

a. Take the day off. This feeling is too good to waste at work.
b. Announce to everyone at work, "I feel like a million bucks!"
c. Channel your positive energy into being a great team member.
d. Set your emotions aside and get to work. You'll enjoy yourself later.

______ **3.** Your usually talkative roommate is quiet today and seems to be looking out the window rather than focusing on the book he's trying to read for school. What are you most likely to do?

a. Tell him, "Focus! That book's not going to read itself."
b. Say that you understand because you've had a hard day too.
c. Ask if anything is bothering him and then listen attentively to what he says.
d. Give him some space. He's probably just tired.

______ **4.** The grade on your research paper is not as high as you had hoped. How are you most likely to respond?

a. Fume about what an idiot the professor is.
b. Post on social media that you are sad and discouraged today.
c. Go over the paper carefully to learn what you might do better next time.
d. Tell yourself, "What's done is done" and try to forget about it.

INTERPRETING YOUR RESPONSES

For insight about your emotional intelligence, see which of the following best describes your answers. (More than one may apply.)

Emotionally Spontaneous If you answered "a" to two or more questions, you tend to display your emotions boldly and spontaneously. This can be an asset in terms of self-expression, but be careful not to let your emotions get the best of you. Your unfiltered declarations may sometimes offend or overwhelm others, and they may prevent you from focusing on what other people are thinking and feeling. Suggestions in this chapter for perception checking and self-monitoring may help you strengthen the empathy and self-regulation components of EI.

Emotionally Self-Aware If you answered "b" more than once, you tend to be aware of your emotions and express them tactfully. You score relatively high in terms of EI. Just be careful to pair your self-awareness with active interest in others. You may feel impatient with people who are not as emotionally aware as you are. Stay tuned for listening tips and strategies in Chapter 5.

EI Champion If you answered "c" to two or more questions, you balance awareness of your own emotions with concern for how other people feel. Your willingness to be self-reflective and a good listener will take you far. Communication strategies throughout the book provide opportunities to build on your already-strong EI.

Emotion-Avoidant If you answered "d" more than once, you tend to downplay emotions—yours and other people's. While this may prevent you from overreacting, it may also make it difficult to build satisfying relationships and to harness the benefits of well-managed emotions. You may feel that others are taking advantage of you, when they actually don't know how you feel. The tips for self-disclosure in Chapter 7 may be especially useful to you.

Identity Management

LEARNING OBJECTIVE 2.6: Describe how personal behavior and the actions of others influence identity management.

Frank Baker was hiking alone one day when he felt his head getting sunburned. Reaching into his pack, he pulled out a pair of underwear and stretched it over his head like a cap. Baker forgot about his unconventional headdress until running into other hikers, who gave him funny looks.[48]

This section focuses on **identity management**—the communication strategies people use to influence how others view them. As Baker's experience shows, no one is perfect at presenting the self they wish others to see. All the same, many of the messages people send are meant to create desired impressions.

Individuals have public and private selves.

So far, we've referred to the "self" as if each person has only one identity. In truth, everyone has several selves, some private and others public. Often, these selves are quite different.

Your **perceived self** is the person you believe yourself to be in moments of honest self-examination. The perceived self is "private" because you are not likely to reveal all of it to another person. You can verify the private nature of the perceived self by reviewing the self-concept list you developed at the start of the chapter. You'll probably find some elements of yourself that you wouldn't disclose to many people, and some that you would not share with anyone. You might, for example, be reluctant to share some feelings about your appearance ("I think I'm unattractive"), your intelligence ("I'm not as smart as I wish I were"), your goals ("The most important thing to me is becoming rich"), or your motives ("I care more about myself than about others").

In contrast to the perceived self, the **presenting self** is a public image—the way you want to appear to others. In most cases, the presenting self you seek to create is a socially approved image: diligent student, loving partner, conscientious worker, and so on. Social norms often create a gap between the perceived and presenting selves. For example, you may present yourself as more confident than you actually feel.

People engage in facework to manage identities.

Sociologist Erving Goffman used the word **face** to describe the presenting self and the term **facework** to describe the verbal and nonverbal ways people try to maintain a positive image.[49] Goffman argued that each person can be viewed as a kind of playwright who creates roles they want others to believe and as a performer who acts out those roles. Depending on the circumstances, you may behave in ways that suggest to others that you are nice, competent, or artistic, for example.

It may seem logical that people would strive for the best face possible—the "nicest person in the world" or the "best artist in town." Two factors discourage this, however. One is an embarrassing loss of face if you can't live up to that image. The other is the way that your face goals make others feel. You have probably known people who acted as if they were "the best," with the unwelcome implication that others were inferior to them. All in all, although everyone wants to be viewed in positive terms, it's face-saving not to overdo it.

Identity management is collaborative.

Identity management is not a solo enterprise. Attaining a particular identity relies on how willing other people are to accept it. If they don't, the results can be frustrating and hurtful. For example, women may be hindered by colleagues who treat them like sex objects or view them as inferior simply because they are women. Or you may find that people assume unfavorable things about you based on your age, physical abilities, ethnicity, appearance, or some other factor. (We'll talk more about stereotypes in Chapter 3.)

At other times, however, people are active agents in helping one another save face. Consider, for example, what you might do if someone you know arrives at a party with their fly unzipped. If you know the person well, you might point it out so they can avoid further embarrassment. Or you might pretend you don't notice. Either way, you're engaged in a cooperative effort to help that person save face, just as you hope others will help you.

People have multiple identities.

In the course of even a single day, you may play a variety of roles: respectful student, joking friend, friendly neighbor, and helpful employee, to suggest just a few. You may even play a variety of roles with the same person. With your parents, for instance, perhaps you acted as a responsible adult sometimes ("You can trust me with the car.") and at other times as a helpless child ("I can't find my shoes!"). Sometimes—perhaps on birthdays or holidays—you were a dedicated family member, and at other times you may have been antisocial and locked yourself in your room. People exercise the same level of versatility in different situations. One scholar pointed out that bilingual Latinxs in the United States often choose whether to use English or Spanish depending on who they are speaking to and the kind of identity they seek in a given conversation.[50]

Identity management may be deliberate or unconscious.

Sometimes you are probably highly aware of managing your identities, as when you are on a job interview or a first date. But in other cases, you may act largely out of habit or an unconscious sense of what is appropriate.[51] For example, people tend to smile and display sympathetic expressions more during in-person conversations than they do on the phone.[52] You probably don't consciously think, "Since the other person can (or can't) see me, I'll alter my nonverbal displays." Reactions like these are often instantaneous and

outside of your conscious awareness. Another kind of unconscious face management involves "scripts" you have developed over time. When you find yourself in familiar situations, such as greeting customers at work or interacting with friends or family members, you probably slip into scripts that fit the occasion.

People differ in their degree of identity management.

Some people are more aware of their identity management behavior than others. As we discussed in Chapter 1, **high self-monitors** pay close attention to their own behavior and to others' reactions, adjusting their communication to create the desired impression. By contrast, **low self-monitors** express what they are thinking and feeling without much attention to the impression their behavior creates.[53] There are pros and cons to both approaches.

High self-monitors are generally:

- Good actors who can act interested when bored, or friendly when they actually feel the opposite. This allows them to handle social situations smoothly, often putting others at ease.
- Good "people-readers" who can adjust their behavior to get a desired reaction from others. For example, they tend to post pictures and messages online that make them seem especially outgoing, which correlates to a higher-than-average number of "likes."[54]
- Unlikely to experience events completely because a portion of their attention is always devoted to viewing the situation from a detached position.
- Hard to read. Even close friends may have a difficult time discerning how a high self-monitor really feels.

Low self-monitors are generally:

- Easy to read. They have a limited repertoire of behaviors, so they act in more or less the same way regardless of the situation. "What you see is what you get" might be their motto.
- Straightforward communicators with clear and consistent ideas about how they feel and who they are. This can make them reliable and honest. But a lack of flexibility often makes them less tactful than high self-monitors.

By now it should be clear that neither extremely high nor low self-monitoring is ideal. There are some situations in which paying attention to yourself and adapting your behavior can be useful, but sometimes, reacting without considering the effect on others is a better approach. This demonstrates again the notion of communicative competence outlined in Chapter 1: *Flexibility is the key to successful communication.*

Social rules influence identity management.

Social rules govern your behavior in a variety of settings. It would be impossible to keep a job, for example, without meeting certain expectations. Salespeople are obliged to treat customers with courtesy, employees must appear reasonably respectful when talking to the manager, and some forms of clothing would be considered outrageous at work. By agreeing to take on a job, you are signing an unwritten contract that you will present a certain face at work, whether or not that face reflects the way you might feel at a particular moment.

Identity management can be goal oriented.

People often manage their identities strategically. You might dress up for a visit to traffic court in hopes that your front (responsible citizen) will convince the judge to treat you sympathetically. Or you might be nice to your neighbors so they will agree to keep their dog off your lawn. It's difficult—even impossible—not to create impressions. After all, you have to send some sort of message. If you don't act friendly when meeting a stranger, you have to act aloof, indifferent, hostile, or in some other manner. If you don't act businesslike, you have to behave in an alternative way—casual, goofy, or whatever. Often, the question isn't whether or not to present a face to others but which face to present.

Identity management isn't necessarily dishonest.

After reading this far, you might think that identity management sounds like a form of manipulation or phoniness. If the perceived self is the "real" you, it might seem that any behavior that contradicts it is dishonest. It's true that there are situations in which identity management is dishonest. A manipulative date who pretends to be single, even though they are married, is clearly unethical and deceitful. So are job applicants who lie about their academic records to get hired. But managing identities doesn't necessarily make you a liar. In fact, it's almost impossible to imagine how you could communicate effectively without making decisions about which front to present in one situation or another. It would be ludicrous for you to act the same way with strangers as you do with close friends, and nobody would show the same face to a 2-year-old as to an adult. Each of us has a repertoire of faces—a cast of characters—and part of being a competent communicator is choosing the best role for the situation. ●

PAUSE TO REFLECT *Which Identities Do You Enact?*

1. Compare the identity you construct when interacting with older family members (e.g., parents, aunts, or uncles) to the identity you construct when spending time with your best friend. How do they differ?

2. What other identities do you construct for different relationships and roles you play?

Identity Management and Social Media

LEARNING OBJECTIVE 2.7: Analyze the challenge of using social media to present a favorable image while still being authentic.

Rachel Leonard had it made. Newly wed to the love of her life, she could relax on her front porch and enjoy a beautiful view of the Blue Ridge Mountains, all the while looking forward to the birth of their first child. Well, to be more accurate, *virtual* Rachel had all of those things.

Rachel's Facebook page included happy wedding pictures, gorgeous mountain scenes, and pregnancy updates. Real-life Rachel was grappling with a difficult pregnancy and a growing realization that she had married the wrong person. And the beautiful scenery? The mountain view straight ahead *was* gorgeous, "but if you looked to the left, you could see this huge factory," she admits, adding, "Of course, I didn't take [or post] pictures of the factory because why would you do that?"[55]

Rachel faced a common dilemma rooted in self-concept, communication, and perception: she wanted to present herself favorably to others. At the same time, she craved the genuine approval of people who understood and accepted her as she was. Concerns such as these are central to the communication choices people make. Here we consider the impact of social media in managing that delicate balance.

Social media can boost self-esteem.

Conventional wisdom suggests that face-to-face communication is richer and more meaningful than mediated messages in terms of boosting self-esteem, but that isn't always true. Research with adults 35 and younger suggests that text-based interactions—such as through emails, texts, and tweets—often contribute to self-esteem more than do in-person and telephone conversations. The reasons are twofold. First, people (at least in that age bracket) tend to disclose things about themselves in writing that they wouldn't share in person. And technology makes it possible to receive support, even from people who aren't available to offer it in person.[56] The caveat is that self-esteem is not boosted when people present an unrealistically positive image of themselves online.

Being genuine matters most.

People tend strategically to post photos that make them appear attractive and socially engaged with others.[57] They may carefully edit social media posts until they make the desired impression.[58] This is okay within limits. But ultimately, confidence arises from a sense of being accepted for the genuine you. College students who accept their own strengths and weaknesses are more likely than their peers to show their true selves on social media. Consequently, they enjoy the security of knowing that others like them for who they really are, imperfections and all.[59] As one social media analyst puts it, stop *trophy hunting*—trying to find that perfect picture or story that will play well on social media—and enjoy your life.[60] Share what happens naturally, not what you have manufactured to impress others.

Self-esteem can enhance emotional resilience.

People who feel good about themselves are more likely than others to believe and enjoy compliments.[61] They are also more resilient in the face of criticism. For example, individuals with healthy self-esteem who are the targets of cyberbullying are more likely than those with low self-esteem to tell others about the bullying and to see bullies as immature and eager to prove their own status.[62] That's not to say that bullying is okay or can always be shrugged off. It does suggest, however, that being silent or self-critical can make unkind comments feel even worse.

The Self, Perception, and Communication

The Self-Concept Defined

- Self-concept includes people's sense of what is unique about them and what makes them similar to others.
- Self-esteem involves people's evaluations of self-worth.

Factors That Influence Communication and Self-Concept

- Significant others
- Mass media
- Culture
- Expectations

Common Errors in Attribution

- Individuals judge themselves more charitably than they judge others.
- People pay more attention to negative impressions than to positive ones.
- When people do perceive positive qualities, they tend to overgeneralize.
- People gravitate to the familiar.

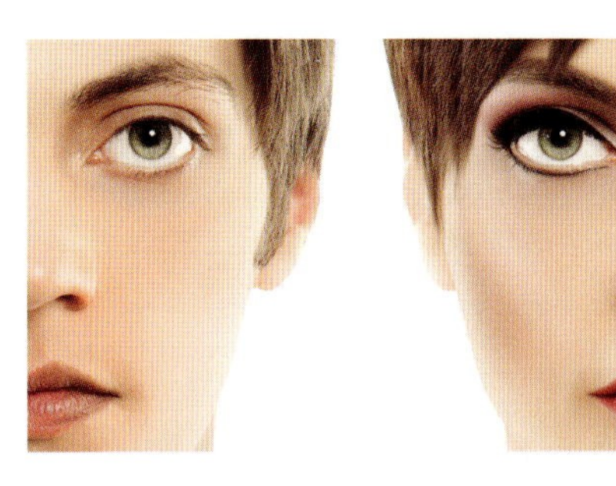

Misconceptions About Gendered Communication

- Myth 1: *Sex* and *gender* are the same.
- Myth 2: Communication styles are either masculine or feminine.
- Myth 3: There is an "opposite" sex.
- Myth 4: Gender roles are rooted in biology.

Emotional Intelligence Includes . . .

- Self-awareness.
- Self-regulation of emotions.
- Internal motivation to persevere.
- Empathy.
- Social skills.

Stages in Perception Checking

- Describe the behavior you noticed.
- Suggest at least two possible interpretations of the behavior.
- Ask for clarification about how to interpret the behavior.

Identity Management Involves . . .

- Public and private selves.
- Collaboration with others.
- Multiple identities.
- Conscious and unconscious effort.
- Degrees of self-monitoring.
- Role expectations.
- Goals.

Identity and Social Media

- Social media can boost self-esteem.
- The ultimate confidence arises from a sense that people accept you as you are.
- Self-esteem can enhance emotional resilience.

Show Your Communication Know-How

2.1: Explain the self-concept and its relation to self-esteem.

Consider people who know you best. How do they enhance your self-esteem? Do they ever challenge it? If so, how?

KEY TERMS: self-concept, self-esteem

2.2: Analyze ways that communication both influences and reflects the self-concept.

How do you compare to "very attractive" people portrayed in the media? Do such comparisons influence the way you think about yourself? If so, how?

KEY TERMS: reflected appraisal, significant others, self-fulfilling prophecy

2.3: Recognize tendencies that lead to distorted perceptions of yourself and others and how those distortions affect communication.

If you get a parking ticket, you might say the space wasn't well marked or nothing else was available. How might your opinion differ if someone takes *your* parking space? Explain the influence of self-serving bias.

KEY TERMS: attribution, self-serving bias, fundamental attribution error, halo effect

2.4: Counteract myths about gendered communication with more accurate information.

How do people's perceptions of your gender influence the way they think about you? How do their perceptions affect the way they communicate with you verbally and nonverbally? What privileges are associated with your gender? What disadvantages?

KEY TERMS: sex, gender, cisgender, transgender, androgynous, undifferentiated

2.5: Explain dimensions of emotional intelligence and practice the technique of perception checking.

Rate yourself from 1 to 10 on each of the five dimensions of emotional intelligence: self-awareness, self-regulation, internal motivation, empathy, and social skills. Which are you best at? Which are you worst at?

KEY TERMS: emotional intelligence (EI), empathy, perception checking

2.6: Describe how personal behavior and the actions of others influence identity management.

Describe a situation in which you were embarrassed—in Goffman's terms, when you lost face. What aspect of your desired social identity was threatened by the episode? How did you respond to save face as much as possible?

KEY TERMS: identity management, perceived self, presenting self, face, facework, high self-monitors, low self-monitors

2.7: Analyze the challenge of using social media to present a favorable image while still being authentic.

If you have a social media presence, does it mostly show you in a genuine way, imperfections and all, or in a way that makes you look as good as possible? What do you think would happen if your social media identity changed?

3 CULTURE AND Communication

Culture Defined

LEARNING OBJECTIVE 3.1: Define culture and coculture and differentiate between in-groups and out-groups.

Cultures may differ even within the same family, neighborhood, and organization. You embody different cultural assumptions throughout the day as you shift between the various roles you play.

While growing up in India, Priya was taught not to smile or make eye contact with strangers, since those actions might be construed as a sexual invitation. On her first day visiting Mexico, Priya shared the hotel elevator with a man who was also a guest there. "The Mexicans are very warm and friendly people," Priya says, "He smiled and greeted me with 'Buenos días.' I wanted to greet him back, but just couldn't. . . . I gave an awkward smile and stayed silent." The man then used a form of sign language to say hello. Priya realized that he mistakenly thought she was Deaf. Even though the encounter was awkward, Priya says she appreciated his friendly manner.[1]

Like Priya, you have probably experienced challenges interacting with people who grew up differently than you, but the rewards can be worth it. Here we explore some key concepts in intercultural communication.

Culture and Coculture

Culture is "the language, values, beliefs, traditions, and customs people share and learn."[2] The episode Priya described involves cultural expectations about how to interact with strangers. Social scientists use the term **coculture** to describe a group that is part of an encompassing culture. For example, you may feel like part of an overarching American culture but also feel membership in youth culture, a Hispanic community, a religious or political group, or many other cocultures.

Salience

Depending on the situation, cultural differences may seem nearly insurmountable or practically nonexistent. For example, if you're on an athletic team with people who are Asian American, African American, Latinx, and European American, cultural differences may seem minimal compared to the shared goal of winning the league championship. But away from the game, cultural traditions (such as how you express emotions or manage conflict) might influence communication. Social scientists use the term **salience** to describe how much weight people attach to cultural characteristics in a particular situation.

In-Group and Out-Group

If you consider everyone you know, you'll probably identify more closely with some than with others. Social scientists use the term **in-group** to describe people we consider to be similar to us and with whom we have an emotional connection. The term **out-group** describes people we view as different and with whom we have little or no sense of affiliation.[3] Context is a factor in group membership. At home, your family members may feel in-group to you, but at a rock concert, your friends may feel more in-group than your family members.

Although cultural norms and values influence communication in powerful ways, there are sometimes greater differences *within* cultures than *between* them. If you've ever met someone from a different part of the world, you may have been surprised by how much you have in common.

Cultural Values and Norms

LEARNING OBJECTIVE 3.2: Analyze how values and norms affect communication between members of different cultures.

Cultures differ along some key dimensions, such as how they define group identity, uncertainty, power, and silence.

Growing up in the Netherlands, Daniëlle didn't anticipate that she would fall in love with a Sudanese man. However, she and her now-husband Hussam connected right away. "Even though we were from different continents, we had an insane amount of things in common," she says. "We both loved to read the same books and liked playing around with graphic design. We understood each other."[4]

Even so, Daniëlle was initially nervous about getting to know Hussam, based on stereotypes she had heard about Arab men. Over time, she says, she learned a valuable lesson: "We are not the stereotypes people have about us. . . . We are all just people, with differences and similarities, strengths and weaknesses, habits and customs."[5]

One way to reduce the uncertainty about communicating with people from different cultures is to better understand key norms and values. Here is a look at five patterns that help distinguish cultures around the world.

Individualism and Collectivism

Members of **individualistic cultures**—including the United States, Canada, and Great Britain—tend to regard people as unique and independent. Idioms such as "Be your own person" and "Stand up for yourself" convey an emphasis on individuality. By contrast, communicators in **collectivistic cultures**—such as those in China, Korea, and Japan—typically put more emphasis on group membership.[6,7] Popular sayings in Japan include "Different body, same mind" and "Child of a frog is a frog," which emphasize shared values and characteristics.

Here are some of the ways that people in individualistic and collectivistic cultures approach communication:

- Members of individualistic cultures are relatively tolerant of conflicts, whereas those in collectivistic cultures place a greater emphasis on harmony.[8,9]
- People in individualistic societies are likely to tout their personal accomplishments, whereas those in collectivistic societies often consider it polite to deny or downplay their talents and achievements. This difference can lead to misunderstandings in the classroom and on job interviews. For example, individualistic Americans may assume that individuals of Asian descent who behave in a humble manner lack confidence or are less capable than others.
- Compared to members of collectivistic cultures, people accustomed to individualism tend to value independence and put less effort into seeing

others' points of view. In one study, Chinese and American players were paired together in a game that required them to take the perspective of their partners.[10] The collectivist Chinese had greater success in perspective taking than did their individualistic American counterparts.

High and Low Context

Members of **low-context cultures** use language primarily to express thoughts, feelings, and ideas as directly as possible. But members of **high-context cultures** rely more on subtle, often nonverbal cues—such as behavior, history of the relationship, and general social rules—to maintain social harmony.[11]

Many cultures in the United States, Canada, northern Europe, and Israel are at the low-context end of the scale. Longtime residents generally value straight talk and grow impatient with "beating around the bush." By contrast, people in most Asian and Middle Eastern cultures fit the high-context pattern. For them, maintaining harmony is important, so communicators avoid speaking directly if doing so may threaten another person's "face" or dignity.[12] One Chinese exchange student in the United States gave this example:

> *Suppose a guy feels bad about his roommate eating his snacks. If he is Chinese, he may try to hide his food secretly or choose a certain time to say, "My snacks run out so fast, I think I need to buy more next time." Before this, he also may think about whether his roommate would hate him if he says something wrong. But Americans may point out directly that someone has been eating their food.*[13]

The roommate from China may feel his displeasure is obvious, based on the situation and his indirect statement. But the American, who may expect his friend to say outright if he is upset, may miss the point.

It's easy to see how the difference between directness and indirectness can present challenges. To members of high-context cultures, communicators with a low-context style can appear inattentive, overly talkative, redundant, and lacking in subtlety. On the other hand, to people from low-context backgrounds, high-context communicators may seem evasive or even dishonest.

Uncertainty Avoidance

Uncertainty may be universal, but cultures have different ways of coping with unpredictable conditions. **Uncertainty avoidance** reflects the degree to which members of a culture feel threatened by ambiguous situations.[14] As a group, residents of some countries (including Singapore, Great Britain, Denmark, Sweden, Hong Kong, and the United States) tend to embrace change, while others (such as natives of Belgium, Greece, Japan, and Portugal) tend to find new or ambiguous situations discomforting.

A culture's degree of uncertainty avoidance is reflected in the way its members communicate. In countries that avoid uncertainty, people are especially concerned with security, so they feel a strong need for clearly defined rules and regulations. People who are different or who express ideas that challenge the status quo are often considered dangerous. By contrast, individuals in cultures that feel less threatened by the new and unexpected are more likely to tolerate—and even honor—those who don't fit the norm. Unconventional people may be lauded as trailblazers and innovators.

Power Distance

Power distance refers to the gap between those with substantial power and resources and those with less. Cultures with low power distance believe in minimizing the difference between social classes. They tend to subscribe to the egalitarian belief that one person is as good as another regardless of their station in life—rich, poor, educated, or uneducated.

Austria, Denmark, Israel, and New Zealand are some of the most egalitarian countries. Most cultures in the United States and Canada value equality, even if that ideal is not always perfectly enacted. For example, Americans may call their bosses by their first names and challenge the opinions of people in higher status positions.

At the other end of the spectrum are countries with a high degree of power distance, such as the Philippines, Mexico, Venezuela, India, Japan, and Singapore.[15] In these countries, it may seem rude to treat everyone the same way. In the Japanese workplace, for example, new acquaintances exchange business cards immediately, which helps establish everyone's relative status. The oldest or highest ranking person receives the deepest bows from others, the best seat, the most deferential treatment, and so on. This treatment isn't regarded as elitist or disrespectful. Indeed, treating a high-status person the same as everyone else would seem rude.

Talk and Silence

Beliefs about the value of talk differ from one culture to another.[16] Members of Western cultures tend to view talk as desirable and use it for social purposes as well as to perform tasks. Silence has a negative value in these cultures. It is likely to be interpreted as lack of interest, or as hostility, anxiety, shyness, or incompatibility.

On the other hand, silence is valued in Asian cultures. Taoist sayings propose that "In much talk there is great weariness" and "One who speaks does not know; one who knows does not speak." Unlike most Westerners, who find silence embarrassing and awkward, traditional Japanese and Chinese individuals tend to believe that remaining quiet is the proper state when there is nothing to be said. To Asians, a talkative person is often considered a show-off or a fake.

Members of some Native American communities also honor silence. For example, traditional members of western Apache tribes may maintain silence when others lose their temper to avoid making the situation worse.[17] Many Apaches also consider silence to be comforting. The idea is that words are often unnecessary in periods of grief, and it is comforting to have loved ones present without the pressure to maintain conversations with them.

It's easy to see how these views of speech and silence can lead to communication challenges when people from different cultures meet. Both the "talkative" Westerner and the "silent" Asian and Native American are behaving in ways they believe are proper, yet each may view the other with disapproval and mistrust. Only when they recognize the dissimilarities in their cultural expectations can they adapt to one another, or at least understand and respect their differences. •

PAUSE TO REFLECT *What Cultural Norms Do You Embrace?*

1. In what ways is your identity shaped by who you are as an individual? In what ways is it shaped by the groups to which you belong (e.g., your family, hometown, college, clubs, religion, and so on)? Do you identify more with the cultural value of individualism or collectivism? ____________________

2. If the vice president of a company where you work initiates a conversation with you in the hallway, in what ways do you demonstrate that there is power distance between you (e.g., in terms of your greeting, behaviors, conversation topics, formality, and so on)? In general, do you mostly embody a high power distance or a belief that all people are equal, regardless of their rank or status? ____________________

3. Imagine that you are hanging out with friends when a lull occurs in the conversation. Do you appreciate the silence or find it uncomfortable? How does your comfort (or discomfort) with silence affect the way you communicate? Does this vary by relationship? If so, how? ____________________

ABOUT YOU *How Much Do You Know About Other Cultures?*

Answer the questions below to test your knowledge about what is culturally appropriate around the world.

_______ **1.** Japanese visitors are in town. You've heard that Japanese custom involves gift giving. What should you know?

a. It's important that gifts be expensive and of the finest quality.
b. Avoid gifts that come in threes, as in three flowers or three candies.
c. It's preferable to sign the accompanying card in green ink rather than black.
d. It is not customary to wrap gifts in Japan.

_______ **2.** You are interacting with a person who is Deaf and who uses an interpreter. What should you do?

a. Address your comments to the interpreter, then look at the Deaf person to see how they react.
b. Maintain eye contact with the Deaf person rather than the interpreter.
c. Offer to communicate in written form so the interpreter will be unnecessary.
d. Speak very slowly and exaggerate the movements your mouth makes.

_______ **3.** While traveling in China, you should be aware of which rule of dining etiquette?

a. It's considered rude to leave food on your plate.
b. You should put your drinking glass on your plate when you finish eating.
c. Cloth napkins are just for show there. Use a paper napkin to wipe your mouth.
d. Avoid sticking your chopsticks upright in your food when you are not using them.

_______ **4.** You are meeting with a group of Arab businesspeople for the first time. What should you know?

a. They favor greetings that involve shaking hands and kissing on each cheek.
b. It's polite to say no if an Arab host offers you coffee or tea.
c. Men tend to be touch avoidant and to stand at least 3 feet from one another during conversations.
d. They consider the left hand unsanitary and hold eating utensils only with their right hands.

INTERPRETING YOUR RESPONSES |
Read the explanations below to see which questions you got right.

Question 1 Gift-giving is an important ritual in Japan, but gifts needn't be extravagant or expensive. The number 3 is fine, but avoid gifts that involve 4 or 9, as these numbers rhyme with the Japanese words for *death* and *suffering*, respectively, and are considered unlucky.[18] Black is associated with death or bad luck, so green ink, which symbolizes good luck, is preferred.[19] Gift wrapping is expected and is even considered an art form. The correct answer is c.

Question 2 Treat Deaf people with the same courtesy as anyone else—maintain eye contact and focus on them.[20] The correct answer is b.

Question 3 Cultures vary in terms of whether it is rude to eat everything or rude not to. In China, leaving a little food on your plate lets your hosts know they have provided plentifully for you. However, sticking your chopsticks upright in your food evokes thoughts of funerals, where it's customary to place a stick of lighted incense upright in a container of rice.[21] The correct answer is d.

Question 4 Members of Arab cultures may shake hands and kiss on each cheek, but usually only with people they already know well. Kisses are not appropriate for an introductory business meeting.[22] It's polite to accept a host's offer of coffee or tea. Men tend to speak at close distances (far closer than 3 feet) unless the conversation involves a woman, in which case it is rude to touch or crowd her.[23] It's considered unclean to eat with one's left hand (even if you are left handed),[24] harkening back to days when the left hand was used for personal hygiene. The correct answer is d.

Communication and Cocultures

LEARNING OBJECTIVE 3.3: Apply the concept of intersectionality to your communication, and identify communication factors that help shape cocultural identity.

Because individuals are members of many cocultural groups simultaneously, their identity arises from a complex interplay of cultural expectations. Here we explore some of the factors at play.

It's overly simplistic to think of individuals as the sum total of their various identities. Imagine, for example, that you are an Italian American person raised in the American Midwest who uses a wheelchair. It's unlikely that a person with similar physiology in a different community or part of the world will experience life in quite the same way as you. The same is true of all aspects of your identity.

Intersectionality theory describes the complex interplay of people's multiple identities. It proposes that each person experiences life at the intersection of multiple factors that give rise to a unique perspective and collection of experiences.[25,26] Intersectionality theorists argue that it's a mistake to focus on one cultural or cocultural dimension in isolation. Instead, identity is shaped by the interplay of many elements simultaneously.[27] With that in mind, treat the following descriptions not as a formula for understanding people, but as a way of exploring qualities that contribute in countless ways to creating cultural diversity.

Race and Ethnicity

Khama Ennis wears a large name tag that identifies her as a physician—as do the other doctors in the emergency department where she works. But Ennis is Black, and that seems to baffle some patients, who make comments such as "Where are you from?" and "You don't look like a doctor."[28] Ennis says she makes an extra effort to be friendly and professional, but she is aware that her White colleagues don't face the same communication hurdles that she does.

The notion of **race** was created hundreds of years ago to reflect differences between people whose ancestors originated in different regions of the world—Africa, Asia, Europe, and so on. Actually, there is no scientific basis for the idea of race.[29] There is more biological diversity between people in general than between one race and another, and superficial qualities such as skin color and hair texture don't actually say anything about a person. As one analyst puts it: "There is less to race than meets the eye."[30]

Ethnicity is a social construct that refers to the degree to which a person identifies with a particular group, usually on the basis of nationality, culture, religion, or some other perspective. For example, people from around the world who speak Spanish may look very different from one another but experience a sense of shared identity.

Although there is no physical basis for race and ethnicity, their impact is powerful at a social level. About 10,000 racial slurs a day appear on Twitter alone.[31] More than half of Black, Latinx, and Asian teens in the United States say they encounter demeaning comments about racial and ethnic groups online.[32] One antidote to prejudice is knowledge.

Regional Differences

It's a bad idea to judge people based on their accents or where they grew up. Individual differences are far too great for that. But seen overall, there are regional cultures. For example, in research about the personality profiles of people in the United States, three "psychological regions" emerged.[33]

- In Middle America (a zone extending southward from Montana and Michigan to Louisiana and over to the Carolinas), people tend to place a high value on being friendly and conventional. That is, they are more likely than residents of other regions to be extroverted, considerate, traditional, and dutiful.
- People on the West Coast and in the Rocky Mountains and Sunbelt (from California and Arizona up through Washington and Idaho) are more often described as relaxed and creative. They are

inclined to value new ideas, innovation, and individualism.

- To outsiders, people raised in the Middle Atlantic and Northeast regions of the country (most of New England) may seem temperamental and even a little anxious or irritable. Insiders typically describe themselves in different terms—as passionate, plain talking, and firm in their convictions.

The differences seem to stem from the degree of cultural diversity in each region (the Western region being particularly diverse), people's choice to move to regions that suit their personalities, and cultural norms that encourage some communication styles and discourage others. Given these differences, it's easy to imagine how a first-year college student from the Midwest might view a new roommate from Massachusetts as unfriendly, and how the New Englander might view a West Coast native as fickle and unfocused.

Sexual Orientation and Gender

As we discussed in Chapter 2, the traditional concept of two "opposite" sexes has given way to a less constrictive, more inclusive notion of gender identity. *Masculine* and *feminine* are but two adjectives in a broad constellation of gender-related qualities. The acronym LGBTQIA+ stands for lesbian, gay, bisexual, transgender, queer or questioning, intersex, asexual and/or aromantic, and more. Other identities include genderfluid, gender independent, gender expansive, and gender diverse.[34]

It is now commonly accepted that gender identity may change over time and is not strictly tied to physical features. For example, transgender individuals don't feel that the biological sex attributed to them at birth is a good description of who they are. And people typically describe themselves as queer if they don't feel that gender adjectives describe them well or if they dislike the idea of gender categorizations in general.[35]

Whereas individuals in some cultures are receptive to diverse gender identities and sexual orientations, others are more disapproving. On average, 1 in 5 hate crimes in the United States targets people on the basis of their sexual orientation or gender identity.[36]

One aspect, but certainly not the only one, of gender identity involves sexual orientation. "Every time I meet someone new I must decide if, how, and when I will reveal my sexual orientation,"[37] reflects Jennifer Potter, a physician who is gay. She says it's often easy to "pass" as heterosexual, but then she experiences the awkwardness of people assuming that she has a boyfriend or husband, and it saddens her when she cannot openly refer to her partner or invite her to take part in social gatherings.

Although they acknowledge the communication dilemmas they face, most LGBTQIA+ individuals don't want the public to see them in tragic terms. Aside from issues of social acceptance, many say their lives are just as happy and productive as anyone else's.

Religion

In some cultures, religion is a defining factor in shaping in- and out-groups. For example, amid fears of international terrorism, peace-loving Muslims living in the West have often been singled out and vilified. Yasmin Hussein, who works at the Arab American Institute, reflects:

> *Many Muslims and individuals of other faiths who were thought to be Muslim have been attacked physically and verbally. Young children have been bullied at schools, others told to go back home and social media has become at times (a lot of the time) an ugly place to be on.*[38]

In an effort to dispel unrealistic stereotypes, tens of thousands of Muslims have joined the #NotInMyName social media movement in which they denounce terrorist groups such as ISIS and condemn violence perpetrated in the name of the religion.

In less extreme but still profound ways, religion may shape how and with whom people communicate. Newcomers to some regions of the United States might find that one of the first questions people ask them is, "What church do you attend?" And members of some religions consider it important to marry within the faith. In a study of young Orthodox Jewish women, for example, many of them said that a man's religious preference is as important, or more important, than his personality.[39]

Communication plays a large role in negotiating the impact of different religious preferences. Religious teens who respect the viewpoints of multiple religions typically date more frequently than their nonreligious peers.[40] And the odds are good for interfaith couples. Studies show that, if they communicate openly and respectfully about matters of faith, they are just as likely as other couples to stay together.[41]

Disability

As in any group, there is no absolute consensus among people with disabilities on the terms they consider most respectful and accurate, but here are some general best practices in terms of communication.

- *Be cautious about supposed euphemisms.* Terms such as "differently abled," "challenged," and "special" are typically not preferred.[42,43] Emily Ladau of the Center for Disability Rights explains that it can feel demeaning "when non-disabled people try to dance around the world 'disabled'" as if it is a "negative quality or derogatory word, when in fact, disabled is what I am."[44]
- *Be sensitive to preferred terminology.* Many people with disabilities prefer "people first" language, such as "a person who is blind" rather than "a blind person." The idea is that a disability is only part, sometimes a very small part, of what makes the person unique. On the other hand, members of some groups—such as many people who are Deaf or Autistic—prefer "identity first" language, such as "Autistic person." They believe that their identity is closely tied with the condition and there is no need to distance themselves from it. "After all, we don't frantically try to avoid saying 'a blond girl,'" say the authors of the Disability in Kidlit blog, who add, "No one is insisting on 'a girl with blond hair' or a 'girl with blondness.'"[45]
- *Avoid judgments.* Don't use language that implies that people with disabilities should be pitied ("victim" or "sufferer") or regarded as special ("heroic" or "inspiring"). Also avoid saying that someone is "wheelchair bound." Instead, say that they use a wheelchair.[46] As accessibility researcher Dot Nary puts it, "I personally am not 'bound' by my wheelchair. It is a very liberating device that allows me to work, play, maintain a household, connect with family and friends, and 'have a life.'"[47]

Political Viewpoints

As one analyst quipped, "Liberals like to have fun. Conservatives like to have fun. Liberals and Conservatives like to have fun with each other . . . unless they're talking about politics."[48] Political discussions have become one of the most contentious examples of intercultural communication in the United States.

Conventional wisdom advises people to steer conversations away from politics and religion, recognizing the sensitive nature of talking about deeply held beliefs. Perhaps for that reason, many people use electronic means to express their views. In the United States, nearly 2 out of 3 people who use social media have posted messages encouraging others to join a political or social cause.[49] Their approach is not always productive, however. About 55 percent of Americans who use social media say they are tired of seeing political messages online, mostly because there seems to be little room for a respectful exchange of ideas.[50]

Some people are invested in turning people against one another online. **Social media trolls** are individuals whose principal goal is to disrupt public discourse by posting false claims and prejudiced remarks, usually behind a mask of anonymity. In a similar but more personal way, **social media snarks** post insulting comments about people to get a rise out of them. You can minimize the hurtful impact of these saboteurs by following the guidance in "Tips & Reminders: 3 Ways to Discuss Politics Responsibly on Social Media." ●

TIPS & REMINDERS

3 Ways to Discuss Politics Responsibly on Social Media

Experts offer the following tips for engaging in responsible political discourse online.[51]

1. **Don't assume that what you read or watch online is true.**

   Sometimes it's difficult to know which sources to trust. As a general rule, check to see if multiple sources with different perspectives are reporting the same information.

2. **Don't troll or snark.**

   It's okay to disagree respectfully, but never post messages that insult or belittle others. As one observer puts it, "Disagreement is perfectly normal," but using those differences to bash others is unacceptable.[52]

3. **Be open minded about different opinions.**

   Resist the temptation to block responsible messages that differ from your own. You'll never learn anything new if you aren't willing to hear about different ways of thinking.

Age and Generation

LEARNING OBJECTIVE 3.4: Explain communication patterns within and between different age groups.

Imagine how odd it would seem if an 8-year-old or a senior citizen started talking, dressing, or otherwise acting like a 20-year-old.

We tend to think of getting older as a purely biological process. But age-related communication reflects culture at least as much as it reflects biology. In many ways, we learn how to "do" being various ages—how to dress, how to talk, and what not to say and do—in the same way we learn how to play other roles in our lives, such as student or employee.

Ideas about aging change over time.

At some points in history, older adults have been regarded as wise, accomplished, and even magical.[53] At others, they have been treated as "dead weight" and uncomfortable reminders of mortality and decline.[54] Today, for the most part, Western cultures honor youth, and attitudes about aging tend to be negative. On balance, people over age 40 are twice as likely as younger people to be depicted in the media as unattractive, bored, and in declining health.[55] And people over age 60, especially women, are still underrepresented in the media. Despite negative stereotypes, the data present a different story. Studies show that, overall, individuals in their 60s are just as happy as those in their 20s.[56]

Stereotypes discourage open communication.

People who believe older adults have trouble communicating are less likely to interact with them. And when they do interact, it's common for them to use simple words and speak slowly. Even when these speech styles are well intentioned, they can have harmful effects. Older adults who are treated as incapable tend to perceive *themselves* to be older and less capable than their peers.[57] And challenging ageism (hurtful stereotypes based on age) presents seniors with a dilemma: Speaking up can be taken as a sign of being cranky or bitter, reinforcing negative assumptions.[58]

Being young has its challenges.

Teens and young adults often experience intense pressure to establish their identity and prove themselves.[59] At the same time, adolescents typically experience what psychologists call a **personal fable**, the belief that they are different from everybody else, and **imaginary audience**, a heightened self-consciousness that makes it seem as if people are always observing and judging them.[60] These beliefs can lead to some classic communication challenges. Teens often feel that their parents and others can't understand them because their situations are unique. They may get annoyed when adults seem to butt into their affairs with "overly critical judgments" and "irrelevant advice." All the while, parents may not understand why their "extensive experience" and "good advice" are rejected.

Generations regard technology differently.

It probably won't surprise you that young adults are more likely than older ones to share personal information online. Older adults are typically more concerned with maintaining their own privacy and that of people they know.[61] As members of Gen Z (born after 1996) enter adulthood, they are paradoxically both more tech-savvy than earlier generations and more nostalgic for simpler times—hence a resurgence in vinyl records, board games, and classic TV shows.[62]

Differences emerge at work.

In the workplace, Millennials (born between 1981 and 1996) tend to have a stronger need for affirming feedback than do members of previous generations.[63] Millennials typically want clear guidance on how to do a job correctly, but they don't want to be micromanaged when they do it. To managers from previous generations, it may seem like a burden to give that much guidance and feedback. They may feel that, "no news is good news," and that not being told that you screwed up is praise enough.

Age is but one of many cultural variations that influence communication. "Tips & Reminders: 4 Ways to Learn More About Other Cultures" may be helpful in bridging the gaps. ●

TIPS & REMINDERS

4 Ways to Learn More About Other Cultures

How can a communicator acquire the culture-specific information that leads to competence? Scholars suggest the following strategies for moving toward a more mindful, competent style of intercultural communication:[64]

1. **Seek out cultural information.**

   There are two main ways to learn about cultures—passive and active. *Passive observation* involves noticing how members of a culture behave and applying these insights. *Active strategies* include reading, watching videos, asking experts and members of the culture how to behave, and taking courses related to intercultural communication and diversity.[65]

2. **Confess your ignorance.**

   When you find yourself at a loss, you might say, "This is new to me. What's the right thing to do in this situation?" While some cultures may not value this sort of candor and self-disclosure, most people are pleased when others attempt to learn the practices of their culture, and they are glad to help.

3. **Get to know people from different backgrounds.**

   Spending time with people from different cultures can lead to reduced prejudice.[66] It can also expand your communication repertoire and adaptability. But exposure alone isn't enough. To benefit, you must have a genuine desire to know and understand others.

4. **Be flexible.**

   The ability to shift gears and adapt one's style to the norms of multiple cultures is called **frame switching.**[67] Frame switching is essential to intercultural communication, and it offers benefits for personal growth as well. Meiga Loho-Noya, who moved to the United States after growing up in Venezuela and Paris, says she feels different interacting with American friends (more outgoing) than with Hispanic friends (more emotionally expressive) or French friends (more formal). Her husband Zac loves that she embodies all of these roles. "Being with someone so different from yourself—it's like you add another dimension to your life," he says.

Talking About Race

LEARNING OBJECTIVE 3.5: **Adopt communication practices that promote understanding between people of different races.**

Some of the most important conversations we have are also some of the most difficult.

George Floyd died in May 2020 after police handcuffed him and then held him down with a knee to his neck. After video of the incident went viral, demonstrations against racism and police brutality were held in every state of the union and in 40 other countries.[68] Even as people of many different races and ethnicities protested together for social justice, the question kept recurring: *Can we sustain a multicultural dialogue about racism beyond this crisis?*

Talking about race isn't easy. "To most of us, [it] is an uncomfortable topic," observes writer Matt Vasilogambros, "and when we do talk about race, it's usually with people who look like us."[69]

Despite the challenges, respectful conversations about race are worthwhile, especially when they occur between people who have historically occupied different places in society. "The best things in life are on the other side of a difficult conversation," encourages Kwame Christian, a specialist on race and civil rights.[70] The suggestions here can help you engage constructively with people whose experiences are different from your own.[71]

Expect strong emotions.

There will almost certainly be a great deal of emotional heat in conversations about race.[72] White people and members of other dominant groups may experience guilt, shame, and defensiveness. People of color may feel angry and vulnerable. It can help to cultivate what writer David Campt calls "mindful courage"—a commitment to listen respectfully, exercising curiosity and humility.[73]

Put yourself in the other person's shoes.

"You may think that someone is making a mountain out of a molehill," says Ijeoma Oluo, author of *So You Want to Talk About Race,* "but when it comes to race, actual mountains are indeed made of countless molehills stacked on top of each other."[74] It's easy to assume that racism doesn't exist if you haven't been the target of it. Interracial conversations are one way to gain insights. Likewise, people of color can recognize that—without open dialogue about it—White people may not realize it when they are granted opportunities and special treatment that others are not.

Don't debate.

Journalist and author Renni Eddo-Lodge says she is tired of talking to many White people about race because, all too often "they try to interrupt, itching to talk over you but not to really listen, because they need to let you know that you've got it all wrong."[75] If you are White, you can avoid this frustrating pattern by focusing your efforts on listening and seeking to understand the experiences of others.

Learn and apologize, if appropriate.

One stumbling block to open communication about race is a fear of saying the wrong thing or being misunderstood. Even with the best motives, people sometimes blunder and cause pain. The real test of good intentions is to learn from those mistakes and do better in the future. Invite people around you to let you know if your words or actions cause pain. And if they point something out, listen, thank them, apologize, and avoid making the same mistake again. If you mean it sincerely, you might say, "Now that you've explained, I can see how my remarks were hurtful. I'm really sorry. I learned a lesson here."

If you hear someone make a hurtful statement (whether or not it's directed at you), a good approach is to remain calm and point out why the person's statement is problematic. For example, if someone says "Black people are always late," Oluo suggests that "you can definitely say, 'Hey, that's racist' but you can also add, 'and it contributes to false beliefs about Black workers that keep them from even being interviewed for jobs.'" The value of this communication approach, says Oluo, is that it calls attention to the harmful effects of racism and reduces the chance that the speaker will say, "It's not that big of a deal, don't be so sensitive."[76]

Don't force the issue.

If you haven't experienced racism, you may have a genuine desire to learn from people who have, but it isn't fair to insist that they tell you. Talking about such a sensitive subject requires a great deal of emotional labor. As writer John Meta puts it, "When you ask a Black person to teach you how to be a better White person, you are scratching a wound."[77] Asking questions can be relatively easy and passive, but Meta points out that answering them can be painful and exhausting.

White people can educate themselves about racism via books, lectures, blogs, and other resources. When people of color are asked questions they would rather not answer, they can suggest resources such as *So You Want to Talk About Race*,[78] *White Fragility*,[79] *Uncomfortable Conversations with a Black Man*,[80] and *Why Are All the Black Kids Sitting Together in the Cafeteria?*[81] Helpful communication strategies are also provided in this book—such as how to avoid and respond to microaggressions (Chapter 4), be a better listener (Chapter 5), and develop friendships with a diverse array of people (Chapter 8).

If all of this feels overwhelming, take heart. Even Ijeoma Oluo, who wrote a book about the subject, finds it difficult to talk about social differences. "I'd love to not talk about race ever again," she attests (p. 45). Yet she keeps the dialogue open because she believes that communication is the key to bridging differences and facilitating change. "Our humanity is worth a little discomfort," she says, 'it's actually worth a *lot* of discomfort."[82] ●

PAUSE TO REFLECT *How Does Talking About Race Make You Feel?*

1. What emotions do you experience when the topic of race comes up? How do you react? ______

2. What communication approaches might you use to talk about race without turning the conversation into a debate? ______

Overcoming Prejudice

LEARNING OBJECTIVE 3.6: Practice thinking mindfully to overcome prejudiced assumptions that influence communication.

One of the greatest barriers to intercultural communication is the sense that everyone should think and act the same way.

We talked in Chapter 2 about the tendency for people to judge themselves and members of their groups more favorably than they judge out-group members. Where intercultural communication is concerned, perceptual biases can lead to intolerance and unfair treatment, but there is hope. Here are four conclusions from the research.

We tend to think our culture is the best.

Ethnocentrism is an attitude that one's own culture is superior to that of others. An ethnocentric person thinks—either privately or openly—that anyone who does not belong to their group is somehow strange, wrong, or even inferior.

We often prejudge and stereotype others.

Ethnocentrism leads to an attitude of **prejudice**—an unfairly biased and intolerant attitude toward others who belong to an out-group. (Note that the root term in *prejudice* is "pre-judge.") An important element of prejudice is **stereotyping**—exaggerated generalizations about a group. Stereotypical prejudices include the obvious exaggerations that all women are emotional, all men are sex-crazed and insensitive, all older people are out of touch with reality, and all immigrants are untrustworthy.

Judgments can lead to unfair treatment.

Preconceived attitudes toward others can lead people to engage in **unfair discrimination**—depriving people of opportunities or equal treatment based on prejudice, stereotypes, or irrelevant factors such as appearance, age, or race. A class action lawsuit against the recruiting firm MVP Staffing alleged that employees marked the applications of Black job candidates with code words to systematically remove them from consideration.[83] It's a serious issue. Researchers in another study found that job applicants were nearly twice as likely to make employers' short list if their résumés were "whitened" first by excluding reference to names, interests, or affiliations that might suggest they were people of color.[84] This was true even when the companies doing the hiring promoted themselves as being diversity friendly.

Mindful thinking can help.

People tend to harbor stereotypes without consciously thinking about them.[85] To avoid that, it's useful to continually remind yourself that every individual reflects a unique collection of experiences and cultures that generalizations cannot describe. As Allison Collins, one reviewer of this book, put it:

> *The issue I find people voicing today is not "don't hate me because I'm gay" or "don't hate me because I'm Black," but more nuanced . . ."Just because I'm gay doesn't mean I hate sports, so accept me both as an individual and as part of a culture," or "Being Black is a huge part of who I am, so just because I'm now getting an advanced degree or living in an affluent neighborhood doesn't mean I don't relate to victims of police brutality or that I don't sympathize with Colin Kaepernick taking a knee."*

Simply asking yourself whether you might be succumbing to unfair thinking can be surprisingly effective. Look for ways to appreciate others beyond obvious cues such as race, gender, age, ability, and sexual orientation.

Coping with Culture Shock

LEARNING OBJECTIVE 3.7: Analyze the stages involved with adapting to communication in a new culture.

When Lynn Chih-Ning Chang came to the United States from Taiwan for graduate school, she cried every day on the way home from class.[86] Becoming comfortable and competent in a new culture or coculture may be ultimately rewarding, but the process isn't easy.

All her life, Chang had been taught that it was respectful and feminine to sit quietly and listen, so she was shocked that American students spoke aloud without raising their hands, interrupted one another, addressed the teacher by first name, and ate food in the classroom. What's more, Chang's classmates answered so quickly that, by the time she was ready to say something, they were already on a new topic. The same behavior that made her "a smart and patient lady in Taiwan," she says, made her seem like a "slow learner" in the United States.[87] Communication theorist Young Yum Kim has studied cultural adaptation extensively and offers the advice that follows.

Don't be too hard on yourself.

After a "honeymoon" phase in which you feel excited to be in a new culture, it's typical to feel confused, disenchanted, lonesome, and homesick.[88] To top it off, you may feel disappointed in yourself for not adapting as easily as you expected. This stage—which typically feels like a crisis—has acquired the labels **culture shock** and **adjustment shock**.[89]

Homesickness is normal.

It's natural to feel a sense of push and pull between the familiar and the novel.[90] Kim encourages people acclimating to a new culture to regard stress as a good sign. It means they have the potential to adapt and grow. With patience, the sense of crisis may begin to wane, and once again, the person may feel energetic and enthusiastic to learn more.

Expect progress and setbacks.

The transition from culture shock to adaptation and growth is usually successful, but it isn't a smooth, linear process. Instead, people tend to take two steps forward and one step back, and to repeat that pattern many times. Kim calls this a "draw back and leap" pattern.[91] Above all, she says, if people are patient and keep trying, the rewards are worth the effort.

Reach out to others.

Communication can be a challenge while you're learning how to operate in new cultures, but it can also be a solution.[92] Blogger Benjamin Decker encourages people to open their minds to the diversity around them. "One of the most interesting individuals and someone I would never picture myself being close to is now a best friend of mine," he says. "You may never know what may come out of a hello, talking to someone you may find odd."[93]

Chang, the Taiwanese student adapting to life in America, learned this firsthand. At first, she says, she was reluctant to approach American students, and they were reluctant to approach her. Gradually, she found the courage to initiate conversations, and she discovered that her classmates were friendly and receptive. Eventually, she made friends, began to fit in, and successfully completed her degree.

Culture and Communication

Culture

- Culture is "the language, values, beliefs, traditions, and customs people share and learn."
- A coculture is a group that is part of an overarching, encompassing culture.
- Cultural differences are salient in some situations but not in others.
- People with whom one identifies are considered in-group and others are out-group.
- Intersectionality theory describes the complex interplay of people's multiple identities.

Cultural Values and Norms

- Individual or collective
- High or low reliance on context
- Comfort level with uncertainty
- Power distance
- How members feel about silence

Communication and Cocultures

- Race and ethnicity
- Regional differences
- Sexual orientation and gender
- Religion
- Ability and disability
- Political viewpoints

Age and Generation

- Ideas about aging change over time.
- Stereotypes discourage open communication.
- Being young has its challenges.
- Generations regard technology differently.
- Differences emerge at work.

Learning About Other Cultures

- Seek out cultural information.
- Confess your ignorance.
- Spend time with people from different backgrounds.
- Be flexible.

Talking About Race

- Expect strong emotions.
- Put yourself in the other person's shoes.
- Don't debate.
- Learn and apologize, if appropriate.
- Don't force the issue.

Overcoming Prejudice

- We tend to think our culture is the best (ethnocentrism).
- We often prejudge and stereotype others.
- Judgments can lead to unfair discrimination.
- Mindful thinking can help reduce bias.

Coping with Culture Shock

- Don't be too hard on yourself.
- Homesickness is normal.
- Expect progress and setbacks.
- Reach out to others.

Show Your Communication Know-How

3.1: Define culture and coculture and differentiate between in-groups and out-groups.

In what situations do you feel like an in-group member? When do people treat you like an out-group member? How do you feel in each of these situations?

KEY TERMS: culture, coculture, salience, in-group, out-group

3.2: Analyze how values and norms affect communication between members of different cultures.

A friend says she is frustrated at work because, although she is the boss, people don't show her respect. Your friend grew up in a culture that observes high power distance, but her coworkers are accustomed to low power distance. How might you explain this cultural difference to your friend using communication examples to show how people might display high and low power distance in a work setting?

KEY TERMS: individualistic cultures, collectivistic cultures, low-context cultures, high-context cultures, uncertainty avoidance, power distance

3.3: Apply the concept of intersectionality to your communication, and identify communication factors that help shape cocultural identity.

List 5 to 10 of your social identities (e.g., your gender, race, occupation, sexual orientation, family, and so on). From the perspective of intersectionality, explain how the interface of these identities (e.g., Black female engineer in the South) gives rise to issues that are different from considering each of these roles separately (e.g., how being a female engineer is different than the sum total of being a female and an engineer and so on).

KEY TERMS: intersectionality theory, race, ethnicity, social media trolls, social media snarks

3.4: Explain communication patterns within and between different age groups.

In what ways does society stereotype people your age? Are these assumptions mostly true or not? How do they affect the way people communicate with you?

KEY TERMS: personal fable, imaginary audience, frame switching

3.5: Adopt communication practices that promote understanding between people of different races.

Imagine a conversation involving people of different backgrounds. When the topic of racism comes up, a Black man says, "I live with racism every day. People on the street look at me in fear. Shopkeepers follow me around as if I am a thief." One member of the group says, "I don't think that's true. You're probably imagining it" and another says, "It's not *my* fault. Why are you acting like I did something wrong?" Using the tips in "Talking About Race," explain why these responses are not helpful and what conversational partners might say or ask instead.

3.6: Practice thinking mindfully to overcome prejudiced assumptions that influence communication.

Speculate about how someone inclined toward ethnocentrism, prejudice, and stereotypical assumptions might regard a woman dressed in a headscarf and a long robe. What means might the person use to get to know the woman as a unique individual instead of making assumptions?

KEY TERMS: ethnocentrism, prejudice, stereotyping, unfair discrimination

3.7: Analyze the stages involved with adapting to communication in a new culture.

Think of a time when you felt homesick or out of place (perhaps at a new job or school). What was most useful to you in terms of adapting to the culture?

KEY TERMS: culture shock, adjustment shock

Language

4

The Nature of Language

LEARNING OBJECTIVE 4.1: Explain how symbols and linguistic rules allow people to achieve shared meaning.

Imagine what life would be like without language to explore new ideas, share your ideas, and accomplish everyday tasks. Language both shapes and reflects our experiences.

Language is powerful. You can probably think of a time when someone's words gave you courage, comforted you, or made you feel special. Alternatively, you may also recall a time when words hurt you or made you feel bad. As we use the term, **language** is a collection of symbols governed by rules and used to convey messages between people. Here are four qualities of language that help explain this definition.

Language is symbolic.

As you read in Chapter 1, **symbols** represent thoughts—usually in the form of words that can be conveyed via speech, writing, or gestures. Most words have no inherent link to what they represent. They only have meaning to the extent that others interpret them in the same way. Consider the word *barf.* In Hindi and Farsi it means snow, which explains why a popular brand of detergent used in the Middle East and India bears that name.[1] However, a soap called Barf probably wouldn't be a big seller in the English-speaking world, where it means vomit.

Meanings are in people, not in words.

Understanding terms such as *dog* and *book* is a fairly straightforward matter. However, even when people speak the same language, they may interpret some words very differently. The term *queer* is an example. At one time, it was used in a negative way to refer to homosexuality. To people who remember that, it may still hurt to be called queer. But in the last 20 years or so, many have embraced the term as an inclusive way to describe anyone who is not cisgender or exclusively heterosexual.[2] Shows such as *Queer Eye for the Straight Guy* were instrumental in reclaiming the term to some extent—giving it a different, more positive meaning than it once had.

A word's **denotative meaning** is its formally recognized definition. But even if you memorized the dictionary, you'd have a hard time knowing exactly how to use and interpret some words. That's because language also involves **connotative meaning**—the thoughts and feelings associated with a term. Connotations are typically positive or negative. For example, you might feel either uplifted or insulted to be called a feminist, liberal, or conservative. In the southern United States, people realize that "bless their heart" may have multiple connotations, ranging from a sincere expression of affection or sympathy ("She's sick again, bless her heart") to an insult ("She's dumber than dirt, bless her heart.").

The lesson here is that misunderstandings result when people assume that others use words in the same way they do. In the end, words don't mean things, people do—and often in widely different ways.

Words affect and reflect reality.

Language affects people's experiences by spotlighting some concepts and making others hard to talk about. Consider pronouns. If you are accustomed to a language in which people are called either *he* or *she*, you probably categorize individuals as male or female, even when you don't consciously think about it. By contrast, some languages exclusively use gender-inclusive pronouns—such as the Finnish pronoun *hän* that refers to any individual. Finnish speakers learning English often say that it requires a mental shift to categorize people by gender. The effects go beyond word choices. Gender equality tends to be greater in cultures that use gender-neutral pronouns than in those that don't.[3]

Language also reflects reality. Again, gender references are a good example. In decades past, many job titles included a masculine suffix (e.g., chairman, policeman, salesman). But when research revealed that females are less likely than males to aspire to careers with "man" in the title,[4,5] many people began to consciously change the words they used (e.g., chair, police officer, salesperson) to support a more inclusive perspective. A similar movement is occurring with the use of *they or their* to refer to one person or more than one—much like the words *you* and *your*, which can also be used either way. Statements such as "A professor should get to know their students" acknowledge that gender is a social construct that includes more than two options—and sometimes gender is irrelevant to the point you are making. *They* has been so impactful that Merriam-Webster Dictionary named it the word of the year in 2019.

Language is governed by rules.

Communicating involves more than knowing a lot of words. You also have to understand their meaning, pronounce them correctly, put them in a coherent order, and know when to say them. Here are four types of rules that provide structure for language.

- **Semantic rules** are guidelines about the meaning of specific words. They make it possible for us to agree that *bikes* are for riding and *books* are for reading. Because semantic rules differ by language, it's possible for the same word to represent different things. For example, if you grew up speaking English, the word *gift* probably brings up pleasant memories, but in German *gift* means poison.[6]
- **Phonological rules** govern how words are pronounced. Can you correctly say comptroller, miniature, sherbet, and assuage? If you pronounced them *con-troller*, *min-ee-a-chore*, *sher-bit*, and *ess-wage*, give yourself top marks in phonology.[7,8] Phonology is more complex than memorizing sounds of the alphabet because the pronunciation of some words depends on their meaning. To illustrate this, say aloud: "A farm can produce produce" and "The present is a good time to present the present." Although phonological rules can be tricky, it's worth the effort to learn them. Mispronounced words can change the meaning of a sentence.
- **Syntactic rules** govern the structure of language—the way symbols should be arranged. Correct English syntax prohibits sentences such as "Have you the cookies brought?"—which is a perfectly acceptable word order in German. Different syntactic rules apply in different situations. You probably wouldn't say aloud to someone, "Need 2 study u can call me later tho bye," but it's acceptable to text that message. Part of the challenge is using proper syntax for the occasion. You are not likely to impress others if you use the casual sentence structure of a text or tweet in a college assignment, job application, or an email to the boss.
- **Pragmatic rules** govern how people use and understand language in everyday interactions.[9] You probably won't find these rules written down, but those familiar with the language and culture rely on pragmatic rules to judge what's appropriate in a particular situation. For example, pragmatic rules help you know when it's okay to laugh, when you should be silent, how to behave at work versus at home, and so on. Pragmatic rules change over time. For example, your grandparents probably considered it impolite to use swear words in most settings. These days, profanity has become more commonplace. A study released in 2016 showed that 1 in 4 Americans use the f-word daily, a steep increase from 10 years earlier.[10] As with all forms of communication, the challenge is to gauge what language is appropriate given the people and situation involved. ●

The Power of Language

LEARNING OBJECTIVE 4.2: Identify ways in which language shapes people's attitudes and reflects how they feel about themselves and others.

The words people use influence how others see them, how they think about themselves, and who fits in.

When Lauren learned that her parents had changed her name when she was a baby, she wondered if life would have been different with the name she'd been given at birth (Tiffany). To try it out, she changed her nickname to Tiffi on social media. As people began addressing her by the new name, she started to behave the way she thought a Tiffi would. "I said yes more—to going out at night, to dating, and to doing things that were edgy for me," she says. "All I could think was: *Lauren would never do this.*"[11]

Naming is one example of how language matters. In addition, in this section we'll examine the power of accents and dialects, powerful and powerless speech, and affiliative language.

Names

Names play a role in shaping and reinforcing a sense of personal identity. Naming a baby after a family member can create a connection between the child and their namesake. Names can also make a powerful statement about cultural identity. Some names suggest a Black identity, whereas others sound more White.[12] The same could be said for Hispanic, feminine/masculine, Hindi, and so on.

Names can also be used as the basis for discrimination. When researchers posted more than 6,000 AirBnB requests that were identical except for the users' first names, they found that would-be guests with Black-sounding names were 15 percent more likely to be declined lodging than those with White-sounding names.[13] A similar pattern appears in employment decisions. In the United States, job applicants with names such as Mohammed and Lakisha typically receive fewer calls from employers than equally qualified candidates with traditionally European names such as Thomas and Susan.[14,15] Because of this potential for discrimination, some people advocate for job applications in which potential employees' names are masked during the review process.[16]

Accents and Dialects

In the classic musical *My Fair Lady,* Professor Henry Higgins helps Eliza Doolittle transform from a lowly flower girl into a high-society woman by replacing her Cockney accent with an upper-crust speaking style. It's not a far-fetched idea.

An **accent** involves pronunciation perceived as different from the local speech style.[17] Accents and **dialects** (versions of the same language that include substantially different words and meanings) can either enhance or detract from speakers' social status. Among English speakers around the world, British accents are typically considered most pleasing to the ear, followed by American, Irish, and Australian accents.[18]

Listeners often assume that accents are linked with particular abilities. In the United States, employers are more likely to hire job candidates who sound as if English is their first language than those who have Asian or Hispanic accents, even when the candidates speak English clearly and proficiently.[19] The power of language is so strong that stereotypes persist with no evidence to support them.[20]

"Powerful" and "Powerless" Speech

Americans typically consider language to be **powerful** when it is clear, assertive, and direct. By contrast, language is often labeled as **powerless** when it suggests that a speaker is uncertain, hesitant, intensely emotional, deferential, or nonassertive.[21]

Speech considered powerful can be an important communication tool. In employment interviews, for example, people who seem confident and assertive usually fare better than those who stammer or otherwise seem unsure of themselves.[22]

It doesn't pay to overdo it, however. Just as an extremely "powerless" approach can feel weak, an overly "powerful" statement can come off as presumptuous and disrespectful. Consider the following statements a student might make to a professor:

I hate to say this, but I ... uh ... I guess I won't be able to turn in the assignment on time. I had a personal emergency and ... well ... it was just impossible to finish it by today. I'll have it in your mailbox on Monday, okay?

I won't be able to turn in the assignment on time. I had a personal emergency, and it was impossible to finish it by today. I'll have it in your mailbox on Monday.

The first statement seems tentative and powerless. In some situations, however, less assertive speakers seem friendlier, more sincere, and less coercive than more assertive ones.[23] The second approach may come across as more direct and powerful, or it may seem presumptuous and disrespectful.

Individuals in some cultures admire self-confidence and direct speech. However, in many cultures, saving face for others is a higher priority, so communicators tend to use ambiguous, less assertive terms. In traditional Mexican culture, it's considered polite to add "*por favor?*" ("if you please?") to the end of requests, such as when ordering food in a restaurant. By contrast, "powerful" declarative statements such as "I'll have the fish" are likely to seem rude and disrespectful—especially when delivered in an assertive tone of voice.[24]

Affiliative Language

One means of demonstrating solidarity with others is through **affiliative language**, which demonstrates a sense of connection between people. Close friends and romantic partners often use nicknames and personal references that signify the nature of their bond.[25] The same process works among members of larger groups, ranging from street gangs to military personnel. Fans of the same sports team may share specialized cheers, greetings, and other linguistic rituals that make it clear they are on the same side. Communication researchers call it **convergence** when people use similar words and ways of speaking.

The opposite is also true. Communicators who want to set themselves apart from others may adopt the strategy of **divergence**, speaking in a way that emphasizes their difference from others. For example, people may use dialect as a way of showing solidarity with one another. Philadelphia natives use the word *jawn* to mean almost anything from a place, to a thing, to a person. Use of the word marks them as locals (or natives), while newcomers are almost certainly confused by statements such as "Pass me the jawn" and "They're building a new jawn downtown."[26] Divergence also operates in other settings. For example, a physician or attorney who wants to establish credibility with a client might use specialized language to create a sense of distance. The implicit message is "I'm different from (and more knowledgeable than) you." ●

PAUSE TO REFLECT *How Does Language Influence You?*

1. Do you believe that your name influences the way others see you? Does it influence how you view yourself? If so, how?

2. Observe a casual conversation and make a mental note of how the participants display "powerful" and "powerless" speech patterns as well as convergence and divergence. Describe the patterns you observe and what effects they seem to have on the conversation.

3. How do your accent, dialect, and use of regional vocabulary reflect the cultures you have been part of? Do you change between different dialects and vocabularies when you interact with different types of people? If so, how and why?

Misunderstandings

LEARNING OBJECTIVE 4.3: Recognize and remedy vague and confusing language.

In addition to being a blessing that enables us to live together, language can be something of a curse.

We all have known the frustration of being misunderstood, and most of us have been baffled by another person's overreaction to an innocent comment. In this section, we examine four reasons people might misunderstand each other even when they are trying to communicate well.

Language is equivocal.

Equivocal words have more than one definition, which can lead to misunderstandings. For example, when a nurse told a patient that he "wouldn't be needing" the clothes he requested from home, the patient interpreted the statement to mean he was near death. But the nurse actually meant he would be going home soon. Other equivocal statements arise from cultural differences. In Britain, if someone says, "I'll knock you up in the morning," it probably means "I'll wake you up in the morning." However, in the United States, the phrase has a quite different meaning—I'll get you pregnant in the morning.

In contrast to equivocal words, which may confuse people unintentionally, an **equivocation** is a deliberately vague statement that can be interpreted in more than one way. If your date asks how you like their new haircut, you might equivocate by saying, "Your hair looks so shiny" rather than admitting that you don't like the style. Equivocations can spare people the embarrassment that might come from a blunt and truthful answer. However, they can also be underhanded, as when an employee calls in sick, saying, "I'm not feeling well" when the truth is that she's exhausted from partying all night.

Meaning is relative.

Relative words gain their meaning by comparison. Is the school you attend large or small? Compared to a university with 60,000 students, it may seem small, but next to one with 2,000 students, it might seem quite large. In the same way, relative words such as *fast* and *slow, smart* and *stupid, short* and *long* depend on comparisons for their meaning. Using relative words without explaining them can lead to communication problems. For instance, if a new acquaintance says "I'll call you soon," when can you expect that to happen?

Have you been disappointed to learn that classes you've heard were "easy" turned out to be hard or that journeys you were told would be "short" were long? The problem in each case came from failing to anchor the relative word to a more precisely measurable one.

Language differs by community.

Social and professional groups tend to develop their own vocabularies. **Slang** is language used by members of a particular coculture or other group. For instance, cyclists who talk about *bonking* are referring to running out of energy. Young people may recognize that *extra* means someone is being overly dramatic, as in "Wearing leather pants to class? She's so extra."

In addition to slang, almost everyone uses some sort of **jargon**—a specialized vocabulary that functions as linguistic shorthand for people with common backgrounds and experiences. Whereas slang tends to be casual and changing, jargon is typically more technical and enduring. Some jargon consists of acronyms—initials used in place of the words they represent. In finance, *P&L* (pronounced P-N-L) translates as "profit and loss," and military people label failure to serve at one's post as being *AWOL*, meaning "absent without leave."

Jargon can be an efficient way to use language for people who understand it. For example, the trauma team in a hospital emergency room can save time, and possibly lives, by speaking in shorthand, referring to *GSWs* (gunshot wounds), *chem 7* lab tests, and so on. But people unfamiliar with the jargon can feel left out or baffled by it. This can happen in many settings, such as classrooms and business meetings, where newcomers may be reluctant to admit that they don't understand the jargon being used.

Language is nuanced.

A **euphemism** is a pleasant term substituted for a more direct but potentially disquieting one. We use euphemisms when we say *restroom* instead of *toilet* or *passed away* instead of *died*. Euphemisms often seem more polite and less anxiety provoking than other words. However, they can be vague and misleading. Terms such as *domestic disturbance* and *battle fatigue* are easy to hear, but they downplay the harsh realities involved. In the same way, being *excessed*, *decruited*, or *graduated* doesn't make the reality of losing one's job any easier.[27] See "Tips & Reminders: 6 Ways to Avoid Misunderstandings" for suggestions on choosing your words carefully. ●

TIPS & REMINDERS

6 Ways to Avoid Misunderstandings

It may be tempting to blurt out statements without thinking, but impetuous word choices can be confusing, hurtful, and downright wrong. Here are some tips to help clarify your language and avoid mix-ups.

1. **Use slang and jargon with caution.**
   For example, if you say "that person needs to get woke" (educated about social issues) or "the SCOTUS is completely out of touch" (referring to the Supreme Court of the United States), make sure others understand what you mean.

2. **Explain your terms.**
   Relative words such as *good*, *bad*, *helpful*, and *happy* mean different things to different people.

3. **Be specific.**
   "It will take me 30 minutes" is better than "It won't take long."

4. **Clarify whom you represent.**
   It can be tempting to present your opinions as if other people share them, as in, "We think you have been slacking off lately." But unless you can say who "we" is and confirm that your opinion is indeed shared, use an "I" statement instead.

5. **Focus on specific behaviors.**
   "It's important that you arrive by 9 o'clock every morning" is clearer than "Be on time."

6. **Be careful with euphemisms and equivocations.**
   If you say "He went to a better place," listeners may wonder if he died, got a better job, or found a higher quality restaurant for dinner.

Facts, Inferences, and Opinions

LEARNING OBJECTIVE 4.4: Distinguish between facts, opinions, and inferences, and avoid using disruptive language.

Misunderstandings are a fact of life. But it's possible to avoid using irresponsible and uncivil language.

When the Pew Research Center asked 5,000 adults to read 10 statements and indicate which were fact and which were opinions, the results were disappointing. About 1 in 4 respondents got most of them wrong, while slightly more than a third got them all right. Especially alarming was the tendency to think that facts they disliked were opinions—and conversely, that opinions they liked were actually facts.[28]

"Chances are, you're not as open-minded as you think," concludes one writer after reviewing the research.[29] **Confirmation bias** is the tendency to reject information that is inconsistent with one's current viewpoint. It's heightened by news outlets that offer slanted versions of the "truth" and by online algorithms that funnel information to people that is consistent with what they have viewed in the past.[30] As a result of all these factors, people can be closed to new ideas and relationships.

Distinguishing between different types of language can help you make well-informed decisions and continue learning throughout your life. Here we explore four strategies for accomplishing at that.

Distinguish between fact and opinion.

Factual statements are claims that can be verified as true or false. By contrast, **opinion statements** are based on the speaker's beliefs. Unlike matters of fact, they can never be proved or disproved. Consider a couple of examples:

Fact: It rains more in Seattle than in Portland.
Opinion: The climate in Portland is better than in Seattle.

Fact: Serena Williams has won 23 Grand Slam titles.
Opinion: Serena Williams is the greatest tennis player of all time.

When factual statements and opinion statements are set side by side, the difference between them is clear. In everyday conversation, however, we often present our opinions as if they are facts. For example, you might exclaim, "It would be a waste of money to buy that wreck of a car!" Such a statement implies that your opinion is fact and anyone who disagrees with it is wrong. You're likely to get an argument or hurt feelings in return. It would be more respectful and less antagonistic to say, "Even if it costs a little more, I think a newer model would be more reliable."

See "Tips & Reminders: 3 Ways to Distinguish Between Facts and Opinions" for experts' guidance.

Don't confuse facts with inferences.

Difficulties arise when people confuse factual statements with **inferential statements**—conclusions arrived at from an interpretation of evidence. Here are a couple of examples:

Fact: He hit a lamppost while driving down the street.
Inference: He was probably texting when he crashed.

Fact: You interrupted me.
Inference: You don't care about what I have to say.

There's nothing wrong with making inferences as long as you identify them as such: "When she stomped out and slammed the door, I thought she was furious." The danger comes when we confuse inferences with facts and make them sound like the absolute truth.

Don't present emotions as facts.

Particularly troublesome are opinion statements meant to incite strong emotional reactions, sometimes called **emotive language**. For example, a statement such as "Worthless bums are ruining our town" is emotionally inflammatory. A more responsible statement might sound something like this: "I worry that the rising number of homeless people will cause families to move away from this area."

One problem with emotive language is that it tends to inspire reactions based more on emotional fervor than rational thought. It may lead you to believe an emotionally charged speaker even if they present no solid evidence. Or it may cause you to react angrily toward someone whose arguments are different than yours. "Overly strong emotional language antagonizes the receiver and wipes away impulses to listen, to stay friends, or even to talk together any further," reflects psychologist Susan Heitler.[31]

Don't resort to insults.

Calling people ugly names is exceptionally hurtful. Not only is it degrading to others, but name calling also damages relationships and discourages an honest give and take. The **fallacy of ad hominem** (translated as *to the person*) involves attacking someone's character rather than debating the issues at hand. (For more about fallacies, see Chapter 14.) Calling an opponent Lyin' Mark or Crooked Diane diverts attention away from the real issues.

Name calling has an ugly past in that insulting language has been used to stigmatize certain groups.[32] It's easy to see the damage of calling people with mental illness *crazy* or labeling a person with a developmental disability *retarded*. The power of prejudiced language to shape attitudes is clear. In a classic study, even those who disapproved of a derogatory label thought less of the group being "described" after they heard the slur.[33]

Social media can encourage personal attacks by creating what some theorists call "webs of hate."[34] Online, it's easy to network with people who have similar prejudices, bolstering the sense that those attitudes are more prevalent than they really are, and creating speech communities in which hateful speech is tolerated or encouraged.

Many people feel that, in today's contentious political climate, it's especially important to think clearly about information and avoid language that alienates and offends. By using language responsibly, you can encourage respectful discourse about diverse perspectives. •

TIPS & REMINDERS

Ways to Distinguish Between Facts and Opinions

There is a place for personal opinions, but it's troublesome when they are misrepresented as facts. Use the guidelines below to determine if information—whether it be in a social media post, news item, or personal conversation—is fact, opinion disguised as fact, or a responsible opinion.[35,36]

1. **If statements meet the following criteria, they are probably facts.**
   - The evidence presented can be objectively proven or verified.
   - The information is current and relevant.
   - Valid sources of information are provided.
   - An effort is made to encourage additional and emerging information.
2. **Opinions disguised as facts tend to include one or more of the following.**
   - Statements seem designed mostly to stir up people's emotions.
   - Claims are not supported with objective information.
   - Arguments are based on an isolated or unusual case.
   - Assertions are overgeneralized or out of date.
3. **Responsible opinions usually have the following qualities.**
   - Statements are clearly acknowledged to be perceptions ("I feel that ...").
   - Assertions are supported with trustworthy information.
   - Respect is shown for other opinions.

Microaggressive Language

LEARNING OBJECTIVE 4.5: Evaluate statements for signs of microaggression and adopt more inclusive language.

Even when people aren't trying to offend, the stereotypes that underlie their comments and questions can be hurtful.

"You speak excellent English."

People often say this to Derald Wing Sue. They aren't trying to be mean, he says. But the implication is clear: They assume that Sue, who was born and raised in Oregon, is an immigrant. "What they are saying is that you are a perpetual alien in your own country, and you are not a true American," Sue says.[37] Although the speaker may mean the words as a compliment, they hurt.

Microaggressive language involves subtle, everyday messages that (intentionally or not) stereotype or demean people on the basis of sex, race, gender, appearance, or some other factor.[38,39] Such language often takes the form of comments, questions, and even supposed compliments. Here are some more examples:

> *"You're really pretty for a dark skin girl."*[40]
>
> *"I wish I was Native, so I could get scholarships and stuff."*[41]
>
> *"What are you ladies gossiping about?"*[42]
>
> *"You're Autistic? ... You seem so normal. I never would have guessed."*[43]
>
> *"My neighbors are lesbians! ... Do you know them?"*[44]
>
> *"Not to be racist, but what are you?"*[45]

Such statements can be painful to the recipients because they are based on assumptions that feel dehumanizing and derogatory. These imply that women with dark complexions aren't usually beautiful, that Native Americans receive free handouts, that women are typically nosy and unkind, that Autistic individuals are not normal, that gay women all know each other, and that a person (typically someone who appears to be nonwhite or multiracial) should explain "what" they are so that the speaker can categorize them.

If you haven't often been the recipient of microaggressive comments, they may seem innocent or trivial on the surface. But put yourself in the shoes of someone who is regularly stamped with a social stereotype that belies their status as a unique individual and marginalizes a group with which they identify. "The 'micro' in microaggresion doesn't mean that these acts can't have big, life-changing impacts," points out Kevin Nadal, a scholar who studies the issue.[46]

Microaggressions present a quandary because people who initiate them aren't necessarily trying to be unkind, and because it can be hard to shift an everyday conversation to talk about stereotypes and prejudice. But the stakes are high. People who are frequently the targets of microaggressive language tend to experience more stress and depression, lower self-esteem, less sense of belonging, and more worry about the future than their peers who don't.[47,48,49]

The good news is that everyone can be part of the solution by engaging in **microresistance**—everyday behaviors that call attention to hurtful language and stereotypes that put some people at a disadvantage. Here are some ways to do that.

Examine your own assumptions.

Avoiding microaggressive language requires that we examine our own assumptions, educate ourselves about what others may find offensive, and be willing to discuss sensitive issues respectfully. **Implicit bias** refers to prejudices and stereotypes that people harbor without consciously thinking about them.[50] For example, imagine that—deep down, without even thinking about it—you assume that fat people are lazy or that people who don't speak English well lack intelligence. Although unconscious, these beliefs can affect the way you think about people and what you say. This may be true of many other ideas as well. You can get a sense of your implicit biases by monitoring your thoughts and by thinking before you speak. Before blurting out "You run like a girl" or "You're really outgoing for an Asian person," stop and ask yourself: *What stereotypes am I harboring and perpetuating?*

Inquire.

If you are Black and someone says, "I can't believe you like country music," you might ask, "Why does that surprise you?" In considering an answer, the speaker might recognize a bias within themselves that they hadn't realized before.

Use humor.

When people tell Derald Wing Sue that he speaks excellent English, he sometimes quips in return, "Thank you, I hope so, I was born here."[51] Sometimes humor is enough, he says, to make a person stop and think.

Point out the underlying assumption.

Giving words to an underlying pattern can be a means of bringing it into conscious awareness. If someone says scornfully, "That's so gay," you might say, "It sounds like you have something against gay people. What's up?"

Be an ally.

An **ally** is someone from a dominant social group (e.g., White, male, cisgender, management) who actively advocates for fair treatment and social justice for others.[52] If you are on a personnel committee at work and diverse candidates are written off as "not management material," you can be an ally by saying, "I think we are overlooking a lot of great candidates because, at some level, we think everyone should be just like us. Let's agree on job-specific qualifications we can apply to everyone equally." Research shows that allies' involvement can go a long way toward changing social viewpoints and helping people who are the targets of microaggression feel less singled out and othered.[53]

Avoid casting individuals as "spokespersons".

Imagine that a teacher says, "Alejandra, you're Hispanic. Tell us about the struggles of Spanish speakers in the United States." Right away, Alejandra is depicted as a "typical" member of a large group that is ostensibly "different" from everyone else. And the question presumes that she is knowledgeable about the issue and willing to discuss it. "That can be very psychologically and emotionally exhausting," points out Kevin Nadal.[54] A better option—whether you are in class, conversing with friends or colleagues, or on social media—is to create an environment in which people are invited to share their experiences, but no one is put on the spot to speak for a particular group.

Choose your battles.

There are times when it's not worth outing a microaggression. Perhaps you don't have the emotional energy to broach a sensitive topic, or you fear the other person will react aggressively toward you. Use good judgment.

Apologize if you mess up.

If you inadvertently make a microaggressive statement, own up to it and offer a sincere apology. "We're all human beings who are prone to mistakes," says Derald Wing Sue.[55] Use the situation as an opportunity to become more aware. Inclusivity coach Pooja Kothari suggests something like this:

> *I said something that I think was offensive. I have thought about it and want to apologize to you. I know my words have an impact and I am sorry for the impact they made on you. I value our friendship/relationship/camaraderie and want you to know I am aware of what I said, I take responsibility for it and am working on it.*[56]

Even if your initial statement was insensitive, your sincere desire to make it right is likely to benefit the relationship and your good name. ●

Gender and Language

LEARNING OBJECTIVE 4.6: Describe the ways in which traditionally masculine and feminine speech patterns are alike and how they differ.

"Why do men want to talk about sex so much?" "Why do women talk on the phone for hours?" "Why won't he tell me how he feels?" These generalizations (which are not necessarily true) appear on websites with titles such as "I Don't Understand Women"[57] and "8 Things We Don't Understand About Men."[58]

Gendered perspectives on language fascinate everyday people as well as researchers. The tricky part can be differentiating between stereotypes and realities. This section explores answers to six questions about gender and language.

Q Is it true, metaphorically speaking, that men are from Mars and women from Venus?

A There's no denying that gender differences can be perplexing. But the sexes aren't actually "opposite" or nearly as different as the Mars–Venus metaphor suggests. As you read in Chapter 2, there is an array of gender identities. Keep in mind that generalities don't describe every person, and terms such as *men* and *women*, although common in the literature, don't begin to describe the true diversity among people.

Q Do women talk more than men?

A Actually, men and women speak roughly the same number of words per day, but women tend to speak most freely when talking to other women, whereas men usually do most of the talking in professional settings.[59]

Q Do men and women talk about different things?

A Yes ... sometimes. This is most true when women talk to women and when men talk to men. Among themselves, women tend to spend more time discussing relational issues such as family, friends, and emotions. Male friends, on the other hand, are more likely to discuss recreational topics such as sports, technology, and nightlife.[60] That is not to say that people of different genders always talk about different things. Nearly everyone reports talking frequently about work, movies, and television.[61]

Q Are women more emotionally expressive than men?

A In the United States, because women frequently use conversation to pursue social needs, they are often said to employ **affective use of language** style, meaning that their language focuses on emotions. Online messages written by women tend to be more expressive than those composed by men.[62] Women's messages are more likely to contain laughter references, emojis, typographical emphasis (italics, boldface, repeated letters), and adjectives. Women are also more inclined than men to ask questions—such as "How do you feel about that?"—that invite another other person to share their feelings. So, the answer is yes, at least in the United States in personal conversations. However, the answer is different in professional settings, where women are more likely to hide their emotions for fear of seeming weak or moody.[63]

That's not to say that men never express emotions. In some cultures, such as in traditional Arab communities, men may be emotionally expressive.[64] And men in the United States are encouraged to show emotions in some situations, such as during sporting events.[65] In addition, in their private lives, men typically do express emotions, but they may do so through actions (such as physical affection and favors) more than words.[66]

Q We've moved beyond traditional gender roles in terms of dating, right?

A Although expectations have changed dramatically over the decades, powerful vestiges of traditional gender roles persist when it comes to romance. Among adults who use the dating app Tinder, men are more likely than women to judge potential partners primarily on the basis of looks,[67] and more men than women say their main intention is to find sex partners rather than dating partners.[68] Similar patterns are evident when people date in person. On first dates and in speed-dating situations, men are more inclined than women to bring up the topic of sex, and women are more likely than men to think that a date is successful if conversation flows smoothly and the tone is friendly.[69,70]

Q Men are more inclined to get right to the point, aren't they?

A It depends on the topic. Men in the United States have traditionally been socialized to adopt an **instrumental use of language**, meaning that the focus is on accomplishing tasks. They tend to emphasize giving directions and solving problems. That's why, when someone shares a problem with them, some men are prone to offer advice, such as "That's nothing to worry about ..." or "Here's what you need to do . . ." Of course, as with every pattern described here, this doesn't apply to everyone or every situation.

By now it's probably clear that neither traditionally masculine nor feminine styles of speech meet all communication needs. You can improve your linguistic competence by switching and combining styles. As you finish this chapter, take the "About You" quiz to see how you typically use language. ●

PAUSE TO REFLECT *How Would You Describe Your Communication?*

1. In what situations do you communicate with the main goal of accomplishing a task? When are you more interested in making an emotional connection with the people around you?

2. In what situations are you likely to talk freely? When are you more likely to be quiet?

ABOUT YOU *How Do You Use Language?*

Answer the questions below to see what orientation is suggested by the way you use language.

______ **1.** Your best friend is upset upon learning that he was not accepted into graduate school. What are you most likely to say?

a. "You seem discouraged. Tell me what's going through your head."
b. "Grad school is overrated. Tons of successful people don't have master's degrees."
c. "There are other great schools. How might I help you apply to them?"
d. "You are an outstanding student. Don't let this get you down. The school that accepts you will be very lucky."

______ **2.** You are planning a sales pitch that could earn your company millions of dollars. What is your pitch most likely to include?

a. A focus on the client's most deeply held values.
b. A list of the reasons your company is better than the competition.
c. Specific features that make your product highly useful and effective.
d. Jargon and other language that shows you understand the client's business.

______ **3.** You hope to meet with a professor to learn more about a topic covered in class. How would you word a meeting request?

a. "I'm excited about the ideas you shared in class. Could I meet with you to learn more?"
b. "This topic is critical to my long-term success. Can I meet with you to learn more about it?"
c. "I'd like to hear what steps you think I should follow to be successful at this. Can we meet?"
d. "I like what you said in class. I know you're busy, but would it be possible to meet and talk more about it?"

______ **4.** Your family is planning a holiday celebration, but you'd like to go skiing with friends instead. How are you most likely to broach the topic with your family?

a. "You've always been so supportive of me. I think you'll understand ..."
b. "Going skiing with my friends is a once-in-a-lifetime opportunity."
c. "The ski trip is an opportunity to make new friends and maybe even some future business contacts."
d. "I'd love to go skiing. But I won't go unless you're 100 percent okay with it."

INTERPRETING YOUR RESPONSES |

Read the explanations below to learn more about your use of language. (More than one may apply.)

Affective If you answered "a" to two or more questions, your language tends to focus on emotions—yours and other people's. This affective approach can make you a sensitive listener and a motivational speaker. Just be sure to balance this strength with awareness of practical concerns.

Emotive If you answered "b" to more than one question, you tend to voice strong opinions. Educated opinions can be useful, but review the discussion about "emotive language" to make sure you don't present your opinions as facts. Doing so can squelch open communication and lead you to overlook alternative ways of understanding the world around you.

Instrumental If you answered "c" to two or more questions, you are inclined to adopt an instrumental approach to language. Your focus on strategies and goals can be highly effective, but you may come off as headstrong in some situations. Make sure you don't lose sight of the emotional (affective) aspects of the issue at hand.

Affiliative If you answered "d" to more than one question, you are disposed toward an affiliative language style. You tend to display convergence (alignment) with other people and avoid actions that might place you at odds. Your thoughtfulness is no doubt appreciated. At the same time, take a stand when it's important to do so. The advice on assertive communication in Chapter 9 may be helpful.

Language

The Nature of Language

- Language is symbolic.
- Meanings are in people, not in words.
- Words affect and reflect reality.
- Language is governed by rules.

The Power of Language

- Names shape and reinforce a sense of personal identity.
- Listeners often associate accents with particular abilities and traits.
- "Powerful" language is clear, assertive, and direct.
- "Powerless" language suggests that a speaker is uncertain and nonassertive, but "powerless" is sometimes a misnomer.
- Affiliative language demonstrates solidarity with others.

Misunderstandings

- Some words are equivocal in that they have more than one definition.
- Equivocation involves a deliberate attempt to be vague.
- Relative words gain their meaning by comparison.
- Slang and jargon differ by community.
- Euphemisms are pleasant alternatives to bolder talk, but they can cause confusion.

Facts, Inferences, and Opinions

- Distinguish between facts and opinions.
- Don't confuse facts with inferences (interpretations).
- Don't present emotions as facts.
- Don't resort to insults.

Microaggressive Language

- Examine your own assumptions.
- Inquire.
- Use humor.
- Point out the underlying assumption.
- Be an ally.
- Avoid casting individuals as "spokespersons."
- Choose your battles.
- Apologize if you mess up.

Gender and Language

- The sexes aren't actually "opposite."
- Men and women speak roughly the same number of words per day, but in different situations.
- Among themselves, women tend to talk more about family, friends, and emotions.
- Male friends are more likely to discuss sports and technology.
- Although ideas are changing, traditional gender roles continue to influence dating customs.
- In the United States, women typically use more affective language and men more instrumental language.

Show Your Communication Know-How

4.1: Explain how symbols and linguistic rules allow people to achieve shared meaning.

Analyze a time when someone thought you were being serious when you were really kidding or vice versa. What pragmatic rules were involved? What were the consequences? How did things work out?

KEY TERMS: language, symbols, denotative meaning, connotative meaning, semantic rules, phonological rules, syntactic rules, pragmatic rules

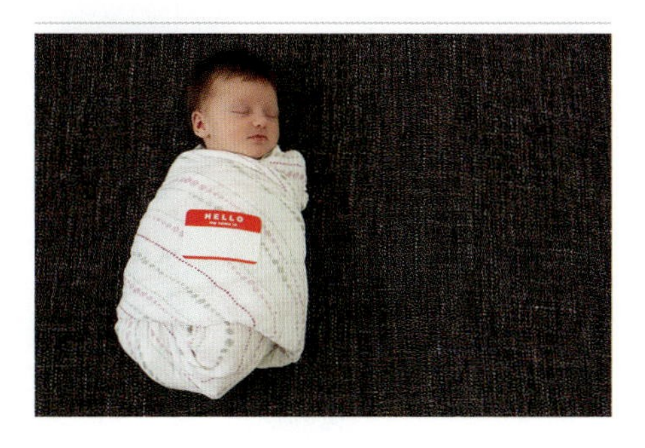

4.2: Identify ways in which language shapes people's attitudes and reflects how they feel about themselves and others.

Describe the same person in five different sentences. What do the descriptions suggest about your opinion of this person? How are others likely to view this person based on your word choices?

KEY TERMS: accent, dialects, powerful language, powerless language, affiliative language, convergence, divergence

4.3: Recognize and remedy vague and confusing language.

Think of a time when someone misunderstood a word you used. How did what you meant compare to their interpretation of the word? How might you avoid causing similar confusion in the future?

KEY TERMS: equivocal words, equivocation, relative words, slang, jargon, euphemism

4.4: Distinguish between facts, opinions, and inferences, and avoid using disruptive language.

Find a news article or social media post and mark elements of it that are fact and those that are opinion. Are the facts trustworthy and verifiable? Are the opinions acknowledged as such and presented with respect for other viewpoints? What improvements might you suggest to encourage civil discourse about the topic?

KEY TERMS: confirmation bias, factual statements, opinion statements, inferential statements, emotive language, fallacy of ad hominem

4.5: Evaluate statements for signs of microaggression and adopt more inclusive language.

Ask several people you know if they have ever had someone say something to them that revealed a hidden bias or stereotype. If so, how did that person feel? What lessons about using language arise from that experience?

KEY TERMS: microaggressive language, microresistance, implicit bias, ally

4.6: Describe the ways in which traditionally masculine and feminine speech patterns are alike and how they differ.

Describe how gender roles influence the way you communicate and what you communicate about. Explain how other factors, such as your major or occupation, influence your communication style. Which factors do you think are most influential?

KEY TERMS: affective use of language, instrumental use of language

5 Listening

The Importance of Listening

LEARNING OBJECTIVE 5.1: Summarize the benefits of being an effective listener.

Listening well takes discipline and skill, but the payoffs are substantial in terms of personal growth and career success.

Of the many qualities that attracted Kiki Hayden to her now-husband Michael, one stood out: *He is a great listener.* When an early conversation revealed a difference of opinion, Michael focused all his attention on what Kiki was saying and then said, "That's a really good point. I hadn't thought of it that way before." The sense that he genuinely cared about what she thought stole Kiki's heart. "Talk about butterflies in my stomach!" she remembers, "My face broke out into a wide grin." To this day, she says, the couple shows their love and respect for one another by listening.[1]

Listening is harder than it seems, but you can become better at it by building your communication skills and avoiding some bad habits. Here are five reasons why it's worth the effort.

Listening makes you a better friend and romantic partner.

While you're getting ready for a social gathering, make sure to clean out your ears, metaphorically speaking. Friends and partners who listen well are considered to be more supportive than those who don't.[2] That probably doesn't surprise you, but this may: Listening well on a date can significantly increase your attractiveness rating.[3,4] The caveat is that you can't *pretend* to listen. Effective listeners are sincerely interested and engaged.

Good listeners aren't easily fooled.

People who listen carefully and weigh the merits of what they hear are more likely than others to spot what some researchers call "pseudo-profound bulls—t"—statements that sound smart but are actually misleading or nonsensical, such as "attention and intention are the mechanics of manifestation."[5] Mindful listening (a topic we'll discuss further shortly) is your best defense.

People with good listening skills are more likely than others to be hired and promoted.

"Listening is more important than speaking," advises a spokesperson for one of the largest career networks sites in the United States. In fact, she ranks the importance of listening among the top five things recruiters wish people knew.[6] (The other four involve dressing appropriately, handling rejection well, being proactive, and being polite and considerate.) Listening skills are also important once you get a job. Because good listeners are typically judged to be appealing and trustworthy,[7] they are especially popular with employers and with customers and clients.[8,9]

Asking for and listening to advice makes you look good.

"Many people are reluctant to seek advice for fear of appearing incompetent," observe researchers who studied the issue.[10] But evidence suggests just the opposite—that people think more *highly* of individuals who ask them for guidance about challenging issues than those who fumble through on their own. Of course, that's just the first step. Making the most of that advice requires good listening skills and follow-through.

Listening is a leadership skill.

Leaders who are good listeners typically have more influence and stronger relationships with colleagues than less attentive leaders do.[11] In fact, leaders' listening skills are often more influential than their speaking skills.[12] As columnist Doug Larson puts it, "Wisdom is the reward you get for a lifetime of listening when you'd have preferred to talk."[13]

Despite these advantages, much of the listening people do is not very effective. They misunderstand others and are misunderstood in return. They become bored and feign attention while their minds wander. They engage in a battle of interruptions without hearing others' ideas. Read on for ways to improve your skills. •

PAUSE TO REFLECT *How Can You Improve as a Listener?*

1 Which of the following apply to you?

a) I frequently feel impatient and wish people would get to the point.
b) I often interrupt when others are speaking.
c) I tend to make snap judgments about people and their ideas.
d) I am often distracted by my phone or my mental to-do list.
e) I am likely to tune out if I don't agree with what the other person is saying.

2 If you chose several items, you aren't unusual. These are common barriers to good listening. But the benefits of improving your listening skills can be tremendous. Write down three ways you might improve the way you listen.

1) ______________________________
2) ______________________________
3) ______________________________

3 If you follow through on the listening goals you have just set, how might it affect your relationships?

____
____
____
____

Misconceptions About Listening

LEARNING OBJECTIVE 5.2: Outline the most common misconceptions about listening, and assess how successfully you avoid them.

Comedian Paula Poundstone once quipped, "It's not that I'm not interested in what other people have to say, it's that I can't hear them over the sound of my own voice."[14] Poundstone is more honest than most in admitting that listening doesn't come easy. But with attention, it's possible.

Here's a good example: Julio was nervous about meeting his wife's coworkers at a party. After fretting about what he might say to impress them, Julio decided to focus instead on what *other* people were saying. He paid close attention to people's words and body language and responded with statements such as "I understand what you're saying. You feel strongly that ..." and "Let me see if I understand what you mean ..."[15] Throughout the party, people told Julio's wife how much they enjoyed talking to him. Julio's behavior shows that he doesn't buy into some common myths about listening.

Myth 1: Hearing and listening are the same thing.

Imagine that a friend says something to you while you're playing a video game or studying for a big test. You may hear what they say but not be listening. **Hearing** involves the physiological ability to perceive sounds in the environment. If you have that ability, hearing occurs automatically when sound waves strike your eardrums and cause vibrations that are transmitted to your brain. By contrast, **listening** occurs when the brain considers stimuli in the environment and gives them meaning. Unlike hearing, listening requires conscious effort and skill. If your mental energy is focused on something else, you may hear what someone is saying but not understand or remember their message.

Myth 2: People only listen with their ears.

Look more closely at the definition of listening and you'll see that it isn't limited to auditory stimuli. Even when people cannot hear, they can be attentive listeners in other ways. The phrase "I listen with my eyes" is common in the Deaf community.[16] It refers not only to sign language but to the ability to gain meaning by using all of the senses.

In the broadest sense, listening can even involve reading. Recall a time when you've quickly scanned a text or email and misunderstood it. Conversely, think about times when you've given a written message such careful attention that you could "hear" the thoughts or feelings behind it.

Myth 3: Listening is a natural process.

Although it may seem that listening is like breathing—a natural activity that people do well—in truth, it's harder to be a good listener than most people think. In the workplace, good listeners are typically more influential than their peers because they are perceived to be more agreeable, open, and approachable than people who listen poorly.[17] However, most people are not the good listeners they think they are. In one survey, 96 percent of professionals said they were good listeners, but 80 percent of them admitted to multitasking while on the phone, a sure sign that they do not give callers their full attention.[18]

Myth 4: All listeners receive the same message.

When two or more people are listening to a speaker, they tend to assume that they hear and understand the same thing. In fact, such uniform comprehension isn't the case. Chapter 2 pointed out many factors that cause people to perceive messages differently. Perhaps you're hungry, preoccupied, or just not interested. Or you may give words a different meaning or significance than someone else does. Your friend might find a joke funny, whereas you consider it silly or even offensive.

Misunderstandings are especially likely when remarks are interpreted out of context. When Fifth Harmony member Normani Kordei called one of her groupmates "very quirky" in an interview, she says she meant it in a good way, but some fans interpreted her remark as an insult and attacked Kordei on social media.[19]

The Listening Process

LEARNING OBJECTIVE 5.3: Describe how each stage in the listening process influences your ability to send and share messages.

No one can be a perfect listener all the time, but the best listeners learn to tune out extraneous factors. The next time you're with friends or at work, take stock of your attention level. Which of your senses are involved in listening? In what ways might you be more attentive?

"I'm a crappy listener," confesses writer Amanda Zantal-Wiener. Or at least she used to be. "Whenever someone spoke to me about something that I found less than fascinating, I had a tendency to tune out," she remembers.[20] These days, she's trying hard to be more attentive, which means staying focused through all of the stages involved in listening well. These stages are represented in the acronym HURIER, which stands for hearing, understanding, remembering, interpreting, evaluating, and responding.[21]

Hearing

In the hearing stage, people receive signals. The degree to which you attend to these signals varies. Sometimes you might give people your undivided attention. At other times, you probably ignore signals. For example, you might tune out your roommates' conversation until you hear your name mentioned, or you might skim your notes rather than focusing on a lecture. As you learned in Chapter 1, even mental distractions can create noise that makes it hard to pay attention.

Understanding

In the **understanding** stage, a listener makes sense of a message. Communication researchers use the term **listening fidelity** to describe the degree to which a listener understands what a sender is attempting to communicate.[22] *High-fidelity listening* occurs when there is a close match between the sender's thoughts and feelings and the receiver's understanding of them. In *low-fidelity listening*, there's a significant mismatch between the two. You might experience low fidelity when your chemistry professor says, "Changes in marine redox structure may be tracked by means of geochemical proxies."[23] Then again, if you know the vocabulary, the meaning may be very clear to you. A good way check the fidelity of your understanding is to paraphrase or ask questions, such as, "If I understand correctly, you're saying that ... " or "Am I right in thinking that ... ?"

Remembering

Although **remembering** also happens after an encounter has passed, it begins in the moment, based on how much information you take in and how you store it for future reference. How often have you been introduced to someone and then realized moments later that you have no recollection of the person's name? People remember only about half of what they hear immediately after hearing it and even less as time passes.[24] Of course, these amounts vary based on the person and the importance of the information.[25] Given the amount of information you are likely to process every day—from instructors, friends, TV, social media, and other sources—the **residual message** (what you remember) is bound to be a small fraction of what you hear.

Interpreting

Whereas understanding involves grasping the literal meaning of a statement, **interpreting** it requires that you take into consideration the situation, the sender's nonverbal behaviors, and other contextual cues. If your boss says, "See me in my office immediately," the literal meaning is clear, but your interpretation may vary from "I must be getting a raise" to "I'm in big trouble."

Evaluating

By this point in the listening process, you may feel that you *understand* the literal message and can *interpret* it in context. In **evaluating**, you go a step further to make a judgment about the message and/or the speaker. You might ask yourself "Is this person sincere?" and "Can I trust this information?"

Responding

In **responding** to a message, you give observable feedback to the speaker. As discussed in Chapter 1, communication is transactional, meaning that people send messages at the same time they receive them. Many people assume that good listeners stay quiet and do nothing. However, one of the most important indications of good listening is feedback—which might include eye contact, facial expressions, asking questions, making relevant comments, sitting up straight, and facing the speaker.[26]

Listening in a Complex World

LEARNING OBJECTIVE 5.4: Develop strategies to minimize listening challenges.

With the number of people and devices clamoring for your attention, it's important to learn techniques that will help you focus.

Are any of the following listening hazards familiar?

- Your phone vibrates while you're listening to a lecture or talking to a friend. You sneak a peek at the screen to see what's up.
- You're binge-watching a long-awaited season of your favorite TV show. A neighbor drops by to warn you about some car break-ins nearby. You know the issue is important, but you find yourself becoming irritated at the interruption.
- Over coffee, a friend complains about having a bad day. You want to be supportive, but you are preoccupied with problems of your own, and you need to get back to work soon to meet a deadline.
- Your boss critiques your work. You think their comments are unfair and you feel the need to defend yourself.
- A family member tells the same story you've heard many times before. You feel obliged to act interested, but your mind is far away.

These are common barriers to good listening, but with effort you can minimize their influence. The most common distractions fall into the following four categories.

Message Overload

Today's world is **multimodal**, meaning that messages are conveyed in many ways—involving a complex array of colors, sounds, images, and words transmitted via numerous communication channels.[27] (In this context, you can think of a mode as a means of expression.) Pause for a moment to consider how many messages are available to you at this moment—perhaps a logo on someone's shirt, the sound of music, the words in this book, the *ping* announcing a new message on your phone, and so on. Even a simple web page is likely to include colors, fonts, images, pop-up messages, and video clips simultaneously clamoring for your attention. All of these represent modes of communication—underscoring what a rich and complicated information environment most people live in today.

The amount of information you are exposed to makes it impossible to listen carefully to everything. But when it's important to listen well, experts suggest that you take a disciplined approach to tuning out distractions. Here are a few strategies that may help:

- Silence your phone while you work on complex tasks.
- Turn off notifications that alert you the moment someone posts a tweet, photo, or video.
- Send clear and brief emails with specific subject lines and think twice before sharing trivial information with everyone you know.[28]

Experts offer additional suggestions in "Tips & Reminders: 3 Ways to Limit Social Media Distractions."

Psychological Noise

Although humans are capable of understanding speech at rates up to 600 words per minute, the average person speaks between 100 and 140 words per minute.[29] Thus, a listener has a great deal of mental "spare time" while someone is talking. It's tempting to use this time to think about personal interests, daydreaming, planning a rebuttal, and so on. You may remember from Chapter 1 that thoughts and feelings that interfere with communication are called psychological noise.

Everyone's mind wanders at one time or another, but excessive preoccupation with your own thoughts can lead to poor listening. To avoid that pitfall, you might devote your mental energy to:

- rephrasing the speaker's ideas in your own words
- considering how the ideas might be useful to you
- asking questions
- paraphrasing what you hear

As writer Amée LaTour puts it, listening well means "accepting that we aren't the center of the universe and that we don't know it all."[30] That may sound harsh, but people who are able to put their concerns aside and focus on others are likely to learn more and enjoy better relationships as a result.[31]

Physical Noise

The world around you presents external distractions that make it hard to pay attention. The sound of traffic, music, others' speech, and the like may interfere with your ability to hear well. You can listen better by removing physical noise whenever possible. Turn off the television, put away your phone, close the window, and so on. Julian Treasure, who studies sound and human communication, lists silence as the first step to better listening. He proposes that quiet time allows people to relax, regroup, and become sensitive to others' words as well as to their subtle nonverbal cues.[32]

Cultural Differences

The behaviors that define a good listener vary by culture and generation. Here are a few examples:

- People in North America are typically most impressed by listeners who ask questions and make supportive statements.[33] The focus is often on words and their meaning—*what* is being said.
- Iranians tend to judge people's listening skills based on their posture and eye contact.[34] As members of a high-context culture (Chapter 3), they are particularly attentive to nonverbal cues—*how* something is said.
- In Italy, interruptions may be regarded favorably as an indication that the listener is engaged and enthusiastic.[35]
- People who grew up texting and tweeting may think that glancing at their phone during a conversation is fine, but their elders may consider that behavior inattentive and disrespectful.

Understanding the challenges and expectations involved in being a good listener should help you adapt to a wide array of people and situations. •

TIPS & REMINDERS

3 Ways to Limit Social Media Distractions

One challenge to serious listening is the influence of social media. By some estimates, most people swipe, stroke, tap, or click their smartphones hundreds or even thousands of times a day.[36] Although social media may make you more tuned in to people who are not near you, it can rob you of presence in the current moment. As a result, you may be a less attentive and less considerate listener. Given that people are not likely to give up their devices any time soon, psychologist and social media analyst Sherry Turkle offers the following tips:[37]

1. **Don't reach for a device every time you get a free moment.**
   Instead, take stock of what you are seeing, feeling, smelling, and hearing. It will make you more attentive to the people and things around you.
2. **Create "device-free zones."**
   By setting devices aside at the dinner table, in the car, or in the living room, you can be alone with your thoughts or carry on a conversation without distractions.
3. **Share your feelings in person every so often.**
   Rather than posting or tweeting your thoughts, consider sharing them face to face. Also, be there in person for a friend in need rather than just posting a message of support on social media.

Hurtful Listening Habits

LEARNING OBJECTIVE 5.5: Identify and manage faulty listening habits that can hurt others and damage relationships.

Although people may mean well, some of their listening and responding styles can upset others.

Shasta was at dinner with a group of friends when she proposed that they take turns sharing one thing about the friendship that they liked and one thing they would like to improve or expand. "Everyone shared really beautiful things," Shasta recalls. "It was super touching." Then, right before it was her turn, the conversation shifted to a different topic. No one seemed to realize that Shasta never got a turn to weigh in. "I felt hurt," she says, looking back.[38]

Here are seven bad habits to overcome if you want to be fully present with the people around you.

Pretending to Listen

Pseudolistening is an imitation of the real thing. When people pseudolisten, they give the appearance of being attentive when they really aren't. They may look people in the eye, nod and smile at the right times, and even answer occasionally. That appearance of interest, however, is a polite way to mask thoughts that have nothing to do with what the speaker is saying.

Tuning In and Out

Selective listeners respond only to the parts of a speaker's remarks that interest them. If you make detailed plans with a friend and then remember only that you're going out to eat, but not where or when, you were probably only listening to part of the message. Everyone is a selective listener from time to time, but it's a habit that can lead to confusion, misunderstandings, and hurt feelings.

Acting Defensively

People who perceive that they are being attacked even when they aren't are **defensive listeners**. For example, if someone says, "I heard you tried the new dessert," a defensive listener may snap back, "I'm entitled to take a break from my diet once in a while!" For suggestions on how to keep your ears open when something pushes your emotional hot buttons, see "Tips & Reminders: 6 Tips for Listening Nondefensively."

Avoiding the Issue

When you steer clear of a sensitive subject, you're being an **insulated listener**. You may not want to hear the boss describe the reasons you didn't get a promotion or listen to your cousin rave about a political candidate you despise. But there are many advantages to listening well, even when the topic makes you uncomfortable. You're likely to earn the boss's respect and learn some valuable tips to help you succeed in the future. You and your cousin may never agree on politics, but by listening well you demonstrate that you care about them as a person.

Online, insulated listening can take the form of blocking and unfollowing people whose beliefs are different than yours. In doing so, you limit your exposure to diverse ideas. "It's worth listening to people you disagree with," urges Zachary R. Wood, who wrote the book *Uncensored* about difficult conversations surrounding race, free speech, and dissenting viewpoints.[39] Wood brings people with diverse beliefs together, not to argue, but simply to listen to one another.

Ignoring Underlying Issues

Insensitive listeners tend to take remarks at face value rather than looking below the surface. An insensitive listener might miss the warble in a friend's voice that suggests she is more upset than her words let on. Or, when a partner complains, "I always take out the trash," an insensitive listener might miss that what's wanted is a thank you.

Being Self-Centered

The next time you're engaged in conversation, consider who has control. **Conversational narcissists** focus on themselves and their interests instead of listening to and encouraging others.[40] One type of conversational narcissist is the **stage hog**, who actively claims more than their fair share of the spotlight. Other narcissists are more passive. They may not interrupt, but neither do they encourage others with supportive comments such as "uh-huh" and "What happened next?"[41] Whatever their approach, conversational narcissists tend to discourage the equal give-and-take that is the hallmark of mutually satisfying conversations.

Talking Too Much

You probably know a few people who love nothing more than the sound of their own voice. Not only does talking too much lead to bad listening, it also robs people of the opportunity to learn from others. As playwright Wilson Mizner once observed, "A good listener is not only popular everywhere, but after a while [they get] to know something."[42]

After reviewing these bad habits, you may feel stunned by the egotism behind many of them. Sometimes people's intentions are truly selfish. More likely, they just haven't learned the skills and discipline involved in being better leaders. Shasta, whose story began this section, says she looks back on the dinner episode and wishes she had been more assertive about sharing her feelings instead of being in a huff because people weren't listening to her as she had hoped.

TIPS & REMINDERS

6 Tips for Listening Nondefensively

It's natural to feel uncomfortable when the boss wants to talk about the deadline you missed or when your roommate is upset because you left a mess. Here are some tips for listening nondefensively, even when the heat is on.[43,44]

1. **Take a deep breath or two and remind yourself of your good qualities.**
2. **Avoid berating yourself with negative self-talk.**
   Thinking "That was such a dumb mistake" or "He will never forgive me" won't help.
3. **Stop expecting perfection.**
   Let go of the idea that you (or anyone) can be perfect.
4. **Thank the speaker for sharing.**
   Even when the words are hard to hear, it's usually better to know what's on other people's minds.
5. **Ask questions.**
   You might say, "Did you feel taken for granted when you saw my dishes in the sink?"
6. **Learn and move on.**
   At the very least, congratulate yourself for handling a difficult situation with sincerity and openness.

Skills for Different Types of Listening

LEARNING OBJECTIVE 5.6: Adapt listening behaviors to specific situations and engage in mindful listening.

Effective listening comes in many forms, each with particular goals and techniques.

Here are five types of listening and experts' tips for doing them well.

Relational Listening

When a pale and disheveled man approached Samarnh Pang at the university where he works, Pang didn't walk away. Instead, he listened as the man described his hardships and explained that many people shun him because he is old and unwashed. "I sensed that this man just needed someone to listen to his stories," Pang says. He was right. After the older man had talked for a while, he smiled and said to Pang, "Son, you are the first person to listen to my stories with kind attention. Thank you for being kind hearted."[45]

The goal of **relational listening** is to emotionally connect with others. Here are some tips for accomplishing that:

- *Allow enough time.* Encouraging others to share their thoughts and feelings can take more than a moment. If you're in a hurry, it may be best to reschedule a relationally focused conversation for a better time. You might say, "I want to give you my undivided attention. Can we meet at 2 o'clock for coffee?"
- *Listen for unexpressed thoughts and feelings.* People don't always say what's on their minds. They might be confused, fearful of being judged, or trying to be polite. However, these unstated messages can be as important as the spoken ones. Consider whether your friend who says, "It's fine. Don't worry about it," really feels that way or is masking hurt and disappointment—or if the new acquaintance who says, "What are you doing tonight?" is interested in making plans with you.
- *Encourage further comments.* You can often strengthen relationships simply by encouraging others to say more. Great teachers harness this power regularly. They know that students often learn more when they ask questions and work through problems than when they are given the answers up front.[46]

Supportive Listening

In **supportive listening**, the primary aim is to help the speaker deal with a personal dilemma. Sometimes the problem is a big one: "I'm not sure this marriage is going to work" or "I can't decide whether to drop out of school." At other times, the issue is more modest. A friend might be trying to decide what birthday gift to buy or where to spend a vacation. Here are some strategies for being a supportive listener:

- *Consider when and how to help.* Before committing yourself to helping another person—even someone in obvious distress—make sure your support is welcome. People may prefer to handle difficult situations on their own.[47] Sometimes the most supportive thing you can do is listen quietly. At other times, running an errand or offering assistance with a task may be more helpful than anything else you could do.[48]
- *Be cautious about offering advice.* Listeners often assume that distressed individuals want pointers on how to solve their problems. However, this assumption is often faulty and can make things worse. As a general rule, only offer advice if the person welcomes it, if you can offer the advice in a way that

doesn't seem belittling, and if you are well qualified to give the advice. Despite your good intentions, it's presumptuous to assume that you have the answers based on your own opinions or experiences.
- *Avoid being judgmental.* It's usually not helpful to place blame or assert your opinion, even when that seems to be supportive in the moment. A classic case of this is bashing a friend's romantic partner after they have broken up or argued. Saying, "What a jerk!" may feel great at the time, but as you have probably experienced, it can lead to hurt feelings and tension if the couple gets back together. It can be even worse when your "supportive" assessment makes the other person feel judged. Statements such as "You've clearly chosen the wrong major" and "If I were you, I would quit that job now" can come off as value judgments that make the speaker even more distressed.

Task-Oriented Listening

The purpose of **task-oriented listening** is to secure information necessary to get a job done. This might involve following instructions at work, hearing tips for mastering a new game or app, getting tips from a coach—the list goes on. Since success often relies on your ability to be a good task-oriented listener, here are some tips to help:

- *Listen for key ideas.* It's easy to lose patience with long-winded speakers, but good task-oriented listeners stay tuned and are able to extract the main points from even a complicated message.
- *Ask questions.* If you're meeting friends at a restaurant that you've never been to, you might ask "What's the menu like?" or "Is it casual or upscale?" In other situations, questions might include, "When is this project due?" or "Who should I ask for more information?"
- *Paraphrase.* **Paraphrasing** means restating in your own words the message you thought the speaker sent, without adding anything new. For example, you might say, "You're telling me to drive down to the traffic light by the high school and turn toward the mountains, is that it?" or "Am I right in thinking your goal is to raise sales by 10%?"
- *Take notes.* As mentioned, listeners usually forget about half of what they hear, so it's smart to take notes instead of relying on your memory. Make sure to take notes right away, record only key ideas rather than scrambling to put down every word, and develop a note-taking format that works for you—whether it's an outline or simply using bold letters, underlining, or asterisks to flag especially important information.

Analytical Listening

The goal of **analytical listening** is to fully comprehend a message. Analytical listeners explore ideas and issues from a variety of perspectives to understand them as fully as possible. Analytical listening is particularly valuable when issues are complicated. Here are some strategies you might use:

- *Listen for information before evaluating.* Most people are guilty of judging a speaker's ideas before they completely understand them. The tendency to make premature judgments is especially strong when the ideas you hear conflict with your own beliefs.
- *Separate the message from the speaker.* At times you may discount the value of a message because of the person who presents it. But even the most boring instructors, the most idiotic relatives, and the most demanding bosses occasionally make good points. If you write off everything a person says before you consider it, you may be cheating yourself out of valuable information.
- *Search for value.* You can find something to appreciate in even the worst situations. If you find yourself in a boring conversation with someone whose ideas you believe are worthless, challenge yourself to learn something useful nevertheless. At the very least, you might ask yourself, "What lessons can I learn from this person that will keep me from sounding the same way myself in other situations?"

Critical Listening

The goal of **critical listening** is to go beyond understanding and analyzing a topic to assess its quality. This skill is especially critical when messages are slanted or inaccurate. Here are some ways to determine if what you're hearing holds up under scrutiny:

- *Examine the speaker's evidence and reasoning.* Trustworthy speakers offer support to back up their statements. For example, a reputable car dealer might share performance statistics from *Consumer Reports*. Unfortunately, outrageous and untrue assertions are rampant as well. To avoid falling for faulty logic and made-up stories, consider whether the source of the information is reliable, whether the information is consistent across many sources, and if it is current and reasonable. (Chapters 12 and 14 offer additional insights on evaluating evidence.)

- *Evaluate the speaker's credibility.* If your longtime family friend, a self-made millionaire, invites you to invest in a start-up business, you might be grateful for the tip. If your deadbeat brother-in-law makes the same offer, you would probably decline. Consider the answers to two questions: Does the speaker have the experience or expertise to qualify as an authority on this subject? and Is the speaker impartial? If the person has a personal stake in the outcome of a topic, consider the possibility of intentional or unintentional bias. (See Chapter 14 for more on credibility.)
- *Assess emotional appeals.* Sometimes emotion alone may be enough to persuade you. You might "lend" your friend $20 even though you don't expect to see the money again soon. In other cases, however, it's a mistake to let yourself be swayed by emotion. Don't agree to a speaker's proposition if their promises seem too good to be true or if there is little evidence to support them. The fallacies described in Chapter 14 will help you recognize flaws in emotional appeals.

We have explored various types of listening, but mindful listening will serve you well no matter what the situation. Learn more in "Tips & Reminders: 4 Tips for Listening Mindfully."

TIPS & REMINDERS

4 Tips for Listening Mindfully

Mindful listening involves being fully present with others—paying close attention to their gestures, manner, and silences, as well as to what they say.[49] It means paying attention to difficult concepts, even when it would be easier to tune out. Mindful listening also involves a commitment to understand other people's perspectives without being judgmental or defensive. This can be difficult, especially when you're busy or when you feel vulnerable yourself. Here are some tips for being more mindful.[50,51,52]

1. **Determine when mindfulness is needed.**

   Sometimes it's okay to be mindless about what you hear. Paying attention to every social media post or every commercial message around you would distract you from more important matters. The problem is being lazy about listening to things that really matter. For example, a college student hurt by his girlfriend's poor listening skills wrote in an online forum, "I have opened up to her about really, really personal things and then two weeks later or within the week ... she's like, 'Oh, you never mentioned it to me.' I just find this really really rude and insulting."[53]

2. **Commit to being fully present.**

   Minimize distractions, including extraneous thoughts and worries. Of course, this isn't always easy. Sometimes enthusiasm for the conversation itself can make people poor listeners. Mark Goulston, author of *Just Listen*, recommends that people hit the reset button when they have failed to be as mindful as they would like to be. For example, he might say to a conversational partner, "In my eagerness to build on what we're talking about, I've raced entirely ahead of the conversation. I'm sorry."[54] Goulston then slows down and renews his commitment to being fully present.

3. **Mentally acknowledge your own feelings.**

   Listening with an open mind can be uncomfortable. You may find yourself becoming angry, sad, impatient, or defensive. A good technique is to acknowledge your emotions but not let them hijack the conversation. You might think to yourself, "I'm feeling angry. I'll set that aside for now and try to understand more fully what this person is sharing with me." It also helps to remember that other people's feelings are real, even if their interpretations are different from yours.[55] Asking questions is a good way to stay curious rather than engaging in knee-jerk emotional reactions.[56]

4. **Be patient.**

   Even when you know the speaker well, resist the temptation to finish their sentences. Instead, allow them the time and freedom to express themselves.[57] Likewise, don't rush the speaker or interrupt. Silence can be helpful when the goal is to pause, think, and understand.

ABOUT YOU *What Are Your Listening Strengths?*

Answer the questions below to gauge which listening approaches you use most.

_______ **1.** Which of the following best describes you?

a. I'm a quick learner who can hear instructions and put them into action.
b. I have an intuitive sense, not just of what people say, but how they are feeling.
c. I'm a good judge of character. I can usually tell whether people are trustworthy or not.
d. I'm a rapid thinker who is often able to jump in and finish people's sentences for them.

_______ **2.** Imagine you are tutoring an elementary school student in math. What are you most likely to do?

a. Focus on clearly articulating the steps involved in solving simple equations.
b. Begin each tutoring session by asking about the student's day.
c. Pay close attention to what the student says to see if they really understand.
d. Feel frustrated if it seems the student isn't listening or isn't motivated.

_______ **3.** A friend launches into a lengthy description of a problem with a coworker. What are you most likely to do?

a. Offer some ideas for discussing the issue with the coworker.
b. Show that you are listening by maintaining eye contact, leaning forward, and asking questions.
c. Read between the lines to better understand what is contributing to the problem.
d. Pretend to listen but tune out after 5 minutes or so.

_______ **4.** If you had your way, which of the following rules would apply to team meetings?

a. Chit-chat would be limited to 5 minutes so the team can get to the point at hand.
b. Everyone would get a turn to speak.
c. People would back up their opinions with clear data and examples.
d. There would be no meetings; they're usually a waste of time.

INTERPRETING YOUR RESPONSES |
Read the explanations below to see which listening approaches you frequently take. (More than one may apply.)

Task Oriented If you answered "a" to more than one question, you tend to be an action-oriented listener. You value getting the job done and can become frustrated with inefficiency. Your task orientation can help teams stay on track. Just be careful that you don't overlook the importance of building strong relationships, which are essential for getting the job done. Tips for group work in Chapter 11 may be especially interesting to you.

Relational/Supportive If you answered "b" more than once, you tend to be a relational and/or supportive listener. It's likely that people feel comfortable sharing their problems and secrets with you. Your strong listening skills make you a trusted friend and colleague. At work, however, this can make it difficult to get things done. Make an effort to set boundaries so people don't talk your ear off.

Analytical/Critical If you answered "c" to more than one question, you often engage in analytical and/or critical listening. You tend to be a skeptical listener who isn't easily taken in by phony people or unsubstantiated ideas. Your ability to synthesize information and judge its merits is a strength. At the same time, guard against the temptation to reach snap judgments. Take time to consider people and ideas thoughtfully before you write them off. The tips for mindful listening in this chapter can help.

Impatient If you answered "d" more than once, you tend to be an impatient or distracted listener. Your frustration probably shows more than you think. Review the tips throughout this chapter for ways to become more focused and active in your listening approach.

Listening

The Importance of Listening

- Listening makes you a better friend and romantic partner.
- Good listeners aren't easily fooled.
- People with good listening skills are more likely than others to be hired and promoted.
- Asking for and listening to advice makes you look good.
- Listening is a leadership skill.

Misconceptions About Listening

- Myth: Hearing and listening are the same thing.
- Myth: People only listen with their ears.
- Myth: Listening is a natural process.
- Myth: All listeners receive the same message.

Stages in the Listening Process

- Hearing
- Understanding
- Remembering
- Interpreting
- Evaluating
- Responding

Common Distractions

- Message overload
- Psychological noise
- Physical noise
- Cultural differences

Limiting Social Media Interruptions

- Don't reach for a device every time you get a free moment.
- Create "device-free zones."
- Share your feelings in person every so often.

Hurtful Listening Habits

- Pretending to listen
- Tuning in and out
- Acting defensively
- Avoiding the issue
- Ignoring underlying issues
- Being self-centered
- Talking too much

6 Tips for Listening Nondefensively

- Remember your good qualities.
- Avoid negative self-talk.
- Stop expecting perfection.
- Thank the speaker for sharing.
- Ask questions.
- Learn and move on.

Types of Listening

- Relational
- Supportive
- Task-Oriented
- Analytical
- Critical

4 Tips for Listening Mindfully

- Determine when to be mindful.
- Commit to being fully present.
- Acknowledge your feelings.
- Be patient.

Show Your Communication Know-How

5.1: Summarize the benefits of being an effective listener.

How might being a better listener benefit you in your career? In your personal life?

5.2: Outline the most common misconceptions about listening, and assess how successfully you avoid them.

Which of the listening myths described in the chapter characterize your attitudes about listening? What can you do to change your thinking and behavior?

KEY TERMS: hearing, listening

5.3: Describe how each stage in the listening process influences your ability to send and share messages.

Think of a time when you heard the words someone said, but you interpreted them differently than was intended. What happened? How did you resolve the misunderstanding?

KEY TERMS: understanding, listening fidelity, remembering, residual message, interpreting, evaluating, responding

5.4: Develop strategies to minimize listening challenges.

Call to mind a time when you were not at your best as a listener. Did any of the challenges described in this chapter play a role? If so, how?

KEY TERM: multimodal

5.5: Identify and manage faulty listening habits that can hurt others and damage relationships.

Under what circumstances are you likely to listen selectively or defensively? How might you overcome that tendency?

KEY TERMS: pseudolistening, selective listeners, defensive listeners, insulated listeners, insensitive listeners, conversational narcissists, stage hogs

5.6: Adapt listening behaviors to specific situations and engage in mindful listening.

How would close friends rate your listening skills in various situations? What skills and approaches described in this chapter might increase your effectiveness?

KEY TERMS: relational listening, supportive listening, task-oriented listening, paraphrasing, analytical listening, critical listening, mindful listening

NONVERBAL

Communication

6

The Nature of Nonverbal Communication

LEARNING OBJECTIVE 6.1: Explain the defining characteristics of nonverbal communication.

Nonverbal communication is sometimes even more potent than what people say. This section covers some fundamental characteristics of communication that do not involve words.

You have probably noticed that there's often a gap between what people say and what they feel. An acquaintance says, "We should do this again sometime" in a way that seems insincere. A speaker tries to appear confident but their body language almost screams "I'm nervous!" You ask a friend what's wrong, and the "nothing" you get in response doesn't ring true.

Then, of course, there are times when someone's message comes through even though they use no words. A look of irritation, a smile, or a sigh can say it all. These examples illustrate communication without words, also known as **nonverbal communication**. Nonverbal communication involves gestures, sounds, facial expressions, use of space, touch, clothing, and more. It also includes audible cues that aren't linguistic—such as humming, sobs, how loudly or quickly someone speaks, and so on. To test your understanding of this definition, answer the following questions:

- Is American Sign Language mostly verbal or nonverbal?
- How about an email?
- How about laughter?

If you answered verbal, verbal, and nonverbal, respectively, you are correct. American Sign Language doesn't require sound, but its vocabulary and sentence structure are word based, thus verbal.[1] Emails are usually verbal for the same reason. (If you imagined an email filled with nothing but emojis, that would indeed be nonverbal.) Laughter involves vocalizing, but doesn't rely on words, so it's nonverbal. These distinctions only begin to convey the richness of nonverbal messages. Here are some other observations about communicating without words.

Nonverbal communication is impossible to avoid.

Even if you try not to send nonverbal cues—perhaps by closing your eyes or leaving the room—others may consider those behaviors meaningful. And think about the last time you involuntarily blushed or stammered. Like it or not, others probably attributed meaning to those nonverbal cues.

Nonverbal behavior is part of identity management.

Chapter 2 explored the notion that people strive to create images of themselves as they want others to view them. A great deal of this identity management occurs nonverbally. Consider what happens when you attend a party. Instead of projecting your desired image verbally ("Hi! I'm attractive, friendly, and easygoing"), you behave in ways that support that identity. You might smile a lot and adopt a relaxed posture. It's also likely that you will dress carefully—even if you're trying to create the illusion that you haven't given a lot of attention to your appearance.

Nonverbal cues help define relationships.

Think about the wide range of ways you behave when greeting another person. Depending on the nature of your relationship, you might wave, nod, smile, pat the other person on the back, give a hug, or avoid all contact. Even trying *not* to communicate can send a message, as when you avoid talking to someone.

Nonverbal behavior is ambiguous.

You've probably seen self-proclaimed experts offer tips about the hidden meaning of nonverbal behavior. Arms crossed? *She's mad.* Eyes looking up? *He's skeptical.* Simplistic interpretations such as these are usually bogus. The reality is that nonverbal cues are difficult to interpret accurately because they can mean more than one thing. To appreciate this, consider the following factors:

- *The context in which the nonverbal behavior occurs.* A smile that might mask nervousness in a job interview might reflect happiness when you're greeted by a friend.
- *The history and tone of your relationship with the sender.* An eye roll might convey playfulness

when things are going smoothly but exasperation if you're in conflict mode.

- *The sender's mood at the time.* A scowl when your housemate is grumpy might say more about their emotional state than anything you've done.
- *Your own feelings.* When you're feeling insecure, almost anything can seem like a threat.

No matter what meaning you think you detect, it's best to consider nonverbal behaviors not as facts, but as clues to be checked out.

Nonverbal communication is influenced by cultural expectations.

As you'll see throughout the chapter, nonverbal cues that are valued in one culture may be offensive or puzzling in another. For example, is it polite to make eye contact with a stranger? What would you think if a classmate put their hand on your arm? Is it okay to show up to a meeting 10 minutes late? Your answers depend on cultural assumptions about what is appropriate.

What happens when a communicator violates expectations? **Expectancy violation theory** proposes that people may react positively or negatively depending on how extreme the behavior is and how they feel about the rule breaker.[2,3] For example, if someone you find attractive gazes at you longer than normal, you may be flattered. But if someone you don't know or like does the same thing, you might feel afraid or uncomfortable. Depending on your reaction, expectancy violation theory predicts that you might either *accommodate* or *compensate* nonverbally. If someone you like invades your personal space, you might lean even closer toward them. That's accommodating. On the other hand, if the violation is unwelcome, you might compensate by moving away, avoiding eye contact, or ignoring the person. The best advice is to think about the implications of your nonverbal cues, proceed slowly, and pay close attention to people's reactions.

Nonverbal communication is essential to success.

It's hard to overstate the importance of effectively sending, receiving, and responding to nonverbal cues. Nonverbal encoding and decoding skills are strong predictors of popularity, attractiveness, and overall well-being.[4] In general, people with good nonverbal communication skills are more persuasive than those who are less skilled, and they have a greater chance of success in settings ranging from careers to poker to romance. For example, when teachers' facial expressions and tone of voice seem encouraging and friendly, their students are usually more motivated and more likely to succeed than if teachers are standoffish.[5] All in all, nonverbal sensitivity is a major part of emotional intelligence (Chapter 2), and researchers have come to recognize that it's impossible to fully understand spoken language without paying attention to nonverbal dimensions as well.[6] ●

PAUSE TO REFLECT *How Nonverbally Savvy Are You?*

1 Which of the following apply to you?

a) I'm a good storyteller. I enjoy spinning a suspenseful or funny tale.
b) I have a hard time judging whether people like my ideas or not.
c) I can usually tell when someone is upset, even if they say things are okay.
d) When I get nervous, I fidget a lot and have trouble maintaining eye contact with people.
e) I usually make a positive first impression on people.
f) Whatever I'm feeling shows on my face, even when I'd rather hide my emotions.

2 The list above includes nonverbal traits typically considered to be effective (items a, c, and e) and others (items b, d, and f) that can pose challenges. What are your greatest strengths and challenges as a nonverbal communicator? (Think in terms of facial expressions, body language, voice, touching behaviors, clothing selections, posture, use of time, and so on.) ____________________

____

Functions of Nonverbal Communication

LEARNING OBJECTIVE 6.2: Describe key functions served by nonverbal communication.

Although verbal and nonverbal messages differ in many ways, they operate together on most occasions. In this section we discuss four key functions of nonverbal cues and how they relate to verbal communication.

Complementing

Nonverbal behavior complements a verbal message when the nonverbal behavior reinforces the content of the verbal message. For example, an apology delivered in a heartfelt tone of voice will probably be more believable than the same words delivered in a monotone. Complementary nonverbal cues can be part of written communication, too. If you've ever added an emoji such as ❤ or ☺ to a message, you probably intended the symbol to complement your verbal message.

Contradicting

Having just talked about nonverbal cues that complement messages, we should also consider those that don't. People sometimes say one thing but display nonverbal cues that suggest the opposite. A classic example is when someone with a red face and bulging veins yells, "I'm not angry!" When verbal and nonverbal messages are at odds, people tend to trust the nonverbal cues more than the words—probably because nonverbal cues seem more spontaneous and harder for the speaker to control.[7,8] This is true in both close relationships and with strangers. Audiences tend to distrust public speakers who display nonverbal cues that are inconsistent with their words.[9]

Substituting

Emblems are deliberate nonverbal behaviors that have precise meanings known to members of a cultural group. For instance, when a friend asks what you thought of a movie, you might respond with a thumbs down gesture to signify "I didn't like it." In the United States, people would probably say that nodding one's head up and down means "yes" and shaking one's head side to side means "no." But beware, the same cues might mean something very different in another culture. (Test your knowledge of culture-specific gestures with the "About You" quiz.)

Regulating

Nonverbal behaviors can also regulate the flow of verbal communication. For example, conversational partners send and receive turn-taking cues. The speakers may use nonverbal fillers—such as *um* or an audible intake of breath—to signal that they would like to maintain their speaking turn.[10] Or they may hold up a finger to suggest that the listener wait to speak. Conversely, long pauses are often taken as opportunities for others to speak. Nonverbal regulators also include signs that you would like to wrap up the conversation. For example, you might say *okaaay* or glance at your phone. ●

Deception and Nonverbal Cues

LEARNING OBJECTIVE 6.3: Analyze the likelihood of identifying deception via nonverbal cues.

People often assume that they can tell if someone is lying, but can they really? Read on to see if your lie-detection antennae are as sensitive as you think.

Q What cues indicate that someone is lying?

A Decades of research show that there is no sure-fire way to detect deception based on nonverbal cues.[11,12] As one writer put it, "There is no unique telltale signal for a fib. Pinocchio's nose just doesn't exist."[13] This helps explain why most people have only about a 50–50 chance of accurately identifying a liar.[14] They tend to be worse at catching deceivers while they participate actively in conversations than when they observe from the sidelines, probably because of the mental energy it takes to manage one's own participation in an encounter.[15]

Q What if the deceiver is a child?

A One researcher tested the conventional wisdom that children are clumsy liars who give themselves away. In a series of experiments, an adult told elementary school children (one at a time) that they could win a prize by guessing the numbers on cards lying face down on a table. The adult then left each child alone with the cards for a few minutes. As you might predict, few youngsters could resist taking a peek. When the experimenter returned and asked the children if they had looked at the cards, some answered truthfully and others lied. Researchers then showed the children's videotaped statements to randomly selected adults to see if they could tell which children were telling the truth. They couldn't. The participants' guesses were no better than chance—even when they were child care professionals or parents who interact with children every day.[16] Of course, deception is easier to spot in younger children who haven't yet gained much experience with deception.

Q Are my odds better if I know the person well?

A Even with loved ones, detecting deception isn't as easy as you might imagine. For the most part, close friends and romantic partners are little better than strangers at detecting when their partners are lying.[17,18]

Q Why is it so hard to detect deception?

A One reason is the ambiguity of nonverbal cues. People who are nervous or defensive may seem cagey even though they are telling the truth. "If someone is asking me a tough question of some sort . . . it can appear as though I am lying," writes one blog contributor, adding, "I struggle to keep up eye contact, I kinda gulp a lot as well."[19] On the other hand, some people are remarkably composed while they lie. Another stumbling block involves preconceived notions. Some people harbor a **truth bias**, meaning that they assume people are telling the truth unless they have a compelling reason to suspect otherwise.[20] Conversely, others have a **deception bias**, meaning that they assume that people (or at least some people) are likely to lie.[21] Either way, internal biases influence the degree to which people either overlook or imagine deception by others.

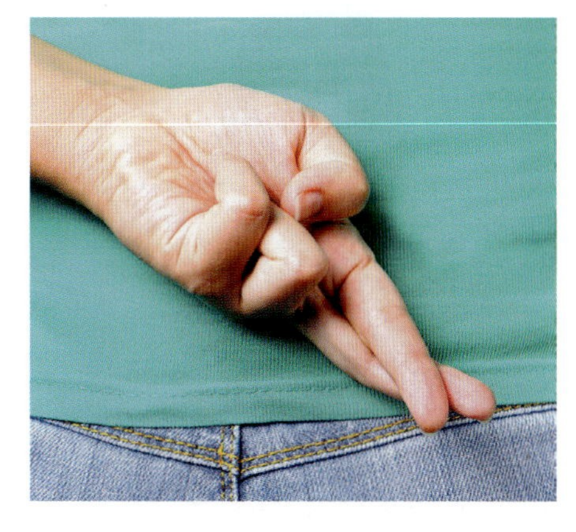

Q When do I have the best chance of catching a lie?

A By now, you probably realize that "common sense" notions about lying are faulty. Liars might avoid eye contact, stutter, stammer, sweat, and so on. But some of them don't. With this awareness in mind, it *is* slightly easier to catch someone in a lie when the deceiver hasn't had a chance to rehearse, feels strongly about the information being hidden, and/or feels anxious or guilty about lying.[22]

Kinesic Nonverbal Communication

LEARNING OBJECTIVE 6.4: Summarize types of kinesic nonverbal behaviors and their impact on interactions.

People send messages with their bodies, faces, voices, and use of touch.

Sometimes nonverbal cues are fairly easy to interpret. Facial expressions that reflect emotions such as happiness and sadness are similar around the world.[23] Other expressions and gestures are culture specific. Here we explain seven types of **kinesic** nonverbal behaviors—nonverbal cues that result from the way people move their faces and bodies.

Posture

There's a reason parents often tell their children to stand up straight. Good posture suggests to others that one is confident and capable.[24] Some evidence indicates that good posture can also make people *feel* more confident. Researcher Amy Cuddy found that adopting a "power pose"—shoulders back, hands on hips, head held high—for 2 minutes before a stressful event such as a job interview helped some people perform better.[25] The idea is to "fake it until you become it," says Cuddy.[26] One caveat is that a confidence boost is most likely among people who *believe* a power pose will work. Skeptics are less likely to experience it.[27]

Because posture sends messages about how alert and vulnerable someone is, criminals may use it to identify targets. In a classic study, researchers showed prison inmates footage of people walking down a city sidewalk and asked them who would be easiest to rob. The inmates consistently selected "easy marks" based, not on their size, but on their nonverbal cues. Those with slouched posture who took small steps and kept their arms close to their bodies were deemed easier targets than others who walked with a confident gait—long strides, head up, and shoulders back.[28]

Fidgeting

You have probably seen a public speaker who looked nervous. Perhaps they fidgeted with their clothing, clasped and unclasped their hands, or played with a pen or paperclip while they spoke. Social scientists call these behaviors **manipulators**, in the sense that they involve manipulating or fiddling with objects or parts of the body.[29] Research confirms what common sense suggests—a greater than normal use of manipulators is often a sign of discomfort. The good news is that you can appear more confident by avoiding the temptation to fidget. If you anticipate a stressful situation, wear clothing that makes you feel confident and comfortable, don't hold anything in your hands, and try to relax your body and use gestures naturally.

Smiling

People who smile are typically regarded as friendlier and less aggressive than those who don't.[30] This can be a powerful advantage when making friends and working on teams. At the same time, people in some situations and cultures are put off by excessive smiling, especially when whole-face grins are involved. Particularly in professional settings, people who smile "too much" may be regarded as less competent and less assertive than others.[31] As with all nonverbal communication, it pays to be mindful of the situation, cultures, and relationships involved.

Eye Contact

The need for eye contact begins at birth. Newborns instinctively lock eyes with their caregivers.[32] But the meaning people give eye contact varies by culture. In Euro-American culture, meeting someone's glance with your eyes is usually taken as a sign of involvement or interest, whereas looking away suggests a desire to avoid contact. However, in some cultures—such as traditional Asian, Latin American, and Native American—it may be considered aggressive or disrespectful to make eye contact with a stranger or authority figure.[33] It's easy to imagine the misunderstandings that occur when one person's "friendly gaze" feels rude to another, and conversely, how "politely" looking away can feel like a sign of indifference.

Expressions of Emotion

Facial expressions and eye contact are often difficult to interpret. That's partly because of the sheer number of expressions people can produce—as many as five per second. **Affect blends** are combinations of two or more simultaneous expressions that show different emotions, such as fearful surprise or angry disgust. This is possible because people tend to display different emotions with different parts of the face. Happiness and surprise usually show in the eyes and lower face; anger in the lower face, brows, and forehead; fear and sadness in the eyes; and disgust in the lower face.

Voice

"That kind of joke can get you in trouble," says the boss with a smile and chuckle. The employee receiving the message wonders if the boss is serious or only kidding. As you have seen, the way people express themselves can be as important as what they say. Social scientists use the term **paralanguage** to describe nonverbal cues that are vocal. These include tone, speed, pitch, volume, laughter, and more. You might use your voice to emphasize particular words, or use disfluencies such as "uh," "um," and "er." Even in writing, you can convey a particular tone through the use of capital letters, exclamation marks, and emojis. Scholars have found that tone has four basic dimensions: funny or serious, formal or casual, respectful or irreverent, and enthusiastic or matter of fact.[34] Even a simple remark such as "That's not what I expected" can be interpreted many ways based on the tone. Thinking about these options can help you choose a tone that supports the message you hope to convey either aloud or in writing.

Touch

Haptics, the study of touch, has revealed what life has probably taught you—that physical contact is highly potent. Romantic partners who frequently touch each other are typically more satisfied with their relationships than couples who don't.[35] Restaurant servers who fleetingly touch the hand or shoulder of diners often receive larger tips.[36] Touch is so important that many people found it difficult to give up handshake greetings during the COVID-19 pandemic. Our hands "speak for us," said writer Robin Givhan, observing that people in many cultures use a handshake to convey "Nice to meet you. We have a deal. It's been a pleasure."[37] To substitute for handshakes, many people adopted haptic alternatives such as fist bumps and elbow taps.

Although touch may be appreciated in some situations, it's annoying or frightening in others. By law, unwelcome touch that is sexually suggestive, excessive, or inappropriate may constitute harassment.[38] One woman was dismayed when a business leader she asked for career advice pulled his chair alongside hers, put his arm around her, and then kissed her on the head rather than shaking hands when they parted. "I was hurt and annoyed," she remembers, "and I was frustrated by the fact that my attempts to forge a professional connection were treated this way."[39] ●

ABOUT YOU *How Worldly Are Your Nonverbal Communication Skills?*

Answer the questions below to test your knowledge of nonverbal communication in different cultures.

______ **1.** In the United States, touching your index finger to your thumb while your other fingers point upward means "OK." But what does it mean elsewhere? (Two of the following are correct.)

a. It signifies money in Japan.
b. People in Greece and Turkey interpret it to mean 30.
c. In France, it means "You're worth zero."
d. It's a compliment in Russia, implying that "you and I are close friends."

______ **2.** People around the world recognize the V sign for "peace" or "victory"—two fingers up, thumb holding down the other fingers, palm facing out. But in many places, the same gesture means something different if you show the back of your hand instead. Which of the following is correct?

a. In Hungary, it's a request for more, as in, "May I have seconds?"
b. In Singapore and Thailand, it means "I'll be right back."
c. If you move your hand from side to side while doing this, it's a polite way to wave goodbye in Germany.
d. In England, New Zealand, and Australia, it's an aggressive insult meaning "Up yours!"

______ **3.** In the United States, people convey "come closer" by alternately extending and curling their index finger in someone's direction. Where might the same gesture be considered a serious insult?

a. Egypt
b. The Philippines
c. Spain
d. Saudi Arabia

______ **4.** The "thumbs up" sign that means "yes" or "job well done" in the United States means something else in other cultures. Two of the following are true. Which ones?

a. It means "It's my turn to talk" in Tahiti and neighboring South Pacific Islands.
b. It means "Up yours!" in Australia, Greece, and the Middle East.
c. It means the number 5 in Japan.
d. In Myanmar, it's a symbol of mourning, meaning "Someone has died."

INTERPRETING YOUR RESPONSES

Read the explanations below to see how many answers you got right.

Question 1 The gesture that means "OK" in the United States means "money" in Japan. But it has a darker meaning in France, where it conveys "You're worth zero." It's risky to use this gesture in other parts of the world as well. In Brazil, Germany, and Russia, it depicts a private bodily orifice; and in Turkey and Greece it's taken as a vulgar sexual invitation. The correct answers are "a" and "c."

Question 2 The palm-forward V sign is popular around the world, especially in Japan, where it's customary to flash a peace sign while being photographed.[40] But a slight variation makes a big difference. Winston Churchill occasionally shocked audiences during World War II by "flipping them off" (knuckles forward) when he really meant to flash a victory sign (palm forward).[41] Years later, U.S. president Richard Nixon made the same mistake in Australia, effectively saying "f— you" to an Australian crowd when he got the gesture wrong.[42] The correct answer is "d."

Question 3 The gesture Americans use to mean "come closer" is offensive in many places, including the Philippines, Slovakia, China, and Malaysia. People in those cultures summon a dog that way, so it's a put-down to use it with a person. Answer "b" is correct.

Question 4 "Thumbs up" has a positive connotation in the United States. Meanwhile, people in Germany and Hungary interpret it to mean the number 1, and people in Japan use it for the number 5. However, the gesture is taken as an insult (akin to "Up yours!") in the Middle East. Both "b" and "c" are correct.

The Impact of Space, Time, and Place

LEARNING OBJECTIVE 6.5: Assess the nonverbal implications of proxemics, chronemics, territoriality, and physical environment.

Nonverbal communication isn't limited to the way people use their faces and bodies. It also involves how they use contextual elements of their environment.

Louise Hung learned some valuable lessons about personal space when she moved to a big city in Japan. Based on her experiences in the United States, Hung expected to feel uncomfortable on Japanese subways, which are often so crowded that people are smashed up against each other. Surprisingly, Hung says, the experience didn't feel weird because passengers compensated in other ways. "What little space you are lucky enough to occupy is regarded with respect by those around you," Hung discovered. Subway passengers in Japan tend to look down and refrain from conversation with strangers. There is a silent agreement that, although they are very close physically, everyone is in their "own world," Hung says.[43]

In this section, we reflect on the ways that people in a variety of cultures use space, time, and place to communicate nonverbally.

Space

The study of the way individuals use space is called **proxemics**. Cultural norms influence proxemics. In many cultures of North America, people position themselves about 4 feet away from casual acquaintances as they converse, but people from the Middle East tend to stand much closer.[44] It's easy to visualize the awkward pattern that might occur when people from these cultures meet. The Middle Easterner would probably keep moving forward to close a gap that feels wide to them, while the American is likely to keep backing away.

Allowing the right amount of personal space is so important that scientists who create interactive robots take proxemics into account. They have found that people tend to be disturbed by robots who get too close, especially if the robot makes consistent "eye contact" with them. However, people don't mind as much if robots whose nonverbal behaviors seem friendly and nonthreatening move into their personal space.[45]

Time

Chronemics is the study of how people use and structure time. Some cultures (such as North American, German, and Swiss) tend to be **monochronic**, meaning that they emphasize punctuality, schedules, and completing one task at a time. Other cultures (such as South American, Mediterranean, and Arab) are more **polychronic**, with flexible schedules in which people pursue multiple tasks at the same time.[46] When a Brazilian American friend threw a party, she invited her Brazilian friends to show up at 5 p.m. and her American friends to show up at 7 p.m. As she expected, they all arrived just after 7 o'clock. That's not to say the Brazilians were rude. From their perspective, it would have been rude to show up at the time specified.

Even within cultures, time is treated differently depending on who is involved. "Important" people, whose time is supposedly more valuable than that of others, may be seen by appointment only, while it's acceptable to intrude without notice on individuals deemed less important.[47]

Territory

Territory involves the tendency to claim places and spaces you consider to be more or less your own. These might include your bedroom, house, or the seat you usually occupy in class. People often use nonverbal markers to declare their territory. You might erect a fence around your yard or spread a blanket on the beach to mark the area as yours, at least temporarily. You may feel annoyed or disrespected if someone encroaches on your territory without permission. Indeed, honoring boundaries is one way of showing respect. People of high status are typically granted more personal territory and privacy than others. You may knock before entering the boss's office, whereas the boss might walk into your work area without hesitating.

Environment

Google, Microsoft, and some other employers offer communication-friendly work environments in which the furniture can be moved at will and there is plenty of space for conversation and group interaction. They know what social scientists have long found to be true: Physical environments shape the communication that occurs within them. Natural light, flexible seating configurations, and views of nature have been shown to enhance learning in the classroom[48] and productivity at work.[49]

TIPS & REMINDERS

Ways to Interpret Nonverbal Cues More Accurately

By now, it's probably clear that there is no magic formula for deciphering people's nonverbal cues. However, it's possible to get better at interpreting them. Here are four tips for doing that.

1. **Focus on behavior.**

   It's easy to overlook important nonverbal cues when you're only listening to the words being spoken. Pay close attention to people's vocal qualities as well as their posture, gestures, facial expressions, and other cues.

2. **Consider the context.**

   A wink may be a sign of romantic interest, a signal to go along with a joke, or a reaction to dust in the air. To make an educated guess, ask yourself: *Which interpretation is most consistent with the sender's other behaviors?* and *Which seems most likely under the circumstances?*

3. **Be willing to change your interpretations.**

   Dating coach Eddy Baller remembers feeling that a woman he liked was uninterested on their first date. "She kept looking around the room, and she would audibly sigh as if she was going to die of boredom," he recalls. To his surprise, she agreed to a second date and they had a lot of fun. His advice: Don't overestimate your ability to read people's "signals."[50]

4. **Use perception checking.**

   Since nonverbal behaviors are ambiguous, it's important to consider your interpretations as educated guesses, not absolute translations. If someone yawns while you're telling a story, they may be bored—or maybe they just had a sleepless night. Perception checking (Chapter 2) is one way to explore the significance of nonverbal cues. As a reminder, here's how it works: Describe the behavior you've noted, share at least two possible interpretations, and ask for clarification about how to interpret the behavior. It might sound like this: *"Last night you left the party early* [behavior]. *I wasn't sure whether you were tired or if something was bothering you* [two options]. *Is anything wrong?"*

PAUSE TO REFLECT *How Do You Use Time?*

1 Which of the following best describes your attendance at class and work meetings?

a) I usually arrive a few minutes early.
b) I tend to arrive exactly at the specified time.
c) I often arrive after the specified time.

2 Do you do mostly use time in a monochronic or polychronic manner? What are the pros and cons of that approach? ______

______

Nonverbal Cues and Attractiveness

LEARNING OBJECTIVE 6.6: Analyze the relationship between nonverbal communication and attractiveness.

The way someone appears can be just as revealing as how they sound and move. Here we explore physical attractiveness, clothing, and tattoos as forms of nonverbal communication.

Attractiveness Advantage

Some observers have coined the phrase "the Tinder trap" (after the popular dating app) to describe the tendency, especially online, to judge individuals primarily or even solely by their appearance. As experience has no doubt taught you, looks aren't a good predictor of a relationship's potential, although they're often the most visible means of creating a first impression.

The benefits of attractiveness go beyond dating. People who are considered physically appealing are more likely than others to be satisfied with life in general.[51] And no wonder. They are more likely than their peers to win elections, be granted a not-guilty verdict in court, influence their peers, and succeed in business.[52,53,54] More than 200 managers in one survey admitted that attractive people get preferential treatment both in hiring decisions and on the job.[55] Researchers in one study even found that people with attractive avatars enjoy an advantage in online job interviews.[56]

What some researchers call the *beauty premium* involves a cause-and-effect spiral. People tend to assume that attractive people are more confident than others, so they treat them as if they are—which can lead attractive people to actually feel more confident than others.[57] And because people tend to smile at attractive people, they tend to smile back, which can boost their attractiveness rating even more.[58] One lesson is that presenting yourself in a confident and friendly manner can improve others' opinions of your appearance, even if you don't consider yourself to be the best looking person in the room.

Clothing

As a means of nonverbal communication, clothing can be used to convey economic status, educational level, athletic ability, interests, and more. Although college-age men often deny that they put much thought into their wardrobes, about 9 in 10 admit that they deliberately choose attire that supports the image they want to convey—such as t-shirts that feature a sports team or musical group, or clothing that makes them seem destined for professional success.[59]

Clothing choices are an important means of nonverbal communication for women as well, but women face several challenges when trying to live up to social standards.

- The latest fashions might not look good on women or be designed to fit them.[60] Clothing ads tend to feature female models who are younger and thinner than the average person.
- Media images tend to suggest that women in skimpy clothing are attractive, but women who dress that way may be taken less seriously than others. In one study, university students judged women in photos to be more intelligent, powerful, organized, professional, and efficient when they were dressed in business clothes rather than in form-fitting or revealing clothing.[61]

- Clothing and shoes that women are expected to wear can be uncomfortable and impractical.[62]

Clothing options may be especially problematic for women who identify as queer.[63] They often say that there are few role models or clothing styles that reflect their identity. As a result, they may feel alienated and ignored whether they shop in the "women's" or the "men's" section. The majority of queer women surveyed said they would appreciate shopping in clothing sections that are not designated for one gender or another.

Even the colors people wear may influence how others perceive them. In one study, experimenters asked people to rate the attractiveness of individuals shown in photos. The pictures of each person were identical, except that the experimenters had digitally changed the color of the models' shirts. Participants considered the models more attractive when they were wearing red or black compared to yellow, blue, or green.[64] Before you load your wardrobe with red and black, however, consider that perceptions vary by context. Patients are significantly more willing to share their social, sexual, and psychological problems with doctors wearing white coats or surgical scrubs than those wearing business dress or casual attire.[65]

Body Art

In the United States, about 40 percent of people age 40 and younger have a tattoo, making indelible body art a common means of self-expression.[66] The most popular reason to get a tattoo is to commemorate an important relationship, life event, or philosophy.[67] When it comes to ink, beauty is in the eye of the beholder *and* the identity of the design wearer. College students tend to consider tattoos more attractive on younger women than on older ones.[68] And when researchers showed people images of the same men with or without tattoos, the respondents tended to rate the tattooed versions as more masculine and aggressive.[69] That can be both good and bad. Overall, heterosexual women in the study considered the tattooed men appealing but not necessarily good husband or father material. On the other hand, gay men did not consider males with tattoos to be any less desirable than others as long-term partners. But beware: So far, a tattoo taboo still reigns in many workplaces. Overall, people with visible tattoos have more difficulty getting hired than others.[70]

Overall Effect

If you aren't extraordinarily gorgeous or handsome by society's standards, don't despair. Evidence suggests that, as people get to know and like one another, they rate each other higher in terms of physical attractiveness.[71] Moreover, people view others as beautiful or ugly not just on the basis of their physical attributes but also on how they behave. Posture, gestures, facial expressions, and other behaviors can increase the attractiveness of an otherwise unremarkable person. And occasionally, physical attractiveness has a downside. Employers sometimes turn down especially good-looking candidates because they perceive them to be threats.[72] All in all, while attractiveness generally gets rewarded, over-the-top good looks can be intimidating.[73] ●

PAUSE TO REFLECT *What Roles Does Appearance Play for You?*

1. In what ways does your appearance influence the ways others communicate with you? ______________________________

2. Describe how you make clothing choices and what image you hope to present to others. ______________________________

3. Do you find tattoos more appealing on some people than on others? If so, describe your preference. ______________________________

Gender and Nonverbal Communication

LEARNING OBJECTIVE 6.7: Illustrate how social ideas about gender influence nonverbal communication.

By now, it's probably clear that cultural expectations have a powerful effect on the way people behave. Here we explore patterns related to gender and nonverbal communication.

Gender Differences

Although differences between the sexes are often smaller than people think, women in general more accurately identify the emotions others display nonverbally.[74] And in some ways, women are more nonverbally expressive than men. Research shows that, compared with men, women tend to:

- Smile more[75]
- Frown less[76]
- Use more emoticons in digital communication[77]
- Show and receive more physical affection[78]

Most communication scholars agree that these differences are influenced more by social conditions than by biological differences. Of particular influence are media and social power structures, which we discuss next.

Media's Influence

Media portrayals tend to reinforce stereotypes about gender and nonverbal communication. These stereotypes are often conveyed via appearance and behavior.

Television programs for children and teenagers commonly define girls in terms of how they look and their ability to attract the attention of boys, and boys in terms of rugged independence and a preoccupation with pursuing girls.[79] The depictions are overwhelmingly heterosexual and consistent with the stereotype that one should be either a "hot girl" or a "cool dude," as one research team put it.[80] Television commercials and video games for all ages feature similar, even more extreme, versions of these themes.[81,82]

High exposure to media is associated with stereotypical beliefs. For example, men who frequently play video games in which women are portrayed as "damsels in distress" are more likely than other men to think women are weak and helpless.[83] Stereotypes affect people's self-image as well. Selfies (photos of oneself) on social media tend to correspond closely with images in the media—females suggestively dressed and smiling, and men emphasizing their physique and emotional control.[84]

Social Structure

Women may demonstrate greater sensitivity than men to nonverbal cues due to their social status. Because women have historically had less power, they have had greater incentive to read men's nonverbal cues than the other way around.[85] You have probably noticed a similar dynamic in work settings, where people are usually more tuned into the boss's moods than the boss is to theirs. It may also be that, because women have traditionally been responsible for child care, they learn to display and decipher nonverbal cues so they can better communicate with young children who are not yet proficient using language.

Commonalities

Despite these differences, men's and women's nonverbal communication patterns have a good deal in common.[86] You can prove this by imagining what it would be like to use radically different nonverbal rules: Standing only an inch away from others, sniffing strangers, or tapping people's foreheads to get their attention would mark you as bizarre no matter your gender. Moreover, according to one study, nonverbal differences are less pronounced in conversations involving LGBTQ+ individuals than those involving heterosexuals, presumably because the former feel less constrained by gender-related stereotypes.[87] All in all, gender and culture have an influence on nonverbal style, but the differences are often a matter of degree and cultural influence.

PAUSE TO REFLECT *What Do Your Nonverbal Cues Suggest?*

1. What might others assume about you if they could see your nonverbal cues right this moment? ____________

2. Do you think people form an accurate first impression of you? Why or why not? ____________

3. Do the nonverbal cues you tend to display reflect traditional gender patterns or not? Explain. ____________

4. In your experience, do people of different genders use emoticons and facial expressions differently, or is gender irrelevant? Describe what you have observed.

Nonverbal Communication

Nonverbal Communication Is . . .

- Impossible to avoid.
- Part of identity management.
- Helpful in defining relationships.
- Ambiguous and cultural.
- Essential to success.

Nonverbal Communication . . .

- Complements verbal messages.
- Contradicts verbal communication.
- Substitutes for words.
- Regulates interactions.

Deception and Nonverbal Cues

- People have only a 50–50 chance of detecting a lie, even when the deceiver is a child.
- Knowing someone well doesn't usually make it easier to detect deception based on nonverbal cues.
- A preconceived bias to think people are truthful (or not) interferes with people's judgment.
- Lies are easiest to catch when the deception is spontaneous and emotional and the deceiver feels bad about lying.

Kinesic Nonverbal Communication

- Good posture sends a message to others and even to yourself.
- Manipulators are fidgety behaviors.
- Smiling (within certain bounds) is advantageous.
- Eye contact may be perceived as friendly or as aggressive.
- An affect blend involves the expression of multiple emotions.
- Haptics reveals pleasurable and unpleasant dimensions of touch.

Space, Time, and Place

- Proxemics involves the use of space and is heavily influenced by culture.
- A monochronic approach emphasizes punctuality and doing one thing at a time.
- A polychronic approach involves simultaneous activities and a fluid sense of time.
- People claim territory in many ways, such as through the use of walls, doors, and personal items.
- Environments either encourage or inhibit open communication.

Interpret Nonverbal Cues by . . .

- Observing behavior.
- Considering context.
- Being willing to change your interpretation.
- Using perception checking.

Nonverbal Cues and Attractiveness

- Good looks are generally an advantage, but extreme attractiveness can intimidate others.
- Clothing colors and style influence perceived attractiveness.
- Tattoos are evaluated differently depending on age and gender but are still discouraged in many work environments.
- People can boost their attractiveness level nonverbally.

Gender and Nonverbal Communication

- Media portrayals emphasize women's appearance and men's ruggedness, and they generally underrepresent gender diversity.
- Women may be especially sensitive to nonverbal cues because traditionally they have been less powerful than men and more responsible for child care.

Show Your Communication Know-How

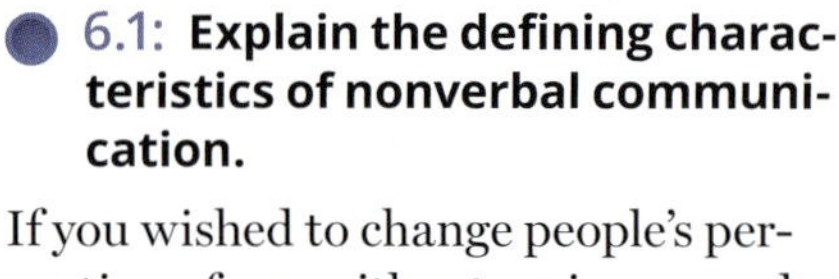

6.1: Explain the defining characteristics of nonverbal communication.

If you wished to change people's perception of you without saying a word, how might you change your typical nonverbal behaviors and appearance?

KEY TERMS: nonverbal communication, expectancy violation theory

6.2: Describe key functions served by nonverbal communication.

Think of a recent conversation. In what ways did your nonverbal cues repeat, substitute, complement, regulate, or contradict the words you used?

KEY TERM: emblems

6.3: Analyze the likelihood of identifying deception via nonverbal cues.

Ask a friend to guess whether you are lying or not when you describe one thing you have in your bag or backpack. (You can either lie or tell the truth.) Was your friend's conclusion correct?

KEY TERMS: truth bias, deception bias

6.4: Summarize types of kinesic nonverbal behaviors and their impact on interactions.

Before an important meeting or event, take 2 minutes alone to strike a power pose with your hands on hips and feet shoulder width apart. Does it make you feel more confident or not?

KEY TERMS: kinesic, manipulators, affect blends, paralanguage, haptics

6.5: Assess the nonverbal implications of proxemics, chronemics, territoriality, and physical environment.

In class or with your family, occupy a seat that someone else usually takes and notice how that person reacts. Do they seem territorial or not?

KEY TERMS: proxemics, chronemics, monochronic, polychronic

6.6: Analyze the relationship between nonverbal communication and attractiveness.

Do you find tattoos attractive or not? Does it matter who has them?

6.7: Illustrate how social ideas about gender influence nonverbal communication.

What factors have shaped how sensitive you are to nonverbal cues? Do gender norms play a role in your case?

COMMUNICATING IN INTERPERSONAL

Relationships

7

Defining Interpersonal Communication

LEARNING OBJECTIVE 7.1: Explain what makes some communication interpersonal.

Not every conversation involves interpersonal communication. To clarify what is and isn't interpersonal, consider a few of the people you are likely to see on a typical day.

Try to guess which of the following encounters exemplifies interpersonal communication.

- In your morning class, you strike up a conversation with a classmate you've just met.
- Later, you take part in a group project meeting that is so lively and productive you can't remember who said what.
- At midday, you pick up lunch and say thanks to the cashier as he hands you the receipt.
- After work, you enjoy a conversation with your roommate, who will understand what a crazy day you have had and no doubt have some funny experiences to share in return.
- Before bed, you exchange texts with someone you met online but have never seen in person.

If you picked the scenario with your roommate, you're right. If you also selected the online relationship, score that one as a maybe for now. The other encounters are important in their own ways, but they don't qualify as interpersonal. To understand why, think of interpersonal communication as the opposite of *impersonal* communication. It is often useful and rewarding to chat with strangers and take part in meetings, but those interactions aren't necessary personal. As we'll use the term, **interpersonal communication** involves interaction between people who are part of a close and irreplaceable relationship in which they treat each other as unique individuals. Let's consider the implications of that definition by returning to the examples you just considered.

You might eventually develop a close relationship with the classmate you just met, but for now, you don't know each other well enough to appreciate one another's unique qualities. Interpersonal relationships require a sense of closeness that doesn't occur instantly. Rather, it evolves over time.

The group project meeting is a good example of effective task-related communication. But since there's no evidence that your colleagues have a close personal attachment, you may assume that it's not interpersonal.

Although interactions with strangers and casual acquaintances serve an important role in life, your exchange with the cashier is not interpersonal because there's no exchange of personal information, and you're not likely to care if a different cashier helps you next time. By contrast, if a different person showed up tomorrow playing the role of your roommate, mother, or brother, you would probably be disoriented and upset.

The conversation with your roommate is interpersonal based on the fact that you are invested in listening to and sharing personal information with each other as unique individuals.

The relationship with your online friend may or may not be interpersonal. It depends—you guessed it—on how much personal information you each share and whether you treat one another as unique individuals.

Of course, it isn't always easy to categorize relationships. On a continuum between impersonal and interpersonal, some relationships fall in the middle. Our main point here is that interpersonal relationships are marked by emotional closeness and a sense of uniqueness. •

Relational Messages

LEARNING OBJECTIVE 7.2: Categorize and explain types of relational messages.

Messages exchanged by relational partners have meaning on two levels—what is actually said and what is implied.

When Lucien asked his friend Haris to go to lunch, Haris said, "Sorry, I'm busy." Throughout the day, Lucien wondered if his friend was actually short on time or whether something was bothering him.

The quandary in this example involves the difference between content and relational meaning. Virtually every verbal statement contains both a **content message**, which focuses explicitly on the subject being discussed (in this case "Sorry, I'm busy"), and a **relational message** that suggests how the parties feel toward one another. If Haris declined the lunch invitation with an apologetic tone of voice, Lucien might interpret it differently than if he sounded angry or frustrated. Because relational messages are often implied rather than stated outright, they can be difficult to interpret accurately.

We focused on language in Chapter 4. Here we consider some of the dimensions communicated on a relational level.

Affinity

The degree to which one person likes another is called **affinity**. Sometimes people indicate feelings of affinity explicitly (as in "Thank you" or "I love you"), but often the clues are nonverbal, such as a pat on the back or a friendly smile. If you ask someone to lunch and they bluntly tell you no, you might assume (rightly or wrongly) that they don't like you.

Immediacy

Whereas affinity involves attraction, **immediacy** reflects the level of engagement between people in a relationship. If two people interact openly and frequently, immediacy is high. If one or both of them is detached and distant, it is low. Affinity and intimacy can interact in different ways. Perhaps you have two friends you really like (high affinity), but you engage with one of them regularly (high immediacy) and the other one very rarely (low immediacy).

Respect

The degree to which you admire another person and hold them in high esteem is known as **respect**.[1] While respect and affinity might seem similar, they're actually different dimensions of a relationship. If you have a charming coworker who goofs off on the job, you may like them but not respect them. Likewise, you might respect a boss or teacher's talents without liking them.[2] In our example, Lucien may have been disappointed that Haris declined lunch but respected him as a busy adult with the right to spend time as he chooses.

Control

In every conversation and every relationship there is some distribution of **control**; that is, the amount of influence exercised by the individuals involved. Control can be shared evenly among relational partners, or one person can have more or less than the other. An uneven distribution of control in some ways isn't necessarily problematic if it balances out in others, but relationships suffer if control is lopsided overall, as when one partner orders the other around or always gets their way.[3] Perhaps Lucien invites Haris to lunch nearly every day and Haris sidestepped the invitation today to have more control over his own schedule.

In the end, we can speculate on Lucien and Haris's feelings, but we are only guessing. Keep this in mind when you evaluate the relational messages of people around you. The impatient tone of voice you take as a sign of anger might be due to fatigue, and the interruption you consider belittling might arise from enthusiasm about your idea. Ultimately, relational meanings are ambiguous and situational. It's a good idea to check your understanding before making assumptions about them.

Metacommunication

LEARNING OBJECTIVE 7.3: Evaluate the advantages and potential pitfalls of engaging in metacommunication.

Try to guess what the following statements have in common: "You seem upset." "I was only joking." "I appreciate your honesty." "I was confused by your text." The answer? They all involve metacommunication.

The term **metacommunication** describes messages that refer to other messages.[4] In other words, metacommunication is communication about communication. You are metacommunicating when you say "I appreciate your honesty" or text "jk" (just kidding). Here are some key things to know about metacommunication.

"She's texting me, but I think she's also subtexting me."

Metacommunication can bring issues to the surface.

With metacommunication, you can call attention to underlying meanings. You might say to a friend, "I think I offended you during our conversation the other day" or ask your partner "Are you quiet because I was late for our date?" In this way, you may be able to show that you care and are paying attention, and you can create opportunities to discuss how you both feel.

Metacommunication can be risky.

As you have no doubt experienced, talking about underlying issues can make relational partners feel vulnerable. If one of you is offended or angry, you are both likely to be sensitive about it. It may help to realize that important issues in a relationship often lie beneath the surface, and ignoring them can make things worse.

Every relationship involves some degree of conflict and misunderstanding. Successful partnerships stand out because the people involved are willing to do the repair work needed to address them, heal, and move on.[5]

The authors of *Difficult Conversations* offer a number of tips that may help:

- take time to think about how you are feeling,
- share your feelings honestly without blaming the other person, and
- listen rather than debating who is right or wrong.[6]

The good news is that, as risky as it feels in the moment, metacommunication can help clear up misunderstandings and keep resentment from festering.

Metacommunication isn't just for problem solving.

Metacommunication doesn't always involve heavy conversations. It's also a good way to reinforce the positive aspects of a relationship, as in "Thanks for praising my work in front of the boss" or "I appreciate it when you listen to me when we disagree." Comments such as this let others know that you value their behavior, and they boost the odds that the other person will continue those behaviors in the future.

Self-Disclosure in Close Relationships

LEARNING OBJECTIVE 7.4: Describe two models of self-disclosure, and apply tips for self-disclosing effectively.

It's important to share personal information as a relationship progresses. The key is to not share too much or too little.

"We don't have any secrets," some people proudly claim. If so, they engage in a great deal of **self-disclosure,** which is the process of deliberately revealing information about oneself that is significant and that would not normally be known by others.

Under the right conditions, self-disclosure can be rewarding.[7] Talking about your feelings and experiences can help you understand yourself better and connect with others at a deeper level. It can be validating to know that others know and like the real you and are willing to share something about themselves in return. At the same time, however, self-disclosure involves an element of vulnerability. What you say might be used against you. It might also make others uncomfortable. You have probably experienced moments of TMI (too much information) when someone shared intimate details that made you feel overwhelmed or embarrassed. Here are two models of self-disclosure that offer insights about relationship development and self-disclosure.

Social Penetration Model

Social psychologists Irwin Altman and Dalmas Taylor describe two ways in which communication can be disclosive.[8] Their **social penetration model** (Figure 7.1) proposes that communication occurs within two dimensions: (a) **breadth**, which represents the range of subjects being discussed; and (b) **depth**, how significant and personal the information is.

For example, as you start to reveal information about your personal life to coworkers—perhaps what you did over the weekend or stories about your family—the breadth of your disclosures is likely to increase. The depth may expand if you shift from relatively nonrevealing messages ("I went out with friends") to more personal ones ("I went on this awful blind date set up by my mom's friend. . . ."). Depth is also reflected in the difference between a relatively casual statement such as "I love my partner" and an emotionally vulnerable statement such as ". . . I don't think my partner loves me back."

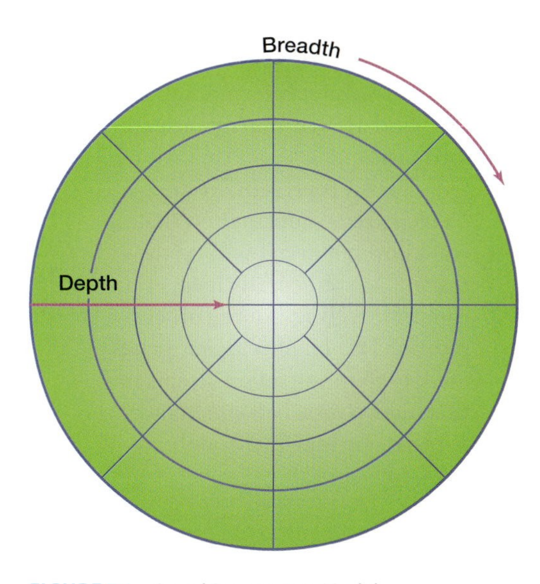

FIGURE 7.1 Social Penetration Model

Each of your personal relationships has a different combination of breadth and depth. As relationships become more intimate, disclosure increases (usually gradually) in both dimensions. Even so, it can be difficult to know how much to share, and how soon. As a rule of thumb, theorists recommend the "Goldilocks principle": Pay attention to the other person's reaction to gauge if you are offering "too much," "too little," or "just right."[9]

The Johari Window

Another model that represents self-disclosure is the **Johari Window**, which describes information based on what individuals know and share about themselves.[10] Imagine a frame that contains everything there is to know about you: your likes and dislikes, your goals, your secrets, your needs—everything.

Of course, you aren't aware of everything about yourself. Like most people, you're probably discovering new things all the time. The Johari Window makes the most sense if you consider it in the context of particular relationships, since you share different information with different people. The Johari Window depicts what you know and think about yourself in quadrants on the left (Figure 7.2) and the part you don't know about in quadrants on the right.

We can also divide this frame in another way. The top row contains the things about you that the other person knows, and the bottom row things about you that you keep to yourself. The full Johari Window presents everything about you divided into four parts. It's worth considering each quadrant in the model separately.

- Quadrant 1 represents information about you that both you and the other person are aware of. This is your *open area*.
- Quadrant 2 represents the *blind area*—information you are unaware of but the other person knows. Perhaps you display talents that aren't obvious to you but are appreciated by the other person. You learn about information in the blind area primarily through feedback.
- Quadrant 3 represents your *hidden area*—information that you know but aren't willing to reveal. Do you secretly have romantic feelings for the other person? Do you have more social anxiety than you let on? Items in this hidden area become known to others primarily through self-disclosure.
- Quadrant 4 represents information that is *unknown* to both you and the other person. For example, even if you are afraid of public speaking now, you may surprise yourself and others by emerging as a confident speaker in the future. Conversely, you may think of someone you consider to be calm—until they panic in a high-stress situation, surprising themselves and those around them.

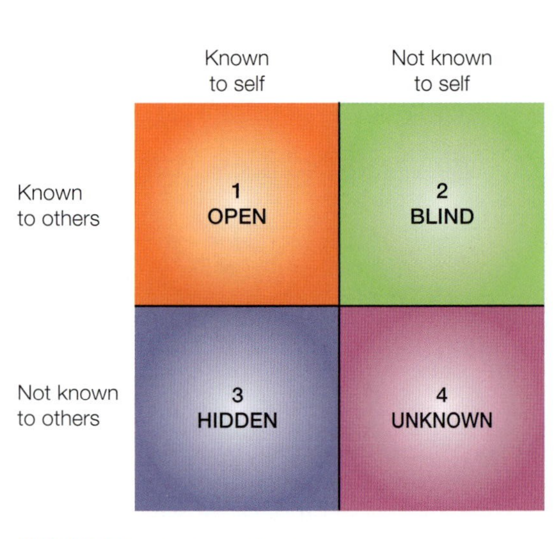

FIGURE 7.2 The Johari Window

The Johari Window presents three main implications for communication.

- Individuals keep some aspects of themselves hidden from others.
- Some secrets are okay, but interpersonal relationships of any depth require that individuals have some open area.
- Through open communication, individuals are likely to learn things about themselves and their relational partners.

To ensure that you share information about yourself in ways that enhance your relationships, see "Tips & Reminders: 7 Questions to Consider Before Self-Disclosing." ●

PAUSE TO REFLECT *Do You Self-Disclose Too Much or Too Little?*

1. Describe a time when you wish you had shared more about yourself or your feelings. ____________________

2. Describe a time when you regretted sharing personal information or your feelings. ____________________

3. What did you learn from the experiences you just described that might help you choose when to self-disclose in the future? ____________________

TIPS & REMINDERS

Questions to Consider Before Self-Disclosing

No style of self-disclosure is appropriate for every situation. However, there are some questions you can ask yourself to determine when and how self-disclosure may be beneficial for you and others.[11]

1. **Is the other person important to you?**

   Disclosure may be the path toward developing a more personal relationship with someone. However, it can be a mistake to share personal information with people you don't trust or know well.

2. **Is the disclosure appropriate?**

   This can be tricky to answer because appropriateness relies on personal preferences and culture. Some North Americans, with their individualistic orientation, are often comfortable disclosing personal information sooner than are people from more collectivistic cultures, such as Japan's.[12] As a result, some North Americans may come off as overly personal, and they may assume that people who do not disclose as quickly are standoffish or uninterested.

3. **Is the risk of disclosing reasonable?**

   You're asking for trouble when you open up to someone who is likely to betray you or make fun of you. On the other hand, knowing that your relational partner is trustworthy and supportive makes it more reasonable to speak up.

Effective self-disclosure is a balancing act, defined and managed by people within a relationship.

4. **Are the amount and type of disclosure appropriate?**

   Telling others about yourself isn't an all-or-nothing decision. Before sharing important information with someone, test their reaction by disclosing something slightly less personal first.

5. **Is the disclosure relevant to the situation at hand?**

   A study of classroom communication revealed that it was ineffective for people to share all their feelings and be completely honest. A better alternative was to establish a relatively honest climate in which pleasant but less disclosive relationships were the norm.[13] Even in close personal relationships, constant disclosure isn't a useful goal. Instead, the level of sharing in successful relationships rises and falls in cycles.

6. **Is the disclosure reciprocated?**

   There's nothing like sharing vulnerable information about yourself only to discover that the other person is unwilling to do the same. Unequal self-disclosure creates an unbalanced relationship.

7. **Will the disclosure be constructive?**

   Self-disclosure can be a vicious tool if not used carefully. Disclosures that are needlessly hurtful toward others may damage your relationships. Comments such as "I've never thought you were very smart" are best left unspoken.

Interpersonal Communication Online

LEARNING OBJECTIVE 7.5: Analyze the advantages and disadvantages of online interpersonal communication.

Communicating with someone online can be either more impersonal or more emotionally intense than interacting in person. Here are some of the pros and cons of online interactions.

Maya and Jad live in different countries and know each other only online. Although they have never met in person, Maya considers Jad one of her closest friends. The two have shared personal experiences—including some they haven't shared with their RL (real life) friends. "I trust him enough to ask things I can't ask face-to-face," Maya says. "I like to think I have found a safe little corner where I can talk and joke with someone who I would not have met otherwise."[14]

Is the communication between Maya and Jad interpersonal? Scholars' early definitions specified that interpersonal communication had to take place in person.[15] Times have changed. Today, virtually nobody disputes the idea that interpersonal communication can occur via emails, messaging, video chats, and social media.[16] Based on Maya's description, her online relationship with Jad does seem to be interpersonal. In this section we consider five of the most rewarding aspects of online interpersonal communication and two of its less appealing qualities.

Online communication helps people stay connected.

Even when people's routines don't mesh, technology can help them stay in touch. Perhaps for this reason, adolescents who use online communication (in moderation) typically have more cohesive friendships than other teens,[17] and long-distance couples who talk frequently on the phone often feel more loving, committed, and confident about their relationships than couples who don't.[18]

Online communication provides for immense diversity.

Most face-to-face communication networks are limited to people in a relatively small geographic region. But the number of people you can befriend online is virtually endless. "I grew up in a fairly small town, so being a sci-fi and comics nerd who loved makeup, '80s and '90s pop music, fancy cake, and sushi pretty much made me a peer group of one," reflects Rachel. Online, however, she has access to "an entire world's worth of people," including many who share her interests and passions.[19]

Online communication can feel non-threatening.

For some people, particularly those who are introverted, mediated channels make it easier to build close relationships.[20] Sociolinguist Deborah Tannen remembers when online communication enhanced her relationship with a reserved colleague. "Face to face he mumbled so I could barely tell he was speaking," Tannen says, "but when we both got on e-mail, I started receiving long, self-revealing messages; we poured our hearts out to each other."[21] Even if you're not shy, you may find some messages easier to send than to say aloud.

Online communication can be validating.

One appealing quality of communication technology is its potential to convey social support. Posting news of the A+ you earned in English is likely to be rewarded almost instantly with "likes" and congratulations. University students who use social media typically experience less stress than their peers, especially when they consider their online friends to be supportive, likeable, and trustworthy.[22]

Online communication has a pause option . . . sometimes.

Many forms of online communication are asynchronous, meaning that they allow you to think about messages and then reply when you are ready. This is an advantage in that you can catch mistakes or avoid blurting out something you would regret later.[23] However, by the same token, asynchronous electronic communication can feel less spontaneous and more calculated. "Arguing over text messages is cheating," asserts one person who feels that relational partners more easily mask their true feelings when technology is in the middle.

Online communication can be distracting.

On the downside, social media use can interfere with in-person relationships. Paying more attention to your devices than to the people around you is known as **phubbing** (a combination of phoning and snubbing).[24] Researchers in one study found that the mere presence of a mobile device—even if it's sitting unused on the table—can have a negative effect on closeness, connection, and conversation quality while people discuss personal topics.[25]

Too much online communication can be isolating.

Although moderate use of social media can boost feelings of connection, that only goes so far. It's possible to have thousands of superficial online "friendships" but few people you can count on during hard times. As a consequence, those who spend excessive time online tend to be lonelier than their peers.[26]

Considering the pros and cons of online communication, most experts agree that moderation is key, and the best relationships often include communication both in person and online.[27] •

PAUSE TO REFLECT *Do You Overuse Social Media?*

1 Which of the following apply to you?

- ☐ Even when I should pay attention, such as in class or at work, I can't resist peeking at my phone.
- ☐ I sometimes engage in activities just because I think they'll make good social media posts.
- ☐ I have more friends online than I do in real life.
- ☐ I often lose track of time while I'm using social media.
- ☐ I'm very anxious about what I'm missing if I can't use my phone for several hours.

2 To some people's way of thinking, if numerous items in question 1 apply to you, you may be using social media excessively.[28,29] Do you feel that social media use interferes with your ability to get things done and to be fully present with the people around you? If so, what might you do to cut down a bit? ______________________________

____

____

____

____

Relational Spirals

LEARNING OBJECTIVE 7.6: Distinguish between positive and negative relational spirals, and practice positive communication strategies.

Personal relationships are a lot like the weather. Some are fair and warm, while others are stormy and cold. Some relationships have stable climates, whereas others change dramatically—calm one moment and turbulent the next.

The term **communication climate** refers to the emotional tone of a relationship. What makes some climates positive and others negative? A short but accurate answer is that communication climate is determined by the degree to which people in a relationship feel valued by each other. When you believe that a relational partner considers you to be important, you are likely to feel good about the relationship. By contrast, the relational climate suffers when you feel unappreciated.

Relational spirals can feel unavoidable.

Making sure your relational partners feel valued may sound simple, but you have probably experienced relationships that seem to have a life of their own—veering into positive or negative territory when you didn't intend for that to happen. A **relational spiral** is a communication pattern in which the messages that relational partners exchange become increasingly negative or positive.[30] See if this sounds familiar: One person says "I always load the dishwasher," to which the other person responds, "That's *nothing*! I always mow the grass, which is a lot harder," leading the first person to exclaim, "I can't believe you're complaining about that. You said you LOVE to mow the grass!" Knowing about the qualities of relational spirals can help you use them to improve, rather than damage, your relationships.

Spirals can be destructive.

Messages that deny the value of another person are **disconfirming.**[31] These might include a dismissive eye roll, a sneer, uncomfortable silence, or a statement such as "You're wrong" or "You don't know what you're talking about." Disconfirming messages can escalate into **conflict spirals** (such as the dishwasher example) in which a statement perceived as an attack leads to a counterattack, and then another, until the communication escalates into a full-fledged argument.[32]

Another type of spiral is less obvious but can also be destructive. Relational partners may engage in **avoidance spirals** in which, rather than fighting, they gradually lessen their dependence on one another, withdraw, and become less invested in the relationship.[33] Perhaps your friend gives you the silent treatment rather than telling you why she's upset, so in frustration, you leave and don't call her for several days. In some cases, partners pass a "point of no return," leading to the end of the relationship.

Spirals can be positive.

The good news is that some types of spirals improve your relationships. Messages that show people they are valued are **confirming.**[34] A hug, a smile, a thank you, or a compliment may confirm to someone that you care about and appreciate them. In **positive spirals**, one person's confirming message leads to a similar response from the other person. Then this positive reaction leads the first person to be even more reinforcing, and so on. Howard Atteberry and Cynthia Riggs experienced this in their real-life love story. When they were young adults, they sent notes back and forth as friends before their lives went in different directions. Then, 62 years later, Howard sent Cynthia a package in the mail containing the notes they had exchanged along with a new note proclaiming his love. It was the beginning of a positive spiral for them. They have been together ever since.[35]

You may wonder how to maximize the confirming aspects of your relationships and minimize what is disconfirming. See "Tips & Reminders: 6 Ways to Avoid Negative Relational Spirals" for experts' suggestions.

TIPS & REMINDERS

Ways to Avoid Negative Relational Spirals

These communication strategies can help you avoid destructive patterns and steer your relationships toward the positive.[36]

1. **Use "I" language.**

   Most people are irritated by judgmental statements such as "You don't know what you're talking about" or "You drink too much." These are often described as **"you" language** because they typically contain an accusatory use of that word. Much better is **"I" language**[37] in which you take ownership of your feelings rather than blaming the other person. Instead of saying, "You are unreliable," you might say, "I feel ignored when you don't respond to my messages for several days." Statements such as this include an account of how you feel and specify a particular behavior by the other person.

2. **Don't be manipulative.**

   Even well-meant manipulation can cause bad feelings. For example, if your friends drop by unannounced with someone they think you will like, you may feel ambushed and wish that they had asked your permission first. Other attempts at manipulation are even less thoughtful. You've probably accepted connections to people on social media only to find yourself bombarded with posts about products they want you to buy or political viewpoints that leave no room for discussion. You'd probably feel less manipulated if your friends were up front about their motives from the beginning.

3. **Don't act superior.**

   Even when a person's knowledge or talents are greater than others' in some way, an attitude of superiority is annoying and belittling. No matter what your relative attributes, it's important to realize that everyone has equal worth as a human being. Rather than declaring, "I wrote a paper on this topic, so I know more than you do," you might say, "My research suggests . . . What has your experience been?"

4. **Use metacommunication.**

   You might keep a negative spiral from worsening by saying "Hold on" or "We're not getting anywhere." Reflection statements such as these can help you and the other person become more mindful about how you are communicating.

5. **Cool off.**

   One quality of a negative relational spiral is that things tend to get out of hand quickly. It's common for both people to feel that they were forced or provoked into responding the way they did. Actually, they were probably responding emotionally without much thought. Taking time to cool off can help. To distinguish between a "cooling off" period and "avoidance," make a firm commitment to discuss the issue at a particular time. "Let the other person know that this conversation is important to you, and that you need to collect your thoughts," suggests therapist Julie Williamson.[38]

6. **Focus on the positive.**

   Even in the midst of a negative spiral, you can often change the momentum by focusing on something you have in common or like about the other person. You might say "We seem to agree that . . ." or "I admire your passion for this topic." People in satisfying relationships tend to maintain at least a 5:1 ratio of positive to negative statements.[39]

Above all, don't panic. It's natural for relationships to have highs and lows. You won't always agree with other people or find their behavior 100 percent acceptable, but your relationships will benefit if you handle inevitable conflicts fairly and respectfully.

ABOUT YOU *What's the Forecast for Your Communication Climate?*

Think of an important person in your life—perhaps a friend, a roommate, a family member, or a romantic partner. Choose the option in each group below that best describes how you communicate with each other.

_____ **1.** When I am upset about something, my relational partner is most likely to:

a. Listen to me and provide emotional support.
b. Say I should have tried harder to fix or avoid the problem.
c. Ignore how I feel.

_____ **2.** When we are planning a weekend activity and I want to do something my partner doesn't want to do, I tend to:

a. Suggest another option we will both enjoy.
b. Beg until I get my way.
c. Cancel our plans and engage in the activity with someone else.

_____ **3.** When my partner and I disagree about a controversial subject, we usually:

a. Ask questions and listen to the other person's viewpoint.
b. Accuse the other person of using poor judgment or ignoring the facts.
c. Avoid the subject.

_____ **4.** If I didn't hear from my partner for a while, I would probably:

a. Call or text to make sure everything was okay.
b. Feel angry about being ignored.
c. Not notice.

_____ **5.** The statement my partner and I are most likely to make during a typical conversation sounds something like this:

a. "I appreciate the way you . . ."
b. "You always forget to . . ."
c. "Were you saying something? I was distracted."

INTERPRETING YOUR RESPONSES

Read the explanations below for a climate report about your relationship.

Warm and Sunny If the majority of your answers are "a," your relational climate is warm and sunny, with a high probability of confirming messages. You seem to be experiencing a positive spiral. Use suggestions throughout this chapter to strengthen and nurture your relationship even more.

Stormy If you answered mostly "b," your relationship tends to be turbulent, with outbreaks of controlling or defensive behavior. Storm warning: You seem to be in a downward escalatory conflict spiral that can damage your relationship. That's not to say it's hopeless, but you may want to consider underlying feelings—yours and the other person's. Guidance on self-disclosure in this chapter may be helpful.

Chill in the Air If most of your answers are "c," beware of falling temperatures. It's natural for people to drift apart sometimes, but your relationship shows signs of chilly indifference and avoidance spiraling. Consider whether you are guilty of the damaging patterns described in this chapter. You may be able to change the weather by engaging in more supportive communication.

Communicating in Interpersonal Relationships

Interpersonal Communication

Interpersonal communication involves two-way interaction between people who are part of a close and irreplaceable relationship in which they treat each other as unique individuals.

Relational Messages Communicate . . .

- How much people like each other (affinity).
- The level of engagement between people (immediacy).
- The esteem people feel for one another (respect).
- The power exercised by one person over another (control).

Metacommunication . . .

- Looks below the surface.
- Can be risky.
- Isn't just for solving problems.

Self-Disclosure Is . . .

- Deliberately revealing information about oneself that is significant and that would not normally be known by others.
- Portrayed in the social penetration model in terms of *breadth* (the range of subjects discussed) and *depth* (how significant and personal the information is).
- Categorized in the Johari Window as everything about a person that is either open, blind, hidden, or unknown within a relationship.

Before Self-Disclosing, Consider . . .

- How important the other person is to you.
- How risky and how appropriate the disclosure is.
- Whether the disclosure will be reciprocated and constructive.

Interpersonal Communication Online Can . . .

- Help people stay connected.
- Connect people with diverse interests.
- Feel nonthreatening.
- Be validating.
- Allow people to think before they respond.
- Be distracting.
- Be isolating.

Relational Spirals . . .

- Involve a pattern in which each person's message reinforces the other's.
- May be confirming or disconfirming.

To Avoid Negative Spirals . . .

- Use "I" language.
- Don't be manipulative.
- Don't act superior.
- Use metacommunication.
- Cool off.
- Focus on the positive.

Show Your Communication Know-How

7.1: Explain what makes some communication interpersonal.

List five instances in which you have communicated with other people in the last week. Which, if any, of these episodes meet the definition of interpersonal communication?

KEY TERM: interpersonal communication

7.2: Categorize and explain types of relational messages.

Draw a 4 × 4 grid. Above each column, write the name of a person you know well (for a total of four names). Using a scale of 1 (low) to 10 (high), indicate in row 1 the amount of affinity you feel for each person, in row 2 how immediate each relationship is, and in row 3 how much you respect each person. In row 4, indicate whether the power balance between you is equal or not. How do the relationships compare? What role does communication play in establishing each of these factors?

KEY TERMS: content message, relational message, affinity, immediacy, respect, control

7.3: Evaluate the advantages and potential pitfalls of engaging in metacommunication.

Think of a time when your feelings were hurt but you didn't say anything. Rewrite the scene using metacommunication to bring your feelings into the open.

KEY TERM: metacommunication

7.4: Describe two models of self-disclosure, and apply tips for self-disclosing effectively.

List some topics (breadth) and details (depth) you might self-disclose to a close friend but probably wouldn't tell your boss or grandparent. Explain why.

KEY TERMS: self-disclosure, social penetration model, breadth, depth, Johari Window

7.5: Analyze the advantages and disadvantages of online interpersonal communication.

In what ways does (or might) online communication allow you to maintain close relationships? In what ways does (or might) it interfere with them?

KEY TERM: phubbing

7.6: Distinguish between positive and negative relational spirals, and practice positive communication strategies.

Identify several disconfirming messages from your own experience and rewrite them as confirming ones. How might these encounters have gone differently if the tone were more positive?

KEY TERMS: communication climate, relational spiral, disconfirming, conflict spirals, avoidance spirals, confirming, positive spirals, "you" language, "I" language

COMMUNICATING WITH

Friends and Family

8

Friendships and Family Ties

LEARNING OBJECTIVE 8.1: Describe factors that influence communication in friend and family relationships.

Friendships and family ties are some of the longest and most influential relationships in people's lives.

"You are more than just my best friend—you are the sister I never knew I needed—you are family." With these words, poet Marisa Donnelly acknowledges the powerful influence of both friends and family.[1] In this section, we explore factors that influence these relationships.

Friendships

Everyone has a story about a friend who has said or done something that made a powerful difference to them. Friendships are unique for a number of reasons:

- Friends typically treat each other as equals—unlike parent–child, teacher–student, or doctor–patient relationships, in which one partner has more authority or higher status than the other.[2]
- People can have as many friends as they want or have time for, in contrast to family and romantic relationships, which are limited in number.
- Friends are relatively free to design relationships that suit their needs. You may have close friends you talk to every day and others you communicate with only once in a while.

Good friends help keep people healthy, boost their self-esteem, and make them feel loved and supported.[3] They also help one another adjust to new challenges and uncertainty.[4] It's not surprising then that people with strong and lasting friendships are happier than those without them.[5]

Family Relationships

In today's world, it's not easy to define what makes a family. We adopt the perspective of theorist Martha Minnow, who suggests that people who share affection and resources as a family and who think of themselves and present themselves as a family *are* a **family**.[6]

Your own experiences probably tell you that this concept of a family might encompass (or exclude) bloodline relatives, adopted family members, stepparents, honorary aunts and uncles, and blended families in which the siblings were born to different parents. This makes it easy to understand why people can be hurt by questions such as "Is he your natural son?" and "Is she your real mother?" Calling some family members "natural" or "real" implies that others are fake or that they don't belong.[7]

Friends *and* Family

We can't close this overview of family and friends without acknowledging that some people are *both*. Sometimes, a parent, uncle, or sibling is also a friend. At other times, as poet Marisa Donnelly reflects, "people with whom we don't share DNA or a roof over our heads" become so close that they are family.[8] This chapter explores how communication influences the way people choose friends, the influence of gender and online communication, and the communication dynamics involving parents and siblings. ●

How People Evaluate Friendship Potential

LEARNING OBJECTIVE 8.2: Explain how people use communication to choose friends.

When she returned to her car after class one day, Jennie found a note on her window that said: *You are beautiful inside and out.*[9] "I never did find out which one of my friends left it for me," Jennie says, "but it is still on my dashboard and means more than anything to me."

When one researcher tracked how new friendships develop, he found that people typically consider themselves friends after spending at least 50 hours of quality time together.[10] It's not a high price to pay for a great relationship, but you can't invest that much time with every person you meet. So how do you decide? Following are seven of the most common reasons to befriend someone.

You have a lot in common.

People typically consider acquaintances friendship material if they remind them of themselves. Coworkers in one study were most likely to pursue friendships with colleagues if they felt they had a lot in common.[11] A quick survey of your friends probably shows that you share many common interests and perspectives. (Despite this tendency, you will see in a moment that there are also good reasons to make friends with people who seem dissimilar to you on the surface.)

You balance each other out.

Differences can strengthen a relationship when they are **complementary**—that is, when each partner's characteristics satisfy the other's needs. For example, when introverts and extroverts pair up as friends, they typically report that the quieter person serves as a steady anchor for the friendship, and the more gregarious partner propels the other to take part in activities they might otherwise avoid.[12]

You like and appreciate each other.

Of course, you aren't drawn toward everyone who likes you, but to a great extent, you probably like people who like you and shy away from those who don't. It's no mystery why this is so. Approval tends to bolster people's self-esteem. It is rewarding in its own right, and it can confirm the part of your self-concept that says, "I'm a likable person."[13]

You admire each other.

It's natural to admire people who are highly competent in something you care about.[14] Forming friendships with talented and accomplished people can inspire you and offer the validating knowledge that someone you look up to admires you back.

You open up to each other.

People who reveal important information about themselves often seem especially likable, provided that what they share is appropriate to the setting and the stage of the relationship.[15] Self-disclosure (Chapter 7) is appealing partly because it's validating to know you aren't alone in your feelings ("I broke off an engagement, myself" or "I feel nervous with strangers, too"). And when people share private information, it suggests that they respect and trust each other.

You interact frequently.

In many cases, proximity leads to liking.[16] For example, you're more likely to develop relationships with students who take the same classes as you than with those in different fields. Proximity allows you to learn about one another and to engage in relationship-building behaviors. Also, people in close proximity may be more similar to you than those who live, work, and play in different places. At the same time, social media allow you to experience "virtual proximity" with people online even if they are not physically nearby.[17]

You find the relationship rewarding.

Friendship is a give and take, and the balance must be right. **Social exchange theory**[18] proposes that people invest in relationships in which the rewards are equal to or greater than the costs. The rewards might include fun, favors, and feeling valued and admired. The costs might involve a sense of obligation, putting up with annoying habits, emotional pain, and so on. According to social exchange theory, people use this formula (usually unconsciously) to decide whether dealing with another person is a "good deal" or "not worth the effort."

At this point, it may seem that individuals who are practically perfect have the best chance of building strong relationships. Actually, perfection isn't required or even desirable. See "Tips & Reminders: 3 Reasons You Don't Have to Be Perfect to Be a Good Friend" to see why.

TIPS & REMINDERS

3 Reasons You Don't Have to Be Perfect to Be a Good Friend

Having just pointed out common considerations when choosing relational partners, a few caveats are in order. Read the following before you fall into the trap of thinking you must be supermodel stunning, Mensa smart, or Olympics-level talented for people to find you appealing.

1. **First impressions can mislead.**

   While it's true that people gravitate to those whose interests and attitudes seem similar to their own, they tend to overestimate how similar they are to their friends and underestimate how similar they are to people they don't know well.[19] In reality, there is strong evidence that superficial similarities such as appearance do not predict long-term happiness with a relationship, and when you're willing to communicate with a range of diverse people, you are likely to find that your differences are not as great as you thought.[20,21]

2. **Perfection can be a turn-off.**

   People tend to like individuals who are attractive and talented, but be uncomfortable around those who are *too* perfect. Let's face it, no one wants to look bad by comparison. In the end, it's more important to be nice than to be flawless.

3. **It's not all about communication, but it's a *lot* about communication.**

   The online dating service eHarmony matches people based on "29 dimensions of compatibility," and other online dating sites make similar promises. You can imagine such compatibility algorithms for finding friends. However, the long-term success of people matched by computer algorithms is no greater than that of people who meet on their own.[22] That's because long-term compatibility relies mostly on how people interact with one another once they start a relationship and encounter stressful issues.

All in all, don't be discouraged if you aren't "perfect" by society's standards. Being perfect is overrated. In the end, being a good friend matters much more.

PAUSE TO REFLECT *What Qualities Matter Most in a Friend?*

1. What qualities do you value most in a friend? ______________________________

2. What would your friends say are your best and worst habits as a communicator? ______________________________

Friendships Can Build Bridges

LEARNING OBJECTIVE 8.3: Summarize how communication in intergroup friendships can overcome prejudice.

It may be easy to communicate just with people who are similar to you, but there are benefits to broadening your circle of friends.

"We went to school where I was in the one percent who were black; Amy was in the one percent Jewish," says Malaika Adero, describing a lifelong friendship that began in the fourth grade.[23] As they have learned, it can be mind-opening to be friends with people from different backgrounds.

The **intergroup contact hypothesis** reflects evidence that prejudice tends to diminish when people communicate with individuals they might otherwise stereotype.[24] For example, a study in the United States showed that college students who have Muslim friends usually have a higher opinion of Muslims than those who don't.[25] Researchers found that positive feelings increased after even a small amount of interaction and continued to grow as the friends spent more time together. A similar pattern has been noted between people of different races,[26] abilities,[27] ages,[28] nationalities,[29] and genders.[30] Intergroup friendships reduce prejudice in three main ways, each of which involves communication.

Stereotypes fade.

As you get to know strangers, preconceived notions about them tend to fall away. Chiarra, an exchange student from Italy, says she was surprised to find that college students in the United States don't all "wear high-fashion clothes and live in huge houses with swimming pools." As she made friends with Americans, Chiarra realized that they have many different personalities and lifestyles. "When I get back to Italy I'll object when people say things about Americans based on TV shows. I know better now," Chiarra says.

Trust grows.

Fear and distrust tend to diminish as you realize how much you have in common with people who seem different from you on the surface.[31] For this reason, some people say that the best antidote to racism is intergroup friendship.[32,33] Musician and author Daryl Davis, who is Black, spent 30 years befriending members of the Ku Klux Klan, a racist hate group. Many of the Klan members whom Davis met had never talked to a Black person before. He reasoned that, if he could lessen people's fear of the unknown by communicating with them, their hate would fade as well. An estimated 200 KKK members left the group after getting to know Davis.[34] Few people may go as far as Davis did, but the power of friendship in dispelling fear and distrust cannot be overstated.

Understanding blooms.

Learning about another person can lead to greater appreciation for them and a better understanding of the challenges they face.[35] Since becoming close friends with Keith, who is

paralyzed, Leah says she knows firsthand how much pain he endures yet how optimistic and energetic he is.[36] She reflects that interacting with Keith has changed the way she approaches other people with disabilities.

The implications of intergroup friendships can be far reaching. People who let go of their stereotypes about one group are often less prejudiced toward other groups as well.[37] As a result, they're more likely to select qualified members of nondominant groups for jobs, promotions, and education opportunities.[38,39] As Jeffrey Tucker puts it: "The more diverse friendship networks we cultivate, the less we think in categories of 'us vs them.'"[40]

Even knowing the importance of intergroup friendships, you might feel shy about initiating them. It's natural to worry that you might say the wrong thing. In Chapter 3, we presented tips for talking about race and ethnicity. "Tips & Reminders: 3 Strategies for Befriending a Wide Range of People" offers some additional tips for overcoming your fears. ●

TIPS & REMINDERS

3 Strategies for Befriending a Wide Range of People

1. **"Accept the awkward."**
   That's the advice of experts who acknowledge that it's natural to feel self-conscious when approaching new people—but who encourage you to do it anyway. "Guess what? You can't have friends without getting vulnerable," says one advisor.[41] A good strategy is to introduce yourself and ask a few nonthreatening questions such as "What are you studying in school?" or "Are you a fan of this artist? . . . Me too!"

2. **Don't fixate on differences.**
   Focus on what you have in common, not just on what makes you dissimilar. For example, if you meet someone who is substantially older or younger than you, don't let that distract you from appreciating them as a unique person. "We're all just people, and we all have our favorite things, our fears, and our shared humanity," says writer Alice Zhang, who encourages others, "Over time, you'll come to see them as a 'friend,' not your 'older friend' or 'younger friend.'"[42]

3. **Be approachable.**
   When you're the one who stands out as different, you can help reduce the stranger barrier by smiling, being friendly, and letting people get to know the real you. Keep in mind that other people probably feel as intimidated as you do, but almost everyone likes to make a new friend.

Types of Friendships

LEARNING OBJECTIVE 8.4: Identify communication patterns that make friendships different from one another.

Friends come in many forms. Some become long-term confidantes whereas others come and go as your lifestyle changes.

Think of several friends in your life—perhaps a new friend, a longstanding one, and a colleague at work. Then consider how they compare on the dimensions described here.

Short-Term Versus Long-Term

Short-term friends tend to change as your life does. You may say goodbye because you move, graduate, or switch jobs. Or perhaps you party less or spend more time off the ball field than you used to. It's natural for your social networks to change as a result. However, long-term friends are with you even when they aren't. Particularly today, with so many different ways to stay in touch, people report that—as long as trust and a sense of connection are there—they feel as close to some of their long-term friends who live far away as to those who are nearby.[43]

Low Disclosure Versus High Disclosure

As you learned in Chapter 7, self-disclosure is associated with greater levels of intimacy such that only a few trusted confidantes are likely to know your deepest secrets. One interesting exception occurs among people who are highly self-disclosive online. They might announce personal news to hundreds of friends and acquaintances with a single post or tweet. This isn't necessarily bad.[44] However, it's easy to cross the line and go public with information you might later wish you had kept private. As one blogger points out, you might have several hundred online "friends," but not all of them need or want to hear that your partner cheated on you last night.[45]

Doing-Oriented Versus Being-Oriented

Some friends experience closeness "in the doing." That is, they enjoy performing tasks or attending events together and feel closer because of those shared experiences.[46] In these cases, different friends are likely to be tied to particular interests—a golfing buddy or shopping partner, for example. Other friendships are "being-oriented." For these friends, the main focus is on simply spending time together, and they meet up just to talk or hang out.[47] Even long-distance, friends may send texts or photos to "be" together when they are miles apart.

Low Obligation Versus High Obligation

There are probably some friends for whom you would do just about anything—no request is too big. For others, you may feel a lower sense of obligation. Culture may play a role. Friends raised in low-context cultures such as the United States' are more likely than those raised in high-context cultures such as China's to express their appreciation for a friend out loud (Chapter 3). For example, friends who are Chinese are more likely to express themselves indirectly—most often by doing favors for friends and by showing gratitude and reciprocity when friends do favors for them.[48] It's easy to imagine the misunderstandings that might occur when one friend puts a high value on words and the other on actions.

Frequent Contact Versus Occasional Contact

You probably see some of your friends on a regular basis. Perhaps you work out, travel, socialize, or FaceTime daily with them. But you might connect with other friends only at reunions or via occasional calls or text messages. Some friends go years without seeing each other and then reconnect as if they were never apart. In "Tips & Reminders: 8 Communication Strategies for Being a Good Friend" you'll find suggestions by communication experts for keeping friendships strong over time. ●

TIPS & REMINDERS

Communication Strategies for Being a Good Friend

Experts suggest the following ways to strengthen your friendships.

1. **Be a good listener.**
   To show how much you care, put aside distractions and pay close attention to your friend's words and nonverbal cues.

2. **Give advice sparingly.**
   Despite your good intentions, offering advice, especially when it's not requested, can come off as insensitive and condescending. A better option is to listen attentively and, if appropriate, ask your friend what options they imagine and what they consider the pros and cons of each.

3. **Share your feelings appropriately.**
   When you feel good about your friendship, say so. And don't be reluctant to let your friend know when you feel hurt or frustrated. It may be tempting to make a snide remark or say "It's nothing" when you feel upset, but that's likely to damage your friendship.[49] Instead, speak up without attacking the other person.

4. **Apologize and forgive.**
   If you slip up—perhaps by forgetting an important date or saying something that embarrasses your friend—admit the mistake, apologize sincerely, and promise to do better in the future.[50] Remembering your goof may inspire you to offer forgiveness rather than harboring a grudge when the tables are turned and your friend makes a mistake.[51]

5. **Be validating and appreciative.**
   Find ways to let your friend know they matter to you.[52] Depending on the relationship, this might involve a thoughtful phone call, spending time together, or remembering a birthday. The best validation comes from knowing what your friend will appreciate most.

6. **Stay loyal in hard times.**
   People who believe their friends are loyal to them typically experience less everyday stress and more physical and emotional resilience than other people.[53] Saying "I'll always be there for you" and backing that up with attentive behaviors can make a world of difference.

7. **Be trustworthy.**
   Two of the most dreaded violations of trust are sharing private information with others and saying unkind things about friends behind their back.[54] Maintain confidentiality and stand up for your friends, even when they aren't around.

8. **Give and take equally.**
   The best friendships are characterized by equal give and take. One payoff of supporting others is the sense that you make a difference in others' lives.[55]

PAUSE TO REFLECT *What Types of Friends Do You Have?*

1. Think of a friend you enjoy being around even if you aren't doing anything special. What makes being together enjoyable? ______________________________

2. Describe a friend for whom you would do almost anything. What about this person inspires your loyalty? ____

ABOUT YOU *What Kind of Friendship Do You Have?*

Think of a particular friend and select the answers below that describe your relationship.

______ **1.** Which of the following best describes the time you spend with this friend?

a. We see each other a lot. I'd really miss our time together if something prevented that.
b. Sometimes we spend time together and sometimes not. It's not a big deal either way.
c. We don't see each other very often, but when we do, we're as in sync as if no time has passed.
d. We haven't spent much time together yet, but I hope we will.

______ **2.** If you were on a long car ride together, what would you most likely talk about?

a. Whatever is on my mind. I can tell this friend anything.
b. Current events or what we've been up to at school or work.
c. Funny memories. We've had many adventures together through the years.
d. Where we grew up, what we're studying in school, and other topics to get to know each other better.

______ **3.** If your friend were in bed with a cold for several days, what would you be most likely to do?

a. Stop by to cheer them up and help out.
b. Send a "get well soon" text.
c. Call to say I wish I could be there in person.
d. It's unlikely that I'd know about it until later.

______ **4.** If this friend said something that hurt your feelings, what would you probably do?

a. Talk about it together and repair the rift.
b. Avoid them for a while.
c. Let it go. It's nothing compared to all we've been through together.
d. Rethink my desire to be friends.

INTERPRETING YOUR RESPONSES

Read the explanations below to reflect on the qualities of your friendship. More than one may apply.

Loyal If you answered "a" more than once, this is a close friend you can count on. You are likely to disclose a great deal to each other and back each other up, even when things are difficult. This is likely to be a long-term relationship with the rewards that come from knowing that someone who knows you well is there for you no matter what.

Independent If you answered "b" two or more times, this is a friendship that doesn't involve a great deal of obligation. You are able to get together when you feel like it without feeling pressured to do so if you don't. Although not as close as some friendships, this one may be valuable, particularly if other commitments claim a lot of your time right now. Not everyone has to be a best friend. Just be careful not to let your desire for independence distance you from forming strong bonds with one or two friends you can always count on.

Far Yet Close If you answered "c" more than once, this seems to be an enduring, long-term friendship that remains strong even though you're not able to be together in person as much as you would like. You are likely to enjoy the benefits of being emotionally connected without much obligation to do things together or for each other. It can be a great feeling to know that distance and time cannot dim the memories you have shared together. At the same time, be sure not to take this friendship for granted. A thoughtful text or call may help you feel close even when you're not together physically.

Evolving If you answered "d" two or more times, it's likely that your friendship is still developing. Your sense of obligation is likely to be low at this stage, as you venture to disclose more about yourselves to each other. It remains to be seen if this will be a short- or long-term relationship, but the benefits of having strong friendships suggest that it may be worth the effort to find out.

Gender and Friendship

LEARNING OBJECTIVE 8.5: Analyze the impact of gender-related expectations on communication between friends.

"Whenever you sense I'm in a bad mood, rather than having me talk it out, you try to make me feel better—usually with jokes and terrible singing."[56] In this open letter to her best friend, Samantha Smith sings the praises of a male friend.

Here we explore answers to some common questions about friendship and gender.

Q Do men and women do friendship differently?

A Although there are many similarities, there are some common differences, especially in same-sex friendships. Traditionally, male–male friendships have typically involved good-natured competition and a focus on tasks and events, whereas female friends have been more likely to treat each other as equals and to engage in emotional support and self-disclosure.[57] These differences don't apply to everyone, of course, but different expectations may help to explain why people are likely to have more same-sex friends than friends of another sex.[58]

Q Can heterosexual men and women be just friends?

A Women typically say yes, but men often give a decidedly iffy answer. In a classic study of 88 college-age male–female friendship partners, most of the women said the friendship was purely platonic, with no romantic interest on either side.[59] However, heterosexual men in the study were more likely to say that they secretly harbored romantic fantasies about their female friends, and they suspected (often wrongly, it seems) that the feeling was mutual. In a more recent study, men and women estimated that underlying sexual interest is present in 6 out of 10 cross-sex friendships, but most were optimistic that the friendships can work.[60]

Researchers speculate that heterosexual men and women get their wires crossed partly because they communicate differently. As we mentioned previously, women usually expect friends to be emotionally supportive and understanding.[61] From the male perspective, this may feel more like romance than friendship. By contrast, men tend to emphasize independence and friendly competition.[62] Those behaviors may not strike women as particularly romantic.

Q Are there advantages to other-sex friendships?

A Yes. For example, men often say that they find it validating when female friends encourage them to be more emotionally expressive than usual, and women say they appreciate the opportunity to speak assertively with their guy friends.[63] In the example that began this section, Samantha says she enjoys having a male friend who doesn't talk a lot about emotions.

Q How does gender diversity figure into friendship?

A Perhaps the greatest byproduct of friendship is a sense of mutual acceptance and respect. For example, gay men who have close friends that are straight are less likely than their peers to perceive that society judges them harshly for being gay.[64] Likewise, college students with at least one friend who is transgender are far less likely than their peers to harbor negative attitudes about transgender people.[65] For those who shy away from transgender or gender-transitioning individuals for fear of causing offense, the advice is clear: "Treat them like you usually do; they're still people. Try to use their preferred pronouns and treat them like they're your friend—because they still are!"[66] ●

Communicating with Friends Online

LEARNING OBJECTIVE 8.6: Compare the way friends communicate in person and online.

The average person has many more online friends than physical ones—double the amount, according to one report.[67] Quantity isn't the only distinction between mediated and offline friendships, however. Here are four common differences.

Many people share more in person, at least at first.

Face-to-face friends are typically more likely than online friends to talk about topics in depth and to share a deep understanding and commitment, especially during the early stages of their relationships.[68] However, as online friendships develop, these differences tend to diminish. There is also some evidence that online relationships can become even more personal, as time goes on, than the in-person variety.[69]

Online communication can be less anxiety provoking.

Online communication can be a comfortable means of befriending people who might otherwise seem intimidating. For example, when a researcher in Turkey interviewed college students from four different parts of the world, the students said they would like to have more international friends, but they felt anxious about approaching them in person.[70] Given the chance, the students were enthusiastic about communicating with people from other countries online. They later reported that online communication reduced their anxiety about saying the wrong thing or encountering communication difficulties. At the same time, although online communication was a good icebreaker, many students said they would like to have in-person relationships with their new international friends as well.

Online communication transcends time and space.

Many friendships thrive by making use of both mediated communication *and* quality in-person time. Especially when busy schedules or distance prevents people from spending as much time together as they would like, staying in touch via social media platforms may keep their relationships alive.[71] A college student determined to remain in touch with childhood friends observes, "There's beauty in knowing friendships can last a lifetime, so long as you choose to preserve them."[72]

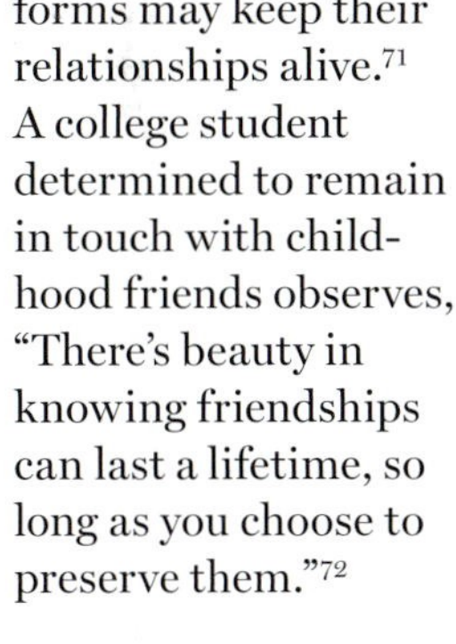

More online communication isn't always better.

The reality is that you probably aren't really friends with all of your online "friends." You may not even know who some of them are. Anthropology professor Robin Dunbar inspired what has become known as **Dunbar's Number** when he documented evidence that, for the most part, people have the mental and emotional energy to keep up with no more than 150 friends at a time.[73] This is not a hard and fast number, of course. At different times in your life, you may have energy for fewer or more friends. The point is that, whereas your online social networks can involve an unlimited number of friends and followers, the number of close friendships you can actually maintain at one time is limited, whether you interact with them online or in person.

Parenting Relationships

LEARNING OBJECTIVE 8.7: Distinguish between different patterns of parent–child communication.

Power and influence play a role in any relationship, but especially in the dynamic between parents and children.

Following are some parenting communication patterns with varying power differentials.

Family Dynamics

Imagine establishing the curfew for teenage members of a family.

- If the family is disposed to manage issues via **conversation,** teens and their parents probably negotiate the curfew by talking openly about it and listening to each other.
- However, if the emphasis is on **conformity**, teens will be expected to follow their parents' rules, beliefs, and values without challenging them.[74]

Most evidence suggests that children who grow up with the conversation approach are better at expressing their emotions confidently and effectively as they grow older.[75,76] As you might imagine, children who don't engage in much give-and-take communication with their parents are usually less comfortable using that style with other people as well.

Among children who grow up with a conformity pattern, the advantage goes to those who perceive that their parents are motivated by love and concern. They tend to grow up to be more emotionally resilient than children who believe their parents control their behavior for selfish reasons.[77]

Parenting Styles

Now let's focus on specific parenting styles.[78]

- **Authoritarian** parents are strict and expect unquestioning obedience. You might characterize this as a "do it because I said so" style. In our curfew example, teens would be expected to follow their parents' rules, beliefs, and values without challenging them.
- **Authoritative** parents are also firm, clear, and strict, but they encourage children to communicate openly with them. These parents have high expectations, but they are willing to discuss them and listen to children's input. Teens and their parents would probably negotiate the curfew by discussing the interests of each side.
- **Permissive** parents do not require children to follow many rules. Based on this approach, parents and children may communicate about other topics, but they probably don't spend a lot of time setting firm guidelines such as curfews.

Most evidence favors the authoritative style in terms of fostering children's happiness and adaptability throughout life.[79] As two researchers put it, authoritative parents provide the dual benefits of structure and compassion—they are "warm, responsive, assertive without being overly intrusive or restrictive."

Sibling Relationships

LEARNING OBJECTIVE 8.8: Compare communication patterns in five types of sibling relationships.

In the midst of what one theorist calls the "playing and arguing, joking and bickering, caring and fighting" of sibling life, children learn a great deal about themselves and how to relate to others.[80]

Just as people who think of themselves as family *are* family, a sibling relationship isn't limited to people who share biological parents. It's much more about shared life experiences. As one person who grew up in a blended family puts it, "You feel beyond annoyed when explaining your family structure and someone says, 'Oh, so you're only half-sisters.' It's tempting, she says, to reply, 'Only? ONLY? Well, you're my half-friend now.'"[81]

Whatever the origin, sibling relationships involve an interwoven, and often paradoxical, collection of emotions. Children are likely to feel both intense loyalty and fierce competition with their brothers and sisters and to be both loving and antagonistic toward them. Here are five types of sibling relationships people might settle into as they become adults.[82]

Supportive

Supportive siblings talk regularly and consider themselves to be accessible and emotionally close to one other. Supportive relationships are most common among siblings who are of similar ages, particularly if they come from large families.[83]

Longing

Longing siblings typically admire and respect one other. However, they interact less frequently and with less depth than they would like. This can be especially difficult for younger siblings who watch older ones move out. One teen lamented when his brother left home: "[I] look at his empty desk, the table where we would sit and talk, and start bawling . . . I know I'll see him again, but nothing will be the same."[84]

Competitive

Competitive siblings behave as rivals, vying for scarce resources such as their parents' time and respect.[85] It's not uncommon for siblings to feel competitive as they grow up. That feeling sometimes extends into adulthood, especially if siblings perceive that their parents continue to play favorites.[86]

Apathetic

Apathetic siblings are relatively indifferent toward one another. They communicate with one another only on special occasions, such as holidays or weddings.

Hostile

Hostile siblings often stop communicating.[87] Unlike apathetic siblings, who may drift apart without hard feelings, hostile siblings usually feel a sense of jealousy, resentment, and anger toward one another.

See "Tips & Reminders: 6 Communication Tips for Strengthening Family Ties" for ways to communicate well with the people you consider family.

TIPS & REMINDERS

Communication Tips for Strengthening Family Ties

Communicating with family members can be a joy and a challenge. Following are some strategies for successful family communication based on experts' advice.

1. **Share family stories.**

   Family stories contribute to a shared sense of identity. They also convey that adversity is an inevitable part of life, and they can suggest strategies for overcoming it.[88]

2. **Listen to each other.**

   People who are involved in reflection and conversation learn how to manage and express their feelings better than those who don't. They tend to have better relationships as a result.[89,90]

3. **Negotiate privacy rules.**

   Privacy violations among family members can have serious consequences.[91] At the same time, too much privacy can lead family members to overlook dangerous behavior and avoid distressing but important topics. Experts suggest that families talk about and agree on privacy expectations and rules. These might involve whether parents "friend" and follow their children on social media, how much the children are allowed to know about their parents' health and financial status, and under what conditions secrets shouldn't be kept.

4. **Coach conflict management.**

   Effective conflict management doesn't just happen spontaneously.[92] It's a sophisticated process that often goes against people's fight-or-flight instincts. Families can help by creating safe environments for discussing issues and striving for mutually agreeable solutions. It's usually more helpful for parents to coach their children through conflict episodes than to take a hands-off approach.[93]

5. **Go heavy on confirming messages.**

   Supportive messages from family members can give individuals the confidence to believe in themselves. Compliments such as "You're a very thoughtful person" and "I know you will do a great job" tend to be self-fulfilling. For example, teens whose parents frequently compliment and encourage them are less likely than others to drop out of high school.[94]

6. **Have fun together.**

   Happy families make it a point to minimize distractions and regularly spend time together. They establish togetherness rituals that suit their busy lives, such as sharing dessert even when they can't eat dinner together,[95] and they share adventures, both large and small.

PAUSE TO REFLECT *How Does Your Family Communicate?*

1. While you were growing up, were decisions such as teen curfews decided mostly through conversation (authoritative) or through conformity with rules set by your parents or guardians (authoritarian)? How do you think that pattern affects the way you communicate as an adult? ______

2. If there is anyone in your life you consider to be a sibling, which of the styles described in this chapter best describes your relationship? How does the nature of your relationship influence the way you communicate?

Communicating with Friends and Family

Friends and Family

- People typically treat friends as equals, they can have numerous friendships, and they can design friendships to suit their mutual needs.
- People who share affection and resources as a family and who think of themselves and present themselves as a family *are* a family.

People Typically Choose to Be Friends if They . . .

- Have a lot in common.
- Balance each other out.
- Like and appreciate each other.
- Admire each other.
- Open up to each other.
- Interact frequently.
- Find the relationship rewarding.

3 Reasons You Don't Have to Be Perfect to Be a Good Friend

- First impressions can mislead.
- Perfection can be a turn-off.
- It's not all about communication, but it's a *lot* about communication.

Friendships Can Build Bridges

When people who are different than one another become friends, it is likely that:

- Stereotypes will fade.
- Trust will grow.
- Understanding will bloom.

Types of Friendships

- Short- or long-term
- Low or high disclosure
- Doing- or being-oriented
- Low or high obligation
- Frequent or occasional contact

8 Communication Strategies for Being a Good Friend

- Be a good listener.
- Give advice sparingly.
- Share feelings respectfully.
- Apologize and forgive.
- Be validating and appreciative.
- Stay loyal in hard times.
- Be trustworthy.
- Give and take equally.

Gender and Friendship

- Male friendships often involve good-natured competition.
- Female friends tend to treat each other more as equals and engage in emotional support.
- Women more often than men feel that heterosexual men and women can be just friends.
- Friendships with people of other genders can be highly rewarding.

Online Friendships Differ from Those in Person in That:

- Many people share more in person, at least at first.
- Online communication can be less anxiety provoking.
- Online communication transcends time and space.
- People are likely to have more online friends than they can keep up with.

Parenting Relationships

- Families may make decisions based on conversations or on conformity with parents' wishes.
- Parenting styles vary from authoritarian, to authoritative, to permissive.

Types of Sibling Relationships

- Supportive
- Longing
- Competitive
- Apathetic
- Hostile

6 Communication Tips for Strengthening Family Ties

- Share family stories.
- Listen to each other.
- Negotiate privacy rules.
- Coach conflict management.
- Share confirming messages.
- Have fun together.

Show Your Communication Know-How

8.1: Describe factors that influence communication in friend and family relationships.

When do you most enjoy communicating with friends? With family members? Are there times when it's challenging? If so, what lessons have you learned?

KEY TERM: family

8.2: Explain how people use communication to choose friends.

List the costs and rewards you associate with a particular friendship. Do the rewards outweigh the costs? If so, how? What role does communication play in managing the balance between costs and rewards in your friendship?

KEY TERMS: complementary, social exchange theory

8.3: Summarize how communication in intergroup friendships can overcome prejudice.

Describe a friendship with someone who is different than you. Do you find that you are less likely to stereotype your friend and members of their group as a result of the relationship? Was it challenging to bridge your differences at first? If so, how?

KEY TERM: intergroup contact hypothesis

8.4: Identify communication patterns that make friendships different from one another.

How would you rate your communication in terms of listening, sharing feelings, apologizing, and forgiving as a friend? What would you like to improve?

8.5: Analyze the impact of gender-related expectations on communication between friends.

In terms of your closest friends, do you most value being together or doing things together? Being emotionally expressive or providing a distraction from worries? Being with a person who is similar to you or connecting with someone who is different? Do you think gender norms play a role in your preferences?

8.6: Compare the way friends communicate in person and online.

Has an online connection ever allowed you to form or strengthen a friendship? If so, what were the advantages and disadvantages of communicating via technology?

KEY TERM: Dunbar's Number

8.7: Distinguish between different patterns of parent–child communication.

Think of a family on television or in the movies that involves interaction between parents and children. Which of the parenting styles described in this chapter best describes them and how?

KEY TERMS: conversation, conformity, authoritarian, authoritative, permissive

8.8: Compare communication patterns in five types of sibling relationships.

How might siblings communicate during family gatherings if they have a longing relationship? An apathetic one? A hostile one?

KEY TERMS: supportive siblings, longing siblings, competitive siblings, apathetic siblings, hostile siblings

COMMUNICATING WITH

Romantic Partners

9

Stages of Romantic Relationships

LEARNING OBJECTIVE 9.1: Distinguish between stages of coming together, staying together, and moving apart as a romantic couple.

Some romances ignite quickly, whereas others grow gradually. Either way, partners are likely to progress through a series of stages as they define what they mean to each other and what they expect.

"Will you accept this rose?" This line from *The Bachelor* and *The Bachelorette* invites a contestant to be part of another round in the reality television game of love. As of publication, viewers have watched 32 couples say "I will" in marriage proposals at the shows' conclusions. However, only five of those couples have actually said "I do."[1] What happens after the show to turn "I love you forever" into "Maybe not"?

Romantic love is the stuff of songs, fairytales, and happy endings. So it might surprise you that the butterflies-in-your-belly sense of romantic bliss isn't a great predictor of happiness. A much better indicator is the effort that couples put into their communication. Sean Lowe, one of the few who found lasting love on *The Bachelor*, describes his wake-up moment: "You leave the show, then you get into the real world and find out like, 'Oh cr–p! Being in a relationship isn't always easy and it actually takes work.'"[2]

Factors such as trust, agreeableness, and emotional expressiveness are primarily responsible for long-term relationship success.[3,4] The communication behaviors that are most effective depend on the stage of the relationship.

Communication scholar Mark Knapp's **developmental model** depicts five stages of intimacy development (coming together) and five stages in which people distance themselves from each other (coming apart).[5] Other researchers have suggested that the middle phases of the model can also be understood as *relational maintenance*—keeping stable relationships operating smoothly and satisfactorily.[6]

Knapp's 10 stages, which can be seen in Figure 9.1, fit into this three-part view of communication in relationships. Consider how well these stages reflect communication in the close relationships you have experienced.

Initiating

The initiating stage occurs when people first encounter one another. In person, this might involve simple conversation openers such as "It's nice to meet you" and "How's it going?" People may also send electronic messages to initiate contact. For example, after noticing Spencer at the gym, Cate sent a private message to him via Instagram to say hi and introduce herself.[7] In the initiating stage, people form first impressions and have the opportunity to present themselves in an appealing manner.

Experimenting

People enter the experimenting stage when they begin to get acquainted by asking questions such as "Where are you from?" and "What do you do?" Viewing a person's social media profiles can also offer insight at this stage. However, if you don't find yourself sharing secrets at this point, don't worry. It can be overwhelming to share personal information too soon. Although small talk and information in online profiles may seem relatively superficial, they provide information that helps people decide who they would like to get to know better.

In the experimenting stage, face-to-face interactions tend to have an edge over online communication. When researchers asked college students to meet a new person either in real life or via technology, those in the face-to-face group more often said they liked the new person, felt they had a lot in common, and wanted to know them better.[8]

Intensifying

In the intensifying stage, truly interpersonal relationships develop as people begin to express how they feel about each other. By definition, romantic **intimacy** requires that partners express themselves through some combination of physical contact, shared experiences, intellectual sharing, and emotional disclosures.[9] If couples are in sync, they may experience heightened intimacy at this stage. But if they aren't, they may feel either pressured or rejected by the other person.

Dating couples often navigate the uncertainty of the intensifying stage by flirting, hinting around, asking hypothetical questions, giving compliments, and being affectionate. They may become bolder and more direct if their partners seem receptive to these gestures.[10]

Even though online relationships may be slow to start, they typically progress just as quickly as other relationships once the partners make contact via video chats or in-person meetings.[11] Switching from cyberspace to face-to-face can be intimidating, however. For experts' suggestions, see "Tips & Reminders: 7 Ways to Transition from Online to In-Person Dating."

Integrating

In the integration stage, couples begin to take on an identity as a social unit. They are likely to be pictured together in social media and to meet each other's families. Couples begin to share possessions and memories—our apartment, our dog, our song. As one observer puts it, you know a relationship is on stable ground when you can have a fight but know that you'll still be together afterward.[12]

Bonding

The bonding stage is likely to involve a wedding, a commitment ceremony, or some other public means of communicating to the world that this is a relationship meant to last. Bonding generates social support for the relationship and demonstrates a strong sense of commitment and exclusivity.

Not all relationships last forever, however. And even when the bonds between partners are strong and enduring, it's sometimes desirable to create some distance. The following stages help accomplish that.

Differentiating

In the differentiating stage, the emphasis shifts from "how we are alike" to "how we are different." For example, a couple who moves in together may find that they have different expectations about doing chores, sleeping late, what to watch on TV, and so on. This doesn't necessarily mean the relationship is doomed. Differences remind partners that they are distinct individuals. To maintain a balance, partners may claim different areas of the home as their personal space and reduce their use of nicknames, gestures, and words that distinguish the relationship as intimate and unique.[13]

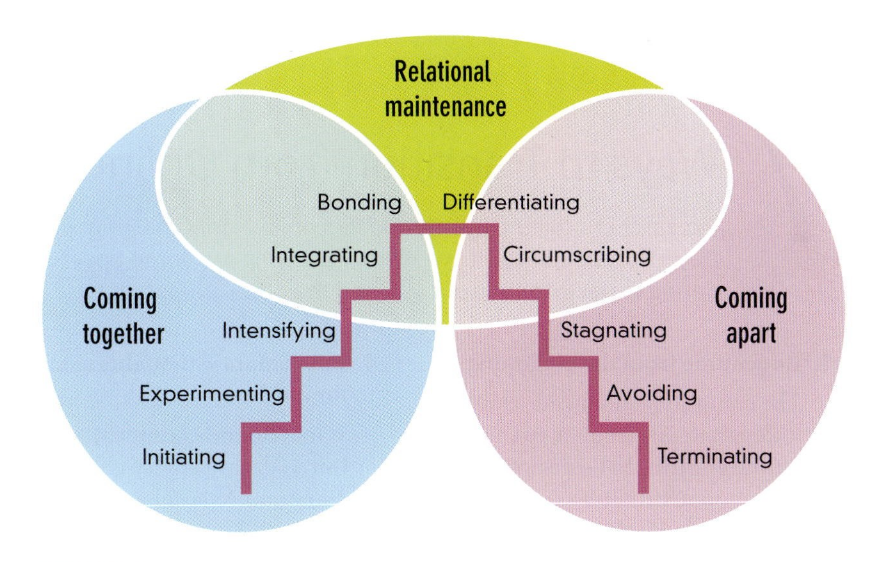

FIGURE 9.1 Relational Development Model

Circumscribing

In the circumscribing stage, communication decreases in quantity and quality. Rather than discuss a disagreement, which requires some degree of energy on both people's part, partners may withdraw mentally by using silence, daydreaming, or fantasizing. They may also withdraw physically by spending less time together, indicating reduced interest and commitment.

Stagnating

If circumscribing continues, the relationship may begin to stagnate. In this stage, partners tend to behave toward each other in familiar ways without much feeling. Like workers who have lost interest in their jobs yet continue to go through the motions, some couples unenthusiastically repeat the same conversations, see the same people, and follow the same routines without any sense of joy or novelty.

Avoiding

When stagnation becomes too unpleasant, partners distance themselves in more overt ways. They might block or unfollow each other on social media, use excuses such as "I've been busy lately," or make direct requests, such as "Please don't come over. I don't want to talk to you."

At this stage, a relationship is in trouble, but it isn't necessarily over. Partners may recognize the warning signs in time to reverse the trend. For example, if they realize they are differentiating or stagnating, they might refresh their relationship by doing more of the things they did while building their relationship, such as going on dates, sharing feelings, and pursuing new experiences together.[14]

Terminating

Characteristics of this final stage include attempts to explain where the relationship went wrong and the desire to break up. Relationships end in many ways—with a cordial conversation, a text, a note left on the table, or a legal document stating the dissolution. This stage can be quite short or drawn out over time.

Not every breakup is forever. A key difference between couples who get together again and those who don't is how well partners communicate about their dissatisfaction and negotiate for a mutually appealing fresh start.[15] Unsuccessful couples deal with their problems by avoidance, indirectness, and reduced involvement. By contrast, couples who repair their relationships more often air concerns and spend time and effort negotiating solutions to problems. •

TIPS & REMINDERS

Ways to Transition from Online to In-Person Dating

Researchers call the transition from online-only chatting to a real-time meetup modality switching. Daters often just call it awkward. Following are some tips from communication researchers and dating experts to help put you and the other person at ease.

1. **Be genuine from the beginning.**
   The computer-enhanced selfie that looks great on screen may cause an online admirer to be disappointed in person. Ultimately, relationships fare best when your mediated self is a close reflection of your in-person self.[16]

2. **Talk on the phone first.**
   If your online connection shows promise, see how a phone call goes before meeting in person.

3. **Be safe.**
   Arrange to meet in a public setting rather than a private home and provide your own transportation. (Avoid your favorite hangouts just in case you'd rather not run into each other again in the future.)[17]

4. **Put romantic thoughts aside for now.**
   It may sound counterintuitive, but as dating advice columnist Jonathan Aslay observes, "most successful long-term relationships are built on a solid friendship."[18] Approaching the encounter as a new friendship can be less anxiety provoking and more realistic than expecting fireworks with someone you barely know.

5. **Begin with a quick and easy meetup.**
   "Don't meet for a meal on your first date," recommends Jennifer Flaa, who met her future husband (plus a host of Mr. Wrongs) online.[19] She suggests meeting for coffee or a drink instead. You can schedule a longer date later, if you like.

6. **Keep the tone light.**
   This isn't the time to make an over-the-top clothing selection, share your deepest secrets, or interrogate your date with highly personal questions. Instead, encourage conversation with casual questions, and share something (but not everything) about yourself.

7. **Be playful.**
   Psychologist Seth Meyers suggests the following techniques to break the ice:[20] Pay your date a sincere compliment, pose fun questions, share a light-hearted story about yourself, and don't forget to smile and laugh. "Let yourself enjoy your first dates,"[21] Meyers suggests.

PAUSE TO REFLECT *Where Does Your Relationship Stand?*

1. Think about the early stages of a past or current relationship. How did the way you communicated early on affect what happened between you? ______

2. As intimacy grew, did you take risks in disclosing? How did your honesty (or reluctance to open up) affect the relationship? What lessons would you like to remember for the future? ______

3. Have you ever experienced a sense of drifting apart? What communication strategies did you use to either increase or reduce the emotional distance? ______

Gender and Intimacy

LEARNING OBJECTIVE 9.2: Describe means of conveying intimate messages that tend to differ by gender.

The internet is loaded with advice on understanding your romantic partner better. It ranges from "just because she says things are fine, don't assume she means it"[22] to "[men] crave hugs and hand-holding too. And no, it doesn't always have to lead to sex."[23] Here's what research suggests about the connection between gender and romantic communication.

Q Is it true that women are better at the lovey-dovey stuff than men are?

A Until recently most social scientists believed that women were better at developing and maintaining intimate relationships than men. This belief grew from the assumption that the most important ingredients of intimacy are sharing personal information and being emotionally supportive. Most research does show that women, taken as a group, prioritize supportive communication (such as listening and comforting) more than men do.[24] But men also value a sense of intimacy.[25] They are just likely to show it in different ways, as through doing favors and showing physical affection.[26]

Q What about sex? Are men and women on the same page?

A Some are. But whereas many women think of sex as a way to express intimacy that has already developed, men are more likely to see it as a way to *create* that intimacy.[27] In this sense, the man who encourages sex early in a relationship or after a fight may view it as a way to build closeness. By contrast, a woman who views personal talk as the pathway to intimacy may resist the idea of physical closeness before the emotional side of the relationship has been developed.

Q Who says "I love you" sooner?

A Evidence suggests that men are likely to fall in love, and to profess their love, sooner than women are.[28] Men are also more likely to believe in love at first sight.[29] These patterns may be common because women have traditionally been taught that caution in romantic situations may help them avoid danger and (in the case of heterosexual sex) unwanted pregnancy. It may also be relevant that men, more than women, consider physical attraction to be a strong predictor of compatibility.[30] One person describes their love-at-first-sight experience this way: "I looked upwards and saw the most beautiful girl I've ever seen in my life ... I didn't even know her name but in that crowd all I could see was her little sweet face, her beautiful eyes, her long hair." Clearly, love at first sight can fizzle into nothing. But as for this couple, they are still together four years later.[31]

Q What are the dynamics when partners are of the same sex?

A Research is limited so far, but much of it suggests that, on average, long-term same-sex partners typically match up well in terms of supportive communication,[32] emotional closeness,[33] and the effort each partner puts into maintaining the relationship. Researchers speculate that, while same-sex couples face mostly the same challenges as anyone else, they have probably been socialized to communicate in similar ways and to have similar expectations.

Given that gender is a social construct—and a fast-changing one—you may or may not relate to the patterns described here. The main point is that social expectations and self-identity can influence why people fall in love and how they express it.

Speaking the Languages of Love

LEARNING OBJECTIVE 9.3: Elaborate on the difference between popular love languages.

If you are in a romantic relationship, how effectively does your partner convey love, and how do you express your feelings?

Relationship counselor Gary Chapman observes that people typically orient to one of five love languages.[34] The odds are that you value all of these to some degree, but you probably give some love languages greater weight than others. Research supports the potency of love languages in promoting harmony.[35,36] The challenge is to communicate your love in a "language" that resonates with your partner.

Affirming Words

Affirmation includes compliments, thanks, and statements that express love and commitment. Even when you know someone loves and values you, it's often nice to hear it in words. The happiest couples continue to flirt with each other, even after they have been together for many years.[37]

Quality Time

Some people show love by completing tasks together, talking, or engaging in some other mutually enjoyable activity. The good news is that, even when people can't be together physically, talking about quality time can be an important means of expressing love. For example, partners separated by military deployments often say they feel closer to each other just talking about everyday activities and future plans.[38]

Gifts

It's no coincidence that people often buy gifts for loved ones on Valentine's Day, birthdays, anniversaries, and other occasions. For some people, receiving a gift—even an inexpensive or free one such as a flower from the garden or a handmade card—adds to their sense of being loved and valued.[39]

Physical Touch

Loving touch may involve a hug, a kiss, a pat on the back, or sex. Touch is potent even in long-term relationships. Researchers in one study asked couples to increase the number of times they kissed each other. Six weeks later, the couples' stress levels and relational satisfaction, and even their cholesterol levels, had significantly improved.[40]

Acts of Service

People may show love by performing favors such as caring for each other when they are sick, doing the dishes, or making meals. Committed couples report that sharing daily tasks is the most frequent way they show their love and commitment.[41] Although each person need not contribute in exactly the same ways, an overall sense that they are putting forth equal effort is essential to long-term happiness.[42]

ABOUT YOU *What's Your Love Language?*

Answer these questions to learn more about the love languages you prefer. If you're in a romantic relationship, consider comparing your answer to your partner's and discussing how you can express your love in ways that will matter the most.

________ **1.** You have had a stressful time working on a team project. The best thing your romantic partner can do for you is:

a. Set aside distractions to spend time with you.
b. Do your chores so you can relax.
c. Give you a big hug.
d. Pamper you with a dessert you love.
e. Tell you the team is lucky to have someone as talented as you.

________ **2.** What is your favorite way to show that you care?

a. Go somewhere special together.
b. Do a favor for your partner without being asked.
c. Hold hands and sit close together.
d. Surprise your partner with a little treat.
e. Tell your loved one how you feel in writing.

________ **3.** With which of the following do you most agree?

a. The most lovable thing someone can do is give you their undivided attention.
b. Actions speak louder than words.
c. A loving touch says more than words can express.
d. Your dearest possessions are things loved ones have given you.
e. People don't say "I love you" nearly enough.

________ **4.** Your anniversary is coming up. Which of the following appeals to you most?

a. An afternoon together, just the two of you.
b. A romantic, home-cooked dinner (you don't have to lift a finger).
c. A relaxing massage by candlelight.
d. A photo album of good times you have shared.
e. A homemade card that lists the qualities your romantic partner loves about you.

INTERPRETING YOUR RESPONSES

For insight about your primary love languages, see which of the following best describes your answers.

Quality Time If you answered "a" to one or more questions, you feel loved when people set aside life's distractions to spend time with you. Keep in mind that everyone defines quality time a bit differently. It may mean a thoughtful phone call during a busy day, a picnic in the park, or a few minutes every evening to share news about the day.

Acts of Service Answering "b" means you feel loved when people do thoughtful things for you such as washing your car, helping you with a repair job, bringing you breakfast in bed, or bathing the children so you can put your feet up. Even small gestures say "I love you" to people whose love language involves acts of service.

Physical Touch Options labeled "c" are associated with the comfort and pleasure you get from physical affection. If your partner texts to say, "Wish we were snuggled up together!" they are speaking the language of touch.

Gifts If you chose "d," you treasure thoughtful gifts from loved ones. Your prized possessions are likely to include items that look inconsequential to others but have sentimental value to you because of who gave them to you.

Words of Affirmation Options labeled "e" refer to words that make you feel loved and valued, perhaps in a card, a song, or a text. To people who speak this love language, hearing that they are loved (and why) is the sweetest message imaginable.

Relational Dialectics

LEARNING OBJECTIVE 9.4: Explain dialectical continua and strategies for managing them.

Relationships can feel like a balancing act. You want connection, but also independence. You want to share your thoughts and feelings, but also to have some privacy. You want the relationship to be fresh, but still have predictable qualities.

The model of **relational dialectics** suggests that partners in close relationships constantly seek a balance between opposing forces such as togetherness versus independence, sharing versus privacy, and comfortable routines versus new adventures.[43] As you read about each set of opposing needs, consider how they operate in your life.

Connection Versus Autonomy

The conflicting desires for togetherness and independence are embodied in the *connection–autonomy dialectic*. One of the most common reasons for breaking up is that one partner doesn't satisfy the other's need for connection:[44]

"We barely spent any time together."

"My partner wasn't committed to the relationship."

"We had different needs."

But couples split up for the opposite reason as well:[45]

"I felt trapped."

"I needed freedom."

Individuals are faced with this dilemma even within themselves. You may desire intimacy, but also feel the need for some time to yourself.

Managing dialectic tensions is tricky because people's needs change over time. Author Desmond Morris suggests that partners repeatedly go through three stages:[46]

"Hold me tight,"

"Put me down," and

"Leave me alone."

In marriages and other committed relationships, for example, the strong "Hold me tight" bonds of the first year are often followed by a desire for independence. This need for autonomy can manifest in many ways, such as making friends or engaging in activities that don't include one's partner. Movement toward autonomy may lead to a breakup, or it can be part of a cycle that allows partners to recapture or even surpass the closeness they had before. For example, you might find that spending some time apart makes you miss and appreciate your partner more than ever. "Tips & Reminders: 7 Strategies for Managing Dialectic Tensions" describes how people (productively or not) try to strike a balance in their relationships.

Openness Versus Privacy

Self-disclosure (Chapter 7) is one characteristic of interpersonal relationships. Yet it's also important to maintain some emotional space between yourself and others. These sometimes-conflicting drives create the *openness–privacy dialectic*. When the drive for openness is strong, you might find yourself asking your partner to share personal information:

"What's on your mind?"

"How are you really *feeling?"*

"Tell me more."

But if you are on the receiving end of such demands and craving a little privacy, you might think or say things like "Stop pushing so hard!" or "Don't try to read my mind!"

Predictability Versus Novelty

Sharing new experiences can keep a relationship fresh and exciting. At the same time, shared routines can create a sense of security. These opposing needs represent different ends of the *predictability-novelty dialectic*. Too much predictability can sap the excitement out of a relationship, whereas too much novelty can lead to uncertainty and insecurity. "I don't know who you are anymore," you might say or hear.

People differ in their desire for stability and surprises—even from one time to another. The classic example is becoming engaged just before graduation or military deployment, when life may seem particularly novel and uncertain. Commitment may balance some of the uncertainty people feel in those situations. However, things may feel *too* predictable once life settles into a new routine.

TIPS & REMINDERS

Strategies for Managing Dialectical Tensions

As you have probably experienced, some strategies for managing dialectical tensions are more productive than others. Consider which of these you might avoid and which you'd like to use more.[47]

1. **Denial**

   One of the least functional responses to dialectical tensions is to deny that they exist. People in denial insist that everything is fine, even if it isn't. They may refuse to deal with conflict, ignoring problems or pretending that they agree about everything.

2. **Selection**

   When partners employ the strategy of selection, they respond to one end of the dialectical spectrum and ignore the other. For example, a couple caught between the conflicting desires for stability and novelty may decide that predictability is the "right" or "responsible" choice and put aside their longing for excitement.

3. **Moderation**

   The moderation strategy is characterized by compromises in which couples back off from expressing either end of the dialectical spectrum. A couple might decide that taking separate vacations is too extreme for them, but they will make room for some alone time while they are traveling together.

4. **Alternation**

   Communicators sometimes alternate between one end of the dialectical spectrum and the other. For example, partners may spend time apart during the week but reserve weekends for couple time.

5. **Polarization**

   In some cases, couples find a balance of sorts by each staking a claim at opposite ends of a dialectic continuum. For example, one partner might give up nearly all personal interests in the name of togetherness, while the other maintains an equally extreme commitment to being independent. In the classic *demand–withdraw pattern*, the more one partner insists on closeness, the more the other feels suffocated and craves distance.[48]

6. **Reframing**

   Couples can also respond to dialectical challenges by reframing them in ways that redefine the situation so that the apparent contradiction disappears. Consider partners who regard the inevitable challenges of managing dialectical tensions as "exciting opportunities to grow" instead of as "relational problems."

7. **Reaffirmation**

   A final strategy for handling dialectical tensions is reaffirmation—acknowledging that dialectical tensions will never disappear and accepting or even embracing the challenges they present. Partners who use reaffirmation view dialectical tensions as part of the ride of life.

PAUSE TO REFLECT *What Dialectic Strategies Do You Use?*

1. Imagine that someone you like prefers to stay home and relax but you crave a busy social life (or vice versa). How are you most likely to manage the dialectical tension that results? Do you think your approach would be helpful? Why or why not? ______________________

2. Have you ever experienced a demand–withdraw pattern in a close relationship? If so, how did you both communicate about the issue? What happened? ______________________

Deception in Romantic Relationships

LEARNING OBJECTIVE 9.5: Analyze the functions served by altruistic lies, evasions, and self-serving lies.

Partners are likely to experience deceit in every stage of their relationship.

When researchers asked college students if they had ever lied to a romantic partner, about 7 in 10 said yes.[49] That may sound problematic, but not all lies are hurtful or malicious. Lies are most likely to damage a relationship when the partners are highly invested in being together, the topic is important, and there have been previous doubts about the deceiver's honesty.[50] Here's a look at three types of lies: altruistic lies, evasions, and self-serving lies.

Altruistic Lies

Altruistic lies are defined, at least by the people who tell them, as being harmless, or even helpful, to the person to whom they are told.[51] For the most part, white lies such as these fall in the category of polite ways to communicate about small matters without causing offense. For example, you might compliment your loved one's new haircut to avoid hurting their feelings.

Nearly half the lies shared by online daters in one study were so-called butler lies: false statements meant to save face for the sender and/or the receiver. For example, a partner might justify not responding right away by saying "I forgot my ringer was off" or "Busy day!"[52] The term *butler* comes from the old-fashioned tradition of asking household employees to make excuses when people weren't ready to socialize. These days, you probably have a phone close at hand 24 hours a day, and there is no buffer between you and the outside world. In essence, we need to provide "polite fictions" in a communication environment that presents more demands than we can fulfill.[53]

Evasions

Evasions, sometimes called *gray lies*, aren't outright mistruths, but they *are* deliberately vague.[54] Some evasions are relatively harmless. For instance, you might tell your partner you were looking up some stuff online without mentioning that you were ordering them a surprise gift.

Some evasions are hurtful, however. Tara was furious when she found out that her boyfriend Michael had been looking up past girlfriends online without telling her.[55] Researchers have coined the term "digital infidelity" to describe cheating via technology. Since there are few hard and fast rules about what qualifies as digital infidelity, the best bet is for romantic partners to discuss their expectations. Here are some questions to consider together:

- Does looking up previous romantic partners online constitute cheating to you? Why or why not?
- If someone in a committed relationship engages in romantic talk online with someone they will never meet in person, do you think that is cheating? Why or why not?
- How about posting sexually provocative comments or photos?

Self-Serving Lies

Self-serving lies are attempts to manipulate a listener into believing something that is untrue—not primarily to protect the listener, but to advance the deceiver's agenda. There are two main types of self-serving deception: lies of omission and lies of fabrication.

Lying by omission involves withholding information that another person deserves to know. If your partner expresses anger after discovering you've had coffee with an ex, you might try to defend yourself by saying, "I didn't lie. I just didn't tell you." When the issue is important, that's not much of a defense.

A *fabrication* is a lie that deliberately misleads another person for your own benefit. For example, you might justify showing up late for an important date by claiming you were tied up at work, when the "work" was an extended happy hour with your colleagues.

Online fabrication may take the form of **catfishing**—creating a false persona to fool others into thinking that they are communicating with a real person. Stephanie Michele thought she was hitting it off with a kind, handsome physician on the Hinge dating app until he gave her a fake phone number and she realized she was being catfished.[56]

It's no surprise that self-serving lies can destroy trust and lead the deceived party to wonder what else their partner might be lying about. However, some couples rebound from serious deceptions, particularly if the lie involves an isolated incident and the wrongdoer's apology seems sincere.[57]

How Partners Express Conflict

LEARNING OBJECTIVE 9.6: Compare and contrast methods of dealing with interpersonal conflict.

Regardless of what people may wish for or dream about, a conflict-free relationship just doesn't exist.

For many people, the inevitability of conflict is depressing. However, effective communicators realize that, although it's impossible to eliminate conflict, there are ways to manage it effectively. The first step is to understand the wide range of communication options available. As you read on, ask yourself which styles you use most often and how they affect the quality of your close relationships.

Nonassertiveness

Anticipating their 10-year wedding anniversary, Alex asked his wife Danielle what she would like. She said, "Just surprise me!" So Alex planned a surprise getaway at a bed and breakfast Danielle likes. She didn't seem thrilled to be there, however. "I asked her what was wrong, and she kept saying, 'Nothing,'" Alex remembers. "Finally, the last day there, she told me she really had her heart set on a new wedding ring. How was I supposed to know that?"[58]

The inability or unwillingness to express one's thoughts or feelings is known as **nonassertion**. A nonassertive person may insist that "nothing is wrong" even when it is. Sometimes nonassertion comes from a lack of confidence. At other times, people lack the awareness or skill to use a more direct means of expression. We might imagine that Danielle felt it would be unseemly to ask outright for a new ring. She might have dropped subtle hints or hoped that Alex would surprise her with a ring because he wanted to give her one, not because she asked him to.

In conflict situations, nonassertion can take a variety of forms. One is *avoidance*—either steering clear of the other person or avoiding the topic, perhaps by talking about something else, joking, or denying that a problem exists. People who avoid conflicts usually believe it's easier to put up with the status quo than to face the problem head-on and try to solve it. *Accommodation* is another type of nonassertive response. Accommodators deal with conflict by giving in, putting others' needs ahead of their own.

While nonassertion won't solve a difficult or long-term problem, there are situations in which accommodating or avoiding is a sensible approach. You might choose to keep quiet if speaking up would risk your job or personal safety, if the conflict is minor, or if you don't know the other person very well. For important or longstanding issues, though, nonassertion rarely helps.

Indirect Communication

Whereas a nonassertive person resists dealing with conflict at all, someone using an indirect style addresses the conflict, but in subtle ways. **Indirect communication** conveys a message in a roundabout manner. The goal is to get what you want without causing hard feelings. If your partner keeps forgetting to turn off the lights, you might say, "That bulb is so dim, it's easy to forget that it's on, isn't it?" The risk of an indirect message, of course, is that the other party will misunderstand or will fail to get the message. There are also times when the importance of an idea is so great that hinting lacks the necessary punch.

Assertiveness

Winston Churchill is said to have proclaimed, "Courage is what it takes to stand up and speak. Courage is also what it takes to sit down and listen."[59] Assertiveness, which represents a balance between high self-interest and high concern for others, involves a good deal of both.

Assertive people handle conflicts by expressing their needs, thoughts, and feelings clearly and inviting others to do the same. Assertive people believe that it's usually possible to resolve problems to everyone's satisfaction.

Here are some tips for being assertive:

- Discuss sensitive issues while you have cool heads rather than in the heat of the moment.

- Ask questions and listen. For example, you might say, "We're often impatient with each other on Monday mornings. I think I'd be less stressed if I plan out my week on Sundays. Is there something we can to do make Monday mornings less stressful for you?"
- Avoid accusations and assumptions. Use "I" language instead. "I was disappointed when you canceled our Friday night plans" is more productive than "You never make time for me."
- Don't be surprised if the process feels uncomfortable. Conflict is inherently emotional, even when you handle it well. It may help to remember that romantic partners who approach conflict in a patient and caring way often feel closer to each other as a result.[60]

Passive Aggression

If you know someone who responds to conflict with unkind humor or snide comments and then acts like they didn't intend to hurt your feelings, you have experienced **passive aggression**, which occurs when a communicator expresses hostility in an ambiguous way. Scholar George Bach describes five types of passive aggressive people:[61]

- *Pseudoaccommodators* only pretend to agree with you. A passively aggressive person might commit to something ("I'll be on time from now on") but not actually do it.
- *Guiltmakers* try to make you feel bad. A guiltmaker will agree to something and then make you feel responsible for the hardship it causes them ("I really should be studying, but I'll give you a ride").
- *Jokers* use humor as a weapon. They might say unkind things and then insist they were "just kidding" and that you are being too sensitive ("Where's your sense of humor?").
- *Trivial tyrannizers* do small things to drive you crazy. Rather than express their feelings outright, they might "forget" to clean the kitchen or put gas in the car just to annoy you.
- *Withholders* keep back something valuable. A withholder might punish others by refusing to show courtesy, affection, or humor.

Direct Aggression

Directly aggressive people show little or no concern for others. A **directly aggressive message** confronts another person in a way that attacks their character, intelligence, or dignity, rather than debating the issues. Aggressive people often use intimidation and insults to get their way. Many directly aggressive responses are easy to spot:

> *"You don't know what you're talking about."*
> *"That was a stupid thing to do."*
> *"What's the matter with you?"*

Other forms of direct aggression rely more on nonverbal cues, such as sneering, shouting, or using intimidating gestures.

Aggressive messages between romantic partners are most common when one person feels they are contributing more than the other.[62] If you are generally tempted to make aggressive statements, see what happens if you bring up an issue in a calm manner instead. Verbal aggressiveness may get you what you want in the short run, but it generally makes a relationship worse over time.[63]

In some cases, aggressive behavior crosses the line. In "Tips & Reminders: 3 Ways to Protect Yourself from an Abusive Partner," you will find advice on what to do if you find yourself in that situation. ●

TIPS & REMINDERS

Ways to Protect Yourself from an Abusive Partner

There are no magic communication formulas to prevent or stop the behavior of an abusive person, but there are steps you can take to protect yourself.

1. **Don't keep abuse a secret.**
   Abusers often isolate their partners from friends and loved ones because it's easier to control them if they don't have a strong network of people who know what's going on.[64] Avoid this trap by keeping close contact and open communication with people you trust. At the very least, tell someone what's happening and ask that person to assist you in getting help.
2. **Have a plan for defense.**
   Program emergency numbers into your phone, and keep it handy. Agree on code words you can mention to trusted people in a conversation, message, or call to let them know you need help without calling attention to your alert. Also avoid sharing passwords that will allow the abuser to access your communication with others or learn your whereabouts.
3. **Don't blame yourself.**
   Abused people often believe they are at fault and that they "had it coming." Remember—*no one deserves abuse.* Abusive people make the choice to be abusive. No one makes them behave that way or prevents them from making that choice.[65] Many resources are available to help you. One source of information and assistance is HealthyPlace (www.healthyplace.com/abuse).

Conflict Patterns That Ruin Relationships

LEARNING OBJECTIVE 9.7: Describe the "Four Horsemen of the Apocalypse" in terms of conflict management.

Unfortunately, people sometimes handle conflict in ways that erode their relationships.

After four decades of studying how couples communicate, psychologist John Gottman can predict with a rate of accuracy approaching 90 percent whether or not a couple is headed toward a breakup.[66] He has identified types of abusive communication that he terms the "Four Horsemen of the Apocalypse" because their continued presence signals that a relationship faces decline and doom.[67] As you read about the Four Horsemen, consider if you are ever guilty of them with partners, friends, roommates, family members, or anyone else you know.

Partners criticize each other.

Whereas it can be healthy for partners tactfully to point out specific behaviors that cause problems ("I wish you would let me know when you're running late"), **criticism** goes beyond that to deliver a personal, all-encompassing accusation such as "You're lazy" or "The only person you think about is yourself."

Partners show contempt.

Contempt takes criticism to an even more hurtful level by mocking, belittling, or ridiculing the other person. Expressions of contempt may be explicit ("People laugh at you behind your back" or "You're disgusting") or nonverbal (sneering, eye rolling, and a condescending tone of voice). Gottman has found that the single best single predictor of divorce is contempt.[68]

Partners are defensive.

When faced with criticism and contempt, it's not surprising that partners react with **defensiveness**—protecting their self-worth by counterattacking ("You're calling me a careless driver? You're the one who got a speeding ticket last month."). Once an attack-and-defend pattern develops, conflict often escalates or partners start to avoid each other.

Partners engage in stonewalling.

Stonewalling is a form of avoidance in which one person refuses to engage with the other. Walking away or giving one's partner the silent treatment conveys the message "You aren't worth my attention." Disengagement may seem like a better alternative than arguing, but it robs partners of the chance to understand each other better.

PAUSE TO REFLECT *How Do You Handle Conflict as a Couple?*

1. If your partner says something that hurts your feelings, how are you likely to respond?

2. How might you react if your partner is upset with you and you don't think you have done anything wrong?

3. Do your answers suggest that you are ever guilty of criticism, contempt, defensiveness, or stonewalling? If so, how might you behave differently to avoid damaging your relationship?

Applying Win–Win Problem Solving

LEARNING OBJECTIVE 9.8: Identify the steps and communication skills involved in win–win problem solving.

Win–win problem solving is typically the most satisfying and relationship-friendly means of resolving conflict.

The goal in **win-win problem solving** is a solution that satisfies both partners' needs. Neither tries to win at the other's expense. Win–win problem solving is a highly structured activity. However, after you have practiced the approach a number of times, it will become more comfortable. You'll then be able to approach conflicts without the need to follow the exact step-by-step approach presented here.

Identify your problem and unmet needs.

Before you speak out, it's important to realize that if something bothers you, the problem is *yours*. Perhaps you're bothered by your partner's tendency to yell at other drivers. Because *you* are the person who is dissatisfied, you are the one with a problem. Realizing this will make a big difference when the time comes to approach your partner. Instead of feeling and acting in a way that blames the other person, you'll be more likely to describe your feelings, which will reduce the chance of a defensive reaction.

Before you voice your problem to your partner, pause to consider why the situation bothers you. Perhaps you're afraid your partner will offend someone you know. Maybe you're worried that excess emotion will lead to unsafe driving, or you'd like to use the drive time as an opportunity for conversation.

Make a date.

Unconstructive fights often start because the initiator confronts someone who isn't ready. A person may not be in the right frame of mind to face a conflict if they are tired, busy with something else, or not feeling well. At times like these, it's unfair to insist on having a difficult discussion. Instead, you might say, "Something's been bothering me. Can we talk about it?" If the answer is "yes," then you're ready to go further. If it isn't, find a time that's agreeable to both of you.

Describe your problem and needs.

Other people can't meet your needs without knowing why you're upset and what you want. It's up to you to describe your problem as specifically as possible without judging the other person. Include a need statement, empathy, and a specific reference to the behavior in question. That might sound something like this:

> *I look forward to riding home from work together because I like the chance to hear about your day and make plans for later [need/desire]. I know you get frustrated with city traffic [empathy], but I feel disappointed when you yell at other drivers instead of talking with me [problem].*

Check your partner's understanding.

After you have shared your problem and described what you need, make sure the other person has understood what you've said. As you may remember from Chapter 5, there's a good chance of your words being misinterpreted, especially in a stressful conflict situation. If your partner says,

"You're telling me I'm a bad driver," you can take the opportunity to say something like, "I'm not judging your driving. I know it's stressful. I'm saying I'd love to have some quality time with you on the ride home."

Ask about your partner's needs.

After you've made your position clear, it's time to find out what would make your partner feel satisfied about the issue. There are two reasons why it's important to discover your partner's needs. First, it's fair. After all, they have as much right to be happy as you do. Second, it's good for the relationship. You are most likely to stay together if you both feel that your needs are being met.

You might learn about your partner's needs simply by asking about them: "Now that you know what I want and why, tell me what you need from me." After your partner begins to talk, your job is to use the listening skills discussed in Chapter 5 to make sure you understand.

Check your understanding of your partner's needs.

Paraphrase or ask questions about your partner's needs until you're certain you understand them. You might say, "It sounds like traffic is extra frustrating on the way home because you feel tired and hungry. Is that how it feels?"

Negotiate a solution.

Now that you understand each other's needs, the goal is to find a way to meet them. First, partner in thinking of as many potential solutions as you can. If possible, write your ideas down so you won't forget any of them.

Next, discuss which solutions might work and which probably wouldn't. Then pick the one that looks best to both of you. If the approach you select doesn't work well, you can change your minds later, but for now keep in mind that a solution is most likely to be effective if you both understand it, support it, and are willing to try it out.

To go back to the driving example, perhaps you decide to meet for dinner and then drive home once rush-hour traffic has subsided. Or, you might take turns driving home. The point is that the solution should meet both of your needs.

Follow up on the solution.

After you have tried your solution for a while, talk about how things are going. You may find that you need to make some changes or even choose a different option. The idea is to keep on top of the problem and continue using creativity to solve it.

All of this being said, win–win solutions aren't always possible. There will be times when even the best-intentioned people simply won't be able to find a way of meeting all their needs. When that happens, compromising may be the most sensible approach. You will even encounter instances when pushing for your own solution is reasonable, and times when it makes sense to willingly accept the loser's role. But even when that happens, the steps we've discussed haven't been wasted. A genuine desire to learn what the other person wants and to try to satisfy those desires will build a climate of goodwill that can help you improve your relationship. •

Communicating with Romantic Partners

Relational Stages

- Initiating
- Experimenting
- Intensifying
- Integrating
- Bonding
- Differentiating
- Circumscribing
- Stagnating
- Avoiding
- Terminating

Begin with a quick and easy meetup.

- Keep the tone light.
- Be playful.

Gender and Intimacy

- Women often regard sex as a way to express intimacy, whereas men are more likely to think that it creates intimacy.
- Same-sex couples often have similar shared expectations and communication styles.

Love Languages

- Affirming words
- Quality time
- Gifts
- Physical touch
- Acts of service

Relational Dialectics

Relationships involve continual negotiation between:

- Connection and autonomy
- Openness and privacy
- Predictability and novelty

Strategies for Managing Dialectical Continua

- Denial
- Selection
- Moderation
- Alternation
- Polarization
- Reframing
- Reaffirmation

Types of Deception

- Altruistic lies
- Evasions
- Self-serving lies

Ways to Express Conflict

- Nonassertiveness
- Indirect communication
- Assertiveness
- Passive aggression
- Direct aggression

Protect Yourself from Abuse

- Don't keep it secret.
- Have a plan for defense.
- Don't blame yourself.

Destructive Conflict Patterns

- Criticism
- Contempt
- Defensiveness
- Stonewalling

Win–Win Problem Solving

- Identify problem and unmet needs.
- Make a date.
- Describe problem and needs.
- Check your partner's understanding.
- Ask about your partner's needs.
- Check your understanding.
- Negotiate a solution.
- Follow up.

Show Your Communication Know-How

9.1: Distinguish between stages of coming together, staying together, and moving apart as a romantic couple.

Think of a romantic relationship you or someone you know has experienced. What stages did you or they experience? What role did communication play in each stage?

KEY TERMS: developmental model, intimacy

9.2: Describe means of conveying intimate messages that tend to differ by gender.

Are you more likely to show people you love them using words or kind deeds? How might gender-related expectations influence how others interpret your behavior?

9.3: Elaborate on the difference between popular love languages.

Which of the love languages described in this chapter resonate most strongly with you? How might you identify the love languages of someone important to you and express yourself that way?

9.4: Explain dialectical continua and strategies for managing them.

Draw a line and label one end "connection" and the other end "autonomy." Think of a particular relationship (it needn't be romantic) and indicate where you are most comfortable on that continuum and where your relational partner is most comfortable. Do the same with the continua of openness and privacy and novelty and predictability. How do you negotiate your differences?

KEY TERM: relational dialectics

9.5: Analyze the functions served by altruistic lies, evasions, and self-serving lies.

Consider a self-serving lie you have communicated in a close relationship. Looking back, would you do anything differently?

KEY TERMS: altruistic lies, evasions, self-serving lies, catfishing

9.6: Compare and contrast methods of dealing with interpersonal conflict.

Are you more likely to talk about your feelings directly or indirectly? Are you satisfied with this approach?

KEY TERMS: nonassertion, indirect communication, assertive, passive aggression, directly aggressive message

9.7: Describe the "Four Horsemen of the Apocalypse" in terms of conflict management.

Have you ever been guilty of contempt or stonewalling? If so, what effect did it have on the relationship?

KEY TERMS: criticism, contempt, defensiveness, stonewalling

9.8: Identify the steps and communication skills involved in win–win problem solving.

Describe an instance of successful conflict management. Which of the steps in win–win problem solving did you use?

KEY TERM: win–win problem solving

10 COMMUNICATING TO Land a Job

Employers Seek Good Communicators

LEARNING OBJECTIVE 10.1: Describe the reasons why good communicators are likely to excel in the workplace.

Employers across the board agree that communication is essential to getting a good job and excelling in the workplace.

Communication skills comprise 7 of the 10 qualities that managers value most highly in employees. Communication ability even outranks technical knowledge.[1] Here are five reasons why good communicators flourish in the professional world.

Good communicators work well in teams.

"Life is a team sport," observes human resource specialist Robert Half.[2] This is especially true in the workplace, where effective teamwork is linked to successful outcomes, high morale, efficiency, problem solving, satisfaction, and loyalty to the organization.[3]

Good communicators enhance customer satisfaction.

Pleasing communication is the number-one factor in consumer satisfaction.[4] Of particular importance are employees' listening skills, empathy, and cultural sensitivity while interacting with clients.[5,6]

Good communicators build public awareness.

Along with promoting the organization during one-on-one interactions, team members can serve as brand ambassadors in front of audiences large and small. They might make sales pitches, inform audiences about the value of a product or service, or advocate for change or public policies. Chapters 12 through 14 will help you refine your public speaking skills.

Good communicators make good leaders.

Leaders spend most of their time communicating—mostly about organizational problems that boil down to poor communication, observes business analyst Matt Myatt.[7] The upshot is that communication is central to what leaders do and what they care about. Research shows that the best leaders are attentive listeners who focus on both tasks and relationships.[8]

Good communicators inspire others.

You have probably been inspired by a manager or colleague you would like to emulate. Phil Dourado remembers a supervisor who offered to resign rather than lay off employees. Instead, the grateful staff worked together to cut costs by 20 percent and keep everyone on board. "We were all fiercely loyal to that boss for ever after," Dourado remembers.[9] ●

Networking Strategies to Find a Job

LEARNING OBJECTIVE 10.2: Engage in networking behaviors conducive to finding a job that matches your skills.

Finding and landing a job you love starts now. Be proactive about developing relationships and asking for advice that might enhance your career.

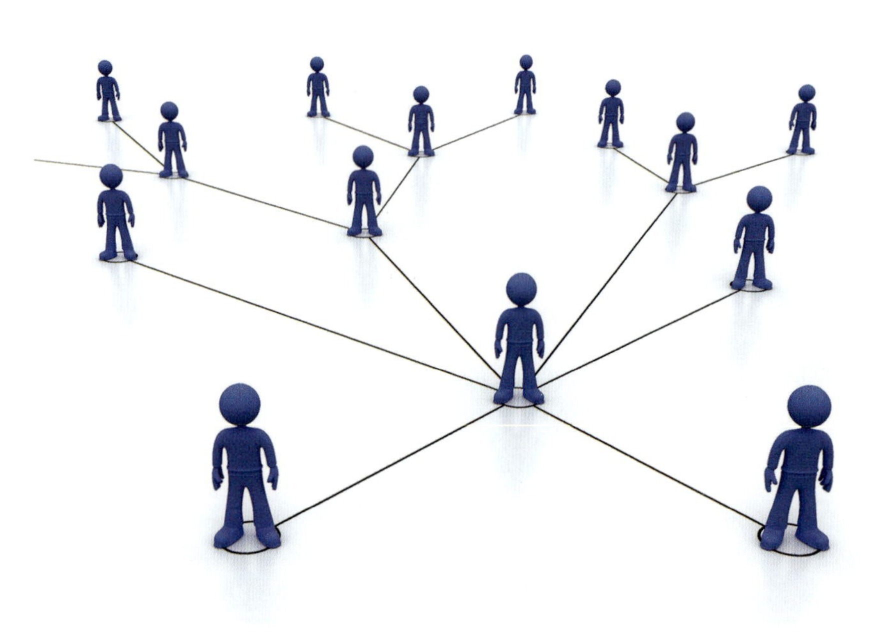

Courtney Baxter was in a state of what she calls "post-graduation anxiety." She was eager to land a job relevant to her degree in gender and international studies, but she was unsure where to begin. On a whim, she emailed Courtney E. Martin, an author whose work about women's issues she had long admired. To her surprise, Martin wrote back with an invitation to meet in person. Baxter arrived with questions about the nature of the field and how she might break in. Martin was so impressed that she arranged for Baxter to meet a colleague at the OpEd Project. That conversation led to a job offer. It's an entry-level position, but Baxter was thrilled to have landed it. "I feel lucky that, at 23, I look forward to work every day," Baxter says of her big break.[10]

As this story shows, jobs in today's competitive workplace go to proactive communicators who develop positive relationships with people in the industry. A whopping 3 out of 4 people in the workplace today obtained jobs with the help of **networking**—the process of meeting people and maintaining relationships.[11] People in your network might give you career advice, tell you about available positions, and put in a good word for you. Of course, networking will only work if others feel that you are worth endorsing. If you're willing to work hard and have the necessary skills to do a job (or are willing to learn), here are several steps you can take to network effectively.

Look for networking prospects.

Besides the people you see every day, you probably have access to a wealth of other contacts. These might include former coworkers, classmates, teammates, social acquaintances, and more.

Engage in online networking.

Numerous websites offer professional networking opportunities. A few of the most popular are LinkedIn, LetsLunch, Opportunity, and Shapr. Most offer basic memberships for free. It's not too early to join a few of these and set up a personal profile—which might include career-relevant projects you have been part of, volunteer work, awards, accomplishments, and interests. Above all, consider how your information will look to people who don't know you well. You may be proud of your membership in the National Rifle Association, Planned Parenthood, or a religious or political group, but a prospective employer might not find your affiliations so admirable. (We'll talk more about managing your online identity in a moment.)

Seek referrals.

Each contact in your immediate network has connections to other people who might be able to help you. Social scientists have verified that the "six degrees of separation" hypothesis is true. The average number of links separating any two people in the world is indeed only half a dozen.[12] You can take advantage of this by seeking people removed from your personal network by just one degree: If you ask 10 people for referrals, and each of them knows three others who might be able to help, you have the potential of support from 30 people.

Conduct informational interviews.

Courtney Baxter, whose story begins this section, had the courage to contact someone in her chosen field.

What followed was an **informational interview**—a meeting in which the interviewer seeks knowledge from someone who can enhance their career success. Interviews of this sort may be conducted in person or via phone or an online meeting format. A good informational interview may help you achieve the following goals:

- Learn more about a job, organization, or field.
- Make a positive impression on the person you are interviewing.
- Gain referrals to other people who might be able to help you.

Unless you know a prospective interviewee well, it's generally best to send your request for a meeting in writing via a letter or email. (A text message is usually too casual.) Keep your message brief. Introduce yourself, explain your reason for wanting the interview, and emphasize that you're seeking information, not asking for a job. Request a specific amount of time for a meeting. (Shorter requests are more likely to be granted.)

After initial pleasantries, be sure to use your limited time to focus on career-related information, such as "What are the three fastest-growing companies in this field?" and "What do you think about the risks of working for a start-up company?"

Often, the best way to get information is to ask straightforward questions, but there are times when it's more gracious to be indirect. For instance, instead of asking "What's your salary?" you might say, "What kind of salary might I expect if I ever held a position like yours?" Listen closely and ask follow-up questions. If the primary question is "Who are the best people to ask about careers in the financial planning field?" a secondary question might be, "What do you think is the best way for me to go about meeting them?"

Show appreciation.

Don't forget to thank the people in your network. Always send a thank-you after the meeting. Beyond that, take the time to maintain relationships and let your contacts know when their help has made a difference in your career advancement. Along with being the right thing to do, your thoughtfulness will distinguish you as the kind of person worth hiring or helping again in the future. ●

TIPS & REMINDERS

5 Strategies to Build a Career-Enhancing Network

1. **Take part in volunteerism and service learning.**
   In addition to gaining experience you may use in a career, you're likely to come in contact with civic and business leaders while working in the community.

2. **Attend lectures, forums, and networking events.**
   Although it's natural to feel a little nervous and out of place at first, networking coach Darrah Brustein says, "Be yourself... The people you connect with when you are authentic are the ones you'll want to stay in touch with."[13] Try to speak personally with several people whose interests are similar to yours. Afterward, send a personal note thanking the presenters and others you meet at the event.

3. **Keep up with local news.**
   There's no better way to know who is involved and what the latest issues are. This can help you identify potential mentors and speak knowledgeably about current topics when you meet them.

4. **Join career-related organizations.**
   Many professional groups offer discounted membership fees for students. Take advantage of the opportunity to meet people in the career field you hope to join. And don't just sit in the back of the room. Volunteer to serve on committees or hold an office. Your hard work will be noticed.

5. **Use online resources.**
   Search LinkedIn or other sites for people who have something in common with you—perhaps those who attended the same school as you or majored in the same discipline. Common interests can be great conversation starters.

Managing Your Online Identity

LEARNING OBJECTIVE 10.3: Cultivate an online identity that appeals to prospective employers.

"Like it or not, your social media accounts are your brand," says one savvy media user.[14]

Just as companies have brands that tell the public what makes them unique, your online identity has the power to shape how others see you. A digital presence is critical in today's job market, so it's important to get it right. According to the *New York Times*, 70 percent of U.S. recruiters have rejected job candidates because of personal information online.[15] Here are experts' tips for creating an online presence that works in your favor.

Showcase your strengths and goals.

Creating an online identity is not about fooling anyone—it's about portraying yourself in an authentic and favorable way. Take stock of your interests, talents, and goals. Make sure that people who encounter you online have a clear sense of who you are.[16]

Build a professional identity.

Your online photos and information should create a sense that you're ready for the career of your choice. For example, hoping to land a job in Washington, DC, Joseph Cadman used LinkedIn to post a profile photo of himself in a suit and tie in front of the Capitol Building.[17] While you're at it, make sure your email address and screen name are dignified. One of the top 10 deal breakers for recruiters is an unprofessional email address.[18]

Avoid embarrassing posts.

When employers review candidates' online presence (as most do), the most common deal breakers are evidence of drinking or partying, posts that are disrespectful toward others, and critical comments about a current or former employer.[19] Even if an off-color meme seems like a harmless joke, do you want it to represent you? Think carefully about everything you post.

Monitor your online presence.

Even information you think is private may be accessible online. Search for yourself on a range of digital platforms (Google, Yahoo!, MSN Search, MetaCrawler, Dogpile, Ask.com) and see what comes up. Also double-check the privacy settings on your social media accounts (although you shouldn't consider them foolproof) and sign up for Google Alerts to receive a notification when your name pops up online. (Create Google Alerts for potential employers while you're at it so you can stay current about them.)

Engage in damage control.

The phrase **digital dirt** refers to unflattering information posted about a person online, whether it's true or not. If possible, remove incorrect, unfair, and potentially damaging information about yourself. If you can't remove it, consider a service such as ReputationDefender.com that will monitor your online identity and ask the managers of offending websites to remove the information.

Beware mistaken identities.

You might find that unfavorable information pops up about someone with the same name as you. One job seeker Googled herself out of curiosity, only to find that the first hit was the Facebook page of a person with the same name whose personal profile was loaded with immature comments. To minimize the chances of being mistaken for someone else, you might include your middle name or initial on your résumé and online.

Don't be scared off.

With all these warnings, you may be tempted to avoid having a digital footprint at all. That's probably unwise. About 7 in 10 employers check out candidates online, and nearly 6 in 10 are reluctant to interview people who have no online presence.[20] The odds are that cultivating an impressive and honest online identity will work in your favor.

Don't stop when you get hired.

Your social media conduct remains important after you are on the job. Never post information that disparages your employer or clients, reveals confidential information, or makes you (hence your employer) look bad.[21] "People are looking," cautions a hiring manager.[22]

TIPS & REMINDERS

6 Steps to Follow When Applying for a Job

The average employer forms an impression of a candidate within a few seconds of looking at their cover letter and résumé, says recruiter Susan Kihn.[23] Here are some strategies for presenting yourself in the best (most accurate) light.

1. **Create a high-quality résumé.**

   A good résumé provides a snapshot of your professional strengths and achievements. Since employers sometimes keep applications on file for the future, be sure to include a permanent phone number and email address. You might use the sample résumé in Figure 10.2 as a content guide, but keep in mind that there are different formats for different purposes. Consult with your school's career services center or type "create résumé" into your favorite search engine to see various options.

2. **Write a confidence-inspiring cover letter.**

   As one expert put it, a cover letter is "an introduction, a sales pitch, and a proposal for further action all in one."[24] Write a letter that provides a brief summary of your interests and experience. The sample cover letter in Figure 10.1 may be useful.

   - If possible, direct your letter to a specific person. (Be sure to get the spelling and title correct.)
   - Indicate the position you are applying for and introduce yourself.
   - Briefly describe your accomplishments as they apply to qualities and duties listed in the job posting.
   - Demonstrate your knowledge of the company and your interest in the job.
   - State the next step you hope to take—usually a request for an interview.
   - Conclude by expressing appreciation to the reader for considering you.

Many employers put cover letters and résumés that include typos or grammatical errors in the 'no' stack.

3. **Edit your materials thoroughly.**

   Many employers put cover letters and résumés that include typos or grammatical errors in the "no" stack. If possible, have a staff member at your school's career center critique your materials. The final documents should be clear, honest, succinct, and free of errors.

4. **Make your materials easily searchable.**

   Many companies use software to electronically scan cover letters and résumés to help identify the most appealing candidates. This software is most likely to spot your qualifications if your materials include words (spelled correctly) that are relevant to job qualifications and if the format you use is easily scannable. Résumés with complicated or unusual design elements may throw off electronic scanners and knock you out of the running. To make your materials most searchable, experts suggest uploading files that use a simple format, a mainstream font (e.g., Arial, Times Roman, Helvetica), and a text-based format such as .doc or .docx.[25,26]

5. **Follow application instructions.**

   There are stories of candidates who do something so unusual that it catches a hiring manager's attention, but it's more likely that failing to follow instructions will create a bad impression. If the posting asks you to submit your materials in PDF format, don't send them as a Google document. If the announcement says "no phone calls," then don't call. As one recruiter puts it: "If you can't follow clear, simple directions, how can I trust that you will be able to give great attention to the details of your job?"[27]

6. **Keep organized records of your communication.**

   Keep a log of everyone you communicate with. Include contact information, when the message was sent or received, and what it was about. Save copies of all written correspondence for future reference.

Preparing for a Job Interview

LEARNING OBJECTIVE 10.4: Prepare to make a good impression during employment interviews.

A successful job interview can be a life-changing experience. It's worth preparing for carefully.

This section offers experts' suggestions for engaging in a **selection interview**—a question and answer session during which a candidate's qualifications are considered. Employment interviews are the most common type of selection interviews, but the same principles apply if you are being considered for a promotion, an award, a scholarship, admission to a graduate program, or another opportunity.

Do research.

Displaying your knowledge of an organization in an interview is a terrific way to show potential employers that you are a motivated and savvy person. In some organizations, failure to demonstrate familiarity with the organization or job is an automatic disqualifier. Along with what you've learned from informational interviews, research the company and industry in advance. Prepare questions about the impact of new regulations on the horizon, recent market shifts, industry innovations, and the like. You are likely to learn a lot and impress the employer in the process.

Prepare for likely questions.

Regardless of the organization and job, most interviewers have similar concerns, which they explore with similar questions. One of the toughest questions to answer is "What is your greatest weakness?"

Whatever response you give, try to show how awareness of your flaws makes you a desirable person to hire. Here are four ways you might respond, but keep in mind that there are endless possibilities. Be sure your answers reflect your own experiences.

- *Describe a weakness that can also be viewed as a strength.* You might say, "When I'm involved in a big project I tend to work too hard, and I can wear myself out."
- *Point out a weakness that seems unrelated to the job and then focus on a strength.* That might sound something like this: "I'm not very interested in accounting. I'd much rather work with people selling a product I believe in."
- *Discuss a weakness the interviewer already knows about.* "I don't have a lot of experience in multimedia design at this early stage of my career. But based on my experience in computer programming and my internship in graphic arts, I know that I can learn quickly."

- *Reference a weakness you have been working to remedy.* "I know being bilingual is important for this job. That's why I've enrolled in a Spanish course."

Some interviewers also ask nontraditional questions to see how well candidates think on their feet, how they handle problems, and how creative they are.[28] Some examples of nontraditional questions include:

> *If you could have any superpower, what would it be?*
>
> *Name five uses for a stapler with no staples in it.*
>
> *If you were a sweater, what kind would you be?*

If asked one of these, it's important to maintain your composure and use your answers to demonstrate qualifications you would like to showcase. For example, one response to the sweater question might be, "I would be attractive but not flashy, so I would have value over time. I would be flexible, so I could be used in many different situations." Notice that the attributes of the sweater would make the candidate a good person to hire.

You may be asked or allowed to make a digital presentation. See "Tips & Reminders: 7 Strategies for Creating a Presentation About Yourself" for guidance.

Know when and where to go.

Don't sabotage an interview before it begins by showing up late. Be sure you're clear about the time and location of the meeting. Research parking or public transportation to be sure you aren't held up by delays. Even if the interviewer is forgiving, a bad start is likely to shake your confidence and impair your performance.

Practice reframing anxiety as enthusiasm.

Feeling anxious about a job interview is natural. Managing your feelings calls for many of the same strategies as managing your apprehension while giving a speech (see Chapter 13). Realize that a certain amount of anxiety is understandable. If you can reframe those feelings as *excitement* about the prospect of landing a great job, the energy can work to your advantage. •

PAUSE TO REFLECT *What Do You Have to Offer?*

1. Find a posting for a job you would like to have one day. What talents and experiences make you a good candidate for the position? ______________________________

2. What can do you to increase your chances of being hired and then succeeding in the position? ______________________________

3. What would potential employers learn about you if they looked you up online? What might worry them? What might impress them? ______________________________

TIPS & REMINDERS

7 Strategies for Creating a Presentation About Yourself

Ask in advance if a brief presentation about your qualifications and experience would be welcome, and if so, follow the advice here to present yourself most favorably.[29,30]

1. **Be audience oriented.**
   Ask who will be present at the interview and what information is most important to them.

2. **Consider technology needs.**
   If the interview is in person, inquire in advance if a projector (and speakers, if necessary) are available in the interview room, or if you might bring your own. Many university media centers or libraries will allow you to check out portable projectors. If the interview will occur via technology, investigate how you might best share your presentation that way.

3. **Follow the principles of good public speaking.**
   Before putting content together, read Chapters 12 through 14 for guidance on creating a professional-quality presentation, such as beginning with an attention getter, developing clear points, presenting strong evidence, and ending memorably.

4. **Focus on relevant accomplishments.**
   The bottom line is how well your talents and accomplishments fit the needs of the organization. Without embellishing, demonstrate with clear evidence how you embody desired qualifications.

5. **Be brief.**
   Your presentation should occupy a small fraction of the time available for the interview. Present yourself clearly and concisely, with professionalism and enthusiasm.

6. **Make your visuals simple.**
   Keep wording to a minimum and use photos, graphics, and video (if applicable) that are professional and simple. If the position involves projects, you might include a brief video clip of you engaged in a professional-quality effort or a photo of the same overlaid with the words "Project Management Experience." Use your spoken words to convey the details.

7. **Practice!**
   Rehearse many times in advance, using a mirror and/or recording device to see how you sound and look to others. Practicing will allow you to speak without notes in a conversational tone during the actual presentation.

PAUSE TO REFLECT *What Should You Include in a Presentation About Yourself?*

1. How might you begin your presentation in an attention-getting way that sets a positive tone and previews what you will cover? ______

2. What three main points can you make to show your qualifications for the position? ______

3. What visual elements might you create that are simple, clear, and effective in making your points? ______

Interviewing and the Law

LEARNING OBJECTIVE 10.5: Develop a strategy for responding to illegal interview questions.

When the interviewer asked, "Do you have children?" Monika was caught off guard. She believed the question was an innocent attempt at small talk. The interviewer may not have realized that it's illegal to ask that. All the same, Monika worried that her answer might jeopardize her chances of getting the job.

What might you do in a similar situation? Here are some suggestions.

Know the law.

Going into an interview, it's important to understand the law and your options as an applicant. Most laws about what topics can be covered in job interviews boil down to two simple principles:

- Employers cannot ask questions about a person's race, religion, gender, sexual orientation, disabilities, national origin, or age. Because it's illegal to judge a candidate based on these qualities, they should never be asked.
- Employers may only ask about topics that are related to the job at hand. Examples of illegal questions include those that ask about any unrelated physical impairments you may have, whether you have children, your religion, or your political affiliation.

Prepare in advance.

Despite the law, there's a good chance that interviewers will ask illegal questions. They are probably uninformed rather than malicious. Still, it's a good idea to prepare in advance for how you might respond. Here are several options:

- *Answer without objecting.* You might choose to answer a question even though you know it's unlawful. Recognize, however, that this could open the door for other illegal questions—and perhaps even discrimination in hiring decisions.
- *Point out the irrelevance.* You might say, "I'm not sure how my marital status relates to my ability to excel in this position."
- *Redirect.* Shift the focus away from a question that isn't job related to one that is. "What you've said so far suggests that age is not as important for this position as knowledge of accounting. Can you tell me more about the kinds of accounting that are part of this job?"
- *Refuse.* You have the option to explain politely but firmly that you will not provide the information requested. You might say, "I'd rather not talk about my religion. That's a very private and personal matter for me" or "That question is illegal and not relevant to the job."
- *Withdraw.* Another choice is to end the interview immediately and leave, stating your reasons firmly but professionally. You might say, "I'm uncomfortable with these questions about my personal life, and I don't see a good fit between me and this organization. Thank you for your time."

The option you choose may depend on several factors, including the apparent intent of the interviewer, the nature of the questions, your desire for the job—and finally, your "gut level" of comfort with the whole situation. Knowing your options going in may help you make an effective split-second decision if the need arises.

Interviewing Best Practices

LEARNING OBJECTIVE 10.6: Demonstrate effective job interviewing skills.

Once an interview begins, it's your chance to shine. Present yourself confidently.

Here are some suggestions for doing your best.

Dress for success.

Most interviewers form their opinions about applicants within the first four minutes of conversation, so it makes sense to look your best.[31] No matter what the job or company, be well groomed and neatly dressed, and don't overdo it with makeup or accessories. The proper style of clothing can vary from one type of job or organization to another, so do some research to find out what the standards are. Avoid wearing anything that seems flashy, flirtatious, or frivolous. Being underdressed or wearing inappropriate clothing can be taken as a sign that you don't take the job or the interview seriously.

Bring copies of your résumé and portfolio.

Arrive a few minutes before the appointed time with materials that will help the interviewer learn more about why you are ready, willing, and able to do the job. Bring extra copies of your résumé. If appropriate, also bring copies of your past work, such as reports you have helped prepare, performance reviews by former employers, drawings or designs you have created for work or school, letters of recommendation, and so on. Besides showcasing your qualifications, items such as these demonstrate that you know how to sell yourself. Also bring the names, addresses, and phone numbers of any references you haven't listed in your résumé.

Mind your manners.

It's essential to demonstrate proper business etiquette from the moment you arrive for an interview. Without realizing it, "you may be riding on the elevator with the head of your interview team," advises one business etiquette expert.[32] Turn off your phone before you enter the building, smile at people, put your shoulders back and head up, and don't fiddle with your clothing, hair, or belongings. In short, behave at all times as the sort of engaged, professional, and attentive coworker everyone wants on their team.

When you meet people, demonstrate an attentive listening posture—shoulders parallel to the other person, eyes focused on the speaker, and facial expressions that show you are paying attention. If multiple people are present, be sure to greet all of them and include them in your comments and eye contact throughout the interview.

Follow the interviewer's lead.

Let the interviewer set the tone of the session. Along with topics and verbal style, pay attention to nonverbal cues such as the interviewer's posture, gestures, vocal qualities, and so on. If they are informal, you can loosen up a bit too, but if the interviewer is formal and proper, you should act the same way.

Keep your answers succinct and specific.

It's easy to ramble in an interview, either out of enthusiasm, a desire to show off your knowledge, or nervousness. But in most cases, long answers are not a good idea. Generally, it's better to keep your responses concise, but provide specific examples to support your statements.

Describe relevant challenges, actions, and results.

Most sophisticated employers realize that past performance can be the best predictor of future success. For that reason, many of them engage in **behavioral interviews**—question and answer sessions that focus on the applicant's past performance (behavior) as it relates to the job at hand. Typical behavioral questions include the following:

- Describe a time you needed to work as part of a team.
- Tell me about a time when you had to think on your feet to handle a challenging situation.
- Describe a time when you were faced with an ethical dilemma and discuss how you handled it.

When asked behavioral questions, answer in a way that shows the prospective employer how your past performance demonstrates your ability to handle the job you are now seeking. "Tips & Reminders: 8 Ways to Respond to Common Interview Questions" provides some useful strategies.

Ask good questions of your own.

Near the end of the interview, you will probably be asked if you have any questions. You might feel as if you already know the important facts about the job, but as we mentioned before, asking questions can yield useful information and show the interviewer that you have done your research. In addition to questions about the organization, here are some that often work well:

- What are the primary results you would like to see me produce?
- What is the biggest challenge or opportunity facing your team now?
- How would you describe the management style I could expect from my supervisors?

It's important to note that most experts feel that it's bad form to ask about salary or benefits during a selection interview unless you are offered the position. You'll have a chance to negotiate after an offer is made.

Follow up after the interview.

Send a prompt, sincere, and personalized note of thanks. A thoughtful and well-written thank-you message can set you apart from other candidates, whereas failing to send one can eliminate you from the running.

- Express your appreciation for the chance to become acquainted with the interviewer(s) and the organization.
- Explain why you see a good fit between you and the job, highlighting your demonstrated skills.
- Let the interviewer know that the conversation left you excited about the chance of being associated with the organization.

Since employment decisions may be made quickly, send a gracious thank-you email the same day as your interview. One recruiter suggests sending the email after 5 p.m., because "by sending the note after working hours you are intimating that you go the extra mile no matter what."[33] In some circumstances, you might also send a handwritten message of thanks. Reread everything you write carefully several times before sending it, and if possible, have a skilled proofreader review it too. One job seeker ruined her chances of employment by mentioning the "report" (instead of "rapport") that she felt with the interviewer. ●

TIPS & REMINDERS

 Ways to Respond to Common Interview Questions

Following are some of the most challenging interview questions asked by potential employers. Review experts' tips for answering them effectively and then brainstorm how you might respond based on your own expectations and career goals.

1. **Tell me something about yourself.**
   This broad opening question gives you a chance to describe which of your qualities (e.g., enthusiasm, self-motivation, good listening skills) can best help the employer. Keep your answer focused on the job for which you are applying. This isn't a time to talk about irrelevant hobbies, your family, or pet peeves.

2. **What makes you think you're qualified to work for this company?**
   This question may sound like an attack, but it's really another way of asking, "How can you help us?" In answering, show how your skills and interests fit with the company's goals. Prepare in advance by making a table with three columns: in one, list your main qualifications; in the next, list specific examples of each qualification; and in the last, explain how these qualifications would benefit the employer.

3. **What accomplishments have given you the most satisfaction?**
   Your accomplishments might demonstrate creativity, perseverance, self-control, dependability, or other desirable attributes. The accomplishments you describe should demonstrate qualities that would help you succeed in the job.

Employers are impressed by candidates who have done their homework about the organization.

4. **Why do you want to work for us?**
   Employers are impressed by candidates who have done their homework about the organization. This offers you the chance to demonstrate your knowledge of the organization and to show how your talents fit with the organization's goals.

5. **Where do you see yourself in five years?**
   This often-posed query is really asking: "How ambitious are you?" "How well do your plans fit with this company's goals?" and "How realistic are you?" Answer in a way that shows you understand the industry and the company. Share your ambitions, but also make it clear that you're willing to work hard to achieve them.

6. **What major challenges have you faced, and how have you dealt with them?**
   What (admirable) qualities have you demonstrated as you have grappled with problems in the past? Perseverance? Calmness? Creativity? The specific problems aren't as important as the way you responded to them. You may even choose to describe a problem you didn't handle well to show how the lessons you learned can help you in the future.

7. **What are your greatest strengths?**
   Link what you say to the job. "I'm a pretty good athlete" isn't persuasive in itself, but you might talk about being a team player, having competitive drive, or having the ability to work hard and not quit in the face of adversity.

8. **What are your salary requirements?**
   Do advance research to determine the prevailing compensation rates in the industry and in your region. Name a salary range and back up your numbers with reasons you think you would be a valuable member of the team. Shooting too high can knock you out of consideration, whereas shooting too low can cost you dearly.

Interviewing by Phone or Video

LEARNING OBJECTIVE 10.7: Effectively prepare for phone or video employment interviews.

In an age when budgets are tight, communication technology is pervasive, and work teams are geographically distributed, it's no surprise that a growing number of interviews are conducted via phone and video conference.

All of the guidelines discussed previously apply to mediated interviews. In addition, the following tips can help you succeed when communication technology is involved.

Present a professional identity.

Your screen name, if you are using one, should be professional and appropriate, not provocative or edgy. Likewise, pay attention to what you wear if it's a video conference. Even if you're at home, dress professionally. In addition, think about what will show behind you. A neutral backdrop (real or virtual) without distractions is ideal. Also minimize background noise. A barking dog or noisy roommate won't increase your odds of impressing a potential employer.

Practice with technology in advance.

Tech problems can end a distance interview before it begins. Follow these tips to ensure that you are ready:

- Make sure you have the right software and are comfortable using it.
- Confirm that you have a solid internet connection with enough speed to handle the conversation.
- Double-check your camera, microphone, and speakers to confirm that they function properly.
- Make sure lighting is sufficient to allow people at the other end to see you clearly. The light source should shine on your face rather than the back of your head (which will cast you in shadow).
- If you're using a phone or tablet, use a stand to avoid distracting jiggles.
- Make sure the camera is at eye level. Looking down is unflattering and can make it seem that you aren't paying attention.

Ensure that you have the right time for the interview.

There's nothing worse than being an hour late. Confirm the time in advance, especially when different time zones are involved (if unsure, search the web for "world clock"). You might send a message such as, "I look forward to speaking with you next Tuesday, March 12, at 8 a.m. Pacific/11 a.m. Eastern."

Ask in advance how long the interview will last.

"Long distance interviews are sometimes meant to be a brief candidate introduction, not a thorough vetting session," says one job search coach. She advises, "If this is the case, be prepared to make the most of this brief first impression!"[34]

Look at the camera, not at the screen.

Looking at your monitor or another device may be tempting, but it will create the impression that you aren't making eye contact with the interviewer. Instead, look directly at the camera. Also remember to smile.

Conduct a dress rehearsal.

Practicing is the best way to ensure that you are prepared. Recruit a trusted friend (or, even better, someone at your school's career center) to play the role of interviewer. Be sure to practice under the actual circumstances of the interview—remotely and with the same equipment and services you'll use for the real thing. Besides ironing out potential glitches, rehearsals should leave you feeling more confident.

Don't panic if technology fails.

Even when you have done everything possible to prepare, technological difficulties can arise. In that case, don't panic. If your online connection is interrupted and you cannot get back to the meeting, immediately call or email the interviewer to explain what's happening. And take heart: Your calm demeanor and quick response may signal to the employer that you will be effective in other tough situations as well.

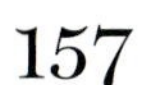

Rose Magnon
[mailing address]
[permanent phone number]
[permanent email address]

January 28, 2022

Renée Robinson, Executive Director
International Society for the Advancement of Children
2525 West 37th Avenue
Landersville, MD 55555

Dear Ms. Robinson,

I am interested in the public relations assistant position at the International Society for the Advancement of Children, as advertised in The *Philanthropy Newsletter*. As the attached résumé shows, I currently serve as a Communication Coordinator at the University of East Florida, in which position I have gained experience that would allow me to make significant contributions to your organization and its mission.

I believe I would be effective in the public relations assistant position at ISAC for three main reasons.

- I am a skilled communicator who crafts messages carefully and adapts well to different audiences and formats. I currently author several newsletters, each designed to reach a specific stakeholder group. I also curate content on numerous social media platforms including Facebook, Instagram, and Twitter. I believe my success in these endeavors would allow me to recruit sponsors for ISAC, coordinate and publicize ISAC events, such as your annual Children's Festival, and share your success stories.
- I have demonstrated success in fundraising. As a volunteer workplace campaign manager, I coordinated fundraising efforts involving 100 volunteers. The result was a portfolio worth more than $800,000. I would enjoy the chance to help coordinate and promote your semiannual Education for All event and other fundraisers.
- I am an accomplished speaker who enjoys interacting with audiences of all sizes. In the last few years, I have won a regional Toastmasters Competition and ranked in the Top 3 at state collegiate debate and forensics tournaments. I would like to use this skill at conferences and civic events to share stories about the good work that ISAC does.

I became interested in the International Society for the Advancement of Children while working on an international project with United Way. I particularly admire your efforts to provide education to children in impoverished areas of the world. My career goal is to coordinate collaborative humanitarian efforts, and I would be honored by the chance to help with the good work that you do.

I have attached my résumé, which includes links to my online portfolio and my LinkedIn profile, where you can see samples of my work. I hope you will consider me for the assistant public relations position. I am available for an interview at your convenience. Thanks very much for your consideration.

Sincerely,
Rose Magnon

FIGURE 10.1 Sample Cover Letter

Rose Magnon

[mailing address]
[permanent email address]
[permanent phone number]
[URLs for online portfolio, LinkedIn page, or other online presence]

PROFILE AND GOALS

I am experienced in using social media to promote mutually beneficial collaborations in the community and with members of other cultures. I hope to pursue a career in the nonprofit sector coordinating humanitarian efforts and securing funding for international partnerships.

EDUCATION

University of East Florida, Oceanview, FL
B.A. in Communication/Public Relations and Minor in Marketing expected in May 2022, 3.86 GPA

EMPLOYMENT EXPERIENCE

Communication Coordinator, University College of Arts, Social Sciences, and Humanities 2019 to present

- Responsible for internal and external college and departmental communication, including production of semi-annual dean's report, social media management, creation and distribution of monthly newsletter, and university/community lecture series.

Director of Student Recruitment (temporary contract) January to August 2018

- Led nationwide marketing effort to recruit university accounting majors to take part in a new online employment platform. My efforts helped to attract 50 new students in 8 months.

ACTIVITIES & VOLUNTEER EXPERIENCE

Co-Chair of Cultural Team for United Way Global Resident Fellowship Program October to December 2019

- Developed partnerships with United Way organizations in Western Australia, France, and South Africa. Wrote influential whitepaper detailing lessons learned and recommendations for future programs.

Workplace Campaign Manager August 2011 to March 2015

- Managed $830,000 workplace campaign portfolio representing 120+ accounts with 130 volunteers. Secured new sponsorships and developed sponsorship campaign materials.

ASSOCIATION MEMBERSHIPS

- Oceanview Young Professionals, Government Affairs Council, 2016 to 2017
- Florida Public Relations Society of America, 2015 to present
- University of East Florida Forensics and Debate Team, 2016 to present

HONORS & AWARDS

- Top 3 finalist in Florida's State Collegiate Debate and Forensic Competition, 2008 and 2009
- Toastmasters Regional Impromptu Speaking Contest, 1st place 2019
- Dean's and President's List every semester since entering college in 2018

FIGURE 10.2 Sample Résumé

Communicating to Land a Job

Good Communicators . . .

- Work well in teams.
- Enhance customer satisfaction.
- Build public awareness.
- Make good leaders.
- Inspire others.

Networking Strategies

- Look for networking prospects.
- Engage in online networking.
- Seek referrals.
- Conduct informational interviews.
- Show appreciation.

Managing Your Online Identity

- Showcase your strengths and goals.
- Build a professional identity.
- Avoid embarrassing posts.
- Monitor your online presence.
- Engage in damage control.
- Beware mistaken identities.
- Don't be scared off.
- Don't stop when you get hired.

6 Steps When Applying for a Job

- Create a high-quality résumé.
- Write a confidence-inspiring cover letter.
- Edit your materials thoroughly.
- Make your materials searchable.
- Follow application instructions.
- Keep organized records of your communication.

Preparing for a Job Interview

- Do research.
- Prepare for likely questions.
- Know when and where to go.
- Reframe anxiety as enthusiasm.

Interviewing and the Law

- It's illegal to ask job candidates about their race, religion, gender, sexual orientation, disabilities, national origin, or age.
- Questions must relate to the job at hand.
- If asked an illegal question, you might answer, redirect the topic, refuse to answer, or leave the interview.

Interviewing Best Practices

- Dress for success.
- Bring copies of your résumé and portfolio.
- Mind your manners.
- Follow the interviewer's lead.
- Keep your answers succinct and specific.
- Describe relevant challenges, actions, and results.
- Ask good questions of your own.
- Follow up after the interview.

Interviewing by Phone or Video

- Present a professional identity.
- Practice with technology.
- Ensure that you have the right time for the interview.
- Ask in advance how long the interview will last.
- Look at the camera, not at the screen.
- Conduct a dress rehearsal.
- Don't panic if technology fails.

Show Your Communication Know-How

10.1: Describe the reasons why good communicators are likely to excel in the workplace.

Describe the best customer service experience you have ever had. What role did communication play in making it memorable?

10.2: Engage in networking behaviors conducive to finding a job that matches your skills.

Make a list of several people you might interview to learn more about your dream job. Then brainstorm a list of questions you might ask them.

KEY TERMS: networking, informational interview

10.3: Cultivate an online identity that appeals to prospective employers.

Search for your name on Google, Yahoo!, and several other search engines. Do you feel that the photos and information revealed by the search would impress prospective employers? If not, how might you change your online image to be more professional? If nothing much shows up about you online, how might you cultivate a greater presence?

KEY TERM: digital dirt

10.4: Prepare to make a good impression during employment interviews.

Brainstorm a list of questions you might ask a prospective employer to show that you understand the industry and organization and are a good candidate for your dream job.

KEY TERM: selection interview

10.5: Develop a strategy for responding to illegal interview questions.

You are in the middle of an interview for a job you really want when the interviewer asks, "Are you married?" or another illegal question. You're afraid your answer might hurt your chances of getting the job. How might you respond?

10.6: Demonstrate effective job interviewing skills.

Rehearse how you might respond to the following questions in a job interview: Why should we hire you? What have been your greatest challenges and victories? What do you want to be doing in five years? What is a difficult problem you have faced in a past job, and how did you handle it.

KEY TERM: behavioral interviews

10.7: Effectively prepare for phone or video employment interviews.

Imagine you're being interviewed via videoconference for a job. List the necessary steps to ensure that the technology will run smoothly. Rehearse how you might respond to the question, "Tell us more about yourself." Remember to pay attention to your posture, facial expressions, and where your gaze falls. Do you feel well prepared for a video interview? Why or why not?

11 COMMUNICATING IN the Workplace

Communication Mistakes to Avoid at Work

LEARNING OBJECTIVE 11.1: Identify and avoid communication blunders at work.

Whereas good communication skills can enhance your career success, some communication behaviors should be on your never-do list at work.

Congratulations! You've landed the job. Now it's time to live up to expectations. No matter what career you have chosen, communicating effectively is a key to success. **Social intelligence** is the capacity to behave appropriately in a range of social relationships and environments, including professional settings.[1] Before we consider how social intelligence can help you communicate effectively in the workplace, it may be helpful to consider what *not* to do. Here are some common blunders to avoid.

Making Fun of People

Some people learn this lesson the hard way. When two women walked into the diner where he worked, Rik wisecracked to a coworker: "Oh look! Fat old ladies in baseball caps!"[2] Then he realized that they were his coworker's mother and aunt. Rik's colleague forgave him, but he says he learned a valuable lesson and swore off insensitive humor forever. It's a good idea. Wisecracks at someone else's expense can be hurtful in any situation. At work, they can be cause for a reprimand, dismissal, or even a lawsuit.

Oversharing

It may seem important to "be yourself," but there are times when disclosing information about your personal life can damage your chances for professional success—or at the very least, annoy people.[3] The "don't overshare" rule applies to online communication, too. Photos of your wild vacation aren't likely to impress your boss, clients, or colleagues. The best rule is to disclose cautiously, especially if the topic is a sensitive one such as religion, political views, or romantic relationships.[4] A trusted colleague may be able to offer advice about how much to share.

Overlooking Cultural Differences

Many Americans display what researchers call "instant intimacy."[5] They often address even new acquaintances, elders, and authority figures by first name. They engage in a great deal of eye contact, touch their conversational partners, and ask personal questions. To people from different backgrounds, these behaviors may seem disrespectful. An Australian exchange student in the United States reflected on her experience this way: "There seemed to be a disproportionate amount of really probing conversations. Things I normally wouldn't chat about on a first conversation."[6] Review Chapter 3 for more guidance on being culturally considerate.

Gossiping

Communicating with integrity isn't always easy. The culture in some organizations involves gossiping, bad-mouthing, and even lying about others. Nevertheless, effective communication means following your own set of principles. It may be helpful to know if someone was promoted, reprimanded, or fired, and why—but malicious gossip can mark you as untrustworthy and can damage team spirit.[7] One executive proposed this test: Before you start talking, stop and ask yourself, "Is it kind?"[8]

Doing Less Than Your Best

You may have heard the phrase "don't sweat the small stuff." In fact, making a good impression requires paying attention to every detail. Show up for work looking as good as you did in the job interview. Another way to stand out is to do more than is required.[9] For example, you might finish a project sooner than anticipated, volunteer to assist with other tasks, offer to deliver a presentation, or tackle a project that keeps getting delayed. The

time that jobs like this take may be worth the good reputation they earn you. If you're frustrated by someone else who is doing less than their best, "Tips & Reminders: 10 Ways to Get Slackers to Do Their Share" presents some strategies that may help.

Losing Your Cool

Patricia is so furious with members of her project group that she sends out an angry group message calling them lazy and irresponsible. Later, she wishes she had handled the situation differently. Losing control under pressure can jeopardize work relationships, your reputation, and your career. "You can't put lava back in the volcano," advises consultant Mark Jeffries.[10] Even if you are usually calm and polite, no one is likely to forget the time you stormed out of a meeting or raised your voice. And if your freak-out takes the form of an email or text, there's a transcript of it that may never go away. To stay collected when you feel yourself getting agitated, take a few deep breaths or a break, and stop to listen and ask questions before responding.[11] And never vent about work-related matters on social media.

Fixating on a Mistake

What if you accidentally say "I love you" while ending a call with your boss? Or your eyes fill with tears during a stressful business meeting? Minor lapses in professionalism are bound to occur, even among people who have been in the workplace for many years. You can usually recover your dignity and your reputation by following these four steps: don't panic, acknowledge the gaffe, apologize, and return to life as usual.[12] For example, you might say, "Sorry about that! I'm in the habit of saying 'I love you' when I talk to my family. Obviously, I didn't mean to end our call that way. I'll be more careful in the future." It's okay to laugh if the other person does, but don't dwell on the mistake. You want other people's opinion of you to be centered on your impressive performance, not on your goof. •

TIPS & REMINDERS

10 Ways to Get Slackers to Do Their Share

Experts offer the following suggestions to make sure everyone on your team does their fair share of the work.[13,14,15]

1. **Focus on the endgame.**
   True motivation arises from a sense of working together toward an important goal.
2. **Match the goal to the group size.**
   Make sure group size and talent match the nature of the task. Lazy behavior is more likely when more people than necessary are involved.
3. **Establish clear goals and responsibilities.**
   Draft a clear action plan to make sure that group members know what's expected of them.
4. **Provide training.**
   Make sure everyone has the training and tools to deliver.
5. **Hold people accountable.**
   Ask team members to regularly share their accomplishments.
6. **Focus on quality.**
   Agree on clear guidelines for high-quality work, and offer feedback at every step.
7. **Ask why.**
   If team members fall behind, ask them why.
8. **Don't overlook poor performance.**
   All team members need to pull their weight, or others may begin to slack off as well.
9. **Guard against burnout.**
   Pay attention to members' emotional states and energy levels to make sure that unrealistic demands aren't sapping their strength.
10. **Celebrate successes.**
    Make sure that even low-visibility tasks are rewarded with praise and recognition.

PAUSE TO REFLECT *How Would You Handle This Communication Mistake?*

1. What advice do you have for Patricia now that she has already sent out the angry group text, and what advice would you offer her teammates who received it?

2. What communication strategies might you suggest so the team can better deal with this conflict and others in the future?

Communication Strategies for Leaders

LEARNING OBJECTIVE 11.2: Demonstrate effective leadership skills based on the situation, goals, and team members' needs.

Think of a leaderless group to which you've belonged. Who did members look to for guidance and direction?

"If you want to become a leader, don't wait for the fancy title or the corner office," advises human resources expert Amy Gallo. "You can begin to act, think, and communicate like a leader long before that promotion."[16] With that in mind, let's consider answers to some essential points about leadership.

Characteristics of Effective Leaders

It may seem that the best leaders are brimming with charisma and self-importance, but leaders who achieve long-term success are not usually like that.[17,18] To the contrary, most are remarkably humble. They are content to let others take the spotlight and quick to say that they are still learning and growing. Leaders as diverse as corporate titans Bill Gates and Warren Buffett, and civil rights heroes Rosa Parks and Nelson Mandela, won hearts and minds through their ideas and actions, not their commanding personalities.

In nearly every environment, successful leaders embody the following characteristics, mostly involving good communication skills:[19]

- good listening
- open to innovation
- able to work well with teams
- skillful at facilitating change
- appreciative of diversity
- honest and ethical

Trait Theories of Leadership

Trait theories of leadership suggest that some people are born with qualities that will make them good leaders, but others are not. In reality, leaders of any personality type can be effective, and the leadership skills people acquire are typically more important than anything they are born with.[20]

Situational Leadership

Most contemporary scholarship supports the principle of **situational leadership**, which holds that a leader's style should change with the circumstances.[21] Those who exercise situational leadership consider the nature of the task, including how prepared team members are to accomplish it, and the team involved, including their relationships with each other and with the leader.[22] The **Managerial Grid** developed by Robert Blake and Jane Mouton (Figure 11.1) portrays leadership on the basis of these two considerations: low to high emphasis on tasks, and low to high emphasis on relationships.[23,24] Here are the management approaches portrayed in the model.

- *Impoverished managers* have little interest in either tasks or relationships. It probably won't surprise you that this approach isn't usually effective.
- *Country club managers* exhibit high regard for relationships but little emphasis on accomplishing tasks. This can be successful, but only if the team is well prepared and highly motivated.

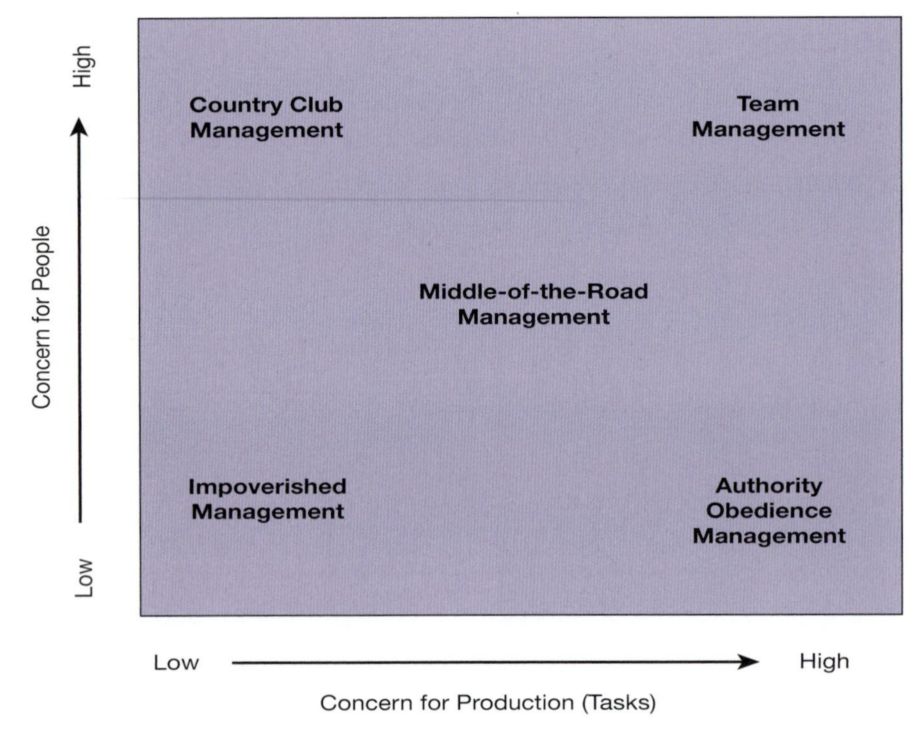

FIGURE 11.1 Managerial Grid

- *Authority-obedience managers* focus almost entirely on tasks and very little on relationships. These types of leaders like to call the shots. This can be useful in emergencies, as when inexperienced team members are handling crises. But over time, most team members prefer to be treated as unique individuals with talents and ideas of their own. Plus, change happens so quickly in today's environment that centralized decision making is usually too slow.
- *Middle-of-the-road managers* display a moderate interest in both tasks and relationships. They're not usually horrible leaders, but they're not great either.
- *Team managers* are typically the most successful of all. They exhibit high regard for both tasks and relationships. This approach has a great deal in common with transformational leadership.

Transformational Leadership

Transformational leadership is defined by leaders' devotion to helping teams fulfill their full potential.[25] Here are the central assumptions of transformational leadership:

- *People want to make a difference.* Transformational leaders believe that if the right people are on board, they will be motivated to accomplish important goals. Therefore, these leaders cultivate strong teams, actively listen to members, consider their feelings, and honor their contributions.
- *Empowerment is essential.* Transformational leaders aren't micromanagers who feel they have all the answers. Instead, they know that the best results come from well-prepared team members with the talent, training, and authority to make most decisions for themselves. The motto of transformational leaders could be, "It's not about me. It's about the *team* and what we accomplish together."
- *Mission is the driving force.* Transformational leaders expect 100 percent effort from everyone on the team because, otherwise, teams cannot live up to their full potential or accomplish their mission.
- *Transparency is key.* Although transformational leaders empower team members to make decisions for themselves as much as possible, when a tough decision is needed, these leaders aren't afraid to make it.[26] In those circumstances, they listen to diverse viewpoints, weigh all the factors, and when they announce a decision, they explain *why* they made it.[27]

It's probably clear that transformational leadership isn't easy. It requires putting one's ego aside and focusing on the team and the mission. Because they are willing to make tough calls, transformational leaders aren't popular with everyone all the time, but even in tough times, team members typically hold these leaders in high regard as being effective, trustworthy, and fair.[28]

Behaviors That Demonstrate Leadership Potential

The following behaviors are good ways to show others that you have strong leadership potential.

- *Stay engaged.* Getting involved won't guarantee that you'll be recognized as a leader, but failing to speak up will almost certainly knock you out of the running.
- *Demonstrate competence.* Make sure your comments identify you as someone who can help the team succeed. Talking for its own sake will only antagonize other members.
- *Be assertive, not aggressive.* It's fine to have a say, but don't try to overpower others. Treat every member's contributions respectfully, even if they differ from yours.
- *Provide solutions in a time of crisis.* How can the team obtain necessary resources? Resolve a disagreement? Meet a deadline? Members who find answers to problems such as these are likely to rise to positions of authority.

ABOUT YOU *What's Your Leadership Style?*

Choose the item in each group that best characterizes your beliefs as a leader.

_______ **1.** I believe a leader's most important job is to:

a. make sure people stay focused on the task at hand.
b. take a hands-off approach so workers can figure things out on their own.
c. make sure the workplace is a friendly environment.
d. help team members build strong relationships so they can accomplish a lot together.

_______ **2.** When it comes to being an employee, I believe that people:

a. accomplish most when leaders set clear expectations.
b. should do their work and let leaders do theirs.
c. are most productive when they are enjoying themselves.
d. have a natural inclination to work hard and do good work.

_______ **3.** As a leader, when a problem arises, I am most likely to:

a. announce a new policy or procedure to avoid the same problem in the future.
b. ignore it; it will probably work itself out.
c. try to smooth things over so no one feels upset about it.
d. ask team members' input on how to solve it.

_______ **4.** If team members were asked to describe me in a few words, I hope they would say that I am:

a. competent and results oriented.
b. removed enough to make decisions without letting my emotions get in the way.
c. pleasant and friendly.
d. respectful and innovative.

_______ **5.** When I see team members talking in the hallway, I am likely to:

a. feel frustrated that they are goofing off.
b. close my door so I can work without interruption.
c. share my latest joke with them.
d. feel encouraged that they get along so well.

INTERPRETING YOUR RESPONSES

For insight about your leadership style, consider which of the following best describes your answers.

Authority-Obedience If most of your answers were "a," you feel that people should stay focused on the job at hand, and you're frustrated by inefficiency and signs that people are "wasting time." The danger is that you will overlook relationships in your zeal to get the job done. This can be counterproductive in the long run since teams often accomplish more than individuals working alone.

Impoverished If the majority of your answers were "b," you tend to take a hands-off approach as a leader, investing neither in relationships nor tasks. You may take pride that you aren't a micromanager, but you're probably going too far in the opposite direction. Team members often need guidance. And even those who work well without much supervision probably crave your attention and appreciation.

Country Club If you selected "c" more than other options, your focus on strong relationships and a pleasant work environment is likely to make you likeable as a person. However, team members may be frustrated by less-than-optimal results. A focus on both relationships *and* tasks may ultimately be more rewarding for everyone involved.

Team or Transformational If you chose "d" most often, you balance an emphasis on results with a respect for the people involved. Although your expectations are high, your support and empowerment are likely to bring out the best in people. Most people consider this to be the ideal leadership style.

Working with a Difficult Boss

LEARNING OBJECTIVE 11.3: Describe strategies for dealing with frustrating leaders.

Sooner or later you're likely to encounter a difficult boss. This person may be unreasonably demanding, blast you with verbal abuse, or engage in passive-aggressive behavior—perhaps being nice to you in person but sabotaging you behind your back. Or your boss may simply be incompetent. What should you do if you encounter such a manager?

While every job and situation is different, here are a few strategies that may help you manage your relationship with a difficult boss.[29]

Rise to the challenge.

Meeting your manager's expectations might make your life easier. If your boss is a micromanager, invite their input. If your boss is a stickler for detail, provide more information than you otherwise would. The extra effort may show your manager that you care and take the job seriously.

Make up for the boss's shortcomings.

If your boss is forgetful, diplomatically remind them of important details. If your boss is disorganized, provide the necessary information before they ask for it.

Seek advice from others.

Gratuitous complaining about your manager is a bad idea. But if other people in your organization have encountered the same problems, you might discover useful information by seeking their advice.

Talk with your boss.

If your best efforts don't solve the problem, consider requesting a meeting with your boss to discuss the situation. Rather than blaming them, use "I" language. For example, "I'm confused when I get different instructions from you and from the division manager" is better than saying, "You aren't following the rules set by your own boss." After explaining how you feel, listen nondefensively to what your boss has to say. Even if you don't like what you hear, you'll know you have given your best effort.

OKAY, STAFF... TELL ME FRANKLY WHAT YOU THINK ABOUT MY SUGGESTION. I WANT TO HEAR YOUR SINCERE OPINIONS. IGNORE THE FACT THAT I CAN FIRE YOU AND THAT I'M EXTREMELY UNFORGIVING.

CartoonStock.com

Maintain a professional demeanor.

Even if your boss has awful interpersonal skills, you'll gain nothing by sinking to the same level. It's best to take the high road, practicing the professional communication skills described elsewhere in this chapter.

Adjust your expectations.

You may not be able to change your boss's behavior, but you can control your attitude about the situation. Sometimes you must accept that there are things over which you have little control. In that case, the challenge is to decide whether you can accept working under less than ideal conditions.

If necessary, make a gracious exit.

If you can't fix an intolerable situation, the smartest approach may be to look for more rewarding employment. If so, leave on the most positive note you can.[30] See "Tips & Reminders: 5 Steps to Leave a Job Without Burning Bridges" for suggestions.

TIPS & REMINDERS

5 Steps to Leave a Job Without Burning Bridges

Many professionals make the mistake of leaving a bad impression when they exit a job. To ensure that a poor reputation and unfavorable reference don't haunt you in the future, follow these steps.[31]

1. **Put it in writing.**

   Write a brief, gracious resignation letter. Include the date you will leave (allow at least two weeks for the transition), a diplomatic explanation for why you are leaving (e.g., "new opportunities for growth"), and a statement of appreciation for what you have learned on the job.

2. **Deliver the news personally.**

   Let the boss know you are leaving before you tell anyone else. If possible, schedule a face-to-face meeting, just the two of you. Give your manager the resignation letter and have a professional and calm discussion together, even if you are leaving under less-than-ideal conditions.

3. **Share the news graciously.**

   Unless instructed otherwise, let your coworkers know you're leaving. When you deliver the news, don't engage in criticism or complaints.

4. **Make the change as easy as possible.**

   Help during the transition. You may be asked to finish key projects, create to-do lists and guides, or train new staff members. Do these things graciously and to the best of your ability as time allows.

5. **Stay positive.**

   Even after you leave, don't complain about your employer. Bad-mouthing your old boss or the company you used to work for won't improve anything, and it's likely to make new colleagues wonder if you might criticize them in the future.

PAUSE TO REFLECT *What Has Shaped Your Leadership Approach?*

1. Think of a leader (either good or bad) who has influenced you in a powerful way. Describe that person's communication style and leadership philosophy. How have they influenced your leadership approach?

2. Describe a difficult decision you have made involving other people. How did you share your decision with the people involved? What communication and leadership lessons did you learn that you can use in the future?

Power in the Workplace

LEARNING OBJECTIVE 11.4: Analyze six types of power in professional settings.

When Omar joined the staff, his great attitude and talent influenced everyone around him. His presence was a good reminder that power is not vested solely in leaders.

Defined as the ability to influence others, **power** comes in many forms. Here are six types of power common in the workplace.[32,33]

Legitimate Power

Legitimate power arises from the title one holds, such as supervisor, professor, or coach. It's sometimes called position power. People with legitimate power are said to be **nominal leaders**. Nominal comes from the Latin word for *name*, meaning that these leaders have been officially named to leadership positions. You can increase your chances of being selected for a leadership role by speaking up without dominating others, demonstrating competence, showing that you respect the group's norms and customs, and gaining the visible support of influential team members.

Expert Power

People have **expert power** when others perceive that they have valuable talents or knowledge. If you're lost in the woods, it makes sense to follow the advice of a group member who has wilderness experience. If your computer crashes at a critical time, you turn to the team member with technical expertise. To gain expert power, make sure that others are aware of your qualifications, be certain to convey accurate information, and don't act as if you are superior to others.

Connection Power

As its name implies, **connection power** comes from a person's ability to develop relationships that help a group reach its goals. For instance, a team seeking guest speakers for a seminar might rely on a well-connected member to line up candidates. To gain connection power, seek out opportunities to meet new people, nurture relationships through open and regular communication, and don't allow petty grievances to destroy valued relationships.

Reward Power

A person with the ability to grant or promise desirable consequences has **reward power**. Rewards come in a variety of forms, including the appreciation you show others. For example, you might offer sincere, positive feedback to a classmate about a presentation they made in class. Your thoughtful words may ultimately be more treasured and memorable than the grade they receive from the instructor.

Coercive Power

The threat or imposition of unpleasant consequences gives rise to **coercive power**. Bosses can coerce members via the threat of a demotion, an undesirable task, or even loss of a job. But peers also possess coercive power. Working with an unhappy, unmotivated teammate can be punishing. For this reason, it's important to keep members feeling satisfied without compromising the team's goals. As a general rule, use rewards as a first resort and punishment as a last resort, make rewards and punishments clear in advance, and be generous with praise.

Referent Power

The basis of **referent power** is the respect, liking, and trust others have for a person. If you have high referent power, you may be able to persuade others to follow your lead because they believe in you or because they're willing to do you a favor. Members acquire referent power by being genuinely likeable and behaving in ways that others in the group admire. To gain referent power, listen to others' ideas and honor their contributions, do what you can to be likable and respected without compromising your principles, and present your ideas clearly and effectively to boost your credibility.

Communication in Small Groups

LEARNING OBJECTIVE 11.5: **Practice communication strategies that minimize the pitfalls and maximize the benefits of groupwork.**

Leaders get a lot of attention, but their influence doesn't count for much without people working together to pursue the vision.

Groups probably play a bigger role in your life than you realize. Some groups are informal, such as friends and family. Others are part of work and school. Project groups, sports teams, and study groups are common types, and you can probably think of more examples that illustrate how central groups are in your life.

Group work can be immensely gratifying or downright miserable.[34] In many cases, the difference comes down to the quality of communication among members. Here are six aspects of group interaction that help explain why some groups succeed and others don't.

Groups are defined by goals and relationships.

For our purposes, a **small group** consists of a limited number of people who interact with one another over time to reach goals. More precisely, small groups embody the following characteristics:

- *Interaction.* Without interaction, a collection of people isn't a group. Students who passively listen to a lecture don't constitute a group until they begin actively to communicate with one another. This is why some students feel isolated even though they spend a great deal of time on a crowded campus.
- *Interdependence.* In groups, members don't just interact—they are interdependent.[35] The behavior of one person affects all the others.[36] When one member behaves poorly, their actions shape the way the entire group functions. On the bright side, positive actions may have ripple effects, too.
- *Time.* A collection of people who interact for a few minutes doesn't qualify as a group. True groups work together long enough to develop a sense of identity and history that shapes their ongoing effectiveness.
- *Size.* Our definition of groups includes the word *small.* Most experts in the field set the lower limit at three members.[37] There is less agreement about the maximum number of people.[38] As a rule of thumb, an effective group is small enough for members to know and react to every other member, and no larger than necessary to perform the task at hand effectively.[39] Small groups usually have between 3 and 20 members.

Group members have different goals.

It's a fact of life that even in high-performing groups, members are never 100 percent in agreement. This is partly because two underlying motives are involved: group goals and individual goals.

- Group goals are the outcomes members collectively seek by joining together. A group goal might be to win a contract, create a product, or provide a service.
- Individual goals are the personal motives of each member. Your individual goals might be to impress the boss, build your résumé, or develop a new skill.

Even when members agree wholeheartedly on the group goal, their individual goals are likely to be somewhat different. That isn't necessarily bad. Sometimes individual goals help the larger group. A colleague seeking an excellent outcome in order to impress the boss will probably help the team excel. However, problems arise when individual motives conflict with the group's goal. Consider a group member who monopolizes the discussion to get attention, or one who engages in **social loafing**—lazy behavior some people use to avoid doing their share of the work.

Groups operate via spoken and unspoken expectations.

All groups have guidelines that govern members' behavior. You can appreciate this by comparing the way you act in class or at work with the way you behave with your friends.

Rules are official guidelines that govern what the group is supposed to do and how the members should behave. They are usually stated outright. In a classroom, rules include how absences will be treated, if late work will be accepted, and so on.

Norms are equally powerful, but they are conveyed by example rather than in words. There are three main types of small group norms.

- **Social norms** govern how members interact with one another (what kinds of humor are and aren't appropriate, how much socializing is acceptable, and so on).
- **Procedural norms** guide operations and decision making ("We always start on time" or "When there's a disagreement, we try to reach consensus before forcing a vote").
- **Task norms** govern how members get the job done ("Does the job

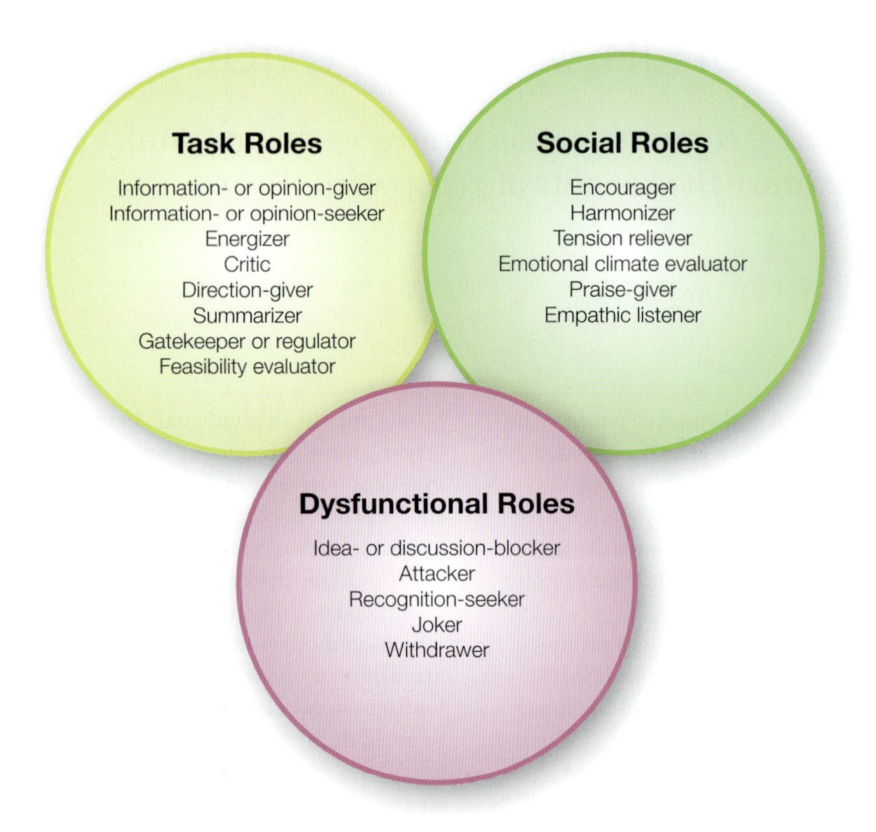

FIGURE 11.2 Roles That Team Members Play

have to be done perfectly, or is an adequate, if imperfect, solution good enough?").

It's important to realize two things about norms. First, a group's norms don't always match what members say is ideal behavior. Consider punctuality. The expectation may be that meetings begin at the scheduled time, but the norm may be to delay for about 10 minutes until everyone arrives. Second, group norms don't emerge immediately or automatically. When people first come together, it's common for them to feel unsure how to behave. Even when groups have been together for a while, members' expectations may not match up perfectly. For example, the group norm may be for members to engage in rousing debates, but some members may wish meetings were calmer and quieter.

Group members play different roles.

Whereas rules and norms establish expectations for how members behave overall, **roles** define patterns of behavior enacted by *particular* members. The next time you see people working in small groups or teams, observe how they behave.

Formal roles are explicitly assigned by an organization or group. They usually come with a label, such as assistant coach, treasurer, or customer service representative. By contrast, **informal roles** (sometimes called "functional roles") are rarely acknowledged by the group in words.[40] Informal group roles fall into two categories: task and social.

- **Task roles** help the group achieve particular outcomes, such as revising workplace policies or hosting an event. Task roles include information seeker, opinion giver, energizer, critic, and so on.
- **Social roles** (also called "maintenance roles") help the relationships among group members run smoothly. For example, someone might encourage shy members to voice their opinions (an encourager), while another might help members with opposing viewpoints reach a consensus (harmonizer).

Not all informal roles are constructive. Some participants may bully others or refuse to participate in offering opinions or ideas. Dysfunctional roles such as these prevent a group from working effectively. As you might expect, research suggests that groups are most effective when people fulfill positive social roles and no one fulfills the dysfunctional ones.[41] See Figure 11.2 for a summary of group roles, good and bad.

Groups develop in stages.

Successful groups often follow a four-stage process when arriving at a decision: orientation, conflict, emergence, and reinforcement.[42] These stages are sometimes characterized as forming, storming, norming, and performing.[43] Knowing them can help curb your impatience and help you feel less threatened when inevitable and necessary conflicts take place.

- In the **orientation (forming) stage**, members approach the problem and one another tentatively. There is little outward disagreement at this stage. Members test out possible ideas cautiously and politely. This doesn't mean that they agree with one another. Rather, they are probably sizing up the situation before asserting themselves.
- After members understand the problem and become acquainted, a successful group enters the **conflict (storming) stage**. Members take strong positions and defend them against those who oppose their viewpoints. Coalitions are likely to form, and the discussion may become polarized. The conflict needn't be personal, however, and it should preserve the members' respect for one another. Even when the climate does grow contentious, conflict seems to be a necessary stage in group development. The give and take of discussion can test

the quality of ideas, and weaker ones may be justly eliminated.[44]

- After a period of conflict, effective groups move to an **emergence (norming) stage**. One idea might emerge as the best one, or the group might combine the best parts of several plans into a new solution. As they approach consensus, members back off from their dogmatic positions. Statements become more tentative again: "That seems like a pretty good idea," "I can see why you think that way."
- Finally, groups may reach the **reinforcement (performing) stage**. At this point, not only do members accept the group's decision, they also endorse it. Even if members disagree with the outcome, they may not voice their concerns at this stage.

Group cohesion boosts commitment. **Cohesiveness** is the degree to which members feel connected with and committed to a group. Compared to groups that lack cohesion, members of highly cohesive groups spend more time interacting and express more positive feelings for one another. They also report more satisfaction and loyalty. Groups can enhance cohesiveness in the following ways.

- *Focus on shared goals.* People draw closer when they share a similar aim or when their goals can be mutually satisfied.
- *Celebrate progress.* While a group is making progress, members tend to feel highly cohesive. But when progress stops, cohesiveness decreases.
- *Minimize competition.* Sometimes strife arises within groups. Perhaps there's a struggle over who will be the leader or decision maker. Whether the threat is real or imagined, the group must neutralize it or face the consequences of reduced cohesiveness.
- *Establish interdependence.* Groups become cohesive when members realize that they must rely on each other to reach their collective goals.
- *Build relationships.* Groups often become close because members like one another. It's a good idea to devote time and energy to building camaraderie and friendship within the group.

Despite the advantages of cohesiveness, it doesn't guarantee success. Members may feel close to one another but not get the job done. You've probably been part of study groups in which the members cared more about hanging out as friends than actually getting down to work. If so, your group was cohesive but not productive.

The suggestions presented here work well with most teams. But occasionally, some team members will try your patience. "Tips & Reminders: 6 Strategies for Dealing with Difficult Team Members" offers some communication strategies that might help.

TIPS & REMINDERS

6 Strategies for Dealing with Difficult Team Members

Sooner or later you'll run across a team member who consistently tests your patience. Perhaps they are whiny, bossy, aloof, aggressive, overly ingratiating, or a know-it-all. Here are some tips from the experts on coping effectively.[45,46]

1. **Keep calm.**
   Some people thrive on goading others and creating drama. Don't play their game.
2. **Look for underlying reasons.**
   Consider what factors might have led the person to feel ignored, hurt, or disrespected.
3. **Talk explicitly about the issue.**
   You might say, "I noticed that you have interrupted me several times. Do you feel that you didn't get a chance to explain your position?"
4. **Lay ground rules.**
   Establishing specific expectations will make it easier to identify and address issues. For example, you might agree that there will be no yelling, interrupting, or maintaining side conversations.
5. **Write down ideas.**
   People may be difficult because they don't feel they're being heard or respected. Write down everyone's ideas on a board or flipchart to capture what people are saying and prevent a potential source of frustration.
6. **Make repercussions clear.**
   When you're coping with a difficult person whose behavior doesn't improve, it's important to be clear about the consequences. This may involve sharing the problem with a boss, or if you have the authority, making the repercussions clear yourself.

Advantages of Group Problem Solving

LEARNING OBJECTIVE 11.6: Assess the advantages of group problem solving.

Groups sometimes get a bad name, yet research consistently shows that, in most cases, groups can produce higher quality solutions than individuals working alone.[47] Here's why.

Groups have more resources than individuals do.

Resources may include space, equipment and supplies, time, interpersonal connections, brain power, and more. Imagine trying to raise money for an important cause. Together, a group is likely to know far more potential contributors than any one person does.

Group members can catch errors.

At one time or another, everyone makes stupid mistakes, like the man who built a boat in his basement and then wasn't able to get it out the door. Working in a group increases the chance that errors like this won't slip by.

Group work enhances buy-in.

Besides coming up with superior solutions, groups may also generate a higher commitment to carrying them out. Members are most likely to accept solutions they have helped create and to work harder to carry out those solutions.

Groups benefit from diverse ideas.

Although people tend to think in terms of "lone geniuses" who make discoveries and solve the world's problems, most breakthroughs are actually the result of collective creativity—people working together to create options no one would have thought of alone.[48]

Groups are best at solving some problems.

Group work isn't always the quickest way to accomplish a task or make a decision. It takes time and effort. But under certain conditions, groups can accomplish more than one person could. Group work is especially effective under the following conditions:[49]

- The job is beyond the capacity of one person.
- Members are in a good position to help one another.
- The issue is important and presents implications for a large number of people.
- There is more than one solution and no easy answer.

Making the Most of Group Meetings

LEARNING OBJECTIVE 11.7: Strategize ways to communicate effectively during group discussions.

Although there are many advantages to group work, even groups with the best of intentions often find themselves unable to reach decisions. At other times, they make decisions that later prove to be wrong.

Though there's no foolproof method of guaranteeing high-quality group work, you can avoid common challenges by using the following approaches.

Encourage equal participation.

Domination by a few vocal or high-status members can reduce a group's ability to solve a problem effectively. You can encourage useful contributions by all members in a variety of ways:

- *Keep the group small.* In groups with three or four members, participation is usually roughly equal, but after the size increases to five or more, there's often a dramatic gap between the contributions of members.[50]
- *Encourage quiet members.* It isn't necessary to go overboard by gushing about a quiet person's brilliant remark, but a word of thanks and acknowledging the value of the person's idea may increase the odds that they will speak up again in the future. You might also assign specific tasks to normally quiet members. The need to report on these tasks guarantees that they will speak up.
- *Ask to hear from other members.* Particularly if one member is talking too much, politely express a desire to hear from others.
- *Question the relevance of off-topic remarks.* If nothing else works, you might say something such as, "I'm sure Saturday's party was awesome! But if we're going to meet the deadline, I think we'd better focus on the task at hand."

Avoid information underload and overload.

Make sure team members know the information and nuances that bear on a problem. At the same time, recognize that too much information makes it hard to sort out what's essential from what isn't. Experts suggest parceling out areas of responsibility.[51] Instead of expecting all members to explore everything about a topic, assign groups to explore particular aspects of it and then share what they learn with the group at large.

Avoid pressure to conform.

If you have ever supported an idea because everyone else seemed to like it or you were tired of debating the issue, you have engaged in **groupthink**, the tendency of some groups to support ideas without challenging them or providing alternatives.[52] The results can range from disappointing to downright tragic.

Groups can minimize the risk of groupthink by adopting the following practices:[53]

- *Recognize the signs of groupthink as they begin to manifest.* If agreement comes quickly and easily, the group may be avoiding a tough but necessary search for alternatives.
- *Minimize status differences.* If the group includes high-status members, they should be careful not to intimidate members into agreeing with them.

- *Develop a group norm that legitimizes disagreement.* After members recognize that questioning one another's positions doesn't signal personal animosity or disloyalty, a constructive exchange of ideas can lead to top-quality solutions.
- *Designate someone to play devil's advocate.* It's this person's job to remind the others about the dangers of groupthink and to challenge group members to consider potentially adverse outcomes of a decision.

Make the most of diversity.

Here are experts' tips for maximizing the benefits and minimizing the challenges of working in multicultural teams:

- *Allow more time than usual.* When members have different backgrounds and perspectives, it can take extra time and effort to understand and appreciate where each person is coming from.
- *Agree on clear guidelines for discussions, participation, and decision making.* If members come to the group with different expectations, it may be necessary to negotiate mutually acceptable ground rules.
- *Use a variety of communication formats.* People may be more or less comfortable speaking to the entire group, putting their thoughts in writing, speaking one on one, and so on. Variety will help everyone have a voice.
- *If possible, involve a distribution of people from various cultures.* Communication is enhanced when people have different perspectives and feel comfortable expressing them.[54]
- *Educate team members about the cultures represented.* People are less likely to make unwarranted assumptions (that a person is lazy, disinterested, overbearing, or so on) if they understand the cultural patterns at play.
- *Open your mind to new possibilities.* Assumptions and too-quick solutions short-circuit the advantage of diverse perspectives.

Even when groups communicate well in person, they may face challenges in a virtual environment. To avoid some common errors, follow the advice in "Tips & Reminders: 9 Ways to Make the Most of Online Meetings."

PAUSE TO REFLECT *How Do You Feel About Group Work?*

1 There are a number of advantages to working in small groups, but there can also be pitfalls. Describe three potential disadvantages of working in small groups. For each, describe a communication strategy you might use to avoid or minimize that disadvantage.

2 Think of the best experience you have had working in a small group. What factors made it a rewarding experience? What role did communication play?

TIPS & REMINDERS

Ways to Make the Most of Online Meetings

Computer-mediated meetings are considered a vital means of communication in 86 percent of North American companies,[55] and the percentage zoomed closer to 100 percent during the COVID-19 pandemic, when a record number of people worked from home. Whether you are new to online meetings or an old pro, these suggestions from the experts are likely to come in handy.

1. **Learn the technology.**

   More than a dozen videoconferencing platforms are in widespread use and more emerge all the time. Familiarize yourself with the technology in advance of a meeting. YouTube is replete with free video tutorials that can help bring you up to speed.

2. **Practice good cybersecurity.**

   To keep meetings secure, require a password to enter, create an electronic waiting room so no one is admitted until the host okays it, and turn off the "join before host" option that might let someone sneak in early.[56]

3. **Set the stage.**

   "Keep in mind that people aren't just seeing you, they're also seeing whatever the camera is pointed at behind you," says tech writer Sean Adams.[57] Keep the area neat and tidy, and whenever possible, limit the presence of other people and pets.

4. **Show your face.**

   Whenever possible, turn on your video camera and let others see you. "In one meeting, I found myself talking to six photographs," laments Ryan, who explains, "The other participants had cameras, but they chose not to use them. I could only wonder if they were actually listening or not." Showing your face is supportive of others, and it shows that you are attentive and engaged. (Make sure lighting is adequate for people to see you clearly.)

5. **Dress head to toe for the camera.**

   Don't be like the telecommuter who logged onto a videoconference wearing a business jacket and pajama pants and then realized once everyone was watching her that she had left important papers on the other side of the room. Dress head to toe for video conferences as you would for in-person meetings.

6. **Develop camaraderie.**

   Communication technology can make it easy to exchange information but hard to make a real connection. Take time to get acquainted with online team members before getting down to business. People tend to be more committed and more accountable when they know their teammates well.[58]

7. **Decide who talks when.**

   Turn-taking cues are less visible online than in person. One strategy is to have participants use a "raised hand" icon or physically hold up a hand when they have something to say. A facilitator can monitor these signals and call on people one by one. The team might also make use of electronic breakout rooms for small group discussions.

8. **Use the mute function wisely.**

   Even relatively quiet sounds add up when everyone's microphone is on. Use the mute function to minimize background noise when you are not speaking. However, be sure to unmute yourself when you speak or laugh. One meeting participant remembers the silence after she told a joke during an online meeting: "No one laughed. Or maybe they did, but everyone was muted. At any rate, I won't do that again."

9. **Pay attention.**

   Although it may be tempting to get other work done during a long-distance meeting, looking away suggests that you are a poor listener and not interested. Position your device so that you can look directly at the camera and display the same listening posture (head up, shoulders back, facing forward) that you would in person.

A Structured Problem-Solving Approach

LEARNING OBJECTIVE 11.8: **Practice the steps involved in systematic problem solving.**

Working through a problem systematically involves a number of steps that help you stop and think, collaborate with others, and consider solutions you might not have thought of otherwise.

In the early 1900s, John Dewey introduced his famous **reflective thinking method**—a systematic, multistep approach to solving problems (Figure 11.3).[59] Since then, other experts have suggested modifications, although it's still generally known as Dewey's method. Although no single approach is best for all situations, a structured procedure usually produces better results than "no pattern" discussions.[60]

Consider the steps described here to be general guidelines, not a precise formula. Depending on the nature of a problem, you may want to focus on some steps more than others.

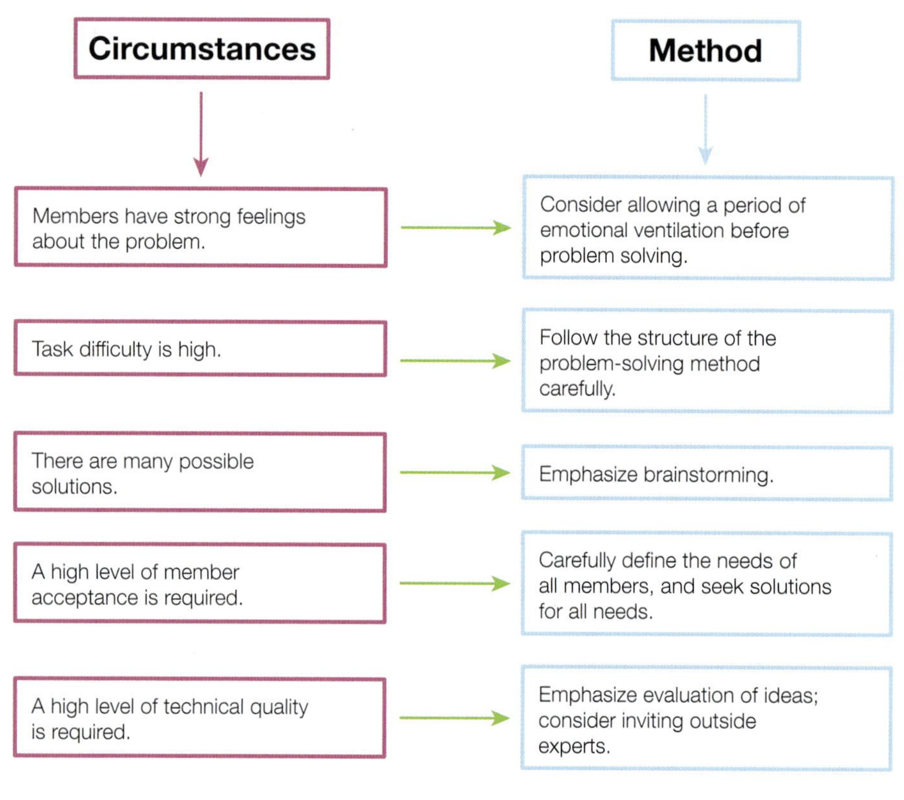

FIGURE 11.3 Problem-Solving Options

Identify the problem.

Sometimes a group's problem is easy to pinpoint. There are many times, however, when the challenge isn't so clear. For example, if a group is meeting to discuss a low-performing employee, it may be helpful to ask why that person is underperforming. It may be because they have personal problems, feel unappreciated by members, or haven't been challenged. The best way to understand a problem is to look below the surface and identify the range of factors that may be involved.

Analyze the problem.

After you have identified the general nature of the problem, examine it in more detail. Word the problem as a broad, open question. For example, if your group is trying to understand why turnover (the number of employees who leave the organization) is high, you might ask yourselves: What factors might be causing employees to feel dissatisfied here? Open-ended questions like this encourage people to contribute ideas and work cooperatively.

Identify criteria for success.

Decide what factors will constitute success. After analyzing the problem, you may set the goal of keeping employee turnover equal to or lower than the norm for your industry. Once you know what you're trying to achieve, you have a better chance of creating goal-oriented solutions and measuring your success.

Gather relevant information.

It's foolish to choose a solution before you know all the options and factors at play. In this stage, you might seek answers to questions such as: How does our current turnover compare to similar companies in this community? How can we measure employee satisfaction? What can we learn from current employees and those who have recently left? and What can we learn from companies with less turnover?

Consider forces for and against.

A force field analysis involves listing the forces in favor of a desired outcome and those that will probably make it difficult to achieve.[61] For example, forces that help you retain good employees might include offering better pay and training.

Challenges might include a transient workforce and the inherent difficulty of the job.

Develop creative solutions.

Propose solutions through brainstorming or by contributing written ideas anonymously. Avoid criticism at this stage. The more ideas generated, the better. Welcome outlandish ideas, since they may trigger more workable ones, and encourage members to "piggyback" by modifying or combining ideas already suggested.

Select an option.

To identify a good solution, ask the following questions: Which solution will best produce the desired changes? Which solution is most achievable? and Which solution contains the fewest serious disadvantages? "Tips & Reminders: 4 Ways to Reach a Group Decision" should help you choose the best method for selecting an option.

Implement the plan.

Everyone who makes New Year's resolutions knows the difference between making a decision and carrying it out. There are several important steps in developing and implementing a plan of action. You should identify specific tasks, determine necessary resources, define individual responsibilities, and provide for emergencies.

Follow up on the solution.

Even the best plans usually require some modifications after they're put into practice. You can improve the group's effectiveness and minimize disappointment by meeting periodically to evaluate progress and revise the approach as necessary. •

TIPS & REMINDERS

4 Ways to Reach a Group Decision

There are several approaches a group can use to arrive at decisions. Here are the advantages and disadvantages of each.

1. **Reach consensus.**

   Consensus occurs when all members of a group support a decision. Full participation can increase the quality of the decision as well as members' willingness to support it. However, consensus building can take a great deal of time, which makes it unsuitable for emergencies.

2. **Let the majority decide.**

   Many people believe the democratic method of majority rule is always superior. That's not always true, however. A majority vote may be sufficient when the support of all members isn't necessary, but in more important matters, it's risky. Even if 51 percent favors a plan, 49 percent might oppose it—hardly sweeping support for any decision that needs everyone's support to work. Decisions made under majority rule are often inferior to decisions hashed out by a group until the members reach consensus.[62]

3. **Rely on the experts.**

   If one or more group members are experts on the topic, you might give them decision-making authority. This can work well if (and only if) their judgment is truly superior.

4. **Honor authority rule.**

   Though it sounds dictatorial, there are times when an executive decision is in order. Sometimes there isn't time for a group to decide, or the matter is so routine that it doesn't require discussion. However, much of the time, group decisions are of higher quality and gain more support from members than those made by an individual.

Communicating in the Workplace

Mistakes to Avoid at Work

- Making fun of people
- Oversharing
- Overlooking cultural differences
- Gossiping
- Doing less than your best
- Losing your cool
- Fixating on a mistake

Leadership Strategies

- Leaders needn't be born with particular traits.
- The Managerial Grid describes leaders in terms of their emphasis on tasks and relationships.
- Transformational leaders recruit strong team members and support their efforts.

Working with a Difficult Boss

- Rise to the challenge.
- Make up for the boss's shortcomings.
- Seek advice from others.
- Talk with your boss.
- Maintain a professional demeanor.
- Adjust your expectations.
- If necessary, make a gracious exit.

How to Leave a Job Without Burning Bridges

- Put it in writing.
- Deliver the news personally.
- Share the news graciously.
- Help with the transition.
- Stay positive.

Types of Power in the Workplace

- Legitimate (formal role)
- Expert (knowledge)
- Connection (relationships)
- Reward (positive reinforcement)
- Coercive (bad consequences)
- Referent (likeable)

Communication in Small Groups

- Group members are motivated by group and individual goals.
- Rules and roles (both official and unspoken) influence teams.
- Groups progress through stages of orientation, conflict, emergence, and reinforcement.

To Deal with Difficult Members . . .

- Keep calm.
- Look for underlying reasons.
- Talk explicitly about the issue.
- Lay ground rules.
- Write down ideas.
- Make repercussions clear.

Groups Can Be Good Problem Solvers Because They . . .

- Have resources.
- Can catch errors.
- Enhance buy-in.
- Have diverse ideas.
- Are best at solving problems.

Make the Most of Group Meetings

- Encourage equal participation.
- Avoid information underload and overload.
- Avoid pressure to conform.
- Make the most of diversity.

Make the Most of Online Meetings

- Learn the technology.
- Practice good cybersecurity.
- Set the stage.
- Show your face.
- Dress head to toe for the camera.
- Develop camaraderie.
- Decide who talks when.
- Use the mute function wisely.
- Pay attention.

Structured Problem Solving

- Identify the problem.
- Analyze the problem.
- Identify criteria for success.
- Gather relevant information.
- Consider forces for and against.
- Develop creative solutions.
- Select an option.
- Implement the plan.
- Follow up on the solution.

Show Your Communication Know-How

11.1: Identify and avoid communication blunders at work.

Think of the worst teammate or coworker you have encountered. Was that person guilty of any of the communication mistakes described in this chapter?

KEY TERM: social intelligence

11.2: Demonstrate effective leadership skills based on the situation, goals, and team members' needs.

Imagine working in an environment that requires you to juggle online and in-person communication. How might you show that you have what it takes to be a leader?

KEY TERMS: trait theories of leadership, situational leadership, Managerial Grid, transformational leadership

11.3: Describe strategies for dealing with frustrating leaders.

If you find yourself working with a boss who is hard to please, what communication strategies might you use to improve the situation?

11.4: Analyze six types of power in professional settings.

Recall the passage "When Omar joined the staff, his great attitude and talent influenced everyone around him." What types of power does Omar seem to have?

KEY TERMS: power, legitimate power, nominal leaders, expert power, connection power, reward power, coercive power, referent power

11.5: Practice communication strategies that minimize the pitfalls and maximize the benefits of groupwork.

Think of a group you have encountered with an underperforming member. What communication strategies might have helped?

KEY TERMS: small groups, social loafing, rules; social, norms, procedural norms, task norms, roles, formal roles, informal roles, task roles, social roles, orientation (forming) stage, conflict (storming) stage, emergence (norming) stage, reinforcement (performing) stage, cohesiveness

11.6: Assess the advantages of group problem solving.

Think of a poorly designed process that frustrates you at school or work. What might the advantages be of having a team look into the problem?

11.7: Strategize ways to communicate effectively during group discussions.

You are part of a group asked to look into the parking problem on campus. One person proposes that the university raise the price of parking tickets, and everyone seems inclined to go along with that idea. What might you do to make sure the group carefully considers a range of options before reaching a decision?

KEY TERM: groupthink

11.8: Practice the steps involved in systematic problem solving.

Consider again the parking problem on campus. Brainstorm how you might structure a team meeting based on the systematic problem-solving method.

KEY TERM: reflective thinking method

12 PREPARING Speeches

Audience Analysis

PAGE 183

How do you seek out information about your audience?

What are the steps involved in analyzing an audience?

Speech Planning

PAGE 186

How can you save time and effort in planning a speech?

What is a purpose statement and why is it important?

Why are organization and structure so important?

Components to Keep in Mind

PAGE 188

How do you make an effective introduction and conclusion?

What role do transitions play in a speech?

How can you be sure your supporting material will be memorable and convincing?

Analyzing Your Audience

LEARNING OBJECTIVE 12.1: Analyze the audience in a given speaking situation.

Political differences have become so severe today that scholars have used the term *toxic polarization* to describe the situation.[1] There seem to be two sides that can't believe or communicate with each other, and each side has not just its own set of opinions, but also its own set of facts and logical rules.[2]

The practice of public speaking was designed to tackle this kind of problem. At its best, public speaking is a process of putting together and presenting messages that bring people together by seeking common ground. This is the point of view taken by former NFL athlete and sports commentator Emmanuel Acho, who is also host of the web series "Uncomfortable Conversations with a Black Man." Acho explains the purpose of his series this way:

> *In the midst of all this chaos in our world so many of y'all have reached out to me—and by y'all I mean white people—asking how can I help, how can I join in, how can I stand with you? So I've created this for you because in order to stand with us and people that look like me you have to be educated on issues that pertain to me and fully educated so that you can feel the full level of pain, so that you can have full understanding. . . . So consider this a safe space to answer so many questions that I've seen from y'all.*[3]

That process of seeking common ground that Acho employs in his series begins with a clear and meaningful analysis of the audience.

The purpose of **audience analysis** is to develop remarks that are appropriate to the characteristics of your listeners, thereby helping you achieve your speaking goal. Just as you have a purpose for speaking, audience members have a reason for gathering. Understanding your listeners' demographics and political affiliation, as well as their attitudes, beliefs, and values, may help you to connect with them, encouraging understanding and influence without sacrificing your own beliefs or objectives.

Demographics and Political Affiliation

Demographics are characteristics of your audience that can be categorized and labeled, such as age, gender, cultural background, educational level, and economic status. In a college class, demographics such as hometown, year in school, and major subject might also be important.

In addition, political affiliation has increasingly become a factor that affects how receptive audiences may be to discussions of certain topics. This information about your audience will help you mention specific ways your information will be interesting or useful to them, and which they'll find persuasive. Demographic characteristics and political affiliation might affect your speech planning in a number of ways. For example:

- *Cultural diversity.* Do audience members vary in terms of race, religion, or national origin? The guideline here might be: *Do not exclude or offend any portion of your audience on the basis of cultural differences.* If one

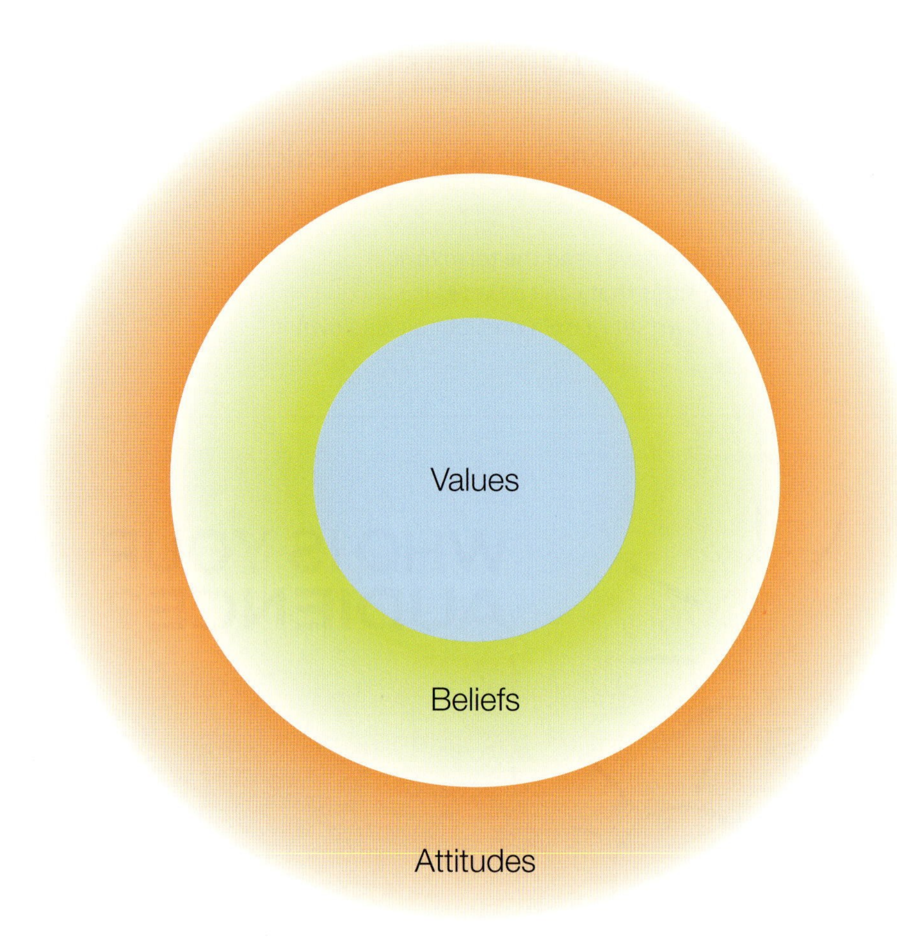

FIGURE 12.1 Structure of Attitudes, Beliefs, and Values

cultural group predominates, you might decide to address it, but remember that the point is to analyze, not stereotype, your audience. If you talk down to any segment of your listeners, you have probably stereotyped them.

- *Gender*. Although masculine and feminine stereotypes are declining, it is still important to think about how gender can affect the way you choose and approach a topic.
- *Age*. Interests vary and change with our age. These differences may run relatively deep; our approach to literature, films, finance, health, and long-term success may change dramatically over just a few years, perhaps from graphic novels to serious literature, from punk to classical music, or from hip-hop to epic poetry.
- *Group membership*. Groups generally form around shared interests among the members. By examining the groups to which your audience members belong, you may be able to surmise their religious beliefs (Catholic Youth Organization, Hillel, or Muslim Students' Association), or occupation (Bartenders Union or National Communication Association). Group membership is often an important consideration in college classes. Consider the difference between a "typical" college day class and one that meets in the evening. At many colleges, the evening students are generally older and tend to belong to civic groups, church clubs, and the local chamber of commerce. Daytime students are more likely to belong to sororities and fraternities, sports clubs, and social action groups.
- *Political affiliation*. One of the most important audience distinctions today involves liberal versus conservative political inclinations. Johnathan Haidt, a psychologist who has studied this phenomenon, suggests that liberals place a higher priority on providing help for people in need, fairness, diversity/inclusivity, and openness to new experiences, whereas conservatives score higher in terms of valuing group membership and loyalty, respecting authority, and maintaining traditions.[4,5]

Analyzing demographics and political affiliations of audience members will help you make an educated guess about their attitudes, beliefs, and values—in essence, what they think.[6] In turn, this will help you develop a speech that speaks to and not at them.

Attitudes, Beliefs, and Values

Attitudes, beliefs, and values reside in human consciousness like the layers of an onion (see Figure 12.1). **Attitudes** lie closest to the surface and reflect a predisposition to view you or your topic in a favorable or unfavorable way. **Beliefs** lie a little deeper and deal with a person's underlying conviction about the truth of an idea. **Values** are deeply rooted feelings about a concept's inherent worth or worthiness.

Since values are the foundation that shapes beliefs and attitudes, experts in audience analysis often try to recognize and appeal to them. As one team of researchers pointed out, "Values have the advantage of being comparatively small in number, and owing to their abstract nature, are more likely to be shared by large numbers of people."[7]

Recall the controversy over mask wearing as the COVID-19 pandemic swept the world. Many people in the United States refused to wear masks in public. One stated reason was framed by the value of personal freedom—the notion that "nobody will tell me how to live my life." Others agreed to wear masks based on the value of altruism: "Show you care: Wear a mask."

To demonstrate the usefulness of appealing to values, one team of researchers conducted a pair of studies. One study dealt with messages surrounding same-sex marriage, while the other dealt with messages pertaining to military spending.[8]

In the first experiment, the researchers shared two messages in favor of same-sex marriage with liberals and conservatives. One message was framed in terms of equality and fairness, while the other was framed in terms of patriotism and loyalty. According to the researchers, "Liberals showed the same support for same-sex marriage regardless of which message they encountered. But conservatives supported same-sex marriage significantly more if they read the patriotism message rather than the fairness one."[9]

In the second experiment, the researchers shared with liberals and conservatives two messages in support of increased military spending. One message was framed in terms of pride and patriotism, while the other was framed in terms of fairness and helping the poor and disadvantaged. According to the researchers, "For conservatives, it didn't matter which message they read; their support for military spending was the same. However, liberals expressed significantly greater support for increasing military spending if they read the fairness message rather than the patriotism one."[10] We look at further ramifications of the process of persuasion in Chapter 14.

Audience Perception of the Occasion

Your audience's perception of the occasion of your speech is based on their expectations. A speech presented in a college class is usually expected to reflect a higher level of thought and intelligence than if you were discussing the same subject with a group of friends over coffee. But this doesn't mean that your speech should be boring or humorless. In fact, wit and humor are indicative of intelligence and may also help you develop a connection with your audience. The sample informative speech in Appendix A of this book was presented by a highly specialized marine biologist. She presents information that is generally new to her highly educated audience, but she does so with wit and a strong personal connection. •

PAUSE TO REFLECT *Where Do You Stand?*

1. What are your own political opinions about issues like business regulation, gun rights, and the separation of church and state? ______________________________

2. How would those opinions be interpreted by someone on the opposite end of the political spectrum? ______________________________

Planning Your Speech

LEARNING OBJECTIVE 12.2: Follow the steps involved with planning a successful speech.

Having analyzed your audience, it's now time to adapt to that audience as you plan your speech. You should choose a topic, define your purpose, write a purpose statement, state your thesis, and gather information with that audience in mind.

Step 1: Choose a topic.

The first question many student speakers face is "What should I talk about?" Try to pick a topic that interests you, that your audience will care about, and that is right for the situation.

Step 2: Define your purpose.

No one gives a speech or expresses *any* kind of message without having a reason to do so. There are three **general purposes** for presenting a public speech:

- *To inform:* To enlighten audience members by teaching them something.
- *To persuade:* To move your audience toward a new attitude or behavior.
- *To entertain:* To relax audience members by providing them with a pleasant listening experience.

While there are distinctive differences among the three basic purposes, there is also considerable overlap. A speech designed to inform an audience will almost certainly need to be entertaining enough to hold listeners' interest. And to persuade audience members, you will most likely have to inform them about your arguments. Even a speech designed purely to entertain might change audience attitudes or teach that audience something new.

Chapter 14 will explore informative and persuasive speaking in more depth. In all types of speaking, however, you should formulate a clear and precise statement of your specific reason for speaking.

Step 3: Write a purpose statement.

Your **purpose statement** should be expressed in the form of a complete sentence that describes your **specific purpose**—exactly what you want your speech to accomplish. There are three criteria for an effective purpose statement:

- *A purpose statement should be result oriented.* Having a result orientation means that your purpose is focused on the outcome you want to accomplish with your audience members. *"After hearing my speech, my listeners will be more likely to listen to people with whom they disagree."*
- *A purpose statement should be specific.* To be effective, a purpose statement should have enough details so that you will be able to measure or test your audience, after your speech, to see if you have achieved your purpose. *"After I'm finished, at least half of my listeners will volunteer to shop for those who have been shut-in during a pandemic."*
- *A purpose statement should be realistic.* It's fine to be ambitious, but you should design a purpose that has a reasonable chance of success. If your purpose is to convince your listeners to adopt a healthier diet, expecting them to become vegetarians would be unrealistic. A more realistic goal might be *"After listening to my speech, the majority of my listeners will opt to consume smaller portions for a week."*

A purpose statement usually is a tool to help you stay focused on your goal as you plan your speech. It's not generally necessary to include your purpose statement word for word in your actual speech.

Step 4: State your thesis.

After you've defined the purpose, you're ready to start planning what is arguably the most important sentence in your entire speech. The **thesis statement** tells your listeners the central idea of your speech and is the one idea that you want audience members to remember after they have forgotten everything else you had to say. The thesis statement for a speech entitled "Winning in Small Claims Court" might be worded like this:

> *Arguing a case on your own in small claims court is a simple, five-step process that can give you the same results you would achieve with a lawyer.*

Unlike your purpose statement, your thesis statement is almost always delivered directly to your audience.

Step 5: Gather information.

It takes time, interest, and knowledge to develop a topic well. Setting aside a block of time to reflect on your own ideas is essential. However, you will also need to gather information from outside sources. Your first instinct may be to do an online search, and that can be a good place to start. However, while you might be tempted to go to Wikipedia as a starting point, it's far better to make a broader search. Keep in mind that many professors forbid using Wikipedia as a primary source because anyone can edit the information found there.

One place to go to gather valid information for a speech is the library, but physical visits aren't necessary today. Most library websites can connect you to databases and reference works that you would otherwise have to pay to subscribe to. However, if you do make a physical visit, you'll find your library to be one of those rare quiet places where you can focus on your task without the usual distractions. You'll also be able to consult with library experts who can help you find and evaluate information.

Another method for gathering information is to conduct a survey of your audience members beforehand to determine their attitudes about a topic. Finally, you might want to interview an expert for facts and perspectives to use in your speech.

Step 6: Double-check your sources. People on all sides of the political spectrum tend to accept disinformation if it conforms to their preconceived prejudices. Sometimes, partisans insist that it doesn't matter to them if the information is true or not, as long as it proves their point. Experts call this **confirmation bias.**[11] Confirmation bias may be so strong that people in its grip will reject information from experts; this has led to a general tendency today to devalue expertise.[12]

Social media has exacerbated the problem of confirmation bias by allowing all of us to exist in what some researchers call a **filter bubble**, in which search engines and social media create echo chambers of information that conform with our beliefs.[13] Because of confirmation bias, remember that if it seems too good to be true, it's probably false, and if it conforms to your preconceived beliefs, you should double-check it for accuracy.

"Hey, that line's moving a lot faster!"

For expert suggestions on things to keep in mind when determining the accuracy of information found online, see "Tips & Reminders: 3 Ways to Evaluate Online Information."

TIPS & REMINDERS

3 Ways to Evaluate Online Information

Consider answers to the following questions when judging whether to use information you find online.

1. **Credibility: Is the information trustworthy?**
   - Who created the site? Don't use anonymous sources.
   - If the sources *are* listed, are their credentials listed?
   - What institution sponsors the site? What is their purpose?
   - Are there obvious proofreading errors/grammatical mistakes? Remember that a sleek site design doesn't guarantee high-quality information, but misspellings and grammatical mistakes are good signs of low quality.
2. **Objectivity: Is the information unbiased?**
   - What is the domain name of the site? The domain names .edu, .gov, and .org are generally more reliable than sites using .com.
   - What opinions (if any) does the author express?
   - If a topic is controversial, are opposing sides equally represented/covered?
   - Does the site have advertising? If so, who appears to be the targets of these ads?
   - Search "Media Bias" online to see if your source is known for being slanted in one political direction. Sites such as AllSides.com have a reputation for being accurate about media bias.[14]
3. **Currency: Is the information up to date?**
   - When was the site created?
   - When was the site last updated?
   - How up-to-date are any links? If any are dead, that is a sign that the information might not be current.

Structuring Your Speech

LEARNING OBJECTIVE 12.3: Create an effective and well-organized speech structure and outline.

Having a clear purpose and thesis as well as interesting and credible information to speak about is important. But if the material isn't well organized, your audience won't understand your message. In addition to making your message clear to your audience, structuring a message effectively is essential to refining your ideas and making them persuasive.

Every speech outline should follow the **basic speech structure** that includes an introduction, body, and conclusion. This structure demonstrates the old aphorism for speakers: "Tell what you're going to say, say it, and then tell what you said." The finer points of your speech structure will be shown in your outlines.

Outlines

Outlines come in all shapes and sizes. Your **working outline** is for your eyes only, and you'll probably create several drafts of it as you refine your ideas. On the other hand, a **formal outline** uses a consistent format and set of symbols to identify the structure of ideas. Another person should be able to understand the basic ideas included in your speech by reading the formal outline. In fact, that's one test of the effectiveness of your outline. Figure 12.2 provides a template for a formal speech outline.

Speaking Notes

Like your working outline, your speaking notes are for your use only, so the format is up to you. Many teachers suggest that speaking notes be in the form of a brief keyword outline, with just enough information listed to jog your memory but not enough to get lost in. They also suggest that you fit your notes on one side of a 3-by-5-inch note card. Others recommend having only your introduction and conclusion or longer quotations on note cards.

Organizational Patterns

An outline should reflect a logical order for your points and one that best develops your thesis. You might arrange your key points from newest to oldest, largest to smallest, best to worst, or in a number of other ways, including by time. For example, if you were discussing the history of racism in America,[15] you might arrange your main ideas in terms of time period:

I. Slavery
II. Jim Crow
III. Today

Chapter 14 will discuss a number of organization patterns specifically designed for persuasion.

INTRODUCTION

I. Introduce your speech topic to your audience:

A. Attention-getter: This statement should make people pay attention and clue them to your topic. It might be a question, quotation, example, anecdote, or statistic.

B. Relevance: Explain why your audience should care about your topic and/or how the information you will impart affects them.

C. Credibility: Tell your audience why they should listen to you and why you are qualified to speak on the topic: personal experience, research, etc.

D. Thesis Statement: Summarize for your audience, in one sentence, the purpose of your speech.

II. Preview: Clue your audience to the main points you will hit upon in your speech. In some instances, this may also serve as a transition to the body of the speech.

BODY: Discuss all of the main and supporting points. Be sure to include transition sentences.

I. First Main point: A single sentence (labeled I., II., III., etc.)

A. Subpoint: A single sentence supporting the main point (labeled A., B., C., etc.)

1. First sub-subpoint: A single sentence supporting the subpoint (labeled 1., 2., 3., etc.)

2. Second sub-subpoint: A single sentence supporting the subpoint (labeled 1., 2., 3., etc.)

B. Second Subpoint: A single sentence supporting the main point (labeled A., B., C., etc.)

II. Second Main point: A single sentence (labeled I., II., III., etc.)

III. Third Main point: A single sentence (labeled I., II., III., etc.)

CONCLUSION

I. Thesis Restatement: Restate your thesis, perhaps in different words.

II. Main Point Review: Remind your audience of the main points you discussed in your speech.

III. Closing Statement: Provide closure in a memorable way.

WORKS CITED/BIBLIOGRAPHY: List all of the references you have used and cited in your speech.

This template does not have to be copied verbatim. Every speech has its own unique structure. See for example, the outlines for the sample speeches in Appendices A (p. 232) and B (p. 237).

FIGURE 12.2 Speech Outline Template

Creating the Introduction

LEARNING OBJECTIVE 12.4: Develop an effective introduction.

The introduction is probably the most important part of your speech. Listeners form their impression of a speaker early. It is therefore essential to make those few moments at the beginning of your speech work to your advantage.

There are five functions of the speech **introduction**. It serves to capture the audience's attention, preview the main points, set the mood and tone of the speech, demonstrate the importance of the topic, and establish credibility.

Capture attention.

There are several ways to capture an audience's attention. See "Tips & Reminders: 9 Ways to Capture the Audience's Attention" to see how you might capture an audience's attention in a speech titled "Communication Between Plants and Humans."

Preview the main points.

After you capture the attention of the audience, an effective introduction will almost always state the speaker's thesis and give the listeners an idea of the upcoming main points.

- Sometimes your preview of main points will be straightforward:

  "I have three points to discuss: They are ________, ________, and__________."

- Sometimes you will not want to refer directly to your main points in your introduction. Perhaps you want to create suspense or a humorous effect, or perhaps you are stalling for time to win over a hostile audience. In that case, you might preview only your thesis:

  "I am going to say a few words about_____________."
  "Did you ever wonder about _____________?"
  "____________ is one of the most important issues facing us today."

Set the tone of your speech.

The introduction is where you establish the mood of your speech. For example, the sample speech in Appendix A of this book was presented by Marah Hardt, a marine biologist. She began her speech with a statement that suggested her speech would be down to earth and conversational:

> *Right now, beneath a shimmering blue sea, millions of fish are having sex. And the way they're doing it and strategies they're using look nothing like what we see on land.*[16]

Demonstrate the importance of your topic to your audience.

Your audience members will listen to you more carefully if your speech relates to them as individuals. Based on your audience analysis, you should state directly *why* your topic is of importance to your audience members. For example, Marah Hardt established the importance of her topic to her audience like this:

> *Sex in the sea is fascinating, and it's also really important, and not just to nerdy marine biologists like me who are obsessed with understanding these salty affairs. It matters for all of us. Today, we depend on wild caught fish to help feed over two billion people on the planet. We need millions of oysters and corals to build the giant reefs that protect our shorelines from rising seas and storms. We depend*

on medicines that are found in marine animals to fight cancer and other diseases. And for many of us, the diversity and beauty of the oceans is where we turn for recreation and relaxation and our cultural heritage.[17]

Establish credibility.

One final consideration for your introduction is to establish your credibility to speak about your topic. One way to do this is to be well prepared. Another is to appear confident as soon as you face your audience. A third technique is to tell your audience about your personal experience with the topic, in order to establish why it is important to you. Elena Abbott, a student at the University of Florida, established her credibility when speaking about how Veterans Administration hospitals treat infertility this way:

> *Last summer, I interned with the American Society for Reproductive Medicine, an organization whose mission is to expand access to infertility care, where I got to focus specifically on the VA system. Doing so put me in rooms with Congressional members and their staffs where I was able to discuss the limited infertility treatment options available to American veterans. . . .*[18]

Chapter 14 will examine the concept of credibility in more detail, especially in terms of persuasive speeches. •

TIPS & REMINDERS

9 Ways to Capture the Audience's Attention

1. **Refer to the audience.**

   The technique of referring to the audience is especially effective if it is complimentary: "Julio's speech last week about how animals communicate was so interesting that I decided to explore a related topic: whether people can communicate with plants!"

2. **Refer to the occasion.**

   A reference to the occasion could allude to the event of your speech: "Our assignment is to focus on an aspect of *human* communication. Given this guideline, it seems appropriate to talk about whether humans can communicate with plants."

3. **Refer to the relationship between the audience and the subject.**

   "It's fair to say that all of us here believe it's important to care for our environment. What you'll learn today will make you care about that environment in a whole new way."

4. **Refer to something familiar to the audience.**

   "Most of us have talked to our pets. Today, you'll learn that there are other conversational partners around the house."

5. **Cite a startling fact or opinion.**

   "See that lilac bush outside the window? At this very moment, it might be reacting to the joys and anxieties that you are experiencing in this classroom." Or "There is now actual scientific evidence that plants appreciate human company, kind words, and classical music."

6. **Ask a question.**

   "Have you ever wondered why some people seem able to grow beautiful, healthy plants effortlessly, whereas others couldn't make a weed grow in the best soil? Perhaps it's because they have better relationships with those plants."

7. **Tell an anecdote.**

   "The other night, while taking a walk in the country, I happened on a small garden that was rich with vegetation. But it wasn't the lushness of the plants that caught my eye. There, in the middle of the garden, was a man who was talking quite animatedly to a giant sunflower."

8. **Use a quotation.**

   "Max Thornton, the naturalist, recently said, 'Psychobiology has proven that plants can communicate. Now humans need to learn how to listen to them.'"

9. **Tell an (appropriate) joke.**

   "We once worried about people who talked to plants, but that's no longer the case. Now we only worry if the plants talk back."

Designing Conclusions and Transitions

LEARNING OBJECTIVE 12.5: Develop an effective conclusion and integrate smooth transitions.

If the introduction is the most important part of your speech, the conclusion and your transitions are a close second and third. Listeners tend to remember best what they hear last, and they tend to understand main points when they are tied together well.

The Conclusion

The **conclusion**, like the introduction, is an especially important part of your speech. The conclusion has three essential functions: to restate the thesis, to review your main points, and to provide a memorable final remark.

You can review your thesis either by repeating it or by paraphrasing it. Or, you might devise a striking summary statement for your conclusion to help the audience remember your thesis. Leah Roberts, a student at Concordia College in New York, gave a speech calling for the insurance industry to cover mental health equally with physical health. She ended her conclusion with this statement:

> *No one should be denied treatment for anorexia because their insurance company doesn't think she is thin enough. No one should be denied a psychiatrist because his insurance doesn't cover one. No mother in North Carolina should have to jump through hoops that would never be tolerated for any other illness. It is time that we start holding our insurance companies accountable for providing mental health care.*[19]

Leah's statement was concise but memorable.

Transitions

Transitions are phrases that connect ideas in your speech by showing how each idea relates to the other. They keep your message moving forward by referring to previous and upcoming points and showing how they relate to one another and the thesis. Transitions usually sound something like this:

> *"Like [previous point], another important consideration in [topic] is [upcoming point]."*

> *"But_______ isn't the only thing we have to worry about. _______ is even more potentially dangerous."*

> *"Yes, the problem is obvious. But what are the solutions? Well, one possible solution is . . ."*

Sometimes a transition includes an internal review (a restatement of preceding points), an internal preview (a look ahead to upcoming points), or both:

> *"So far we've discussed _______, _______, and _______. Our next points are _______, _______, and _______."*

PAUSE TO REFLECT *How Did You Come to That Conclusion?*

1. Think back to an effective speech that you heard, and then search for the transcript online. On close inspection, did the conclusion play an important role in helping you recall this speech as effective?

   ____

   ____

2. In what way did the speaker try to make the conclusion effective? Why did it affect you the way it did?

   ____

   ____

Types of Supporting Material

LEARNING OBJECTIVE 12.6: Choose supporting material that makes your ideas clear, memorable, and convincing.

It is important to organize ideas clearly and logically. But clarity and logic by themselves won't guarantee that you'll amuse, enlighten, or persuade others; these results call for the use of supporting materials. The facts and information that back up and prove your ideas and opinions are the flesh that fills out the skeleton of your speech.

Supporting material clarifies your ideas, proves your points, and generally makes your speech more interesting and memorable. Supporting material can take the form of definitions, examples, statistics, analogies/comparison–contrast, anecdotes, and quotations/testimonies.

Definitions

It's a good idea to give your audience members definitions of your key terms, especially if those terms are unfamiliar to them or are being used in an unusual way. Sometimes, a main point or even an entire speech can be built around a definition. For example, Maria Mendes Pinto, a student at the University of Nebraska-Omaha, presented a speech entitled "'Underage Women' Do Not Exist" that dealt with how one term was used in media and the legal system:

> *"Underage women" is a clear contradiction, given that by definition a woman is an adult, while an underage person is a minor, unable to consent to sex.*[20]

Examples

An **example** is a specific case that is used to demonstrate a general idea. Examples can be either factual or hypothetical, personal or borrowed. Anthony Adams, a student at Monmouth College, used the following example in his speech "On Neurodiversity and Race":

> *Kayleb Moon-Robinson was in the sixth grade when he was arrested for, charged with, and convicted of a felony for pushing away an officer who came to arrest him for . . . kicking a trash can. Kayleb is both autistic and Black, and serves as a grim reminder of the consequences of the intersection between race and neurotypicality.*[21]

Hypothetical (or fictional) examples can often be more powerful than factual examples, because they ask audience members to imagine something, thus making them active participants in the thought. Saeed Malami, a student at Lafayette College in Pennsylvania, drew on a fictional example in his speech on child slavery in the chocolate business:

> *Willy Wonka's chocolate factory held the secret to his success. By some miracle, he was able to churn out the greatest chocolate in the world. Kids and adults alike loved every bite. And here's the miracle: He did all this without employing a single person. How? Oompa Loompas. They served him and did all his bidding without complaining. At least that's how the story is told. . . . Here's a retelling of the story in one word: Slavery. That's how Willy Wonka got his chocolate. And here is how the big chocolate industry gets its chocolate today in two words: child slavery.*[22]

Saeed's full speech appears in Appendix B of this book.

Statistics

Statistics are numbers that are arranged or organized to show that a fact or principle is true for a large percentage of cases. Statistics are actually collections of examples, which is why they are often more effective as proof than are isolated examples. Abigail Banks, a student at Oklahoma City University, used statistics in her speech about sexual assault on college campuses:

> *Sexual assault and understanding sexual consent is a big issue in the United States. One in five women and one in sixteen men will face sexual assault while in college. Every 98 seconds an American is sexually assaulted. And 54% of sexual assaults are reported by people ages 18-34, according to the Rape, Abuse, and Incest National Network (RAINN), the largest anti-violence network in the United States.*[23]

Because statistics can be powerful proof, you should make sure that they make sense and that they come from a credible source. You should also cite the source of the statistic when you use it. And to achieve maximum effect, you should reduce the statistic to a concrete image if possible. For example, $1 billion in $100 bills would be about the same height as a sixty-story building. Using concrete images such as this will make your statistics more than "just numbers" when you use them.

Analogies/Comparison–Contrast

We use **analogies**, or comparisons, all the time, often in the form of figures of speech, such as similes and metaphors. A simile is a direct comparison that usually uses *like* or *as*, whereas a metaphor is an implied comparison that does not use *like* or *as*. So if you said that the rush of refugees from a war-torn country was "like a tidal wave," you would be using a simile. If you said "a tidal wave of refugees," you would be using a metaphor.

Analogies are extended metaphors. They can be used to compare or contrast an unknown concept with a known one. For example, here's how one writer made her point against separate Academy Awards for men and women:

> *Many hours into the 82nd Academy Awards ceremony . . . the Oscar for best actor will go to Morgan Freeman, Jeff Bridges, George Clooney, Colin Firth, or Jeremy Renner. Suppose, however, that the Academy of Motion Picture Arts and Sciences presented separate honors for best white actor and best non-white actor, and that Mr. Freeman was prohibited from competing against the likes of Mr. Clooney and Mr. Bridges. Surely, the Academy would be derided as intolerant and out of touch; public outcry would swiftly ensure that Oscar nominations never again fell along racial lines. Why, then, is it considered acceptable to segregate nominations by sex, offering different Oscars for best actor and best actress?*[24]

Anecdotes

An **anecdote** is a brief story with a point, often (but not always) based on personal experience. The word *anecdote* comes from a Greek term meaning "unpublished item." Sean Keagan, a student at Seton Hall University, used a brief anecdote to illustrate contamination in the recycling industry:

> *After 20 years, Gary Gilliam considered himself a seasoned professional in the recycling industry. That also meant that Gary was no stranger to bad recycling especially when a hand grenade came down the recycling conveyor belt. He admitted . . . that it came as a bit of a surprise.*[25]

Quotations/Testimony

Using a familiar, artistically stated saying will enable you to take advantage of someone else's memorable wording. For example, if you were giving a speech on personal integrity, you might quote Mark Twain, who said, "Always do right. This will gratify some people, and astonish the rest." A quotation like that fits Alexander Pope's definition of "true wit": "What was often thought, but ne'er so well expressed."

You can also use quotations as **testimony**, to prove a point by using the support of someone who is more authoritative or experienced on the subject than you are. Anglea Paola Vasquez Rojas, a student at Las Positas College in California, used testimony on both sides of the issue to make a point about how difficult it is for undocumented students to explain their status to their teachers:

> *In May of 2017, Jin Park, an undocumented student, told* The Harvard Gazette, *"When I was growing up in New York City, my family always told me to be mindful of my surroundings, to keep quiet about being undocumented, and to avoid busy streets where I might encounter immigration agents." Reinforcing this sentiment, in June of 2017, Tom Homan, acting-director of Immigration and Customs Enforcement, also known as ICE, said, "If you entered this country illegally, you should be looking over your shoulder and you should be worried."*[26]

Styles of Support

Most of the forms of support discussed in the preceding section could be presented in either of two ways: through narration or through citation. **Narration** involves telling a story with your information. You put it in the form of a small drama, with a beginning, middle, and end. For example, Abbie Perry, a student at the University of Nebraska, Omaha, used narration in her speech on the dangers of alcohol addiction:

> *Melissa Carter is a single mother of three and works overtime to make ends meet. Every night she makes dinner and stops at a store to pick up a bottle of wine. But when she*

gets home and starts drinking, she can't stop. For years, Melissa has been battling alcohol addiction. She told me in a personal interview last week that her binges would get so bad at times she once ended up in a hospital with a .5 blood alcohol level and is lucky to be alive.[27]

Citation, unlike narration, is a simple statement of the facts. Citation is shorter and more precise than narration, in the sense that the source is carefully stated. Citation should always include such phrases as "According to the July 25, 2021, edition of *Time* magazine," or "As Mr. Smith made clear in an interview last April 24." Abbie Perry cited testimony later in her speech on alcohol addiction:

> *In her book,* A Prescription for Alcoholics, *author Linda Burlison reminds us that there are medical reasons for addiction and approved medications to treat them. But we don't prescribe them, making alcoholism the most dangerous disease in the United States that doesn't get treated.*[28]

Some forms of support, such as anecdotes, are inherently more likely to be expressed as narration. Statistics, on the other hand, are nearly always cited rather than narrated. However, when you are using examples, quotation/testimony, definitions, and analogies, you often have a choice.

PAUSE TO REFLECT *What Kind of a Gatherer Are You?*

1. What is your own style of gathering material for a school assignment, whether it be a speech, a paper, or simply curiosity about something that came up in class? Which type of supporting material do you think you prefer, and use most often? ______________________

2. Think ahead to a speech you gave or might give in this class or elsewhere. What personal experiences do you have that would make an interesting example or anecdote? ______________________

3. When speaking to a friend, did you ever search online for an answer to a question that came up in your conversation? What was it about the question that made you curious enough to look it up? ______________________

Preparing Speeches

Analyzing Your Audience

- Audience demographics are used to analyze characteristics of your audience that can help you mention specific ways your information will be interesting or useful to your listeners.
- Audience attitudes and beliefs are important, but experts in audience analysis suggest that speakers concentrate on values because they are more likely to be shared by large numbers of people.
- Audience perception of the occasion, in a college class, requires a high level of thought and intelligence without being boring or humorless.
- Consider your audience members' political affiliations, and how they differ from your own.

Planning Your Speech

- Choose a topic that is appropriate to you, your audience, and the occasion.
- Define your purpose with a well-worded purpose statement.
- Write a purpose statement that is result oriented, specific, and realistic.
- State your thesis as the most important take-away for your audience.
- Gather information that is credible, objective, and current.
- Beware of misinformation!

3 Ways to Evaluate Online Information

- Is the information trustworthy?
- Is the information unbiased?
- Is the information up to date?

Structuring Your Speech

- Outline your speech as you plan it so your ideas will be effectively organized.
- Use notes to help you remember key information while you are speaking.
- Organize your ideas in a logical pattern that will help you effectively develop your thesis.

An Introduction Should . . .

- Capture the audience's attention.
- Preview your main points.
- Set the mood and tone of your speech.
- Demonstrate the importance of your topic.
- Establish your credibility.

9 Ways to Capture the Audience's Attention

- Refer to the audience.
- Refer to the occasion.
- Refer to the relationship between the audience and the subject.
- Refer to something familiar to the audience.
- Cite a startling fact or opinion.
- Ask a question.
- Tell an anecdote.
- Use a quotation.
- Tell an (appropriate) joke.

Conclusions and Transitions

- Your conclusion should restate your thesis, review your main points, and provide a memorable final remark.
- Transitions connect the ideas in your speech by showing how each idea relates to the other.

Types of Supporting Material

- Definitions
- Examples
- Statistics
- Analogies/comparison–contrast
- Anecdotes
- Quotations/testimony

Style of Supporting Material

- Narration (telling a story with your information)
- Citation (a simple statement of the facts)

Show Your Communication Know-How

12.1: Analyze the audience in a given speaking situation.

Think about the class you are in now. If your classmates were an audience, which of their characteristics would you consider when planning a speech to deliver to them? What would be their purpose in listening and their demographics, attitudes, beliefs, values, and perception of the occasion?

KEY TERMS: audience analysis, demographics, attitudes, beliefs, values

12.2: Follow the steps involved with planning a successful speech.

What topic would you choose for the next speech you would present in your class? What would your purpose be? How would you formulate your thesis statement?

KEY TERMS: general purposes, purpose statement, specific purpose, thesis statement, confirmation bias, filter bubble

12.3: Create an effective and well-organized speech structure and outline.

Describe the process you would use to structure your next speech for this class.

KEY TERMS: basic speech structure, working outline, formal outline

12.4: Develop an effective introduction.

In your next speech introduction, how will you gain your audience's attention, preview your main points, set the mood and tone of the speech, demonstrate the importance of your topic to the audience, and establish your credibility?

KEY TERM: introduction

12.5: Develop an effective conclusion and integrate smooth transitions.

Outline the main points you might include if you were writing a speech about the process you follow to study for a test. How would you use transitions to show how one point relates to the others?

KEY TERMS: conclusion, transitions

12.6: Choose supporting material that makes your ideas clear, memorable, and convincing.

Think about your next speech for this class. How could you use each of the following: definitions of key terms, examples, statistics, analogies, anecdotes, quotations, and testimony?

KEY TERMS: example, hypothetical (or fictional) examples, statistics, analogies, anecdote, testimony, narration, citation

13 PRESENTING Speeches

Managing Speech Anxiety

LEARNING OBJECTIVE 13.1: Describe the sources of debilitative stage fright and ways to overcome speech anxiety.

The terror that strikes many beginning speakers at the mere thought of giving a speech is commonly known as *stage fright,* and is called *speech anxiety* by communication scholars.[1] Whatever term you choose, it's important to realize that this fear of speaking in front of others can be managed.[2]

Facilitative and Debilitative Anxiety

The first step in feeling less apprehensive about speaking is to realize that a certain amount of nervousness is not only natural but also helpful. Just as totally relaxed actors or musicians aren't likely to perform at the top of their potential, speakers think more rapidly and express themselves more energetically when they experience **facilitative speech anxiety**.

It is only when the level of anxiety is intense that it becomes unhelpful in two ways. First, the strong emotion keeps you from thinking clearly.[3] This has been shown to be a problem even in the preparation process: Students who are highly anxious about giving a speech often find the preliminary steps, including research and organization, to be more difficult.[4] Second, intense fear leads to an urge to do something, anything, to make the problem go away. This urge to escape often causes a speaker to speed up delivery, which in turn leads to mistakes, which only add to the speaker's anxiety.

Debilitative speech anxiety occurs when an intense level of apprehension about speaking before an audience results in poor performance. The two main sources of debilitative speech anxiety are past negative experiences and irrational thinking.[5]

Past Negative Experiences and Irrational Thinking

Many of us are uncomfortable doing *anything* in public, especially if we know others are going to be evaluating our talents and abilities. An unpleasant experience in one type of performance can cause you to expect a future similar situation to be unpleasant.[6] You might come to expect paralyzing mental blocks, for example, or rude audience members. These expectations can become reality through the self-fulfilling prophecies discussed in Chapter 2.

A traumatic failure at an earlier speech and low self-esteem from critical parents during childhood are common examples of experiences that can cause later speech anxiety. But not everyone who has bungled a speech or had critical parents is debilitated in the future. To understand why some people are affected more strongly than others by past experiences, see "Tips & Reminders: 4 Types of Irrational Fears About Public Speaking."

TIPS & REMINDERS

Types of Irrational Fears About Public Speaking

Cognitive psychologists argue that it is not events that cause people to feel nervous but rather the beliefs they have about those events. Certain irrational beliefs leave people feeling unnecessarily apprehensive. Psychologist Albert Ellis lists several such beliefs, or examples of **irrational thinking**, which we will call "fallacies" because of their illogical nature.[7]

1. **Fallacy of Catastrophic Failure**

   People who succumb to the **fallacy of catastrophic failure** assume that, if something bad can happen, it probably will. One way to escape this fallacy is to take a more realistic look at the situation. Will audience members really boo you off the stage? Will they really think your ideas are stupid? Even if you do forget your remarks for a moment, will that make your entire speech a disaster? It helps to remember that nervousness is more apparent to the speaker than to the audience.[8] Beginning public speakers, when congratulated for their poise during a speech, are apt to say, "Are you kidding? I was dying up there."

2. **Fallacy of Perfection**

   Speakers who succumb to the **fallacy of perfection** expect to deliver a flawless presentation. While such a standard of perfection might serve as a target and a source of inspiration, it is not realistic to believe you will write and deliver a perfect speech, especially as a beginner. And, remember, audiences don't expect you to be perfect either.

3. **Fallacy of Approval**

   The **fallacy of approval** is based on the idea that it is vital to gain the approval of everyone in the audience. It is rare that even the best speakers please everyone, especially on topics that are at all controversial. To paraphrase Abraham Lincoln, you can't please all the people all the time, and it is irrational to expect you will.

4. **Fallacy of Overgeneralization**

   The **fallacy of overgeneralization** might also be labeled the fallacy of exaggeration, because it occurs when a person blows one poor experience out of proportion, or when a speaker treats occasional lapses as if they were the rule rather than the exception. This sort of mistake usually involves extreme labels, such as:

   "I always forget what I want to say."
   "I can never come up with a good topic."
   "I can't do anything right."

PAUSE TO REFLECT *Are You Thinking Rationally?*

1. When you get up to give a speech, do you experience any of the fallacies just discussed? ______

2. How can you use a previous negative experience to your advantage in your next speaking opportunity? ______

ABOUT YOU *Do You Suffer from Speech Anxiety?*

Answer these questions to measure your speech anxiety.

_______ **1.** What is your overall level of anxiety about speechmaking?

a. What anxiety? I love being the center of attention.
b. I won't lie. I don't relish the idea of making a speech, but I'll be fine as long as I'm prepared.
c. I am terrified! I would literally rather do anything else besides give a speech.

_______ **2.** Are you in control of your speech anxiety, or is your speech anxiety in control of you?

a. I'm definitely in control. I've got nerves of steel!
b. I feel like I'm in control some of the time, but anxiety could take over if something goes wrong.
c. What control? Anxiety definitely takes over when it comes to making speeches.

_______ **3.** What level of sweating/sweaty palms do you experience while speaking?

a. I'm dry as can be. No sweaty palms here.
b. I might sweat a little but it's nothing that a little deodorant or hand washing won't cure!
c. Get me another shirt, please! I tend to sweat a ton when I'm speaking.

_______ **4.** What level of rapid breathing do you experience while speaking?

a. None. I'm breathing slow and steady ... it's like meditation to me.
b. Sometimes my breathing speeds up, but if I take a few deep breaths I can calm right down.
c. Anyone have an oxygen mask? I feel like I am hyperventilating!

_______ **5.** What level of restless energy do you experience while speaking?

a. I'm in the zone, poised and ready with just the right amount of energy.
b. A little. I just want to get started and get it over with.
c. I feel like I need to run a marathon in the opposite direction of this speaking engagement.

_______ **6.** Do you ever forget what you want to say while speaking?

a. Never. I know exactly what I want to say, and I say it.
b. Sometimes I forget the exact words I practiced, but as long as I have my notes handy I can quickly get back on track.
c. Did I even write a speech? I go blank ... like I didn't even prepare at all.

INTERPRETING YOUR RESPONSES |
Give yourself one point for every A, two points for every B, and three points for every C.

6 to 9 Points You have nerves of steel. You love being the center of attention and having everyone's eyes on you, and you're probably a natural public speaker. Regardless, the strategies in the next section can help you be even better.

10 to 13 Points You are the typical public speaker. While it's not your favorite thing to do, you will likely be okay as long as you are well prepared. Read the strategies discussed in "Tips & Reminders: 5 Ways to Overcome Debilitative Speech Anxiety" to learn how to further improve your skills.

14 to 18 Points It's probably no surprise to you that you experience a significant amount of anxiety about public speaking. But the good news is you can use the strategies in the Tips & Reminders section to get over your fears and get better. Believe it or not, some of the greatest speakers of all time have considered themselves highly anxious.

TIPS & REMINDERS

5 Ways to Overcome Debilitative Speech Anxiety

While irrational thinking or bad past experiences may make you apprehensive about speaking, you can take several steps to manage and often minimize speech anxiety.

1. **Use nervousness to your advantage.**

   A little nervousness can actually help you deliver a successful speech. Being completely calm can take away the passion that is one element of a good speech. It's important to control your anxiety but not eliminate it completely.

2. **Understand the difference between rational and irrational fears.**

   Fears based on irrational thinking aren't constructive. It's not realistic to expect that you'll deliver a perfect speech, and it's not productive or rational to indulge in catastrophic fantasies about what might go wrong. If you haven't prepared for a speech, however, that is a legitimate and rational fear.

3. **Maintain a receiver orientation.**

   Paying too much attention to your own feelings, even when you're feeling good about yourself, will take energy away from communicating with your listeners. Concentrate on your audience members rather than on yourself. Focus your energy on keeping them interested and on making sure they understand you.

4. **Keep a positive attitude.**

   Build and maintain a positive attitude toward your audience, your speech, and yourself as a speaker. Some communication consultants suggest that public speakers should concentrate on three statements immediately before speaking:

   I'm glad I have the chance to talk about this topic.

   I know what I'm talking about.

   I care about my audience.

   Repeating these statements (until you believe them) can help you maintain a positive attitude. Another technique for building a positive attitude is known as **visualization**.[9] This technique has been used successfully with athletes. It requires you to use your imagination to visualize the successful completion of your speech. Visualization can help make the self-fulfilling prophecy discussed in Chapter 2 work in your favor.

5. **Be prepared!**

   Preparation is the most important key to controlling speech anxiety. You can feel confident if you know from practice that your remarks are well organized and supported and your delivery is smooth. Researchers have determined that anxiety peaks just before speaking, reaches its second highest level at the time the assignment is announced and explained, and is lowest while you prepare your speech.[10] You should take advantage of this relatively low-stress time to work through the problems that would tend to make you nervous during the actual speech. For example, if your anxiety is based on a fear of forgetting what you are going to say, make sure that your notes are complete and effective and that you have practiced your speech thoroughly. If, on the other hand, your great fear is "sounding stupid," then get started early with lots of research.

Choosing a Type of Delivery

LEARNING OBJECTIVE 13.2: Distinguish among four different types of speech delivery.

One of your first considerations in being prepared is selecting the right way to deliver your speech.

There are four basic types of delivery: extemporaneous, impromptu, manuscript, and memorized. Each type creates a different impression and is appropriate under different conditions. Any speech may incorporate more than one of these types of delivery.

Manuscript

Manuscript speeches are read word for word from a prepared text. They are necessary when speaking for the record, as at legal proceedings or when presenting scientific findings. The greatest disadvantage of a manuscript speech is the lack of spontaneity. For that reason, it's best to avoid speaking from a script unless it's absolutely necessary.

Memorized

As the name suggests, **memorized speeches** are learned by heart. They're even more problematic than manuscript speeches: If you forget your lines, your audience will know immediately. Furthermore, memorized lines can sound artificial and insincere. While memorization may be necessary on special occasions when exact language is essential, it's best to avoid this approach.

Impromptu

Impromptu speeches fall at the opposite end of the delivery spectrum. They're delivered spontaneously, without preparation. You have to adopt this approach when someone asks you to share your thoughts to a group without providing advance notice. Impromptu speaking can be a training aid that teaches you to think on your feet and organize your thoughts quickly. But it's also risky: It can be hard to organize and deliver your ideas smoothly without advance preparation.

Extemporaneous

Extemporaneous speeches are planned in advance but don't depend on word-for-word delivery. This type of speech is easier to deliver because you can speak naturally in a direct, spontaneous manner. Extemporaneous speeches are conversational in tone, which means that they give the audience members the impression that you are talking to them, directly and honestly. Extemporaneous speaking is the most common type of delivery, and for most instructors, it's the *only* type of delivery allowed in the classroom.

Selecting Visual Aids

LEARNING OBJECTIVE 13.3: Describe the different types of visual aids that may be used in a speech.

No matter which type of delivery you use, another integral part of the preparation process is deciding whether or not to use visual aids. **Visual aids** are graphic devices that may be used to illustrate and support speech ideas. There are many types of visual aids. The most common are objects and models, diagrams, and word and number charts.

Objects and Models

Sometimes the most effective visual aid is the actual *object* you are talking about. This is true when you are talking about something that is portable enough to carry and simple enough to use during a demonstration, such as a small piece of weight-training equipment if you are talking about physical training. **Models** are scaled representations of the object you are discussing and are used when that object is too large (the new campus arts complex) or too small (a DNA molecule) or simply doesn't exist anymore (a *Tyrannosaurus rex*).

Diagrams

A **diagram** is any kind of line drawing that shows the most important properties of an object. Blueprints and architectural plans are common types of diagrams, as are maps and organizational charts. A diagram is most appropriate when you need to simplify a complex object or phenomenon and make it more understandable to the audience. Figure 13.1 is a diagram showing the relationship of the three primary characteristics of electricity, in which power is measured in volts, current is measured in amps, and resistance is measured in ohms. These three characteristics could be subpoints for one of the main points of an informative speech, and each aspect of electricity could be pointed out as they are discussed. This type of diagram therefore serves as a memory aid for the speaker as well as a comprehension guide for the audience.

Word and Number Charts

Word charts and **number charts** are visual depictions of key facts or statistics. Your audience will understand and remember these facts and numbers better if you present them visually. Many speakers list their main statistics in word or number charts.

- *Organizational charts.* **Organizational charts** are word charts showing the relationship of the various items. A word chart listing different types of cousins might look like Figure 13.2. Organizational charts are often used to show the hierarchies in business management positions.
- *Pie charts.* **Pie charts** are shaped as circles with wedges cut into them. They are used to show divisions of any whole: where your tax dollars go, percentages of the population involved in various occupations, and so on. Pie charts are often made up of percentages that add up to 100 percent. Usually, the wedges of the pie are organized from largest to smallest. The pie chart in Figure 13.3 represents one person's perception of the spending patterns of a typical college student.
- *Bar charts.* **Bar charts** compare two or more values by stretching them out in the form of horizontal rectangles. **Column charts**, such as the one shown in Figure 13.4, perform the same function as bar charts but use vertical rectangles.
- *Line charts.* A **line chart** maps out the direction of a moving point; it is ideally suited for showing changes over time. The time element is usually placed on the horizontal axis so that the line visually represents the trend over time. Figure 13.5 is a line chart.
- *Flow charts.* A **flow chart** is a diagram that depicts a process with boxes and arrows that represent the steps in a process. Figure 13.6 represents one speaker's perception of the steps involved in the decision to order takeout.

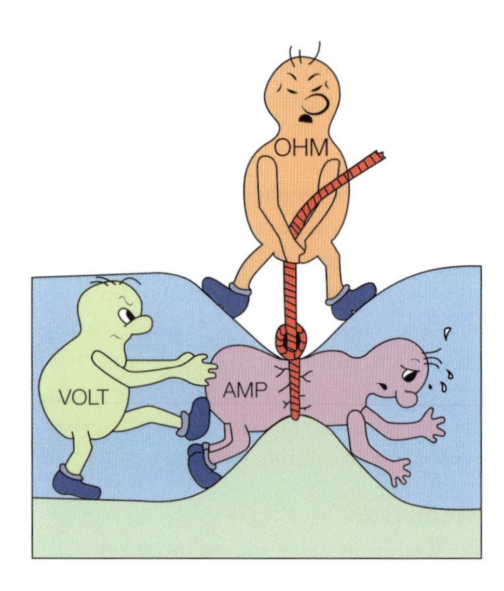

FIGURE 13.1 Diagram: How Electricity Works

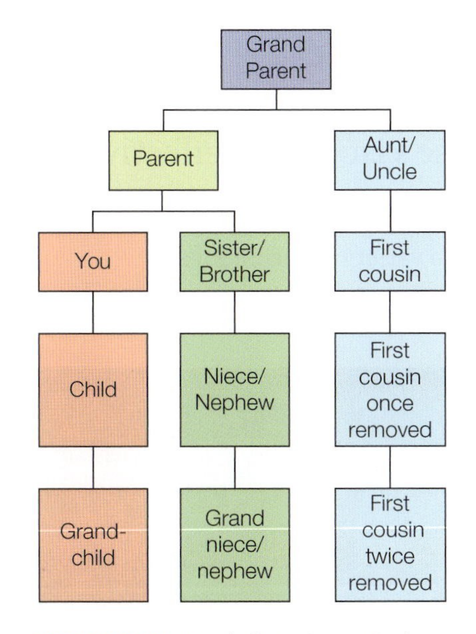

FIGURE 13.2 Word Chart: Cousin Explainer

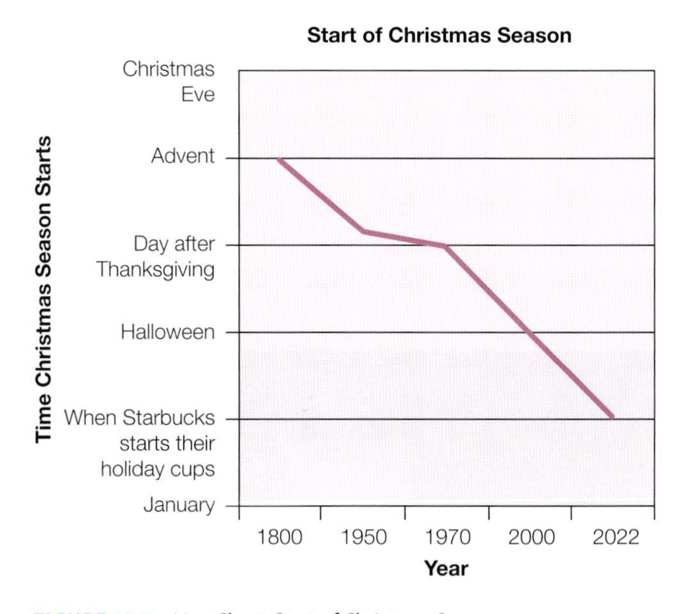

FIGURE 13.5 Line Chart: Start of Christmas Season

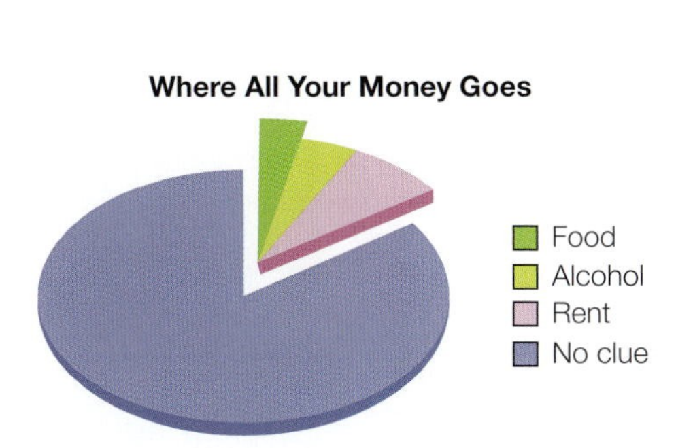

FIGURE 13.3 Pie Chart: Where All Your Money Goes

FIGURE 13.6 Flow Chart: Should You Get Up to Check What's in the Fridge or Order Takeout?

FIGURE 13.4 Column Chart: Appropriateness to Dress in Zombie Costume

Using Visual Aids

LEARNING OBJECTIVE 13.4: Learn to use visual aids effectively.

Many types and variations of visual aids can be used in any speech, and a variety of techniques can be used to present these aids. Each technique has its unique advantages and disadvantages.

Presentation Software

Presentation software can produce visual aids for any type of presentation or speech. Microsoft PowerPoint is the industry standard in this field. It was one of the earliest applications with easy to use, customizable templates for creating slides that could be projected onto a screen via digital projector. Prezi and Google Slides are other popular tools.[11]

In its simplest form, presentation software lets you build an effective **slide deck** out of your basic outline. You can choose color-coordinated backgrounds and consistent formatting that match the tone and purpose of your presentation. Most presentation software programs contain a clip art library that allows you to choose images to accompany your words. They also allow you to import images and video from outside sources and to build your own charts.

Whichever platform you choose, avoid making the content redundant by reading exactly what is on the screen to your audience—a phenomenon known as "death by PowerPoint." Instead, use presentation software to present examples, illustrations, and key points that help your audience keep track of your ideas while you move your speech from idea to idea at a comfortable pace.

The sample informative speech in Appendix A uses a deck of slides to project photographic examples. If you would like to learn more about using presentation software, you can find several Web-based tutorial programs.[12]

Audio and Video Clips

Audio and video files can supply information that can't be presented any other way. For example, you might include a brief YouTube clip to show the audience what divers found in an underwater shipwreck, if that's what your speech is about.

In most cases you should use video and audio clips sparingly. The general rule when using these media is: *Don't let them get in the way of the direct, person-to-person contact that is the primary advantage of public speaking.*

Whiteboards and Chalkboards

Low-tech visual aids can be effective for informal presentations, or when computers and projectors are not available. Sometimes, these low-tech options are an appreciated alternative for audiences that already feel media-saturated, and some speakers prefer them because they allow for more spontaneous audience contact.

The major advantage of whiteboards and chalkboards is their spontaneity. With them you can create your visual aid as you speak, including items generated from audience responses. Along with the odor of whiteboard markers and the squeaking of chalk, a major disadvantage of these media is the difficulty of preparing visual aids on them in advance, especially if several speeches are scheduled in the same room at the same hour.

Flip Pads and Poster Boards

Flip pads are like oversized writing tablets attached to a portable easel, and poster boards are rigid sheets that can be set up on the same type of easel. Both of these techniques enable you to combine the spontaneity of the whiteboard with a portability that enables you to prepare visuals in advance. However, flip pads and poster boards are bulky, and preparing professional-looking exhibits on them requires a fair amount of artistic ability.

Handouts

The major advantage of handouts is that audience members can take away the information they contain after your speech. For this reason, handouts are excellent memory and reference aids. The major disadvantage is that they are doubly distracting when distributed during a speech: first, when they are passed out, and second, when they are in front of audience members while you have gone on to something else. If you do pass around handouts during a speech, make sure they are set up for note-taking, and encourage your audience to do that. Otherwise, it's best to pass them out at the end of the speech so audience members can take them when they leave. •

TIPS & REMINDERS

5 Rules for Using Visual Aids Effectively

No matter which visual aids you use, you should talk to your audience, not to your visual aid. Some speakers become so wrapped up in their props that they turn their backs on their audience and sacrifice eye contact. Here are some additional guidelines.

1. **Keep visual aids simple.**

   Your goal is to clarify, not confuse. Use only key words or phrases, not sentences. The "rule of seven" states that each exhibit you use should contain no more than seven lines of text, each with no more than seven words. Keep all printing horizontal. Omit all nonessential details.

2. **Consider the size of visual aids.**

   Visual aids should be large enough for your entire audience to see at one time but portable enough for you to get them out of the way when they are no longer pertinent.

3. **Make visual aids attractive.**

   Visual aids should be visually interesting and as neat as possible. If you don't have the necessary artistic or computer skills, try to get help from a friend or from the audiovisual center at your college.

4. **Be sure visual aids are appropriate.**

   Visuals must be appropriate to all the components of the speaking situation—you, your audience, and your topic—and they must emphasize the point you are trying to make. Don't make the mistake of using a visual aid that looks good but has only a weak link to the point you want to make, such as showing a map of a city transit system while talking about the condition of the individual cars.

5. **Be in control of your visual aids at all times.**

   Test all electronic media in advance, preferably in the room where you will speak. Just to be safe, have non-electronic backups ready. Be conservative when you choose demonstrations: Wild animals, chemical reactions, and gimmicks meant to shock a crowd can often backfire.

Visual Aspects of Delivery

LEARNING OBJECTIVE 13.5: **Explain the visual components of delivery and use them to improve your performance.**

Audience members are more likely to trust your nonverbal communication than the words you speak. If you tell them, "It's great to be here today," but you stand slouched over with your hands in your pockets and a bored expression on your face, they are likely to discount what you say. If, instead, you approach a subject with genuine enthusiasm, your audience is likely to sense it and to feed off of that enthusiasm.

You can show enthusiasm through your **visual aspects of delivery**, including your appearance, movement, posture, facial expression, and eye contact.

Appearance

Appearance is not a presentation variable as much as a *preparation* variable. Some communication consultants suggest new clothes and new hairstyles for their clients. In case you consider any of these, be forewarned that you should be attractive to your audience but not flashy. Research suggests that audiences like speakers who are similar to them, but they prefer the similarity to be shown conservatively.[13] Speakers, it seems, are perceived to be more credible when they look businesslike.

Movement

The way you walk to the front of your audience will express your confidence and enthusiasm. After you begin speaking, however, nervous energy can cause your body to shake and twitch, and that can be distressing both to you and to your audience. One way to control involuntary movement is to move voluntarily. Don't feel that you have to stand in one spot or that all your gestures need to be carefully planned. Simply get involved in your message, and let your involvement create the motivation for your movement. That way, when you move, you will emphasize what you are saying in the same way you would emphasize it if you were talking to a group of friends.

Movement can also help you maintain contact with all members of your audience. Those closest to you will feel the greatest contact. This creates what is known as the "action zone" in a typical classroom—the center area at the front of the room. Movement enables you to extend this action zone, to include in it people who would otherwise remain uninvolved. Without overdoing it, you should feel free to move toward, away from, or from side to side in front of your audience.

Posture

Generally speaking, good posture means standing with your spine relatively straight, your shoulders relatively squared off, and your feet angled out to keep your body from falling over sideways. In other words, rather than standing at military attention, you should be comfortably erect.

Good posture can help you control nervousness by allowing you to breathe properly; when your brain receives enough oxygen, it's easier for you to think clearly. Good posture also increases audience contact because audience members will feel that you are interested enough in them to stand formally, yet relaxed enough to be at ease with them.

Facial Expression

The expression on your face can be more meaningful to an audience than the words you say. Try it yourself with a mirror. Say, "You're a terrific audience," for example, with a smirk, with a warm smile, with a deadpan expression, and then with a scowl. It just doesn't mean the same thing. Like your movement, your facial expressions will reflect your genuine involvement with your message.

Eye Contact

Eye contact is perhaps the most important nonverbal facet of delivery. Eye contact not only increases your direct contact with the audience but also can be used to help you control your nervousness. Direct eye contact is a form of reality testing. The most frightening aspect of speaking is the unknown. How will the audience react? Direct eye contact allows you to test your perception of the audience as you speak. By deliberately establishing contact with any apparently bored audience members, you might find that they are interested; they just aren't showing that interest because they don't think anyone is looking.

To maintain eye contact, you could try to meet the eyes of each member of your audience squarely at least once during any given presentation. After you have made definite eye contact, move on to another audience member. You can learn to do this quickly, so you can visually latch on to every member of a good-sized group in a relatively short time. ●

TIPS & REMINDERS

4 Steps to Practicing a Speech

Preparation is one of the keys to controlling speech anxiety, and one of the best ways to be prepared is to practice. To get to know your material and feel comfortable with your presentation, we recommend that you go through these steps.

1. **Present the speech to yourself.**
   "Talk through" the entire speech, including your examples and forms of support. Don't skip through parts of the speech as you practice by using placeholders such as "This is where I present my statistics."

2. **Record yourself.**
   Because you hear your own voice partially through cranial bone structure, you are sometimes surprised at what you sound like to others. Video is an effective way to gauge what you look and sound like.[14]

3. **Present the speech in front of a small group of friends or relatives.**[15]
   A friendly audience can be honest without being discouraging!

4. **Give the speech to at least one listener in the room (or a similar room) in which you will present the final speech.**
   It's good to get a feel for your actual venue, and to make sure there's enough ventilation.

Auditory Aspects of Delivery

LEARNING OBJECTIVE 13.6: Explain the auditory components of delivery and use them to improve your performance.

As you read in Chapter 6, your paralanguage—the way you use your voice—says a good deal about you, especially about your sincerity and enthusiasm. Controlling your vocal characteristics will also decrease your nervousness.

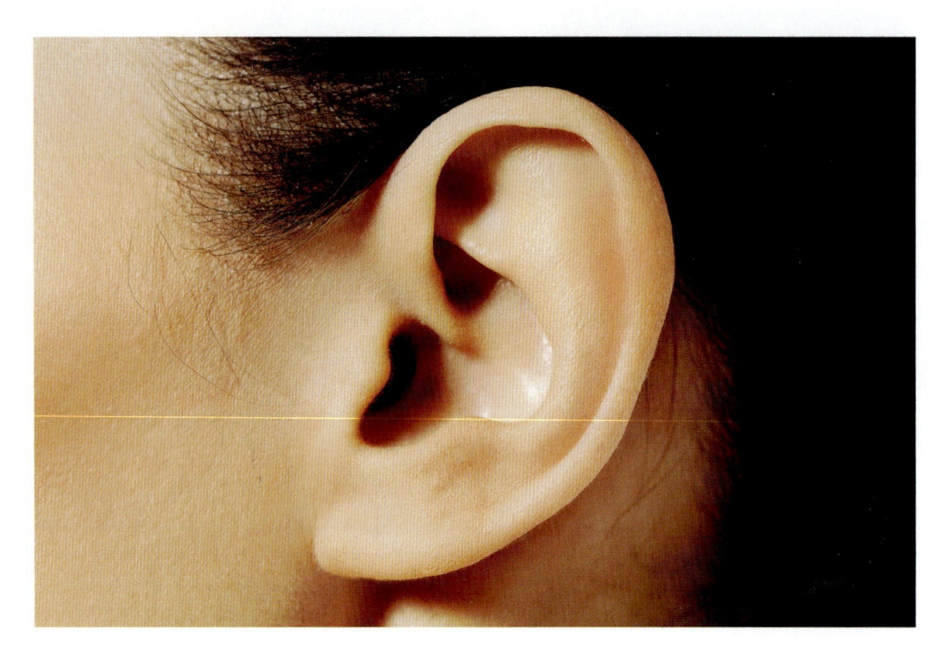

You can control your voice by recognizing and using appropriate volume, rate, pitch, and articulation.

Volume

The loudness of your voice is determined by the amount of air you push past the vocal folds in your throat. The key to controlling volume, then, is controlling the amount of air you use. The key to determining the right volume is audience contact. Your delivery should be loud enough so audience members can hear everything you say, but not so loud that they feel you are talking to someone in the next room. Too much volume is seldom the problem for beginning speakers. Usually they either are not loud enough or have a tendency to fade out or mumble at the end of a thought. Keep in mind that words you whisper or scream will be emphasized by their volume.

Rate

There is a range of personal differences in speaking speed, or **rate**. Daniel Webster, the 19th-century American statesman, is said to have spoken at around 90 words per minute, whereas one actor who is known for his fast-talking commercials speaks at about 250. Normal speaking speed is between 120 and 150 words per minute—about the same rate as a television newscaster would speak. If you talk much more slowly than that, you may lull your audience to sleep. Faster speaking rates are sometimes stereotypically associated with speaker competence,[16] but if you speak too rapidly, you will be unintelligible. Once again, your involvement in your message is the key to achieving an effective rate. If you pause or speed up, your rate will suggest emphasis.

Pitch

The highness or lowness of your voice—**pitch**—is controlled by the frequency at which your vocal folds vibrate as you push air through them. Because taut vocal folds vibrate at a greater frequency, pitch is influenced by muscular tension. This explains why nervous speakers have a tendency occasionally to "squeak," whereas relaxed speakers seem to be more in control.

Pitch will tend to follow rate and volume. As you speed up or become louder, your pitch will have a tendency to rise. If your range in pitch is too narrow, your voice will have a singsong quality. If it is too wide, you may sound overly dramatic. You should control your pitch so that your listeners believe you are talking with them rather than at them. Once again, your involvement in your message should take care of this naturally for you.

Articulation

The final auditory nonverbal behavior, articulation, is perhaps the most important. For our purposes here, **articulation** means pronouncing all the parts of all the necessary words and nothing else. Careful articulation means using your lips, teeth, tongue, and jaw to bite off your words, cleanly and separately, one at a time.

TIPS & REMINDERS

Ways to Improve Your Articulation

What follows are some tips for careful, not standardized, articulation.

1. **Say the entire word.**

   The most common mistake in articulation is **deletion**, or leaving off part of a word. The most common deletions occur at the ends of words, especially *-ing* words. *Going, doing,* and *stopping* become *goin', doin',* and *stoppin'*. Parts of words can be left off in the middle, too, as in *terr'iss* for *terrorist, innernet* for *internet,* and *asst* for *asked.*

2. **Pronounce each sound correctly.**

   Substitution takes place when you replace part of a word with an incorrect sound. The ending *-th* is often replaced at the end of a word with a single *t*, as when *with* becomes *wit*. The *th-* sound is also a problem at the beginning of words, as *this, that,* and *those* have a tendency to become *dis, dat,* and *dose*. (This tendency is especially prevalent in many parts of the northeastern United States.)

3. **Don't add extra sounds.**

   The articulation problem of **addition** is caused by adding extra parts to words, such as *incentative* instead of *incentive, athalete* instead of *athlete,* and *orientated* instead of *oriented*. Sometimes this type of addition is caused by incorrect word choice, as when *irregardless* is used for *regardless.* Another type of addition is the use of "tag questions," such as *you know*? or *you see*? or *right*? at the end of sentences. To have every other sentence punctuated with one of these barely audible superfluous phrases can be annoying. Probably the worst type of addition, or at least the most common, however, is the use of *uh, umm, like,* and *anda* between words. *Anda* is often stuck between two words when *and* isn't even needed. If you find yourself doing that, you might want to pause or swallow instead.[17]

4. **Speak clearly.**

   Slurring is caused by trying to say two or more words at once—or at least overlapping the end of one word with the beginning of the next. Word pairs ending with *of* are the worst offenders in this category. *Sort of* becomes *sorta, kind of* becomes *kinda*, and *because of* becomes *becausa*. Word combinations ending with *to* are often slurred, as when *want to* becomes *wanna*. Sometimes even more than two words are blended together, as when *that is the way* becomes *thatsaway*.

PAUSE TO REFLECT *How Is Your Articulation?*

1. Go over the guidelines for good articulation, and think about your circle of friends and acquaintances. Who among them has the best articulation? By what criteria?

2. Among that same group, who has the worst articulation? By what criteria?

3. Finally, where do you place yourself among the best and the worst? Again, what are the criteria you use to judge yourself?

Virtual Delivery

LEARNING OBJECTIVE 13.7: Identify best practices for delivering a speech virtually.

When college classes moved from in-person to video conferencing during the COVID-19 pandemic many students did not want to be seen on video. As one student put it, "Online is different. Everyone can see you."[18] In a typical in-person class, most of the time is spent with students looking forward, at the instructor.

On the other side of the remote setup, instructors noticed that it was much easier and more effective to teach a class when everyone's video monitors were on. Without that, they didn't know if the students were actually there. Many college instructors asked their students not only to keep their cameras on, but to follow certain guidelines, such as:

- Sitting in a well-lit room.
- Using a virtual background to hide surroundings.
- Ensuring sufficient lighting on the face, which should be the brightest spot in the frame. You can increase the lighting by adjusting the lighting on your computer or screen.
- Setting up the head shot in advance with eyes framed along the imagined upper third line (full face and shoulders, not too much head room).
- When speaking, alternating the gaze between the camera lens (for virtual eye contact) and the faces on the screen (to see audience reactions).

Many of these guidelines apply to virtual speech delivery as well. Increasingly, students and others are being asked to deliver online presentations. While many of the guidelines for presenting in-person speeches apply to online presentations as well, online presentations often involve additional considerations. For advice on presenting in virtual settings, see "Tips & Reminders: 6 Tips for Online/Virtual Delivery of Speeches."

TIPS & REMINDERS

Tips for Online/Virtual Delivery of Speeches

Several online sites provide tutorials for giving online presentations, but here are just a few general guidelines:

1. **Try out various web-conferencing platforms.**

   While Zoom, Microsoft Teams, and WebEx are the most popular, there are dozens of platforms that can be used for online meetings.[19] All have different nuances in the ways they set up the screen and allow users to participate.

2. **Schedule a run-through before the actual event.**

   This will help you ensure the presentation is not too long or too short, and it will enable you to iron out any technical issues or glitches. Most conferencing platforms will allow you to record the session, even if there are only one or two participants, so you can view your presentation in advance and analyze ways to improve it.

3. **Use dynamic visuals.**

   All of the visual aids mentioned earlier are available in online versions. Online whiteboards, for example, can be especially effective for virtual team collaboration. Action shots are better than still images when possible. If you plan to show video, keep it short and on point.

4. **Keep the slides simple.**

   Avoid slides with a lot of text.

5. **Keep it entertaining.**

   Employ stories and/or humor to keep the audience engaged.

6. **Start and end on time.**

   People are busy, and many may have other activities or meetings before or after your presentation; show them respect by sticking to the allotted time. Also, consider putting a recorded version of the final version online via a file-sharing platform such as Dropbox for those who missed the live presentation.

Presenting Speeches

Managing Speech Anxiety

- Speakers think more rapidly and express themselves more energetically when they experience facilitative speech anxiety.
- Debilitative speech anxiety is detrimental and stems from negative past experiences or irrational fears.

4 Types of Irrational Fears About Public Speaking

- Fallacy of catastrophic failure
- Fallacy of perfection
- Fallacy of approval
- Fallacy of overgeneralization

5 Ways to Overcome Debilitative Speech Anxiety

- Use nervousness to your advantage.
- Be rational.
- Be receiver oriented.
- Be positive.
- Be prepared.

Types of Delivery

- Manuscript
- Memorized
- Impromptu
- Extemporaneous

Types of Visual Aids

- Objects and models
- Diagrams
- Word and number charts
- Organizational charts
- Pie charts
- Bar and column charts
- Line charts
- Flow charts

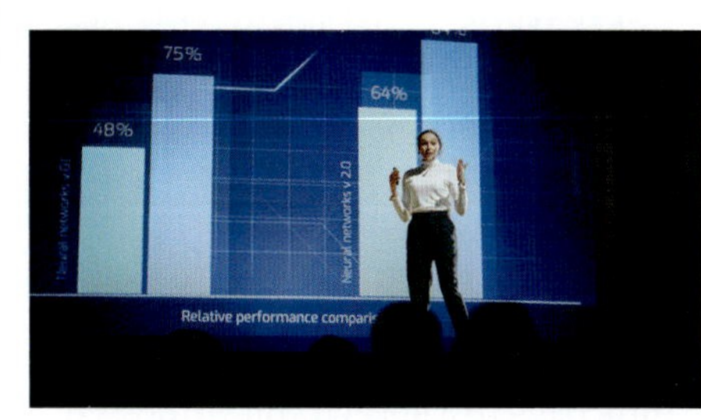

Media for Presenting Visual Aids

- Presentation software
- Audio and video clips
- Whiteboards and chalkboards
- Flip pads and poster boards
- Handouts

5 Rules for Using Visual Aids Effectively

- Keep them simple.
- Consider their size.
- Make them attractive.
- Make sure they are appropriate.
- Control them at all times.

Visual Aspects of Delivery

- Appearance
- Movement
- Posture
- Facial expression
- Eye contact

4 Steps to Practicing a Speech

- Present it to yourself.
- Record it.
- Present it to a small group of friends.
- Present it in the room in which it will be given.

Auditory Aspects of Delivery

- Volume
- Rate
- Pitch
- Articulation

4 Ways to Improve Your Articulation

- Say the entire word.
- Pronounce each sound correctly.
- Don't add extra sounds.
- Speak clearly.

Virtual Delivery

- Sit in a well-lit room.
- Use a virtual background.
- Ensure sufficient lighting.
- Set up the head shot in advance
- Alternate your gaze between the camera lens and the faces on the screen.

6 Tips for Online/Virtual Speeches

- Try out various web-conferencing platforms.
- Schedule a run-through before the actual event.
- Use dynamic visuals.
- Keep the slides simple.
- Keep the speech entertaining.
- Start and end on time.

Show Your Communication Know-How

13.1: Describe the sources of debilitative stage fright and ways to overcome speech anxiety.

Everyone experiences a certain degree of stage fright. What is your personal process for making it work in your favor, rather than against you?

KEY TERMS: facilitative speech anxiety, debilitative speech anxiety, irrational thinking, fallacy of catastrophic failure, fallacy of perfection, fallacy of approval, fallacy of overgeneralization, visualization

13.2: Distinguish among four different types of speech delivery.

Explain why you chose the type of delivery that you did for a speech you gave or might give.

KEY TERMS: manuscript speeches, memorized speeches, impromptu speeches, extemporaneous speeches

13.3: Describe the different types of visual aids that may be used in a speech.

For a speech that you gave or might give, what visual aids would be most effective and why?

KEY TERMS: visual aids, models, diagram, word charts, number charts, organizational charts, pie charts, bar charts, column charts, line chart, flow chart

13.4: Learn to use visual aids effectively.

Think back to a speech you witnessed in which the visual aids were particularly effective or ineffective. What made the difference?

KEY TERM: slide deck

13.5: Explain the visual components of delivery and use them to improve your performance.

Practice your speech using at least three of the methods discussed in this chapter. How could you improve your performance visually?

KEY TERM: visual aspects of delivery

13.6: Explain the auditory components of delivery and use them to improve your performance.

Practice your speech using at least three of the methods discussed in this chapter. How could you improve your performance in terms of its sound?

KEY TERMS: rate, pitch, articulation, deletion, substitution, addition, slurring

13.7: Identify best practices for delivering a speech virtually.

Practice your speech with a friend or classmate on Zoom or another video conferencing platform. What about your delivery surprises you?

SPEAKING TO INFORM AND

Persuade

14

Informing Versus Persuading

LEARNING OBJECTIVE 14.1: Distinguish between speeches to inform and to persuade.

In the age of social media, many people are confused about the differences among information, disinformation, and persuasion.[1] Online "news reports" and "informative messages" are often blatantly, and sometimes sneakily, persuasive, while some well-written opinion pieces can be profoundly informative. When it comes to speeches, however, there are relatively straightforward guidelines for distinguishing between the overall focus of an informative and a persuasive presentation.

Informative Speeches

Informative speaking goes on all around you, whether it's a professor giving a lecture, a news anchor detailing the latest budget stalemate, or a friend giving you a play-by-play of last night's game. Speeches are considered informative if their primary purpose is to describe, explain, or instruct. In addition, informative speeches tend to be noncontroversial, and informative speakers do not focus on trying to change the audience's attitudes.

- *An informative topic tends to be noncontroversial.* For example, if you were to give a speech about hospital births and home-based midwife births, you would describe what the practitioners of each method believe and do without criticizing either method or boosting one over the other. The goal is to present information that is objective and will not engender conflict. If speakers *do* present a controversial topic, they will explain all sides of the issue and will not ask the audience to pick a side.
- *The informative speaker does not intend to change audience attitudes.* For example, an informative speaker might explain how a new social media app works but not try to "sell" that app to the audience. Persuasive speaking, on the other hand, seeks to change audience attitudes or behavior.

Persuasive Speeches

Persuasion is the process of motivating someone, through communication, to change a particular belief, attitude, or behavior. It is not the same as coercion or forcing someone to do something. **Persuasive speaking** can be classified three different ways. First, it can be classified by type of proposition, such as facts (whether something is true or false), value (whether some idea, person, or object has worth), or policy (whether a specific course of action should be taken). Persuasion can also be categorized based on the desired outcome, whether it is to convince an audience of something or to go further and move audience members to behave in a certain way. Finally, persuasion can be classified based on the directness of the appeal, whether it is an outright request or a more indirect one.

- *Persuasion is usually incremental.* When it is successful, persuasion generally succeeds over time. One persuasive speech may be but a single step in an overall persuasive campaign. The best example of this is the various communications that take place during the months of a political campaign. Candidates watch the opinion polls carefully, adjusting their appeals. The best persuaders are always building on the persuasion that came before.

- *Persuasion can be ethical.* Even when they understand the difference between persuasion and coercion, some people are still uncomfortable with the idea of persuasive speaking. They may associate it with pushy salespeople or unscrupulous politicians. And it's true; persuasive speaking can be and often is used by unethical speakers for unethical purposes. However, it is also through persuasion that we may influence others' lives in worthwhile ways. Whether it's convincing a loved one to seek treatment, friends to volunteer for a worthwhile cause, or an employer to hire you for a job, persuasion can be ethical. Persuasion is considered ethical if it is in the best interests of the audience and it does not depend on false or misleading information to change the audience's attitude or behavior.

Overlap Between Informative and Persuasive Speeches

There is some overlap between informative and persuasive speeches. Persuasive speeches also inform (about arguments, evidence, and so on) and informative speeches might change an audience's mind. The sample speech in Appendix A, for example, dealing with the sex lives of fish, also mentions humanity's disruption of the aquatic ecosystem, and might change some minds about that topic. The overall focus of the speech, however, is informative.

PAUSE TO REFLECT *How Do You Distinguish Between Informative and Persuasive Speaking?*

1. Think of a topic for a speech. How would you structure the speech if you were trying to inform your audience on this topic? How would you structure the speech if you were trying to persuade them of something related to this topic?

2. Aristotle insisted that persuasion had to balance logic and ethics with emotion. What arguments have you found in real life that fail to follow this guideline?

3. Tune into either Fox News or CNN and wait for the first story on today's political news. Would you consider this story to be informative or persuasive? Why?

4. Think of a memorable TV commercial and find it on YouTube. What percentage of the ad is informative, and what percentage is persuasive?

Techniques of Informative Speaking

LEARNING OBJECTIVE 14.2: Explain the techniques of informative speaking and use them to present an effective informative speech.

The techniques of informative speaking are based on a number of principles of human communication in general, and public speaking specifically, that help an audience understand and care about your speech. The first step is to make it easy for your audience to listen.

Define a specific informative purpose.

As mentioned in Chapter 12, any good speech must be based on a purpose statement that is result oriented, specific, and realistic. This is especially true for an informative speech. An **informative purpose statement** is generally worded to stress the results you are trying to achieve: audience knowledge, ability, or both:

> *After listening to my speech, my audience will be able to identify the four reasons that online memes go viral.*
>
> *After listening to my speech, my audience will be able to recall at least three reasons that the Electoral College should be abolished.*

Notice that each of these purpose statements uses a specific verb such as *recall*, *identify*, or *discuss* to point out what the audience will be able to do after hearing the speech. Other key verbs for informative purpose statements include these:

> *Accomplish | Choose | Explain | Name | Recognize |*
>
> *Analyze | Contrast | Integrate | Operate | Review |*
>
> *Apply | Describe | List | Perform | Summarize*

A clear informative purpose statement will lead to a clear thesis statement, which presents the central idea of your speech. Sometimes your thesis statement will just preview the central idea:

> *Understanding why memes go viral could make you very wealthy someday.*
>
> *If the Electoral College were not in the Constitution, it would be unconstitutional.*

Setting a clear informative purpose will help keep you focused as you prepare and present your informative speech.

Use clear, simple language.

Another technique for effective informative speaking is to use clear language, which means using precise, simple wording and avoiding jargon. As you plan your speech, use words that are familiar to your audience. Important ideas do not have to sound complicated. Along with simple, precise vocabulary, you should also strive for a direct, short sentence structure. For example, in the sample informative speech in Appendix A, Marah J. Hardt wants to establish common examples of sequential hermaphroditism in fish. As an expert, there are many ways she could do that using scholarly scientific jargon, but instead she says this:

> *I bet nearly all of you have at some point had a seafood dish made up of an individual that started life as one sex and transitioned to another. Oysters? Grouper? Shrimp? Seeing some heads nodding, yeah.*

Emphasize important points.

One key principle of informative speaking is to stress the important points in your speech. This can be done through repetition and the use of signposts.

- *Repetition* is one of the age-old rules of learning. Humans are more likely to understand information that is stated more than once. This is especially true in a speaking situation, because audience members usually cannot go back to reread something they have missed. Of course, simply repeating something in the same words likely would bore audience members who actually are paying attention, so effective speakers learn to say the same thing in more than one way. E. Paige Allbright, a student at Western Kentucky University, used this technique when she wanted to establish the scope of America's childcare problem:

> *America is in a childcare crisis. Families with young children face impossible choices: pay significant portions of their income for childcare . . . or leave the workplace. Half of U.S. families reported difficulty in finding childcare, whose costs have doubled in the last two decades.*[2]

Repeating an idea in different words can be effective when you use it to emphasize important points.[3] It can be ineffective, however, when used with obvious, trivial, or boring points or when repeated to excess. There is no sure rule for making certain you have not overemphasized a point. You just have to use your best judgment.

- *Signposts* are another way to emphasize important material. **Signposts** are words or phrases that emphasize the importance of what you are about to say. You can state, simply enough, *"What I'm about to say is important,"* or you can use some variation of that statement: *"But listen to this . . ."* or *"The most important thing to remember is . . ."* or *"The three keys to this situation are. . . ."*

Generate audience involvement.

The final technique for effective informative speaking is to get the audience involved in your speech. **Audience involvement** is the level of commitment and attention that listeners devote to a speech. Educational psychologists have long known that the best way to teach people something is to have them do it. Social psychologists have added to this rule by proving, in many studies, that participating in an interaction increases audience comprehension of, and agreement with, the message being presented.

There are many ways to encourage audience involvement in your speech. One way is to follow the rules for good delivery by maintaining enthusiasm, energy, and eye contact. Another way is to ask your audience members to apply a general principle to themselves: "What would you do if . . ." or "How would you feel if . . ." Two of the most effective methods are having your audience actually do something during your speech or holding a question-and-answer period.

For example, you can have listeners actively do something during your speech through **audience participation**. If you were giving a demonstration on isometric exercises (muscle-building exercises, which don't require too much room for movement), you could have the entire audience stand up and do one or two sample exercises. If you were explaining how to fill out a federal income tax form, you could give each class member a sample form to fill out as you explain it. Outlines and checklists can be used in a similar manner for just about any speech. Figure 14.1 shows how one student used audience participation to demonstrate the various restrictions that were once placed on voting rights. ●

TIPS & REMINDERS

3 Ways to Make It Easy for the Audience to Listen

Keep in mind the complex nature of listening, discussed in Chapter 5. It's not always easy for your audience members to hear, pay attention, understand, and remember. This means that, as you plan your speech, you should consider techniques that recognize the way human beings process information.

1. **Limit the amount of information you present.**

   You probably won't have enough time to transmit all your research to your audience in one sitting. It's better to make careful choices about three to five main ideas you want to get across and then develop those ideas fully. Too much information leads to overload and a lack of attention on your audience's part.

2. **Transition from familiar to newer information.**

   Based on your audience analysis (Chapter 12), you should move members of the audience from information that is likely to be familiar to them to newer information. If you are giving a speech about how the stock market works, you could compare the daily activity of a broker with that of a salesperson in a retail store, or you could compare the idea of capital growth (a new concept to some listeners) with interest earned in a savings account.

3. **Transition from simple to more complex information.**

   Just as you move audience members from the familiar to the unfamiliar, you can move them from the simple to the complex. An average college audience, for example, might be able to understand the complexities of genetic modification if you begin with the concept of inherited characteristics.

Voting is something that a lot of us may take for granted. Today, the only requirements for voting are that you are a U.S. citizen aged 18 or older who has lived in the same place for at least 30 days and that you have registered. But it hasn't always been that way. Americans have had to struggle for the right to vote. I'd like to illustrate this by asking everyone to please stand.

[Wait, prod class to stand.]

I'm going to ask some questions. If you answer no to any question, please sit down.

- Have you resided at the same address for at least one year? If not, sit down. Residency requirements of more than 30 days weren't abolished until 1970.
- Are you white? If not, sit down. The 15th Amendment gave non-whites the right to vote in 1870, but many states didn't enforce it until the late 1960s.
- Are you male? If not, sit down. The 19th Amendment only gave women the right to vote in 1920.
- Do you own a home? If not, sit down. Through the mid-1800s only property owners could vote.
- Are you Protestant? If not, sit down. That's right. Religious requirements existed in the early days throughout the country.

Source: Voter registration project, New York Public Interest Research Group, Brooklyn College chapter, 2018.

FIGURE 14.1 Using Audience Participation

TIPS & REMINDERS

Ways to Handle a Question-and-Answer Period

One way to increase audience involvement is to answer questions at the end of your speech. You should encourage your audience to ask questions and keep four guidelines in mind as you answer them.

1. **Listen to the substance of the question.**

   Don't zero in on irrelevant details. Instead, listen for the big picture—the basic, overall question that is being asked. If you are not really sure what the substance of a question is, ask the questioner to paraphrase it. Don't be afraid to let the questioners do their share of the work.

2. **Paraphrase confusing or quietly asked questions.**

   Use the active listening skills described in Chapter 5. You can paraphrase the question in just a few words: "If I understand your question, you are asking ______. Is that right?"

3. **Avoid defensive reactions to questions.**

   Even if the questioner seems to be calling you a liar or stupid or biased, try to listen to the substance of the question and respond to that, rather than the possible personal attack.

4. **Answer the question briefly.**

   Then check the questioner's comprehension of your answer by observing their nonverbal response or by asking, "Does that answer your question?"

Techniques of Persuasive Speaking

LEARNING OBJECTIVE 14.3: Explain the techniques of persuasive speaking and use them to present an effective persuasive speech.

The guidelines for informative speaking also form the foundation for persuasive speaking. To be persuasive, however, you also need a clear persuasive purpose and to recognize where your audience's attitudes differ from your own.

Set a specific persuasive purpose.

Remember that your objective in a persuasive speech is to move the audience to a specific, attainable attitude or behavior. In a **speech to change attitudes**, the purpose statement should stress an attitude:

After listening to my speech, audience members will agree that we need to form a New People's Party.

In a **speech to change behavior,** the purpose statement will stress behavior:

After listening to my speech, audience members will sign my petition to include candidates from the New People's Party on the ballot for our next election.

Your purpose statement should always be specific, attainable, and worded from the audience's point of view. "The purpose of my speech is to save the whales" is not a purpose statement that has been carefully thought out. Your audience members wouldn't likely be able to jump into the ocean and save the whales, even if they wanted to. However, they might be able to support a specific piece of legislation by signing a letter to your local congressional representative.

A clear, specific purpose statement will help you stay on track throughout all the stages of preparing your persuasive speech. Because the main purpose of your speech is to have an effect on your audience, you have a continual test that you can use for every idea and every piece of evidence. The question you ask is, "Will this help me to get the audience members to think/feel/behave in the manner I have described in my purpose statement?" If the answer is "yes," you forge ahead.

Adapt to your specific audience.

In a persuasive speech, you should appeal to the values of the audience whenever possible, even if they are not *your* strongest values. This does not mean you should pretend to believe in something. It does mean, however, that you stress those shared values that are felt most forcefully by the members of the audience.[4]

In addition, you should use audience analysis (Chapter 12) to predict the type of response you are likely to get. Sometimes you have to pick out one part of your audience—a **target audience** comprising the subgroup you must persuade to reach your goal—and aim your speech mostly at those members. Some audience members might be so opposed to what you are advocating that you have no hope of reaching them. Still others might already agree with you, so you don't need to persuade them. A middle portion of your audience members might be undecided or uncommitted, and they would be the most productive target for your appeals.

Establish common ground and credibility.

Establishing **common ground**—stressing as many similarities as possible between yourself and your audience members—helps prove that you understand your audience and gives them a reason to listen to you. By showing areas of agreement, you make it easier for the audience to consider settling your one disagreement—the one related to the attitude or behavior you would like them to change.

Establishing common ground also builds some credibility with the audience. **Credibility** refers to the believability of a speaker; it is a perception in the minds of the audience. Members of an audience form judgments about the credibility of a speaker based on their perception of many characteristics, including competence, character, and charisma.[5]

- *Competence* refers to the speaker's expertise on the topic. Sometimes this competence can come from personal experience that leads your audience to regard you as an authority on the topic. For example, if everyone in the audience knows you've earned big profits in the stock market, they will probably take your investment advice seriously. The other way to be seen as competent is to be well prepared with a speech that is well researched. Emma González, the activist who fought for gun control after her high school was the site of a shooting with multiple fatalities, spoke about both her experience and her preparation to speak on her topic:

The students at this school have been having debates on guns for what feels like our entire lives. AP Gov had three debates on this topic this year. Some discussions on the subject even occurred during the shooting while students were hiding in the closets.[6]

- *Character* involves the audience's perception of your ethics and integrity. Again, Emma González offered some insight into her moral courage when she said,

Every single person up here today, all these people, should be home grieving. But instead, we are up here standing together because if all our government and President can do is send thoughts and prayers, then it's time for victims to be the change that we need to see.

- *Charisma* is the audience's perception of your enthusiasm (how you deliver your remarks) and likability (which includes how friendly and genuine you are). History and research have shown that audiences are more likely to be persuaded by a charismatic speaker. Emma González bolstered her perceived charisma when she said,

We are going to be the kids you read about in textbooks. Not because we're going to be another statistic about mass shooting in America, but because . . . we are going to change the law. That's going to be Marjory Stoneman Douglas in that textbook and it's going to be due to the tireless effort of the school board, the faculty members, the family members and most of all the students. . . .

The idea that credibility is important in persuasion is not new. Aristotle insisted upon it more than 2,000 years ago. He also established that it is important to recognize and appeal to an audience's emotions and logical reasoning, a triad we turn to next.

Draw upon Aristotle's Triad.

Aristotle proposed that the three requirements of persuasion are logos, ethos, and pathos.

Logos is the idea of a logical appeal, one based on formal reasoning.

The idea of **ethos** is that the speaker has the audience's best interests in mind at all times. It involves being ethical about your intentions and honestly believing that what you propose is best for your audience.

The idea of **pathos** is to speak to the heart as well as the head. Aristotle warned that political leaders who used only emotions rather than reasoning and ethical standards were dangerous. We have seen this play out throughout history, and we can see it in the political polarization that society suffers from today. If people desperately want to believe something because of the emotions involved, they will believe it even if it is both untrue and ultimately not in their best interests. Researchers call this **confirmation bias**, because it involves a confirmation of emotions the audience already believes. Thus, if coal miners already believe that environmental regulations have cost them their jobs, they can be persuaded to vote for the candidate who will ban those regulations, even if the jobs were actually lost because of automation and a lower demand for coal as a fuel. The politicians who use these kinds of arguments might be extremely effective persuaders, but they are neither logical nor ethical. The rest of this chapter takes a closer look at logic and ethics.

TIPS & REMINDERS

3 Types of Persuasive Appeals

The Greek philosopher Aristotle divided the means of persuasion into three types of appeals: ethos, pathos, and logos. Consider the following questions to make sure you are using all three in your persuasive speeches.

1. **Logos (Logic)**
   Have you made logical arguments to appeal to the audience's sense of reasoning? This was Aristotle's favorite, and is the most important form of appeal that we will discuss in this chapter.
2. **Ethos (Credibility) or Ethical Appeal**
   Have you established your credibility as a speaker so that the audience believes you to be trustworthy?
3. **Pathos (Emotions)**
   Have you used emotional appeals effectively to make your case?

Logic, Ethics, and the Art of Persuasion

LEARNING OBJECTIVE 14.4: Use logical reasoning to create an effective argument that is ethical and persuasive.

Persuasive speaking has been defined as "reason-giving discourse." Its principal technique involves proposing claims and then backing up those claims with proof. **Proof** includes explanations of why your claims are true, along with evidence in the form of the supporting material discussed in Chapter 12.

STEP 1: Structure your basic argument.

One of the keys to delivering a persuasive speech is structuring your basic argument carefully. A sample structure of the body of a persuasive speech is outlined in Figure 14.2. With this structure, if your objective is to change attitudes, concentrate on the first two components: establishing the problem and describing the solution. If your objective is to change behavior, add the third component, describing the desired audience reaction. There are, of course, other structures for persuasive speeches. However, the steps outlined in Figure 14.2 can easily be applied to most persuasive topics.

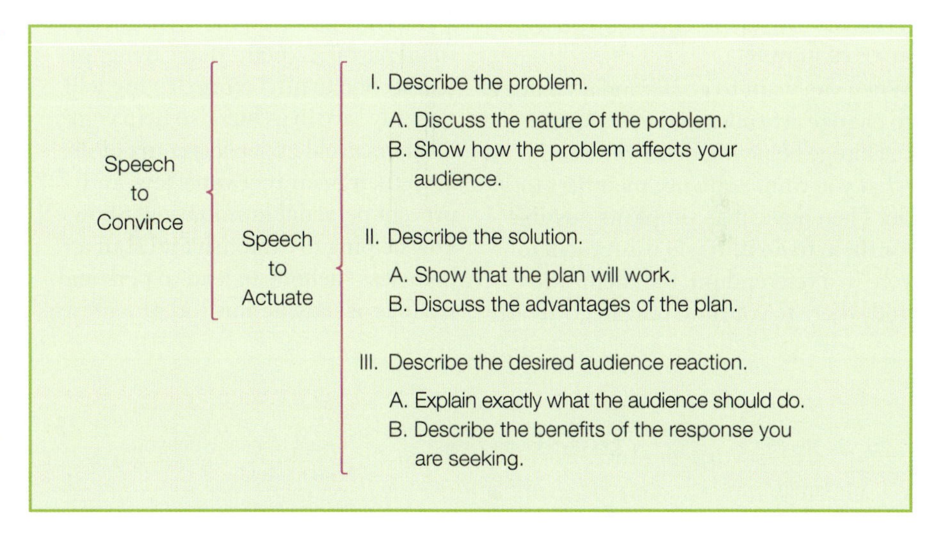

FIGURE 14.2 Sample Structure for a Persuasive Argument

STEP 2: Describe the problem.

In order to convince audience members that something should be changed, you have to show them that a problem exists and that it affects them in some way. For example, if your thesis were "This town needs a shelter for homeless families," you would show that there are, indeed, homeless families (perhaps through the use of statistics) and that the plight of these homeless families is serious (perhaps using an effective anecdote). However, it's not enough to prove that a problem exists. Your next challenge is to show listeners that the problem affects them in some way.[7]

If your prespeech analysis shows that audience members may not feel sympathetic to your topic, explain why your topic is, indeed, a problem that they should recognize. For example, in a speech about the plight of the homeless, you might establish that most homeless people are not lazy, able-bodied drifters who choose to panhandle and steal instead of work. You could cite respected authorities, give examples, and maybe even show photographs to demonstrate that some homeless people are hardworking but unlucky parents and innocent children who lack shelter owing to forces beyond their control.

STEP 3: Describe the solution.

Your next step in persuading audience members is to convince them that there is an answer to the problem you have just introduced. Skeptical listeners might agree with the desirability of your solution but still not believe that it has a chance of succeeding. In the homeless speech discussed previously, you would need to prove that the establishment of a shelter can help unlucky families get back on their feet—especially if your audience analysis shows that some listeners might view such a shelter as a way of coddling people who are too lazy to work. When you want to change audience behavior, describe exactly what you want audience members to do. Then make it as simple as possible for them to do it.

You should also describe in specific terms how your solution will lead to the desired changes. This is the step in which you paint a vivid picture of the benefits of your proposal. In the speech proposing a shelter for homeless families, the benefits you describe would probably include these:

- Families will have a safe place to stay, free of the danger of living on the street.

- Parents will have the resources that will help them find jobs: an address, phone, clothes washers, and showers.
- The police won't have to apply antivagrancy laws (such as prohibitions against sleeping in cars) to people who aren't the intended target of those laws.
- The community (including your listeners) won't need to feel guilty about ignoring the plight of unfortunate citizens.

STEP 4: Describe the desired audience response.

When you want to go beyond a strategy to change attitudes and use a strategy to change behavior, describe exactly what you want audience members to do. Then make it as simple as possible for them to do it. If you want them to vote in a referendum, tell them when and where to vote and how to go about registering, if necessary (some activists even provide transportation). If you're asking them to support a legislative change, *you* write the letter or draft a petition and ask them to sign it. The speaker in the sample speech in Appendix B wanted to convince his audience to boycott slave-produced chocolate. To do so, he handed out samples of slave-free chocolate and cards that showed his audience how to obtain it.

While your solution might be important to society, your audience members will be most likely to adopt it if you can show that they will get a personal payoff. Explain that saying "no" to a second drink before driving will not only save lives but also help your listeners avoid expensive court costs, keep their insurance rates low, and prevent personal humiliation. Show how helping to establish and staff a homeless shelter can lead to personal feelings of satisfaction and provide an impressive demonstration of community service on a job-seeking résumé.

STEP	FUNCTION	IDEAL AUDIENCE RESPONSE
❑ 1. Attention	to get audience to listen	"I want to hear what you have to say."
❑ 2. Need	to get audience to feel a need or desire	"I agree. I have that need/desire."
❑ 3. Satisfaction	to tell audience how to fill need or desire	"I see your solution will work."
❑ 4. Visualization	to get audience to see benefits of solution	"This is a great idea."
❑ 5. Action	to get audience to take action	"I want it."

FIGURE 14.3 Monroe's Motivated Sequence

Sample Outline Using Monroe's Motivated Sequence

There are many ways to expand the structure of argument. One of them is **Monroe's Motivated Sequence,** which was proposed by a scholar named Alan Monroe in the 1930s.[8] In this structure, shown in Figure 14.3, the problem is broken down into an attention step and a need step, and the solution is broken down into a satisfaction step, a visualization step, and an action step. In a speech on "Organ Donation," the motivated sequence might break down like this:

I. The attention step draws attention to your subject.
Someday, someone you know may be on an organ donation list; it might even be you.

II. The need step establishes the problem.
There is a shortage of life-saving organs.

III. The satisfaction step proposes a solution.
Organ donation benefits both the donor's family and the recipient.

IV. The visualization step describes the results of the solution.
Donating an organ could be one of the greatest gifts you could ever give.

V. The action step is a direct appeal for the audience to do something.
Sign an organ donor card today.

Structuring Reasoning Within Your Argument

LEARNING OBJECTIVE 14.5: **Determine how to make a logical and rational persuasive appeal by using claims and subclaims and backing them up with evidence.**

To make a persuasive appeal, it's useful to structure your argument with solid reasoning. **Reasoning** is defined as the process of making claims and backing them up, logically and rationally. In its purest form, argumentation provides an audience with a series of statements, backed up with support, that lead to the conclusion the speaker is trying to establish. The primary components of reasoning are claims, subclaims, and evidence.

Claims and Subclaims

A **claim** is an expressed opinion that the speaker would like the audience to accept. Within a persuasive speech, several claims and subsidiary claims, or **subclaims**, are usually advanced. These are organized according to the rules of outlining discussed in Chapter 12.

In a speech on the health hazards of fast food, one claim might be backed up as follows:

A. *Sugary drinks are bad for you.*
  1. *They contain empty calories, which are stored within the body as fat.*
  2. *They rot your teeth.*
  3. *They actually make you thirstier.*

Some subclaims might need further sub-subclaims to back them up:

3. *Sugary drinks make you thirstier.*
  a. *Sugared drinks are absorbed more slowly than water.*
  b. *You need fluid to digest the sugar. So sugar actually causes you to lose fluid.*
  c. *The caffeine that's in many sugary drinks is a mild diuretic, so it also increases water loss.*

The structure of every argument is different. Even the *same* argument might be structured differently for different audiences. A claim that will be accepted at face value by one audience will need a number of subclaims with another audience. Take the following proposition:

We should do away with the tolls on our local bridge.

If you were speaking to your town's fellow residents, who were uniformly fed up with the inconvenience of those tollbooths, you might be able to advance the following claim without subclaims backing it up:

A. *The traffic delays caused by the tollbooths are bad for the community.*

However, were you to advance the same argument to a group of state legislators, some of whom had no experience with the tollbooths or the delays they cause, you might have to back up your claim with subclaims:

A. *The traffic delays caused by the tollbooths are bad for the community.*
  1. *The delays harm local businesses.*
  2. *The delays waste fuel.*
  3. *The delays increase air pollution.*

For the same proposition with a third audience—one concerned about the income produced by the tolls—you might have to add a second claim:

B. *The same revenue could be generated through taxes.*

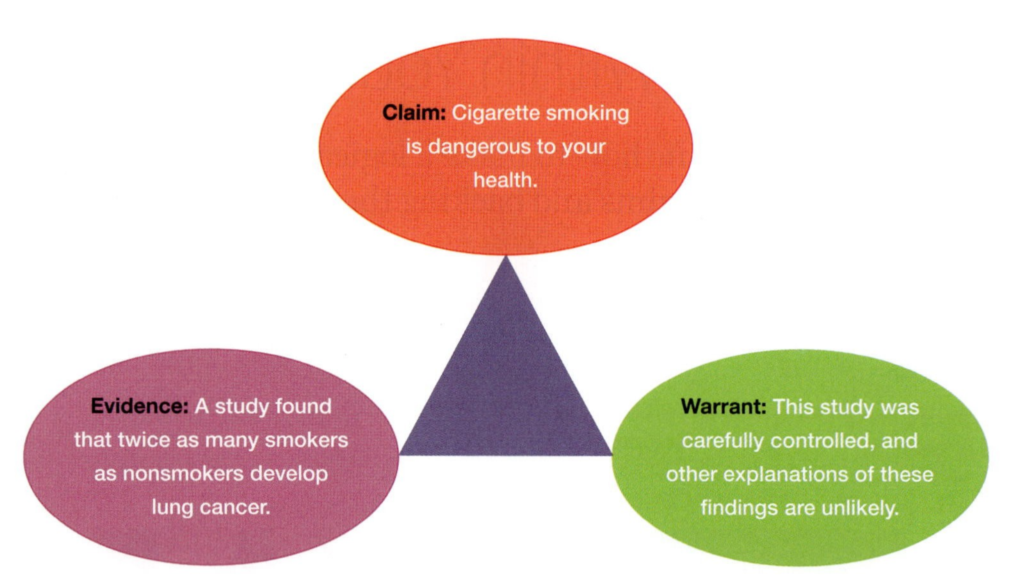

FIGURE 14.4 The Toulmin Model

For yet another audience, you might have to back up that claim with subclaims:

B. *The same revenue could be generated through taxes.*
   1. *Only a slight increase in real estate taxes would be necessary.*
   2. *Residents would be willing to pass such a tax proposal, because they hate the traffic tie-ups.*

Evidence

Evidence is supporting material that the speaker uses to prove any type of claim. All the forms of support discussed in Chapter 12 can be used to back up your persuasive arguments. Your objective in finding evidence is not to find supporting material that just clarifies your ideas, but to find the perfect example, description, analogy, anecdote, statistic, or quotation to establish the truth of your claim in the minds of this specific audience.

The Toulmin Model

In its most basic form, a model of argument proposed by philosopher Stephen Toulmin calls for every claim to be supported not only with evidence but also with a warrant that ties the claim and evidence together.[9] A *warrant*, in this sense, is a statement that justifies the use of evidence for a particular claim. The **Toulmin model** is demonstrated in Figure 14.4. The point of the Toulmin model is that every claim you make has to be examined to see if it needs evidence to back it up, and all the evidence you use needs to be examined to see if it needs a warrant to justify it in light of the claim. Sometimes neither the evidence nor the warrant needs to be stated out loud. For example, a typical college audience would accept the following claim today:

Cigarette smoking is dangerous to your health.

After all, such an audience would be familiar with the research linking smoking to respiratory and heart diseases. However, if you were speaking to a group of tobacco company executives, you might need evidence to back up that claim, and a warrant to prove that the evidence is justified in light of the claim.

If you check your reasoning by applying the Toulmin model to each claim you make, you reduce the chances that your audience will discount what you say because of a weak link between claim and evidence. One final way to check your reasoning is to look for possible fallacies. Notice the way all of the rules of reasoning are used in the outline in Figure 14.5, which one student presented on Suicide Survivor Support.[10] ●

Suicide Survivor Support

INTRODUCTION

I. Attention-getter: My father's suicide had a powerful impact on my family.
II. Thesis statement: We can change the stigma of suicide if we stop survivors from suffering alone.
III. Preview main points.

BODY

I. We need to recognize the reasons suicide survivors (family and friends of those who commit suicide) do not receive the help they deserve.
   A. The deficiencies in survivor support can be found on a societal level.
      1. Society's refusal to use the word *suicide* sets up a social stigma.
      2. Religious doctrine increases this social stigma.
      3. Even media guidelines increase the stigma.
   B. The deficiencies in survivor support can be found on an economic level.
      1. Survivors are left with funeral, counseling, and living expenses.
      2. Survivors might not be eligible for life insurance payouts.
      3. Survivors might not use the money they do receive wisely.
II. We need to examine the impact of that lack of help.
   A. A suicide can cause more grief than most normal deaths.
   B. A suicide can cause post-traumatic stress disorder.
III. We need to examine some possible solutions.
   A. Survivor support solutions can and should be facilitated on a societal level.
      1. One part of the solution would be to require insurance companies to give back the premiums that were paid before the suicide.
      2. Another part of the solution would be to use the word *suicide* when talking to survivors.
   B. Survivor support solutions can and should be facilitated on an individual level.
      1. If you have a friend who is a survivor, just be there for him or her.
      2. If you are a survivor yourself, share your story with others in similar situations.
         a. Make survivors realize that they are not at fault for what happened.
         b. Become part of a LOSS team.
         c. Make sure you also get the help you need.

CONCLUSION

I. Review main points.
II. I have seen firsthand how a suicide can destroy a family.
III. I know my dad would have wanted us to move on and know that everything is okay.

FIGURE 14.5 Speech Outline

TIPS & REMINDERS

Fallacies and How to Avoid Them

It's essential to ensure that the claims and arguments you make within the speech are logical and sound. A **fallacy** (from the Latin word meaning "false") is an error in logic. Although the original meaning of the term implied purposeful deception, most logical fallacies are not recognized as such by those who use them. Scholars have devoted lives and volumes to the description of various types of logical fallacies.[11] Here are some of the most common ones to keep in mind and avoid when building your persuasive argument:[12]

1. **Attack on the Person Instead of the Argument** (*Ad Hominem*)

   In an ***ad hominem* fallacy** the speaker attacks the integrity of a person in order to weaken the argument. Consider this one: "All this talk about 'family values' is hypocritical. Take Senator ________, who made a speech about the 'sanctity of marriage' last year. Now it turns out he was having an affair with his secretary, and his wife is suing him for divorce." Although the senator certainly seems to be a hypocrite, his behavior doesn't necessarily weaken the merits of family values.

2. **Reduction to the Absurd** (*Reductio ad Absurdum*)

   A ***reductio ad absurdum* fallacy** unfairly attacks an argument by extending it to such extremes that it looks ridiculous. "If we allow the administration to raise tuition this year, soon they will raise it every year, and before long only the wealthiest students will be able to go to school here." This extension of reasoning doesn't make sense: One tuition increase doesn't mean that others will occur. This policy might be unwise or unfair, but the *ad absurdum* reasoning doesn't prove it.

3. **Either–Or**

   An **either-or fallacy** sets up false alternatives, suggesting that, if the inferior one must be rejected, then the other must be accepted. "Either we outlaw alcohol in city parks or there will be no way to get rid of drunks." This reasoning overlooks the possibility that there may be other ways to control public drunkenness besides banning all alcoholic beverages.

4. **False Cause** (*Post Hoc ergo Propter Hoc*)

   A ***post hoc* fallacy** mistakenly assumes that one event causes another because they occur sequentially. For example, one critic of education pointed out that the increase in sexual promiscuity among adolescents began about the same time that the courts prohibited prayer in public schools. A causal link in this case may exist: Decreased emphasis on spirituality could contribute to promiscuity. But it would take evidence to establish a *definite* connection between the two phenomena.

5. **Appeal to Authority** (*Argumentum ad Verecundiam*)

   An ***argumentum ad verecundiam* fallacy** involves relying on the testimony of someone who is not an authority in the case being argued. Relying on experts is not a fallacy, of course. A professional athlete could be the best person to comment on what it takes to succeed in organized sports. But an *ad verecundiam* fallacy occurs when the athlete tells us why we should buy a certain kind of automobile. When considering endorsements and claims, it's smart to ask yourself whether the source is qualified to make them.

6. **Bandwagon Appeal** (*Argumentum ad Populum*)

   An ***argumentum ad populum* fallacy** is based on the notion that, if many people favor an idea, you should, too. Of course, the mass appeal of an idea *can* be a sign of its merit. If most of your friends have enjoyed a film or a new book, there is a good chance that you will, too. But in other cases, widespread acceptance of an idea is no guarantee of its validity. In the face of almost universal belief to the contrary, Galileo reasoned accurately that the Earth is not the center of the universe, and he suffered for his convictions. The lesson here: When faced with an idea, don't just follow the crowd. Consider the facts and make up your own mind.

ABOUT YOU *Can You Identify Common Fallacies?*

Identify the logical fallacies in the following examples.

______ **1.** We have to keep controversial speakers from campus or there will be violent protests.

a. Reduce to absurdity
b. Appeal to authority
c. Either–or
d. Bandwagon

______ **2.** If we don't convict these defendants, we might as well put out a sign that says "criminals welcome here."

a. *Ad hominem*
b. False cause
c. Bandwagon
d. Reduce to absurdity

______ **3.** I'm going to try that new McDonald's megaburger. Beyoncé says she loves it.

a. Either–or
b. Appeal to authority
c. Bandwagon
d. False cause

______ **4.** Most people believe we have too much freedom of speech. It is time to consider revoking the First Amendment.

a. Bandwagon
b. *Ad hominem*
c. Reduce to absurdity
d. Appeal to authority

______ **5.** Of course Louie thinks marijuana should be legalized. Louie is a college dropout who hasn't held a job in more than a year.

a. Bandwagon
b. Either–or
c. Reduce to absurdity
d. *Ad hominem*

______ **6.** The President's policies resulted in peace with North Korea. They haven't attacked us since he became president.

a. Reduce to absurdity
b. False cause
c. Bandwagon
d. Either–or

INTERPRETING YOUR RESPONSES

Give yourself one point for each correct answer (they appear below). Then score yourself as follows:

6 Correct You're as logical as Mr. Spock on *Star Trek* (which is to say, very logical). Don't forget to use emotional appeals in your persuasive speech.

4–5 Correct You're about average. You understand how to recognize some logical fallacies, but you should probably review the section on fallacies one more time.

0–3 Correct Oops. You have not quite learned how to recognize logical fallacies. Review the section on fallacies, and find some additional guidelines on fallacies online!

Answers 1. c; 2. d; 3. b; 4. a; 5. d; 6. b

Speaking to Inform and Persuade

Information or Persuasion?

- Speeches are informative if they seek to describe, explain, or instruct about a noncontroversial topic, without trying to change audience beliefs, attitudes, or behavior.
- Speeches are persuasive if they seek to change audience beliefs, attitudes, or behavior, usually about a controversial topic.

To Deliver an Effective Informative Speech . . .

- Define a specific purpose.
- Use clear, simple language.
- Emphasize important points.
- Generate audience involvement.

3 Ways to Make It Easy for the Audience to Listen

- Limit the amount of information you present.
- Transition from familiar to newer information.
- Transition from simple to more complex information.

4 Ways to Handle a Question-and-Answer Period

- Listen to the substance of the question.
- Paraphrase confusing or quietly asked questions.
- Avoid reacting defensively.
- Answer briefly and then check to see if your answer was helpful.

To Deliver an Effective Persuasive Speech . . .

- Prepare a persuasive purpose statement.
- Adapt to your specific audience.
- Establish common ground and credibility.
- Follow Aristotle's Triad by balancing emotion with logic and ethics.

3 Types of Persuasive Appeals

- Logos (logic)
- Ethos (credibility) or ethical appeal
- Pathos (emotions)

To Formulate Effective Arguments . . .

- Structure your argument with problems, solutions, and desired audience behaviors.
- Use Monroe's Motivated Sequence.

To Bolster the Reasoning Within Your Argument . . .

- Back up your claims with evidence.
- Use the Toulmin Model to tie claims and evidence together with a warrant.

6 Fallacies to Avoid

- Attack on the person instead of the argument (*ad hominem*)
- Reduction to the absurd (*reductio ad absurdum*)
- Either–or
- False cause (*post hoc ergo propter hoc*)
- Appeal to authority (*argumentum ad verecundiam*)
- Bandwagon appeal (*argumentum ad populum*)

Show Your Communication Know-How

14.1: Distinguish between speeches to inform and persuade.

Describe the characteristics of your current speech assignment. Which type of speech will it be, based on those characteristics? If it's informative, how could you make it persuasive, or vice versa?

KEY TERMS: informative speaking, persuasion, persuasive speaking

14.2: Explain the techniques of informative speaking and use them to present an effective informative speech.

Describe the techniques of informative speaking that seem easiest and hardest for you to implement. Why do you think some of the techniques are more difficult than others?

KEY TERMS: informative purpose statement, signposts, audience involvement, audience participation

14.3: Explain the techniques of persuasive speaking and use them to present an effective persuasive speech.

Think back to a speech that impressed you with its persuasiveness. This might be a speech that you found online, on TV, in person, or in the classroom. Did the speaker adapt to the audience and attempt to establish common ground? If so, how? If not, how could that speech have been improved in terms of these characteristics?

KEY TERMS: speech to change attitudes, speech to change behavior, target audience, common ground, credibility, logos, ethos, pathos, confirmation bias

14.4: Use logical reasoning to create an effective argument that is ethical and persuasive.

Consider your current or most recent persuasive speech assignment. How would you use Aristotle's Triad to make sure that you balanced emotion, logic, and ethics?

KEY TERMS: proof, Monroe's Motivated Sequence

14.5: Determine how to make a logical and rational persuasive appeal by using claims and subclaims and backing them up with evidence.

Consider your current or most recent speech assignment. What claims would you have to make to convince members of your class? How would you back up those claims?

KEY TERMS: reasoning, claim, subclaims, evidence, Toulmin Model, fallacy, *ad hominem* fallacy, *reductio ad absurdum* fallacy, either–or fallacy, *post hoc* fallacy, *argumentum ad verecundiam* fallacy, *argumentum ad populum* fallacy

Appendix A Sample Informative Speech

The Quirky Sex Lives of Ocean Creatures

Marah J. Hardt, the author of *Sex in the Sea*, is a highly specialized coral reef ecologist. She is also the research codirector for Future of Fish, a nonprofit organization with the following mission statement:

> A majority of the world's fish stocks are fully exploited or overexploited at a time when 37 percent of the global population (2.8 billion people) lives in coastal communities. Many of these communities depend on the health of the oceans for their livelihoods, and the issue of overfishing is as much a human problem as it is an environmental one. Reducing overfishing requires both better business practices and natural resource conservation.[1]

Hardt is also a skilled storyteller, which helps her to educate the public about the complexities of ocean ecosystems. To ensure audience interest, she focuses her speeches on interesting but little-known aspects of fish life.

As a storyteller, Hardt says that she "seeks to peel back the shimmering surface of the sea to reveal the wonders that lie beneath—and highlight the opportunities that exist for fostering a responsible and beneficial relationship between people and the ocean."[2]

This speech was presented at the TEDxMileHigh conference in November 2019.

The Quirky Sex Lives of Ocean Creatures[3]

Marah J. Hardt

1. Right now, beneath a shimmering blue sea, millions of fish are having sex. And the way they're doing it and strategies they're using look nothing like what we see on land.

The audience actually cheers at Marah's introduction. Sex is one of those topics that most people find inherently interesting.

2. Take parrotfish. In this species, all fish are born female, and they look like this:

Photos illustrate concepts and provide visual interest, so Marah begins with a striking visual example.

3. Then later in life, she can transition into a male and she'll look like this:

But it's not just a spectacular wardrobe change. Her body can reabsorb her ovaries and grow testes in their place. In just a few weeks, she'll go from making eggs to producing sperm.

Marah increases audience involvement and interest by relating her topic to their diet. She acknowledges the audience reaction, making her speech conversational and interactive.

4. It's pretty impressive, and in the ocean it's also pretty common. In fact, I bet nearly all of you have at some point had a seafood dish made up of an individual that started life as one sex and transitioned to another. Oysters? Grouper? Shrimp? Seeing some heads nodding, yeah.

Here, Marah provides a hypothetical example told as an anecdote.

5. But not all fish that change sex start as females. Those clown fish we know from "Finding Nemo"? They're all born male. So in the real world, when Nemo's mother died, Nemo's dad Marlin would have transitioned into Marlene—and Nemo would have likely mated with his father turned mother.

6. Yeah. You can see why Pixar took a little creative license with the plotline, right?

Marah notices a slight giggle here, so she reacts to it and turns it into a full laugh line.

7. So sex change in the ocean can happen in either direction and sometimes even back and forth, and that's just one of the many amazing strategies animals use to reproduce in the ocean. And trust me when I say it's one of the least surprising.

8. Sex in the sea is fascinating, and it's also really important, and not just to nerdy marine biologists like me who are obsessed with understanding these salty affairs. It matters for all of us. Today, we depend on wild caught fish to help feed over two billion people on the planet. We need millions of oysters and corals to build the giant reefs that protect our shorelines from rising seas and storms. We depend on medicines that are found in marine animals to fight cancer and other diseases. And for many of us, the diversity and beauty of the oceans is where we turn for recreation and relaxation and our cultural heritage.

Marah establishes the importance of her topic to her audience with four carefully worded reasons. She also refers to herself as a "nerdy marine biologist" to admit to the audience that her frame of reference is different from theirs, and that she is taking this into consideration.

9. In order for us to continue to benefit from the abundance that ocean life provides, the fish and coral and shrimp of today have to be able to make fish and shrimp and coral for tomorrow. To do that, they have to have lots and lots of sex.

10. And until recently, we really didn't know how sex happened in the sea. It's pretty hard to study. But thanks to new science and technology, we now know so much more than even just a few years ago, and these new discoveries are showing two things. First, sex in the sea is really funky. Second, our actions are wreaking havoc on the sex lives of everything from shrimp to salmon.

11. I know. It can be hard to believe. So today, I'm going to share a few details about how animals do it in the deep and how we may be interrupting these intimate affairs, and what we can do to change that.

12. So, remember those sex-changing fish? In many places in the world, we have fishing rules that set a minimum catch size. Fishers are not allowed to target tiny fish. This allows baby fish to grow and reproduce before they're caught. That's a good thing.

13. So fishers go after the biggest fish. But in parrotfish, for example, or any sex changer, targeting the biggest fish means that they're taking out all the males. That makes it hard for a female fish to find a mate or it forces her to change sex sooner at a smaller size. Both of these things can result in fewer fish babies in the future.

14. In order for us to properly care for these species, we have to know if they change sex, how, and when. Only then can we create rules that can support these sexual strategies, such as setting a maximum size limit in addition to a minimum one. The challenge isn't that we can't think of these sex-friendly solutions. The challenge is knowing which solutions to apply to which species, because even animals we know really well surprise us when it comes to their sex lives.

15. Take Maine lobster. They don't look that romantic, or that kinky. They are both.

Audience laughter.

16. During mating season, female lobsters want to mate with the biggest, baddest males, but these guys are really aggressive, and they'll attack any lobster that approaches, male or female. Meanwhile, the best time for her to mate with the male is right after she's molted, when she's lost her hard shell. So she has to approach this aggressive guy in her most vulnerable state. What's a girl to do? Her answer? Spray him in the face repeatedly with her urine.

More laughter.

17. Under the sea, pee is a very powerful love potion. Conveniently, lobsters' bladders sit just above their brains, and they have two nozzles under their eye stalks with which they can shoot their urine forward. So the female approaches the male's den and as he charges out she lets loose a stream of urine and then gets the hell out of there. Only a few days of this daily dosing is all it takes for her scent to have a transformative effect. The male turns from an aggressive to a gentle lover. By the week's end, he invites her into his den. After that, the sex is easy.

18. So how are we interrupting this kind of kinky courtship? Well, the female's urine carries a critical chemical signal that works because it can pass through seawater and lobsters have a smell receptor that can detect and receive the message. Climate change is making our oceans more acidic. It's the result of too much carbon dioxide entering seawater. This changing chemistry could scramble that message, or it could damage the lobsters' smell receptors. Pollution from land can have similar impacts. Just imagine the consequence for that female if her love potion should fail. These are the kinds of subtle but significant impacts we're having on the love lives of these marine life.

19. And this is a species we know well: lobsters live near shore in the shallows. Dive deeper, and sex gets even stranger. Fanfin anglerfish live at about 3,000 feet below the surface in the pitch-black waters, and the males are born without the ability to feed themselves. To survive, he has to find a female fast.

20. Meanwhile, the female, who is 10 times bigger than the male, 10 times, she lets out a very strong pheromone with which to attract mates to her. So this tiny male is swimming through the black waters smelling his way to a female, and when he finds her, he gives her a love bite. And this is when things get really weird. That love bite triggers a chemical reaction whereby his jawbone starts to disintegrate. His face melts into her flesh, and their two bodies start to fuse. Their circulatory systems intertwine, and all his internal organs start to dissolve except for his testes.

Laughter.

21. His testes mature just fine and start producing sperm. In the end, he's basically a permanently attached on-demand sperm factory for the female.

Laughter.

22. It's a very efficient system, but this is not the kind of mating strategy that we see on a farm, right? I mean, this is weird. It's really strange. But if we don't know that these kinds of strategies exist or how they work, we can't know what kind of impacts we may be having, even in the deep sea.

23. Just three years ago, we discovered a new species of deep-sea octopus where the females lay their eggs on sponges attached to rocks that are over two and a half miles deep. These rocks contain rare earth minerals, and right now there are companies that are building bulldozers that would be capable of mining the deep-sea floor for those rocks. But the bulldozers would scrape up all the sponges and all the eggs with them. Knowingly, and in many cases unknowingly, we are preventing successful sex and reproduction in the deep. And let's be honest, dating and mating is hard enough without somebody coming in and interrupting all the time, right? I mean, we know this.

24. So today, while I hope you will leave here with some excellent bar trivia on fish sex, I also ask that you remember this: we are all far more intimately connected with the oceans than we realize, no matter where we live. And this level of intimacy requires a new kind of relationship with the ocean, one that recognizes and respects the enormous diversity of life and its limitations. We can no longer think of the oceans as just something out there, because every day we depend on them for our food security, our own health and wellness, and every other breath we take. But it is a two-way relationship, and the oceans can only continue to provide for us if we in turn safeguard that fundamental force of life in the sea: sex and reproduction.

25. So, like any relationship, we have to embrace some change for the partnership to work. The next time you're thinking about having seafood, look for sustainably caught or farmed species that are local and low on the food chain. These are animals like oysters, clams, mussels, small fish like mackerel. These all reproduce like crazy, and with good management, they can handle a bit of fishing pressure. We can also rethink what we use to wash our bodies, clean our homes, and care for our lawns. All of those chemicals eventually wash out to sea and disrupt the natural chemistry of the ocean. Industry also has to play its part and take a precautionary approach, protecting sexual activity where we know it exists and preventing harm in the cases where we just don't yet know enough, like the deep sea. And in the communities where we live, the places we work, and the country in which we vote, we must take bold action on climate change now.

In this final paragraph, Marah throws in a quick persuasive appeal. It isn't the focus of her speech, but it fits in well and the audience responds, "Yeah!"

Appendix B Sample Persuasive Speech

Child Slavery in the Chocolate Industry

The following persuasive speech was presented by Saeed Malami, a student at Lafayette College in Pennsylvania. With it, he won first place in persuasive speaking at the Interstate Oratorical Association annual conference at West Chester University in April 2019.

Saeed immigrated from Nigeria to attend school at Lafayette, where he became interested in the forensic team that competed in tournaments at other colleges. At first, he shied away from persuasive speaking, because all of the topics seemed to be about events happening in the United States and Saeed didn't feel that he knew enough about the new country he found himself in. When his coach suggested child slavery as a topic, it immediately resonated with Saeed. "This is a West African problem," he said, "and that's where I come from."

Saeed came up with the following purpose statement:

> After listening to my speech, my audience will be able to identify slave-free chocolate and choose it over the brands that are not slave-free.

Saeed collected his material from a wide range of sources, including an interview at a local artisanal chocolate maker. He became more involved in his topic as he did more research. His coach, Scott Placke, explains, "The topic was something he cared about initially but grew to care about more deeply the more research he did on it. There's no way to be involved in the process of researching and performing and not caring."[1] Saeed adds, "The topic remains dear to me; I've since stopped eating chocolate from major brands and a lot of my friends and family have done the same."[2]

Saeed used a simple problem-effect-solution organizational structure, as seen in the following outline (numbers in brackets correspond to paragraphs of the speech):

Introduction [1–4]

I. Attention Getter: Willy Wonka had slaves [1–2]
II. Thesis: Today's big chocolate industry acquires its chocolate with child slavery. [2–3]
III. Preview of Main Points: [3–4]
   A. We must first expose the problem: Big Chocolate.
   B. We must then unravel the effects: Child Slavery.
   C. We must offer some personal solutions: Munch and Mobilize.

Body [5–20]

I. Big Chocolate is the problem. [5–8]
   A. Chocolate manufacturers are part of a near-invisible cocoa supply chain. [5–8]
      1. Small slave farms sell the beans to pisteurs (motorcyclists).
      2. Pisteurs then sell the beans to a cooperative.
      3. Cooperatives then sell the beans to conglomerates.
      4. Conglomerates then sell the processed beans to chocolate manufacturers.
   B. Chocolate manufacturers have plausible deniability. [9–10]
      1. The supply chain is made up of anonymous middlemen.
      2. The path from the bean to bar is untraceable.
      3. Big Chocolate maintains supposed ignorance as to how their cocoa is grown.
II. Big Chocolate affects cocoa growers in a variety of ways. [11]
   A. Their practices create poverty.
   B. Their practices encourage child slavery.
III. Big Chocolate can be impacted by our personal solutions.
   A. We must Munch responsibly.
   B. We must Mobilize effectively.
   C. We must Boycott Big Chocolate.

Conclusion [21–22]

I. While Willy Wonka may have gotten away with using slaves, we should not allow big chocolate companies to do the same.
II. While we enjoy chocolate, we should make it less of a guilty pleasure.

As you read this speech, notice how Saeed structures his argument while he follows the various guidelines for persuasive speaking in Chapter 14.

Child Slavery in the Chocolate Industry[3]

Saeed Malami

1. Willy Wonka's chocolate factory held the secret to his success. By some miracle, he was able to churn out the greatest chocolate in the world. Kids and adults alike loved every bite. And here's the miracle: He did all this without employing a single person. How? Oompa Loompas. [show photo] They served him and did all his bidding without complaining.

Allusion to a classic movie, with a photo as a visual aid.

2. At least that's how the story is told. Here's a retelling of the story in one word: Slavery. That's how Willy Wonka got his chocolate. And here is how the big chocolate industry gets its chocolate today in two words: child slavery.

The thesis statement is presented with a dramatic twist.

3. UNICEF first detailed in 1998 how farmers in Ivory Coast enslaved children from neighboring countries and forced them to work on cocoa farms. Now, twenty years later, this problem has grown to 2.2 million children illegally laboring in the West African cocoa industry, as revealed by the Cocoa Barometer Report. Every major chocolate manufacturer has condemned child slavery and has "executed" a plan to eliminate it. Yet this problem is as big as it has ever been. And it is growing.

A powerful item of evidence is introduced early on.

4. No Kit Kat bar, no Oreo cookie, and no Hershey's Kiss is worth condemning a child to slavery. So we must first expose Big Chocolate, then unravel these companies' effects on cocoa growers, and finally offer some personal solutions. Because as the *Washington Post* of July 7, 2018 argues, for many people, like those of us in this room, "chocolate is synonymous with indulgence, a treat to be relished. But for millions ... it's a synonym for poverty."

Preview of main points.

5. Collectively, Americans eat over 100 pounds of chocolate every second of every day, so we need to look at the causes of this problem: a near-invisible cocoa supply chain and plausible deniability.

Evidence; introduction of the first main point and two subpoints.

6. Recently *Raconteur* magazine revealed how cocoa beans are grown in thousands of small, individual slave farms across West Africa. A report by Mighty Earth explains that motorcyclists, called pisteurs, buy the beans from the farmers and transport them to a cooperative. The cooperatives are large warehouses with bulk capacity who purchase the beans in cash from the pisteurs.

As he develops his idea, Saeed bolsters his credibility with research-based evidence.

7. The cooperatives then sell the beans again, in this instance to one of three corporate conglomerates: Olam, Cargill, and Barry Callebaut. Those conglomerates in turn ship and process the raw beans into cocoa powder and butter that gets sold to the chocolate manufacturers that we know and adore.

8. The key here is the supply chain of several anonymous middlemen. Regardless of where the cocoa is made, it ends up in one "big pile." As such, the path from the bean to bar is untraceable.

9. Companies such as Mars, Hershey, and Nestlé maintain a strategy of plausible deniability as to how their cocoa is grown. Given this absurdly extensive supply chain, they claim to be unable to audit for child slavery. See no evil. Hear no evil. These major international companies even claim further to champion human rights, having all churned out reports condemning child slavery.

10. Yet their shadowy supply chains remain intact. The industry newsletter *Supply Chain Dive* explains that their sustainable cocoa promises have been empty, with a steady growth of child labor and decline in farmer income in the countries over the past 10 years. Furthermore, a *New Food Economy* article laments, "Big Chocolate has failed to move to child slavery-free cocoa production primarily because such a model is far less profitable—but deniability is free."

***Supply Chain Dive* is a newsletter that covers topics such as logistics, freight, and procurement for manufacturing industries.**

11. There are two effects Big Chocolate companies have on individual growers: First, poverty. And second, child slavery.

Introduction of second main points, with two subpoints.

12. First, poverty is directly linked to modern slavery. The *Business for Good* podcast of January 1st, 2019, states that the "consensus definition of modern slavery is . . . exploitation and forced labor." The previously cited *Raconteur*

Definition as support.

article reports that the average cocoa-growing household in West Africa earns about 78 cents a day. That is an extremely low level of income, even by West African standards, and it keeps farmers in perpetual poverty while it keeps children out of school without the skill development they would need to earn a living for themselves in the future.

13. Second, child slavery—crass, brutal, and dehumanizing—is thriving in the very lands that were once the starting point of the transatlantic slave trade. Now the masters are corporate giants. *Fortune* produced a documentary exposé entitled "Behind a Bittersweet Industry" that details an average child's workday on a chocolate plantation. Work begins on the farms at 6 a.m. in the morning and ends well after dark. Children use chainsaws to clear the forest, and machetes to cut open the cocoa pods. Their hands are sliced with scars from several misses in swinging at the pod because every strike has the potential to slice their flesh. The children are malnourished from only eating bananas and corn paste. They sleep on wooden planks and have no access to clean water. As one child who had been working on a cocoa farm said of chocolate consumers, "They are enjoying something that I suffered to make. They are eating my flesh."

Detailed description as support.

14. We must not despair. We have the ability to take this issue into our hands. For this, I have a 2-step solution that's as simple as an M&M. Munch and Mobilize.

Introduction of final main point: The solution, with a catchy mnemonic.

15. The first step is to munch. But instead of munching on that Hershey bar, let's do as the aforementioned *Business for Good* podcast suggests: rethink the supply chain.

16. Some socially responsible upstarts are committing to 100% child-slavery-free production of cocoa by refusing to purchase from the anonymous "big pile" and instead purchasing—at a higher price—cocoa from a separate, transparent pile. A real living wage and an end to child slavery is the result. A *Forbes* magazine article from last November tells about one such company, Tony's Chocolonely.

17. Despite slightly lower profit margins this socially conscious business model still makes money showing that other companies can do it as well. Tony's can be purchased online or from a growing number of vendors such as Whole Foods. If you would like to try a bite feel free to grab a sample of either milk or dark from me after this speech.

Chocolate samples offered to enhance audience involvement. Saeed would later joke about "bribing the judges" with the samples.

18. So here's the deal. We also need to mobilize. On this side of this card (show card), labeled STOP, I have provided a QR Code that links you to chocolate companies who still use child slavery supply chain in their production, including Mars, Nestlé, Hershey, Cadbury, and Godiva. On the other side of the card, labeled ENJOY, is a QR code that links you to several chocolate companies that are committed to ethical cocoa production. Join these companies in taking a stand against the use of child slavery.

The cards are shown as a visual aid during the speech and given out as handouts, with the sample chocolates, at the end of the speech.

19. So I am suggesting a boycott, to create the sense of urgency needed for Big Chocolate to stop its marriage to child slavery. Search for the hashtag I created, #BOYCOTTSLAVECHOCO (show card) and join dozens of others who are already committing to end child slavery.

The Hashtag leads to Saeed's Twitter feed with more information on the boycott.

20. In addition, many tournaments put out candy for competitors and judges. While this is appreciated, I have asked the organizers of this tournament to refrain from putting out slave-produced chocolate. I would also ask those of you who organize tournaments to do the same. We can all do our part here in the forensics community. Munch and Mobilize. M&M!

Direct appeal for action that is relevant to this audience.

21. Today, we have exposed Big Chocolate, its effects on cocoa growers, and some solutions. So while Willy Wonka may have gotten away with enjoying the fictional inhuman labor of making chocolate using oh so dear Oompa Loompas, we should not allow big chocolate companies to do the same in our real world.

Conclusion with summary of main points . . .

22. While this speech may have left a dark bittersweet taste in your mouth, it is important so when you indulge in some chocolatey pleasure, it's a little less guilty.

. . . and a final bon mot (a witty remark) to help his audience remember his main point.

Notes

CHAPTER 1

1. Manusov, V., Stofleth, D., Harvey, J. A., & Crowley, J. P. (2020). Conditions and consequences of listening well for interpersonal relationships: Modeling active-empathic listening, social-emotional skills, trait mindfulness, and relational quality. *International Journal of Listening, 34*(2), 110–126.
2. Okoto, E., Washington, M. C., & Thomas, O. (2017, September). The impact of interpersonal communication skills on organizational effectiveness. *International Journal of Language and Linguistics, 4*(3), 28–32.
3. Wikaningrum, T., & Yuniawan, U. A. (2018, October). The relationship among leadership styles, communication skills, and employee satisfaction: A study on equal employment opportunity in leadership. *Journal of Business and Retail Management Research, 13*(1), 138–147.
4. Liu, N., Zhang, Y. B., & Wiebe, W. T. (2017). Initial communication with and attitudes toward international students: Testing the mediating effects of friendship formation variables. *Journal of Intercultural Communication Research, 46*(4), 330–345.
5. Schwantes, M. (2017, June 13). These 3 billionaires agree: You need this skill to be successful. *Inc.* https://www.inc.com/marcel-schwantes/these-3-billionaires-agree-you-need-this-1-critical-skill-to-be-successful.html.
6. Gergen, K. J. (1991). *The saturated self: Dilemmas of identity in contemporary life*. Basic Books. Quote appears on p. 158.
7. Shannon, C. E., & Weaver, W. (1949). *The mathematical theory of communication*. University of Illinois Press.
8. See, for example, Dunne, M., & Ng, S. H. (1994). Simultaneous speech in small group conversation: All-together-now and one-at-a-time? *Journal of Language and Social Psychology, 13,* 45–71.
9. Wang, A. B. (2017, April 5). Nivea's "White Is Purity" ad campaign didn't end well. *The Washington Post*. https://www.washingtonpost.com/news/business/wp/2017/04/05/niveas-white-is-purity-ad-campaign-didnt-end-well/.
10. The issue of intentionality has been a matter of debate by communication theorists. For a sample of the arguments on both sides, see Greene, J. O. (Ed.). (1997). *Message production: Advances in communication theory*. Erlbaum; Motley, M. T. (1990). On whether one can(not) communicate: An examination via traditional communication postulates. *Western Journal of Speech Communication, 54,* 1–20; Bavelas, J. B. (1990). Behaving and communicating: A reply to Motley. *Western Journal of Speech Communication, 54,* 593–602; and Stewart, J. (1991). A postmodern look at traditional communication postulates. *Western Journal of Speech Communication, 55,* 354–379.
11. For an in-depth look at this topic, see Cunningham, S. B. (2012). Intrapersonal communication: A review and critique. In S. Deetz (Ed.), *Communication yearbook* 15 (pp. 597–620). Sage.
12. Brothers convince little sister of zombie apocalypse. (2016, April 11). YouTube. https://www.youtube.com/watch?v=-hVWEefD5ag.
13. Porter, R. (2020, March 16). TV ratings: "American Idol," "60 Minutes" grow. *Hollywood Reporter*. https://www.hollywoodreporter.com/live-feed/american-idol-60-minutes-tv-ratings-sunday-march-15-2020-1284831.
14. Johnson, S. (2009, June 5). How Twitter will change the way we live. *Time*. http://williamwolff.org/wp-content/uploads/2014/01/johnson-time-2009.pdf.
15. Stinson, A. (2018, March 8). Is it bad to look at your phone right when you wake up? It might be sabotaging your day. *Elite Daily*. https://www.elitedaily.com/p/is-it-bad-to-look-at-your-phone-right-when-you-wake-up-it-might-be-sabotaging-your-day-8437383. Quote appears in para.1.
16. Smartphone statistics: For more users, it's a "round-the-clock" connection. (2017, January 26). *ReportLinker*. https://www.reportlinker.com/insight/smartphone-connection.html.
17. Vraga, E., Bode, L., & Troller-Renfree, S. (2016). Beyond self-reports: Using eye tracking to measure topic and style differences in attention to social media content. *Communication Methods and Measures, 4*(2–3), 149–164.
18. Brown, K. (n.d.). Top 9 reasons why I love social media. *Significantly Successful*. https://significantlysuccessful.com/top-9-reasons-love-social-media/. Quote appears in para. 10.
19. Whelan, E., Islam, A. K. M. N., & Brooks, S. (2020). Is boredom proneness related to social media overload and fatigue? A stress–strain–outcome approach. *Internet Research, 30*(3), 869–887.
20. Bowden-Green, T., Hinds, J., & Joinson, A. (2020, October). How is extraversion related to social media use? A literature review. *Personality and Individual Differences, 164,* nonpaginated epublication.
21. Warner, E. L., Kirchhoff, A. C., Ellington, L., Waters, A. R., Sun, Y., Wilson, A., & Cloyes, K. G. (2020, May). Young adult cancer caregivers' use of social media for social support. *Psycho-Oncology*, nonpaginated epublication.
22. Seiter, C. (2019, January 18). The psychology of social media: Why we like, comment, and share online. *Buffer*. https://buffer.com/resources/psychology-of-social-media. Quote appears in para. 16.

23. Harris, T. (2018, January 25). What your notifications do to your brain, and what to do about it. *Thrive Global*. https://thriveglobal.com/stories/what-your-notifications-do-to-your-brain-and-what-to-do-about-it-2/. Quote appears in para. 2.
24. Social media, social life: Teens reveal their experiences, 2018. *Common Sense Media*. https://www.commonsensemedia.org/research/social-media-social-life-2018.
25. Clement, J. (2020, April 22). *Global social media account ownership from 2013 to 2018. Statistica*. https://www.statista.com/statistics/788084/number-of-social-media-accounts/.
26. Anderson, M., & Jiang, J. (2018, May 31). Teens, social media & technology 2018. Pew Research Center. https://www.pewresearch.org/internet/2018/05/31/teens-social-media-technology-2018/.
27. Roomer, J. (2019, July 31). 3 reasons why you shouldn't check your phone within 1 hour of waking up. *Medium*. https://medium.com/personal-growth-lab/3-reasons-why-you-shouldnt-check-your-smartphone-within-1-hour-of-waking-up-6ccb1264ec74. Quote appears in para. 13.
28. Sabik, N. J., Falat, J., & Magagnos, J. (2020). When self-worth depends on social media feedback: Associations with psychological well-being. *Sex Roles, 82*(7/8), 411–421.
29. Fang, J., Wang, X., Wen, Z., & Zhou, J. (2020, August). Fear of missing out and problematic social media use as mediators between emotional support from social media and phubbing behavior. *Addictive Behaviors, 107*, 1–7.
30. Seiter, C. (2019, January 18). The psychology of social media: Why we like, comment, and share online. *Buffer*. https://buffer.com/resources/psychology-of-social-media. Quote appears in the third to last paragraph.
31. Heckendorn, K. (n.d.). 19 times social media was not worth the embarrassment. *Diply*. http://diply.com/embarrassing-social-media-fails. The scenario appears in the post "1. Not the best first impression."
32. Singer, N. (2013, November 9). "They loved your G.P.A., then they saw your tweets." *New York Times*. http://www.nytimes.com/2013/11/10/business/they-loved-your-gpa-then-they-saw-your-tweets.html. Quote appears in para. 2.
33. Bauerlein, M. (2009, September 4). Why Gen-Y Johnny can't read nonverbal cues. *Wall Street Journal*. http://online.wsj.com/article/SB1000142405297020386320457434848493483201758.html.
34. Watts, S. A. (2007). Evaluative feedback: Perspectives on media effects. *Journal of Computer-Mediated Communication, 12*(2), 384–411. See also Turnage, A. K. (2007). Email flaming behaviors and organizational conflict. *Journal of Computer-Mediated Communication, 13*(1), 43–59.
35. See Wiemann, J. M., Takai, J., Ota, H., & Wiemann, M. (1997). A relational model of communication competence. In B. Kovacic (Ed.), *Emerging theories of human communication*. SUNY Press. These goals, and the strategies used to achieve them, needn't be conscious. See Fitzsimons, G. M., & Bargh, J. A. (2003). Thinking of you: Nonconscious pursuit of interpersonal goals associated with relationship partners. *Journal of Personality and Social Psychology, 84*, 148–164.
36. Light, J., & McNaughton, D. (2014). Communicative competence for individuals who require augmentative and alternative communication: A new definition for a new era of communication? *Augmentative & Alternative Communication, 30*(1), 1–18.
37. Teel, C. M. (2013, March 3). 8 English words you should never use abroad. *SmarterTravel*. https://www.smartertravel.com/8-english-words-you-should-never-use-abroad/.
38. Bruno, G., & Gareth, R. (2014, July). Do we notice when communication goes awry? An investigation of people's sensitivity to coherence in spontaneous conversation. *Plos ONE, 9*(7), E103182.
39. Wang, S., Hu, Q., & Dong, B. (2015). Managing personal networks: An examination of how high self-monitors achieve better job performance. *Journal of Vocational Behavior, 91*, 180–188.
40. Vikanda, P. (2018). Excessive use of Facebook: The influence of self-monitoring and Facebook usage on social support. *Kasetsart Journal of Social Sciences, 39*(1), 116–121.
41. Koenig Kellas, J., Horstman, H. K., Willer, E. K., & Carr, K. (2015). The benefits and risks of telling and listening to stories of difficulty over time: Experimentally testing the expressive writing paradigm in the context of interpersonal communication between friends. *Health Communication, 30*(9), 843.
42. Confusing sentences that actually make sense. (2017, April 7). *Grammarly*. https://www.grammarly.com/blog/confusing-sentences-actually-make-sense/. Quote appears in item 3.
43. Smith, J. L., Ickes, W., & Hodges, S. (Eds.). (2010). *Managing interpersonal sensitivity: Knowing when—and when not—to understand others*. Nova Science Publishers.

CHAPTER 2

1. Birkeland, M. S., Breivik, K., & Wold, B. (2014, January). Peer acceptance protects global self-esteem from negative effects of low closeness to parents during adolescence and early adulthood. *Journal of Youth and Adolescence, 43*, 70–80.
2. Back, M., Mund, M., Finn, C., Hagemeyer, B., Zimmermann, J., & Neyer, F. J. (2015). The dynamics of self-esteem in partner relationships. *European Journal of Personality, 2*, 235–249.
3. Zhang, L., Zhang, S., Yang, Y., & Li, C. (2017). Attachment orientations and dispositional gratitude: The mediating roles of perceived social support and self-esteem. *Personality & Individual Differences, 114*, 193–197.
4. Luerssen, A., Jhita, G. J., & Ayduk, O. (2017). Putting yourself on the line: Self-esteem and expressing affection in romantic relationships. *Personality & Social Psychology Bulletin, 7*, 940–956.
5. Baumeister, R. F. (2005). *The cultural animal: Human nature, meaning, and social life*. Oxford University Press; and Baumeister, R. F., Campbell, J. D., Krueger, J. I., & Vohs, K. D. (2003). Does high self-esteem cause better performance, interpersonal success, happiness, or healthier lifestyles? *Psychological Science in the Public Interest, 4*, 1–44.
6. Vohs, K. D., & Heatherton, T. F. (2004). Ego threats elicit different social comparison process among high and low

self-esteem people: Implications for interpersonal perceptions. *Social Cognition, 22,* 168–191.
7. Rosenthal, R., & Jacobson, L. (1968). *Pygmalion in the classroom.* Holt, Rinehart and Winston.
8. Slater, A., & Tiggeman, M. (2014, December). Media matters for boys too! The role of specific magazine types and television programs in the drive for thinness and muscularity in adolescent boys. *Eating Behaviors, 14*(4), 679–682.
9. López-Guimerà, G., Levine, M. P., Sánchez-Carracedo, D., & Fauquet, J. (2010). Influence of mass media on body image and eating disordered attitudes and behaviors in females: A review of effects and processes. *Media Psychology, 13,* 387–416.
10. Duvall, S. (2011, November 17). *Top 10 countries celebrating female obesity.* http://www.toptenz.net/top-10-countries-celebrating-female-obesity.php.
11. Holmes, J. G. (2002). Interpersonal expectations as the building blocks of social cognition: An interdependence theory perspective. *Personal Relationships, 9,* 1–26.
12. Gray, C. M. (n.d.). How I (finally) got over my fear of public speaking. *The Muse.* https://www.themuse.com/advice/how-i-finally-got-over-my-fear-of-public-speaking. Quote appears in para. 6.
13. Summarized in Hamachek, D. E. (1982). *Encounters with others.* Holt, Rinehart and Winston (pp. 23–30).
14. For a review of these perceptual biases, see Hamachek, D. (1992). *Encounters with the self* (3rd ed.). Harcourt Brace Jovanovich. See also Bradbury, T. N., & Fincham, F. D. (1990). Attributions in marriage: Review and critique. *Psychological Bulletin, 107,* 3–33. For information on the self-serving bias, see Shepperd, J., Malone, W., & Sweeny, K. (2008). Exploring causes of the self-serving bias. *Social and Personality Psychology Compass, 2/2,* 895–908.
15. Williams, R. (2014, June 30). Are we hardwired to be positive or negative? *Psychology Today.* https://www.psychologytoday.com/blog/wired-success/201406/are-we-hardwired-be-positive-or-negative.
16. Thorndike, E. L. (1920). A constant error in psychological ratings. *Journal of Applied Psychology, 4*(1), 25–29.
17. Talamas, S. N., Mavor, K. I., & Perrett, D. I. (2016). Blinded by beauty: Attractiveness bias and accurate perceptions of academic performance. *PLOS ONE, 11*(2), 1–18.
18. Zhang, Y., Kong, F., Zhong, Y., & Kou, H. (2014). Personality manipulations: Do they modulate facial attractiveness ratings? *Personality and Individual Differences, 70,* 80–84.
19. Bacev-Giles, C., & Haji, R. (2017). Person perception in social media profiles. *Computers in Human Behavior, 75,* 50–57.
20. Herrick, L. (2014, June 17). Respecting political differences: As told by a liberal living in a sea of conservatives. *Huffington Post.* https://www.-huffingtonpost.com/lexi-herrick/respecting-political-diff_b_5500406.html. Quote appears in para. 2.
21. Williams, P. S. (2017, December 19). I've lived as a man & a woman—here's what I learned. TED. https://www.youtube.com/watch?v=lrYx7HaUlMY. Quotes are at 2:30 mins and 7:55 mins, respectively.
22. Andreas, O., Eleni, K., Kimmo, S., & Ivanka, S. (2016). Testosterone and estrogen impact social evaluations and vicarious emotions: A double-blind placebo-controlled study. *Emotion, 4,* 515–523.
23. Hyperprolactinemia diagnosis and treatment: A patient's guide. (2011, February). *Hormone Health Network.* http://vsearch.nlm.nih.gov/vivisimo/-cgi-bin/query-meta?v%3Aproject=medlineplus&-query=estrogen+and+testosterone&x=-1171&y=-97.
24. Heilbrun, C. G. (1973). *Toward a recognition of androgyny.* Knopf.
25. Sveinsdóttir, Á. K. (2011). The metaphysics of sex and gender. In C. Witt (Ed.), *Feminist metaphysics: Exploring the ontology of sex, gender and the self* (pp. 47–65). Springer.
26. Bianchi, A. (2018). *Becoming an ally to the gender-expansive child: A guide for parents and carers.* Jessica Kingsley Publishers.
27. Francis, B., & Paechter, C. (2015). The problem of gender categorisation: Addressing dilemmas past and present in gender and education research. *Gender and Education, 7,* 776–790.
28. Kott, L. J. (2014, November 30). For these Millennials, gender norms have gone out of style. National Public Radio. https://www.npr.org/2014/11/30/363345372/for-these-millennials-gender-norms-have-gone-out-of-style.
29. Francis, B., & Paechter, C. (2015). The problem of gender categorisation: Addressing dilemmas past and present in gender and education research. *Gender and Education, 7,* 776–790.
30. Scharrer, E., & Blackburn, G. (2018). Cultivating conceptions of masculinity: Television and perceptions of masculine gender role norms. *Mass Communication & Society, 21*(2), 149–177.
31. Blackburn, G., & Scharrer, E. (2019). Video game playing and beliefs about masculinity among male and female emerging adults. *Sex Roles, 80*(5/6), 310–324.
32. Weinberg, F. J., Treviño, L. J., & Cleveland, A. O. (2019). Gendered communication and career outcomes: A construct validation and prediction of hierarchical advancement and non-hierarchical rewards. *Communication Research, 46*(4), 456–502.
33. Baldoni, J. (2017). Why I'm done trying to be "man enough." TED. https://www.ted.com/talks/justin_baldoni_why_i_m_done_trying_to_be_man_enough/up-next?referrer=playlist-how_masculinity_is_evolving#t-117247. Quotes are at 16:20 mins and 15:45 mins, respectively.
34. Sandberg, S. (2013). *Lean in: Women, work, and the will to lead.* Knopf.
35. National Center for Educational Statistics. (2018). Table 318.30. Bachelor's, master's, and doctor's degrees conferred by postsecondary institutions, by sex of student and discipline division: 2016–17. https://nces.ed.gov/programs/digest/d18/tables/dt18_318.30.asp.
36. Huang, J., Krivkovich, A., Starikova, I., Yee, L., & Zanoschi, D. (2019, October 15). Women in the workplace 2019. https://www.mckinsey.com/featured-insights/gender-equality/women-in-the-workplace-2019.

37. Staley, O. (2016, September 27). Here's new ammunition from McKinsey for women fighting for equality in the workplace. *Quartz*. https://qz.com/793109/a-mckinsey-and-lean-in-report-on-women-in-the-workplace-study-shows-women-are-still-trailing-men-in-opportunities/.
38. Ban bossy—I'm not bossy. I'm the boss. (2014, March 9). #banbossy. https://www.youtube.com/watch?v=6dynbzMl-Ccw&list=UUgjlS2OBBggUw92bqzjAaVw. Quote is at 1:07 mins.
39. Williams, P. S. (2017, December 19). I've lived as a man & a woman—here's what I learned. TED. https://www.youtube.com/watch?v=lrYx7HaUlMY. Quote is at 15:20 mins.
40. Goleman, D. (2006). *Emotional intelligence: Why it can matter more than IQ*. Bantam.
41. Rao, V. (2010, December 20). What are some good examples of emotional intelligence? *Quora*. https://www.quora.com/What-are-some-good-examples-of-emotional-intelligence.
42. Kozina, A., & Mleku, A. (2016). Intrinsic motivation as a key to school success: Predictive power of self-perceived autonomy, competence and relatedness on the achievement in international comparative studies. *Solsko Polje, 27*(1/2), 63–88.
43. Sachan, D. (n.d.). The science of giving yourself a pep talk. *Head Space*. https://www.headspace.com/blog/2017/10/08/giving-yourself-pep-talk/. Quote appears in para. 15.
44. Preece, J. (2004). Etiquette, empathy and trust in communities of practice: Stepping-stones to social capital. *Journal of Universal Computer Science, 10*(3), 294–302.
45. Stiff, J. B., Dillard, J. P., Somera, L., Kim, H., & Sleight, C. (1988). Empathy, communication, and prosocial behavior. *Communication Monographs, 55*, 198–213.
46. Bradberry, T. (2018, January 11). What are some good examples of emotional intelligence? *Quora*. https://www.quora.com/What-are-some-good-examples-of-emotional-intelligence.
47. Ramanauskas, K. (2016). The impact of the manager's emotional intelligence on organisational performance. *Management Theory & Studies for Rural Business & Infrastructure Development, 38*(1), 58–69.
48. Baker, F. (2019, October 24). Most embarrassing moments. *Echo*. https://www.echoak.com/2019/10/most-embarrassing-moments/.
49. Goffman, E. (1959). *The presentation of self in everyday life*. Doubleday; and Goffman, E. (1971). *Relations in public*. Basic Books.
50. Urciuoli, B. (2009). The political topography of Spanish and English: The view from a New York Puerto Rican neighborhood. *American Ethnologist, 10*, 295–310.
51. Leary, M. R., & Kowalski, R. M. (1990). Impression management: A literature review and two-component model. *Psychological Bulletin, 107*, 34–47.
52. Chovil, N. (1991). Social determinants of facial displays. *Journal of Nonverbal Behavior, 15*, 141–154.
53. Snyder, M. (1979). Self-monitoring processes. In L. Berkowitz (Ed.), *Advances in experimental social-psychology* (pp. 85–128). Academic Press; and Snyder, M. (1983, March). The many me's of the self-monitor. *Psychology Today*, p. 34f.
54. Hall, J. A., & Pennington, N. (2013). Self-monitoring, honesty, and cue use on Facebook: The relationship with user extraversion and conscientiousness. *Computers in Human Behavior, 29*, 1556–1564.
55. Vedantam, S. (2017, May 2). Why social media isn't always very social. *Hidden Brain*. Transcript at http://www.npr.org/2017/05/02/526514168/why-social-media-isnt-always-very-social. Quotes appear in para. 9.
56. Gonzales, A. L. (2014). Text-based communication influences self-esteem more than face-to-face or cellphone communication. *Computers in Human Behavior, 39*, 197–203.
57. Siibak, A. (2009). Constructing the self through the photo selection: Visual impression management on social networking websites. *Cyberpsychology: Journal of Psychosocial Research on Cyberspace, 3*, article 1. http://www.cyberpsychology.eu/view.php?cisloclanku=2009061501&article=1.
58. Hancock, J. T., & Durham, P. J. (2001). Impression formation in computer-mediated communication revisited: An analysis of the breadth and intensity of impressions. *Communication Research, 28*, 325–347.
59. Yang, C.-C., Holden, S. M., & Carter, M. D. K. (2017). Emerging adults' social media self-presentation and identity development at college transition: Mindfulness as a moderator. *Journal of Applied Developmental Psychology, 52*, 212–221.
60. Desta, Y. (2015, March 13). Obsessing over the perfect social media post is ruining your life, study says. Mashable. http://mashable.com/2015/03/13/social-media-ruining-your-life/#qbjK5m5pKaq3.
61. Kille, D. R., Eibach, R. P., Wood, J. V., & Holmes, J. G. (2017). Who can't take a compliment? The role of construal level and self-esteem in accepting positive feedback from close others. *Journal of Experimental Social Psychology, 68*, 40–49.
62. Dredge, R., Gleeson, J. M., & de la Piedad Garcia, X. (2014). Risk factors associated with impact severity of cyberbullying victimization: A qualitative study of adolescent online social networking. *Cyberpsychology, Behavior & Social Networking, 17*(5), 287–291.

CHAPTER 3

1. Swaminathan, P. (2017, February 16). What was your most embarrassing moment as a foreigner in another country? Quora. https://www.quora.com/What-was-your-most-embarrassing-moment-as-a-foreigner-in-another-country#!n=18. Quotes appear in the posting by Swaminathan.
2. Samovar, L. A., & Porter, R. E. (2007). *Communication between cultures* (6th ed.). Wadsworth.
3. Tajfel, H., & Turner, J. C. (1986). The social identity theory of inter-group behavior. In S. Worchel & L. W. Austin (Eds.), *Psychology of intergroup relations*. Nelson-Hall.
4. van de Kemenade, D. (2013). Life lessons learnt from my intercultural relationship. [Personal blog.] http://www.daniellevandekemenade.com/life-lessons-learnt-from-my-intercultural-relationship//. This quote appears in para. 5, and the next one in para 12.
5. van de Kemenade, D. (2013). Quote appears in Life Lesson 1.

6. Triandis, H. C. (1995). *Individualism and collectivism*. Westview.
7. Merkin, R. (2015). The relationship between individualism/collectivism. *Journal of Intercultural Communication, 39*, non-paginated.
8. Cai, D. A., & Fink, E. L. (2002). Conflict style differences between individualists and collectivists. *Communication Monographs, 69*, 67–87.
9. Croucher, S. M., Galy-Badenas, F., Jäntti, P., Carlson, E., & Cheng, Z. (2016). A test of the relationship between argumentativeness and individualism/collectivism in the United States and Finland. *Communication Research Reports, 33*(2), 128–136.
10. Wu, S., & Keysar, B. (2007). Cultural effects on perspective taking. *Psychological Science, 18*, 600–606.
11. Hall, H. T. (1959). *Beyond culture*. Doubleday.
12. Chen, Y.-S., Chen, C.-Y. D., & Chang, M.-H. (2011). American and Chinese complaints: Strategy use from a cross-cultural perspective. *Intercultural Pragmatics, 8*, 253–275.
13. Bin "Robin" Luo, profiled in R. B. Adler, G. Rodman, & A. du Pré. (2014). *Understanding human communication* (12th ed.). Oxford University Press. Quote appears on p. 82.
14. Hofstede, G. (2001). *Culture's consequences: Comparing values, behaviors, institutions, and organizations across nations* (2nd ed.). Sage.
15. Hofstede (2001).
16. Dailey, R. M., Giles, H., & Jansma, L. L. (2005). Language attitudes in an Anglo-Hispanic context: The role of the linguistic landscape. *Language & Communication, 25*(1), 27–38.
17. Basso, K. (2012). "To give up on words": Silence in Western Apache culture. In L. Monogahn, J. E. Goodman, & J. M. Robinson (Eds.), *A cultural approach to interpersonal communication: Essential readings* (2nd ed., pp. 73–83). Blackwell.
18. Kelly, N. (2013, July 30). Bad-luck numbers that scare off customers. *Harvard Business Review*. https://hbr.org/2013/07/the-bad-luck-numbers-that-scar.
19. A quick guide: Gift giving in Japan—dos and don'ts. Zooming Japan. http://zoomingjapan.com/culture/gift-giving-in-japan/.
20. Working with sign language interpreters: The DOs and DON'Ts. (2014, September 29). Interpreting Services. http://www.signlanguagenyc.com/working-with-sign-language-interpreters-the-dos-and-donts/.
21. How to eat in China—Chinese dining etiquette. (n.d.) China Highlights. https://www.chinahighlights.com/travelguide/chinese-food/dining-etiquette.htm.
22. DiMeo, D. F. (n.d.). Arabic greetings and good-byes. *Arabic for Dummies*. http://www.dummies.com/languages/arabic/arabic-greetings-and-good-byes/.
23. Body language in Arab cultures. (n.d.). Word Press Culture Convo. https://tbell7.wordpress.com/2012/10/23/body-language-in-arab-cultures/.
24. Traveling in a Muslim country. (n.d.). Embassy of the United Arab Emirates. https://www.uae-embassy.org/about-uae/travel-culture/traveling-muslim-country.
25. Bowleg, L. (2008). When black + lesbian + woman ≠ black lesbian woman: The methodological challenges of qualitative and quantitative intersectionality research. *Sex Roles, 59*(5/6), 312–325. Quote appears on p. 312.
26. DeFrancisco, V. P., & Palczewski, C. H. (2014). *Gender in communication*. Sage.
27. Orbe, M., Allen, B. J., & Flores, L. A. (Eds.). (2006). The same and different: Acknowledging the diversity within and between cultural groups (International and Intercultural Communication Annual, XXIX). Washington, DC: National Communication Association.
28. Ennis, K. (2020, June 11). As a Black ER doctor, I see racism every day. It doesn't have to be that way. *Washington Post*. https://www.washingtonpost.com/lifestyle/2020/06/11/let-me-explain-racism-i-face-an-er-doctor-protests-give-me-hope/. Quotes appear in paras. 7 and 13, respectively.
29. Kolbert, E. (2018, March 12). There's no scientific basis for race—It's a made-up label. *National Geographic*. https://www.nationalgeographic.com/magazine/2018/04/race-genetics-science-africa/.
30. Ten things everyone should know about race. (2003). *Race: The power of an illusion*. Public Broadcasting System, California Newsreel. http://www.pbs.org/race/000_About/002_04-background-01-x.htm.
31. Anti-social media: 10,000 racial slurs a day on Twitter, finds Demos. (2014, February 7). Demos. https://demos.co.uk/press-release/anti-social-media-10000-racial-slurs-a-day-on-twitter-finds-demos-2/.
32. Tynes, B. M. (2015, December). Online racial discrimination: A growing problem for adolescents. American Psychological Association. https://www.apa.org/science/about/psa/2015/12/online-racial-discrimination.
33. Rentfrow, P. J., Gosling, S. D., Jokela, M., Stillwell, D., Kosinski, M., & Potter, J. (2013). Divided we stand: Three psychological regions of the United States and their political, economic, social, and health correlates. *Journal of Personality and Social Psychology, 105*(6), 996–1012.
34. The gender spectrum. (2013, Summer). Teaching tolerance: A project of the Southern Poverty Law Center. http://www.tolerance.org/gender-spectrum. Quote appears in para. 9.
35. What is LGBTQ? (n.d.). Iknowmine.org, sponsored by Alaska Native Tribal Health Consortium, Community Health Services. http://www.iknowmine.org/for-youth/what-is-glbt.
36. Latest hate crime statistics released. (2016, November 14). U.S. Federal Bureau of Investigation. https://www.fbi.gov/news/stories/2015-hate-crime-statistics-released.
37. Potter, J. E. (2002). Do ask, do tell. *Annals of Internal Medicine, 137*(5), 341–343. Quote appears on p. 342.
38. Hussein, Y. (2015, December 12). Are you afraid to be Muslim in America? *Huffington Religion*. http://www.huffingtonpost.com/yasmin-hussein/are-you-afraid-to-be-muslim-in-america_b_8710826.html. Quote appears in para. 8.
39. Milevsky, A., Shifra Niman, D., Raab, A., & Gross, R. (2011). A phenomenological examination of dating attitudes in ultra-Orthodox Jewish emerging adult women. *Mental Health, Religion & Culture, 14*, 311–322.

40. Bartkowski, J. P., Xiaohe, X., & Fondren, K. M. (2011). Faith, family, and teen dating: Examining the effects of personal and household religiosity on adolescent romantic relationships. *Review of Religious Research, 52,* 248–265.
41. Reiter, M. J., & Gee, C. B. (2008). Open communication and partner support in intercultural and interfaith romantic relationships: A relational maintenance approach. *Journal of Social & Personal Relationships, 25,* 539–559.
42. Ladua, E. (n.d.). 4 disability euphemisms that need to bite the dust. Center for Disability Rights. http://cdrnys.org/blog/disability-dialogue/the-disability-dialogue-4-disability-euphemisms-that-need-to-bite-the-dust/.
43. Wright, E. (2020, February 11). Whatever you do don't call me differently abled. *The Startup*. https://medium.com/swlh/whatever-you-do-dont-call-me-differently-abled-d947ac029801.
44. Ladua, E. (n.d.). 4 disability euphemisms that need to bite the dust. Center for Disability Rights. http://cdrnys.org/blog/disability-dialogue/the-disability-dialogue-4-disability-euphemisms-that-need-to-bite-the-dust/. Quote appears in para. 2.
45. Duyvis, C., & Whaley, K. (2016, July 8). Introduction to disability terminology. Disability in Kidlit. http://disabilityinkidlit.com/2016/07/08/introduction-to-disability-terminology/. Quote appears in the fourth bulleted point of the "Disability Terminology" section.
46. Koester, N. (2019, January 19). Choosing the right words. National Center on Disability and Journalism. https://ncdj.org/wp-content/uploads/2019/01/Choosing-the-Right-Words.pdf.
47. Koester (2019). Quote appears on slide 20.
48. Miller, G. (2015, January 11). There's only one real difference between liberals and conservatives. *The Huffington Post*. http://www.huffingtonpost.com/galanty-miller/theres-only-one-real-diff_b_6135184.html. Quote appears in final paragraph.
49. Pew Research Internet Project. (2012). Social media and political engagement. http://www.pewinternet.org/2012/10/19/social-media-and-political-engagement.
50. Anderson, M., & Auxier, B. (2020, August 19). 55 percent of U.S. social media users say they are "worn out" by political posts and discussions. Pew Research Center. https://www.pewresearch.org/fact-tank/2020/08/19/55-of-u-s-social-media-users-say-they-are-worn-out-by-political-posts-and-discussions/.
51. Rainie, L., Anderson, J., & Albright, J. (2017, March 29). The future of free speech, trolls, anonymity and fake news online. Pew Research Center: Internet & Technology. http://www.pewinternet.org/2017/03/29/the-future-of-free-speech-trolls-anonymity-and-fake-news-online/.
52. Editorial: Don't be a troll. (2017, April 9). *Iowa State Daily*. http://www.iowastatedaily.com/opinion/editorials/article_f2edd1e8-1d45-11e7-9ccf-ebde4f9f215c.html. Quote appears in para. 3.
53. Fitch, V. (1985). The psychological tasks of old age. *Naropa Institute Journal of Psychology, 3,* 90–106.
54. Gergen, K. J., & Gergen, M. M. (2000). The new aging: Self construction and social values. In K. W. Schae & J. Hendricks (Eds.), *The societal impact of the aging process* (pp. 281–306). Springer.
55. Bailey, T. A. (2010). Ageism and media discourse: Newspaper framing of middle age. *Florida Communication Journal, 38,* 43–56.
56. Frijters, P., & Beatoon, T. (2012). The mystery of the U-shaped relationship between happiness and age. *Journal of Economic Behavior & Organization, 82,* 525–542.
57. Chasteen, A. L., Pichora-Fuller, M. K., Dupuis, K., Smith, S., & Singh, G. (2015). Do negative views of aging influence memory and auditory performance through self-perceived abilities? *Psychology & Aging, 30*(4), 881–893.
58. Harwood, J. (2007). *Understanding communication and aging: Developing knowledge and awareness*. Sage.
59. Kroger, J., Martinussen, M., & Marcia, J. E. (2010). Identity status change during adolescence and young adulthood: A meta-analysis. *Journal of Adolescence, 33,* 683–698.
60. Galanaki, E. P. (2012). The imaginary audience and the personal fable: A test of Elkind's theory of adolescent egocentrism. *Psychology, 3,* 457–466.
61. Kezer, M., Sevi, B., Cemalcilar, Z., & Baruh, L. (2016). Age differences in privacy attitudes, literacy and privacy management on Facebook. *Cyberpsychology, 10*(1), 52–71.
62. Rickes, P. C. (2016). How Gen Z will continue to transform higher education space. *Planning for Higher Education*, 4, 21.
63. Myers, K. K., & Sadaghiani, K. (2010). Millennials in the workplace: A communication perspective on Millennials' organizational relationships and performance. *Journal of Business and Psychology, 25*(2), 225–238.
64. Berger, C. R. (1979). Beyond initial interactions: Uncertainty, understanding, and the development of interpersonal relationships. In H. Giles & R. St. Clair (Eds.), *Language and social psychology* (pp. 122–144). Blackwell.
65. Carrell, L. J. (1997). Diversity in the communication curriculum: Impact on student empathy. *Communication Education, 46,* 234–244.
66. Pettigrew, T. F., & Tropp, L. R. (2000). Does intergroup contact reduce prejudice? Recent meta-analytic findings. In S. Oskamp (Ed.), *Reducing prejudice and discrimination: Social psychological perspectives* (pp. 93–114). Erlbaum.
67. Benet-Martínez, V., Leu, J., Lee, F., & Morris, M. (2002). Negotiating biculturalism: Cultural frame switching in biculturals with oppositional versus compatible cultural identities. *Journal of Cross-Cultural Psychology, 33,* 492–516.
68. List of George Floyd protests outside the United States. (2020). Wikipedia. https://en.wikipedia.org/wiki/List_of_George_Floyd_protests_outside_the_United_States.
69. Vasilogambros, M., & National Journal. (2015, April 10). Why is it so hard to talk about race? *The Atlantic*. https://www.theatlantic.com/politics/archive/2015/04/why-is-it-so-hard-to-talk-about-race/431934/. Quote appears in para. 3.
70. Liu, J. L. (2020, June 5). Talking about racial inequality at work is difficult—here are tips to do it thoughtfully. CNBC. https://www.cnbc.com/2020/06/05/how-to-thoughtfully-talk-about-racial-inequality-with-your-coworkers.html. Quote appears in para. 8.
71. Oluo, I. (2018). *So you want to talk about race*. Seal Press.

72. Wilson, B. L. (2020, June 8). I'm your Black friend, but I won't educate you about racism. That's on you. *The Washington Post*. https://www.washingtonpost.com/outlook/2020/06/08/black-friends-educate-racism/.
73. Campt, D. (2020, April 27). Message to White allies from a Black anti-racism expert: You're doing it wrong. Medium. https://medium.com/progressively-speaking/message-to-white-allies-from-a-black-racial-dialogue-expert-youre-doing-it-wrong-39c09b3908a5.
74. Oluo, I. (2018). *So you want to talk about race*. Seal Press. Quote appears on p. 221.
75. Eddo-Lodge, R. (2017, May 30). Why I'm no longer talking to White people about race. *The Guardian*. https://www.theguardian.com/world/2017/may/30/why-im-no-longer-talking-to-white-people-about-race. Quote appears in para. 4.
76. Oluo, I. (2019). *So you want to talk about race*. Seal Press. Quotes in this paragraph appear on p. 40.
77. Meta, J. (2017). On allies asking to be taught about race. https://medium.com/@johnmetta/when-you-walk-into-the-valley-933ff8c079c0.
78. Oluo, I. (2019). *So you want to talk about race*. Seal Press. Quotes in this paragraph appear on p. 40.
79. DiAngelo, R. (2018). *White fragility: Why it's so hard for White people to talk about racism*. Beacon Press.
80. Acho, E. (2020). *Uncomfortable conversations with a Black man*. Flatiron Books.
81. Tatum, B. D. (2017). *Why are all the Black kids sitting together in the cafeteria? And other conversations about race*. Basic Books.
82. Oluo, I. (2019). *So you want to talk about race*. Seal Press. Quote appears on p. 168.
83. Stack, L. (2016, December 6). Black workers' suit accuses job agency of favoring Hispanic applicants. *New York Times*. https://www.nytimes.com/2016/12/06/us/lawsuit-alleges-discrimination-against-blacks-at-national-job-agency.html.
84. Kang, S. K., DeCelles, K. A., Tilcsik, A., & Jun, S. (2016). Whitened résumés: Race and self-presentation in the labor market. *Administrative Science Quarterly, 61*(3), 469–502.
85. See, for example, Otten, M., & Banaji, M. R. (2012). Social categories shape the neural representation of emotion: Evidence from a visual face adaptation task. *Frontiers in Integrative Neuroscience, 6*, 9.
86. Chang, L. C.-N. (2011). My culture shock experience. *ETC: A Review of General Semantics, 68*(4), 403–405.
87. Chang (2011).
88. Oberg, K. (1960). Cultural shock: Adjustment to new cultural environments. *Practical Anthropology, 7*, 177–182.
89. Oberg (1960).
90. Kim, Y. Y. (2008). Intercultural personhood: Globalization and a way of being. *International Journal of Intercultural Relations, 32*, 359–368.
91. Kim (2008).
92. Kim, Y. Y. (2005). Adapting to a new culture: An integrative communication theory. In W. B. Gudykunst (Ed.), *Theorizing about intercultural communication* (pp. 375–400). Sage.
93. Decker, B., (2016, January 19). The key to making friends in college. Odyssey. https://www.theodysseyonline.com/the-key-to-making-friends-in-college. Quotes appear in para. 3 and 6, respectively.

CHAPTER 4

1. People wash their clothing in Barf every day. (2009, June 17). *Adweek*. https://www.adweek.com/creativity/people-wash-their-clothing-barf-every-day-14028/.
2. What is LGBTQ? (n.d.). The Lesbian, Gay, Bisexual & Transgender Community Center. https://gaycenter.org/about/lgbtq/.
3. Prewitt-Freilino, J. L., Caswell, T. A., & Laakso, E. K. (2012). The gendering of language: A comparison of gender equality in countries with gendered, natural gender, and genderless languages. *Sex Roles, 66*(3/4), 268–281.
4. Vervecken, D., & Hannover, B. (2015). Yes I can! Effects of gender fair job descriptions on children's perceptions of job status, job difficulty, and vocational self-efficacy. *Social Psychology, 46*(2), 76–92.
5. Lee, J. K. (2015). "Chairperson" or "chairman"?—A study of Chinese EFL teachers' gender inclusivity. *Australian Review of Applied Linguistics, 38*(1), 24–49.
6. Be careful—it's a gift! (2011). Languages. BBC. http://www.bbc.co.uk/languages/yoursay/false_friends/german/be_careful__its_a_gift_englishgerman.shtml.
7. Pous, T. (2017, February 22). Do you know how to pronounce these common words? *BuzzFeed*. https://www.buzzfeed.com/terripous/are-you-pronouncing-these-common-words-correctly.
8. Assuage. (n.d.). Dictionary.com. http://www.dictionary.com/browse/assuage.
9. Pearce, W. B., & Cronen, V. (1980). *Communication, action, and meaning*. Praeger. See also Barge, J. K. (2004). Articulating CMM as a practical theory. *Human Systems: The Journal of Systemic Consultation and Management, 15*, 193–204; and Griffin, E. M. (2006). *A first look at communication theory* (6th ed.). McGraw-Hill.
10. New survey shows Americans believe civility is on the decline. (2016, April 15). Associated Press National Opinion Research Center (NORC) for Public Affairs Research. https://web.archive.org/web/20190930205735/http://www.apnorc.org/PDFs/Rudeness/APNORC%20Rude%20Behavior%20Report%20%20PRESS%20RELEASE.pdf.
11. DePino, L. (2019, August 9). How I came to my own name. *New York Times*. https://www.nytimes.com/2019/08/09/well/family/how-i-came-to-own-my-name.html. Quotes appear in paras. 21 and 22.
12. Borget, J. (2012, November 9). Biracial names for a biracial baby. Baby Center [blog]. https://web.archive.org/web/20160413055708/http://blogs.babycenter.com/mom_stories/biracial-baby-names-110912.
13. Edelman, B., Luca, M., & Svirsky, D. (2017). Racial discrimination in the sharing economy: Evidence from a field experiment. *American Economic Journal: Applied Economics, 9*(2), 1–22.

14. Derous, E., Ryan, A. M., & Nguyen, H. D. (2012). Multiple categorization in resume screening: Examining effects on hiring discrimination against Arab applicants in field and lab settings. *Journal of Organizational Behavior,* 33(4), 544–570.
15. Bertrand, M., & Mullainathan, S. (2004). Are Emily and Greg more employable than Lakisha and Jamal? A field experiment on labor market discrimination. *The American Economic Review, 4,* 991–1013.
16. No names, no bias? (2015, October 31). *The Economist.* http://www.economist.com/news/business/21677214-anonymising-job-applications-eliminate-discrimination-not-easy-no-names-no-bias.
17. Derwing, T. M., & Munro, M. J. (2009). Putting accent in its place: Rethinking obstacles to communication. *Language Teaching, 42*(4), 476–490.
18. Waxman, O. B. (2015, February 10). This the world's hottest accent. *Time.* http://time.com/3702961/worlds-hottest-accent/.
19. Hansen, K., & Dovidio, J. F. (2016). Social dominance orientation, nonnative accents, and hiring recommendations. *Cultural Diversity and Ethnic Minority Psychology, 22*(4), 544–551.
20. Bennett, K. (2016, September 9). Why do British accents sound intelligent to Americans? *Psychology Today.* https://www.psychologytoday.com/blog/modern-minds/201609/why-do-british-accents-sound-intelligent-americans.
21. Erickson, B., Lind, E. A., Johnson, B. C., & O'Barr, W. M. (1978). Speech style and impression formation in a court setting: The effects of "powerful" and "powerless" speech. *Journal of Experimental Social Psychology, 14,* 266–279.
22. Parton, S., Siltanen, S. A., Hosman, L. A., & Langenderfer, J. (2002). Employment interview outcomes and speech style effects. *Journal of Language and Social Psychology, 21,* 144–161.
23. Reid, S. A., Keerie, N., & Palomares, N. A. (2003). Language, gender salience, and social influence. *Journal of Language and Social Psychology, 22,* 210–233.
24. Manners in Spanish—The basics of being polite in Spanish-speaking cultures. (2011). How to learn Spanish online: Resources, tips, tricks, and techniques. http://howlearnspanish.com/2011/01/manners-in-spanish/.
25. See, for example, Bell, R. A., & Healey, J. G. (1992). Idiomatic communication and interpersonal solidarity in friends' relational cultures. *Human Communication Research,* 18, 307–335; and Bell, R. A., Buerkel-Rothfuss, N., & Gore, K. E. (1987). Did you bring the yarmulke for the Cabbage Patch Kid? The idiomatic communication of young lovers. *Human Communication Research, 14,* 47–67.
26. Blevins, J. (2016, March 25). Read this: The history of "jawn," Philadelphia's all-purpose word. A.V. Club. Retrieved from https://www.avclub.com/read-this-the-history-of-jawn-philadelphia-s-favori-1798245587.
27. Peters, M. (2017, January 27). The hidden dangers of euphemisms. British Broadcasting Corporation. http://www.bbc.com/capital/story/20170126-the-hidden-danger-of-euphemisms (site discontinued).
28. Mitchell, A., Gottfried, J., Barthel, M., & Sumida, N. (2018, June 18). Distinguishing between factual and opinion statements in the news. Pew Research Center. https://www.journalism.org/2018/06/18/distinguishing-between-factual-and-opinion-statements-in-the-news/.
29. Epstein, D. (2019, July 20). Chances are, you're not as open-minded as you think. *Washington Post.* https://www.washingtonpost.com/opinions/chances-are-youre-not-as-open-minded-as-you-think/2019/07/20/0319d308-aa4f-11e9-9214-246e594de5d5_story.html. Quote appears in the title.
30. Obermeyer, Z., Powers, B., Vogeli, C., & Mullainathan, S. (2019, October 25). Dissecting racial bias in an algorithm used to manage the health of populations. Science. https://science.sciencemag.org/content/366/6464/447.full.
31. Heitler, S. (2012, October 2). The problem with over-emotional political rhetoric. *Psychology Today.* https://www.psychologytoday.com/blog/resolution-not-conflict/201210/the-problem-over-emotional-political-rhetoric. Quote appears in para. 2.
32. For a discussion of racist language, see Bosmajian, H. A. (1983). *The language of oppression.* University Press of America.
33. Kirkland, S. L., Greenberg, J., & Pysczynski, T. (1987). Further evidence of the deleterious effects of overheard derogatory ethnic labels: Derogation beyond the target. *Personality and Social Psychology Bulletin, 12,* 216–227.
34. Saleem, H. M., Dillon, K. P., Benesch, S., & Ruths, D. (2016). A web of hate: Tackling hateful speech in online social spaces. https://dangerousspeech.org/a-web-of-hate-tackling-hateful-speech-in-online-social-spaces/. Workshop on Text Analytics for Cybersecurity and Online Safety. Quote appears in title.
35. McClure, L. (2017, January 12). How to tell fake news from real news. TED-Ed [blog]. http://blog.ed.ted.com/2017/01/12/how-to-tell-fake-news-from-real-news/.
36. Difference between facts and opinions. (n.d.). Difference Between. http://www.differencebetween.info/difference-between-facts-and-opinions.
37. Connley, C. (2018, April 25). 4 workplace microaggressions that can kill your confidence—and what to do about them. CNBC Make It. https://www.cnbc.com/2018/04/25/workplace-microaggressions-can-kill-your-confidence-heres-what-to-do.html. Quote appears in para. 2 under item 1.
38. Sue, D. W., Capodilupo, C. M., Torino, G. C., Bucceri, J. M., Holder, A. M. B., Nadal, K. L., & Esquilin, M. (2007). Racial microaggressions in everyday life: Implications for clinical practice. *American Psychologist, 62,* 271–286.
39. Sue, D. W. (2010). *Microaggressions in everyday life: Race, gender, and sexual orientation.* John Wiley & Sons.
40. Nigatu, H. (2013, December 9). 21 racial microaggressions you hear on a daily basis. BuzzFeed. https://www.buzzfeed.com/hnigatu/racial-microagressions-you-hear-on-a-daily-basis. Quote appears in photo 18.
41. Mason, S. A. Microaggressions: The little things people say. (2013, November 6). YouTube. https://www.youtube.com/watch?v=ScOA-_tsi-Y. Quote is at 39 seconds.
42. Montana, S. (2017, April 14). A micro-list of microaggressions against women in the workplace. CRN. https://web.archive.

org/web/20170612162545/https://wotc.crn.com/blog/a-micro-list-of-microaggressions-against-women-in-the-workplace. Quote appears in para. 8.

43. Mason, S. A. Microaggressions: The little things people say. (2013, November 6). YouTube. https://www.youtube.com/watch?v=ScOA-_tsi-Y. Quote is at 2:08 mins.
44. Mason (2013). Quote is at 2:42 mins.
45. Mason (2013). Quote is at 3 mins.
46. Limbong, A. (2020, June 9). Microaggressions are a big deal: How to talk about them and when to walk away. NPR. https://www.npr.org/2020/06/08/872371063/microaggressions-are-a-big-deal-how-to-talk-them-out-and-when-to-walk-away. Quote appears in para. 5.
47. Parsons, A. (2017). The effect of microaggressions, predominantly White institutions, and support service on the academic success of minority students. *Perspectives* (University of New Hampshire), 1–10.
48. Nadal, K. L., Wong, Y., Griffin, K. E., Davidoff, K., & Sriken, J. (2014). The adverse impact of racial microaggressions on college students' self-esteem. *Journal of College Student Development, 55*, 461–474.
49. Hollingsworth, D. W., Cole, A. B., O'Keefe, V. M., Tucker, R. P., Story, C. R., & Wingate, L. R. R. (2017). Experiencing racial microaggressions influences suicide ideation through perceived burdensomeness in African Americans. *Journal of Counseling Psychology, 64*, 104–111.
50. Joll, C., & Sunstein, C. R. (2006). The law of implicit bias. *California Law Review, 94*(4), 969–996.
51. Connley, C. (2018, April 25). 4 workplace microaggressions that can kill your confidence—and what to do about them. CNBC Make It. https://www.cnbc.com/2018/04/25/workplace-microaggressions-can-kill-your-confidence-heres-what-to-do.html. Quote appears in para. 4 under item 1.
52. Broido, E. M. (2000, January/February). The development of social justice allies during college: A phenomenological investigation. *Journal of College Student Development, 41*, 3–18.
53. Sue, D. W., Alsaidi, S., Awad, M. N., Glaeser, E., Calle, C. Z., & Mendez, N. (2019). Disarming racial microaggressions: Microintervention strategies for targets, white allies, and bystanders. *American Psychologist, 1*, 128–142.
54. Limbong, A. (2020, June 9). Microaggressions are a big deal: How to talk about them and when to walk away. NPR. https://www.npr.org/2020/06/08/872371063/microaggressions-are-a-big-deal-how-to-talk-them-out-and-when-to-walk-away. Quote appears in para. 1 under "Is there a risk. …"
55. Limbong (2020). Quote appears in para. 3 under "If someone says …".
56. Kothari, P. (n.d.). How to fix a microaggression you didn't mean to commit. Ellevate. https://www.ellevatenetwork.com/articles/8034-how-to-fix-a-microaggression-you-didn-t-mean-to-commit. Quote appears in Item 3.
57. Hudson, P. (2015, January 16). "I don't understand women"—well read on for the full explanation. *Mirror*. https://www.mirror.co.uk/lifestyle/dating/i-dont-understand-women---4993587.
58. 8 things we don't understand about men. (n.d.). *Wewomen*. https://web.archive.org/web/20130726043224/http://www.wewomen.com/understanding-men/what-women-don-t-understand-about-men-questions-and-answers-d30896x64063.html.
59. Mehl, M. R., Vazire, S., Ramírez-Esparza, N., Slatcher, R. B., & Pennebaker, J. W. (2007, July). Are women really more talkative than men? *Science, 317*, 82.
60. Sehulster, J. R. (2006). Things we talk about, how frequently, and to whom: Frequency of topics in everyday conversation as a function of gender, age, and marital status. *The American Journal of Psychology, 119*, 407–432.
61. Sehulster (2006).
62. Fox, A. B., Bukatko, D., Hallahan, M., & Crawford, M. (2007). The medium makes a difference: Gender similarities and differences in instant messaging. *Journal of Language and Social Psychology, 26*, 389–397.
63. Pfafman, T. M., & McEwan, B. (2014). Polite women at work: Negotiating professional identity through strategic assertiveness. *Women's Studies in Communication, 37*(2), 202–219.
64. Gesteland, R. R. (2012). *Cross-cultural business behavior: A guide for global management* (5th ed.). Copenhagen Business School Press.
65. Menchhofer, T. O. (2015, April). Planting the seed of emotional literacy: Engaging men and boys in creating change. *The Vermont Connection, 24*(4), nonpaginated online version. http://scholarworks.uvm.edu/cgi/viewcontent.cgi?article=1197&context=tvc.
66. Schoenfeld, E. A., Bredow, C. A., & Huston, T. L. (2012). Do men and women show love differently in marriage? *Personality & Social Psychology Bulletin, 11*, 1396–1409.
67. Dai, M., & Robbins, R. (2021). Exploring the influences of profile perceptions and different pick-up lines on dating outcomes on Tinder: An online experiment. *Computers in Human Behavior, 117*, nonpaginated.
68. Lopes, M. R., & Vogel, C. Gender differences in online dating experience. (2019). In A. Hetsroni & M. Tuncez (Eds.), *It happened on Tinder: Reflections and studies on internet-infused dating* (pp. 31–47). Institute of Network Cultures. http://www.tara.tcd.ie/bitstream/handle/2262/91343/Lopes-Vogel-IHoT-2019.pdf?sequence=1.
69. Cohen, M. M. (2016). It's not you, it's me … no, actually it's you: Perceptions of what makes a first date successful or not. *Sexuality & Culture, 20*(1), 173–191.
70. Cohen (2016).

CHAPTER 5

1. Hayden, K. (2019, June 14). When she knew: He really listens. *Verily*. https://verilymag.com/2019/06/dating-advice-marriage-listening-conversation. Quotes appear in paras. 2 and 3, respectively.
2. Bodie, G. D., Vickery, A. J., & Gearhart, C. C. (2013). The nature of supportive listening: Exploring the relation between supportive listeners and supportive people. *International Journal of Listening, 27*, 39–49.

3. Fletcher, G. O., Kerr, P. G., Li, N. P., & Valentine, K. A. (2014). Predicting romantic interest and decisions in the very early stages of mate selection: Standards, accuracy, and sex differences. *Personality & Social Psychology Bulletin, 4*, 540–550.
4. What women want from men: A good listener. (2012, October 3.) Ingenio advisor blogs. http://www.ingenio.com/CommunityServer/UserBlogPosts/Advisor_Louise_PhD/What-Women-Want-from-Men—A-Good-Listener/630187.aspx (site discontinued). Quote appears in para. 3.
5. Gordon, P., James Allan, C., Nathaniel, B., Derek J. K., & Jonathan A. F. (2015). On the reception and detection of pseudo-profound bullshit. *Judgment and Decision Making, 10*(6), 549–563. Quote appears on p. 550.
6. Suzuno, M. (2014, January 21). 5 things recruiters wish you knew about career fairs. After College. http://blog.aftercollege.com/5-things-recruiters-wish-knew-career-fairs/. Quotes in appear in tip 2 and in the title, respectively.
7. Kalargyrou, V., & Woods, R. H. (2011). Wanted: Training competencies for the twenty-first century. *International Journal of Contemporary Hospitality Management, 23*(3), 361–376.
8. Davis, J., Foley, A., Crigger, N., & Brannigan, M. C. (2008). Healthcare and listening: A relationship for caring. *International Journal of Listening, 22*(2), 168–175.
9. Pryor, S., Malshe, A., & Paradise, K. (2013). Salesperson listening in the extended sales relationship: An exploration of cognitive, affective, and temporal dimensions. *Journal of Personal Selling & Sales Management, 33*(2), 185–196.
10. Brooks, A. W., Gino, F., & Schweitzer, M. E. (2015). Smart people ask for (my) advice: Seeking advice boosts perceptions of competence. *Management Science, 61*(6), 1421–1435. Quote appears on p. 1421.
11. Brockner, J., & Ames, D. (2010). Not just holding forth: The effect of listening on leadership effectiveness. *Social Science Electronic Publishing*. http://papers.ssrn.com/sol3/papers.cfm?abstract_id=1916263.
12. Ames, D., Maissen, L. B., & Brockner, J. (2012). The role of listening in interpersonal influence. *Journal of Research in Personality, 46*, 345–349.
13. Listening quotes. (n.d.) Wise old sayings. http://www.wiseoldsayings.com/listening-quotes/. Quote appears sixth.
14. Poundstone, P. (2017). *The totally unscientific study of the search for human happiness*. Algonquin Books. Quote appears on p. 189.
15. Bond, A. B. (2005, August 25). The power of listening: A true story. Care2. https://web.archive.org/web/20081011020728/http://www.care2.com/greenliving/power-of-listening-true-story.html. Quotes appear in para. 3. (Julio is a pseudonym for the person described.)
16. Ceraso, S. (2011, April 25). "I listen with my eyes": Deaf architecture and rhetorical space. Humanities, Arts, Science, and Technology Alliance and Collabatory. https://www.hastac.org/blogs/stephceraso/2011/04/25/i-listen-my-eyes-deaf-architecture-and-rhetorical-space.
17. Ames, D., Maissen, L. B., & Brockner, J. (2012, June). The role of listening in interpersonal influence. *Journal of Research in Personality, 46*, 345–349.
18. Accenture research finds listening more difficult in today's digital workplace. (2015, February 26). Accenture. https://newsroom.accenture.com/industries/global-media-industry-analyst-relations/accenture-research-finds-listening-more-difficult-in-todays-digital-workplace.htm.
19. Robertson, R. R. (2016, October 12). Normani Kordei opens up about her struggle with cyberbullies and racist trolls. *Essence*. http://www.essence.com/celebrity/normani-kordei-cyberbullies-racist-trolls.
20. Zantal-Wiener, A. (2017, October 1). 6 phrases that demonstrate active listening. HubSpot. https://blog.hubspot.com/marketing/phrases-for-active-listening. Quotes appear in paras. 1 and 3, respectively.
21. Brownell, J. (2010). *Listening: Attitudes, principles, and skills* (5th ed.). Allyn & Bacon.
22. Powers, W. L., & Witt, P. L. (2008). Expanding the theoretical framework of communication fidelity. *Communication Quarterly, 56*, 247–267; Fitch-Hauser, M., Powers, W. G., O'Brien, K., & Hanson, S. (2007). Extending the conceptualization of listening fidelity. *International Journal of Listening, 21*, 81–91; Powers, W. G., & Bodie, G. D. (2003). Listening fidelity: Seeking congruence between cognitions of the listener and the sender. *International Journal of Listening, 17*, 19–31.
23. Sperling, E. A., Wolock, C. J., Morgan, A. S., Gill, B. C., Kunzmann, M., Halverson, G. P., & … Johnston, D. T. (2015). Statistical analysis of iron geochemical data suggests limited late Proterozoic oxygenation. *Nature, 523*, 451–454. Quote appears on p. 451.
24. Nichols, R. G. (1948). Factors in listening comprehension. *Speech Monographs, 15*, 154–163.
25. Cowan, N., & AuBuchon, A. M. (2008). Short-term memory loss over time without retroactive stimulus interference. *Psychonomic Bulletin and Review, 15*, 230–235.
26. Fontana, P. C., Cohen, S. D., & Wolvin, A. D. (2015). Understanding listening competency: A systematic review of research scales. *International Journal of Listening, 29*(3), 148–176.
27. Kress, G. R. (2010). *Multimodality: A social semiotic approach to contemporary communication*. Taylor & Francis.
28. Hemp, P. (2009, September). Death by information overload. *Harvard Business Review* online. https://hbr.org/2009/09/death-by-information-overload.
29. Drullman, R., & Smoorenburg, G. F. (1997). Audio-visual perception of compressed speech by profoundly hearing-impaired subjects. *Audiology, 36*, 165–177.
30. LaTour, A. (n.d.). What it means to be a good listener. *Good Choices Good Life*. http://www.goodchoicesgoodlife.org/choices-for-young-people/listen-up/. Quote appears in last paragraph of "Why We Don't Listen" section.
31. Odenweller, K., Rittenour, C., Myers, S., & Brann, M. (2013). Father-son family communication patterns and gender ideologies: A modeling and compensation analysis. *Journal of Family Communication, 13*(4), 340–357.
32. Treasure, J. (2011, July). 5 ways to listen better. TEDGlobal 2011. https://www.ted.com/talks/julian_treasure_5_ways_to_listen_better/transcript.

33. Imhof, M. (2003). The social construction of the listener: Listening behaviors across situations, perceived listener status, and cultures. *Communication Research Reports, 20*, 357–366.
34. Zohoori, A. (2013). A cross-cultural comparison of the HURIER Listening Profile among Iranian and U.S. students. *International Journal of Listening, 27,* 50–60.
35. Italian culture. (n.d.). Cultural Atlas. https://culturalatlas.sbs.com.au/italian-culture/italian-culture-business-culture.
36. Winnick, M. (2016, June 16). Putting a finger on our phone obsession. Dscout. https://blog.dscout.com/mobile-touches.
37. Turkle, S. (2012, April 21). The flight from conversation. *New York Times*. http://www.nytimes.com/2012/04/22/opinion/sunday/the-flight-from-conversation.html.
38. Nelson, S. (2014, May 2). The problem: My friend doesn't ask me about my life! Shasta's Friendship Blog. http://www.girlfriendcircles.com/blog/index.php/2014/05/the-problem-my-friend-doesnt-ask-me-about-my-life/. Quotes appear in paras. 2 and 5, respectively.
39. Wood, Z. R. (2018, April). Why it's worth listening to people you disagree with. TED. https://www.ted.com/talks/zachary_r_wood_why_it_s_worth_listening_to_people_we_disagree_with. Quote appears in title.
40. Vangelisti, A. L., Knapp, M. L., & Daly, J. A. (1990). Conversational narcissism. *Communication Monographs, 57*, 251–274.
41. Derber, C. (2000). *The pursuit of attention: Power and ego in everyday life* (2nd ed.). Oxford University Press.
42. Wilson Mizner quotes. (n.d.). Brainy Quote. http://www.brainyquote.com/quotes/authors/w/wilson_mizner.html.
43. Halvorson, H. G. (2010, August 17). Stop being so defensive! A simple way to learn to take criticism gracefully. *Psychology Today*. https://www.psychologytoday.com/blog/the-science-success/201008/stop-being-so-defensive.
44. Valdes, A. (2012, June 19). 8 tips to help you stop being defensive. *Mamiverse*. http://mamiverse.com/8-tips-to-help-you-stop-being-defensive-13577/.
45. Pang, S. (2012). Be a good listener. *Great Inspiring Stories.* http://lifeaward.blogspot.com/2012/08/be-good-listener.html. Quote appears in para. 3.
46. Huerta-Wong, J. E., & Schoech, R. (2010). Experiential learning and learning environments: The case of active listening skills. *Journal of Social Work Education, 46*, 85–101.
47. Guo, J., & Turan, B. (2016). Preferences for social support during social evaluation in men: The role of worry about a relationship partner's negative evaluation. *Journal of Social Psychology, 156*(1), 122–129.
48. Olson, R. (2014). A time-sovereignty approach to understanding carers of cancer patients' experiences and support preferences. *European Journal of Cancer Care, 23*(2), 239–248.
49. Chapman, S. G. (2012). *The five keys to mindful communication: Using deep listening and mindful speech to strengthen relationships, heal conflicts, and accomplish your goals*. Shambhala Publications.
50. Dean, M., & Street, J. L. (2014). Review: A 3-stage model of patient-centered communication for addressing cancer patients' emotional distress. *Patient Education and Counseling, 94*, 143–148.
51. Shafir, R. Z. (2003). *The Zen of listening: Mindful communication in the age of distraction*. Quest Books.
52. Chapman, S. G. (2012). *The five keys to mindful communication: Using deep listening and mindful speech to strengthen relationships, heal conflicts, and accomplish your goals*. Shambhala Publications.
53. Girlfriend literally never listens to me. (2012, July 8). *The Student Room*. http://www.thestudentroom.co.uk/showthread.php?t=2075372. Quote appears in first paragraph.
54. Green, S. (2015, August 13). Become a better listener. *Harvard Business Review*. https://hbr.org/ideacast/2015/08/become-a-better-listener.html. Quote appears in para. 18.
55. Halvorson, H. G. (2010, August 17). Stop being so defensive! A simple way to learn to take criticism gracefully. *Psychology Today*. https://www.psychologytoday.com/blog/the-science-success/201008/stop-being-so-defensive.
56. Valdes, A. (2012, June 19). 8 tips to help you stop being defensive. *Mamiverse*. http://mamiverse.com/8-tips-to-help-you-stop-being-defensive-13577/.
57. Hennessey, F. (2016). The skill of mindful listening. PsychCentral. https://psychcentral.com/lib/the-skill-of-mindful-listening/.

CHAPTER 6

1. Knapp, M., & Hall, J. A. (2010). *Nonverbal communication in human interaction* (6th ed.). Wadsworth.
2. Burgoon, J. K., & Hale, J. L. (1988). Nonverbal expectancy violations: Model elaboration and application to immediacy behaviors. *Communication Monographs, 55,* 58–79.
3. Guerrero, L. K., & Bachman, G. F. (2008). Relational quality and relationships: An expectancy violations analysis. *Journal of Social and Personal Relationships, 23*(6), 943–963.
4. Research supporting these claims is cited in Burgoon, J. K., & Hoobler, G. D. (2002). Nonverbal signals. In M. L. Knapp & J. A. Daly (Eds.), *Handbook of interpersonal communication* (3rd ed., pp. 240–299). Sage.
5. Bambaeeroo, F., & Shokrpour, N. (2017). The impact of the teachers' non-verbal communication on success in teaching. *Journal of Advances in Medical Education & Professionalism, 5*(2), 51–59.
6. Jones, S. E., & LeBaron, C. D. (2002). Research on the relationship between verbal and nonverbal communication: Emerging interactions. *Journal of Communication, 52,* 499–521.
7. Argyle, M. F., Alkema, F., & Gilmour, R. (1971). The communication of friendly and hostile attitudes: Verbal and nonverbal signals. *European Journal of Social Psychology, 1*, 385–402.
8. Çalşkan, N. (2009). The body language behaviours of the chairs of the disputes according to the disputants. *Education, 129*(3), 473–487.
9. Gillis, R. L., & Nilsen, E. S. (2017). Consistency between verbal and non-verbal affective cues: A clue to speaker credibility. *Cognition and Emotion, 4*, 645–656.
10. Patel, S., & Scherer, K. (2013). Vocal behavior. In M. L. Knapp & J. A. Hall (Eds.), *Nonverbal communication* (pp. 167–204). De Gruyter Mouton.

11. Vrij, A. (2006). Nonverbal communication and deception. In V. Manusov & M. L. Patterson (Eds.), *Sage handbook of nonverbal communication* (pp. 341–359). Sage.
12. Levine, T. R., Clare, D. D., Green, T., Serota, K. B., & Park, H. S. (2014, July). The effects of truth-lie base rate on interactive deception detection accuracy. *Human Communication Research, 40*(3), 350–372.
13. Lock, C. (2004). Deception detection: Psychologists try to learn how to spot a liar. *Science News Online, 166*, 72.
14. DePaulo, B. M., Lindsay, J. J., Malone, B. E., Muhlenbruck, L., Charlton, K., & Cooper, H. (2003). Cues to deception. *Psychological Bulletin, 129,* 74–118; and Vrig, A., Edward, K., Roberts, K. P., & Bull, R. (2000). Detecting deceit via analysis of verbal and nonverbal behavior. *Journal of Nonverbal Behavior, 24*, 239–263.
15. Dunbar, N. E., Ramirez, A., Jr., & Burgoon, J. K. (2003). The effects of participation on the ability to judge deceit. *Communication Reports, 16,* 23–33.
16. Lee, K. (2016). Can you tell if a kid is lying? TED. https://www.ted.com/talks/kang_lee_can_you_really_tell_if_a_kid_is_lying/transcript.
17. Knapp, M. L. (2006). *Lying and deception in close relationships.* Cambridge University Press.
18. Morris, W. L., Sternglanz, R. W., Ansfield, M. E., Anderson, D. E., Snyder, J. H., & DePaulo, B. M. (2016). A longitudinal study of the development of emotional deception detection within new same-sex friendships. *Personality & Social Psychology Bulletin, 2*, 204–218.
19. Look like I'm lying when I'm being honest. (2012, August 9). PsychForums.com. http://www.psychforums.com/social-phobia/topic94977.html. Quote appears in post by EarlGreyDregs.
20. Levine, T. R. (2014). Truth-default theory (TDT): A theory of human deception and deception detection. *Journal of Language & Social Psychology, 33*(4), 378–392.
21. Ein-Dor, T., Perry-Paldi, A., Zohar-Cohen, K., Efrati, Y., & Hirschberger, G. (2017). It takes an insecure liar to catch a liar: The link between attachment insecurity, deception, and detection of deception. *Personality & Individual Differences, 113,* 81–87.
22. Vrig, A., Akehurst, L., Soukara, S., & Bull, R. (2004). Detecting deceit via analyses of verbal and nonverbal behavior in children and adults. *Human Communication Research, 30,* 8–41.
23. Matsumoto, D. (2006). Culture and nonverbal behavior. In V. Manusov & M. L. Patterson (Eds.), *Sage handbook of nonverbal communication* (pp. 219–235). Sage.
24. Glass, L. (2012). *The body language advantage*. Fair Winds Press.
25. Cuddy, A. C., Wilmuth, C. A., Yap, A. J., & Carney, D. R. (2015). Preparatory power posing affects nonverbal presence and job interview performance. *Journal of Applied Psychology, 100*, 1286–1295.
26. Waters, H. (2013, December 13). Fake it 'til you become it: Amy Cuddy's power poses, visualized. *TED Blog*. http://blog.ted.com/fake-it-til-you-become-it-amy-cuddys-power-poses-visualized/. Quote appears in title.
27. Crede, M., & Phillips, L. A. (2010). Revisiting the power pose effect: How robust are the results reported by Carney, Cuddy, and Yap to data analytic decisions? *Social Psychological and Personality Science, 8*(5), 493–499.
28. Grayson, B., & Stein, M. (1981, Winter). Attracting assault—victims' nonverbal cues. *Journal of Communication, 31*(1), 68–75.
29. Ekman, P. (1985). *Telling lies: Clues to deceit in the marketplace, politics, and marriage*. Norton.
30. Wang, Z., Mao, H., Li, J., & Liu, F. (2016). The insidious effects of smiles on social judgments. *Advances in Consumer Research, 44,* 665–669.
31. Wang, Z., Mao, H., Li, Y. J., & Liu, F. (2017). Smile big or not? Effects of smile intensity on perceptions of warmth and competence. *Journal of Consumer Research, 5*, 787–805.
32. Farroni, T., Csibra, G., Simion, F., & Johnson, M. H. (2002). Eye contact detection in humans from birth. *Proceedings of the National Academy of Sciences of the United States of America, 99*(14), 9602–9605.
33. Akechi, H., Senju, A., Uibo, H., Kikuchi, Y., Hasegawa, T., & Hietanen, J. K. (2013). Attention to eye contact in the West and East: Autonomic responses and evaluative ratings. *Plos ONE, 8*(3), 1–10.
34. Meyer, K. (2016, July 17). The four dimensions of tone of voice. Nielsen Norman Group. https://www.nngroup.com/articles/tone-of-voice-dimensions/.
35. Gulledge, N., & Fischer-Lokou, J. (2003). Another evaluation of touch and helping behaviour. *Psychological Reports, 92,* 62–64.
36. Jacob, C., & Guéguen, N. (2014). The effect of compliments on customers' compliance with a food server's suggestion. *International Journal of Hospitality Management, 40*, 59–61.
37. Givhan, R. (2020, May 18). The handshake will return. It's too much a part of who we are. *Washington Post*. https://www.washingtonpost.com/lifestyle/style/handshake-greeting-germs-elbow-bump/2020/05/15/e341acb6-9465-11ea-91d7-cf4423d47683_story.html. Quotes appear in paras. 6 and 3, respectively.
38. U.S. Department of State. (n.d.). Sexual harassment policy. Washington, DC: Author. https://www.state.gov/s/ocr/c14800.htm.
39. My story: I was sexually harassed at an informational interview. (n.d). The Muse. https://www.themuse.com/advice/my-story-i-was-sexually-harassed-at-an-informational-interview. Quote appears in para. 7.
40. Burnett, S. (2014, August 4). Have you ever wondered why East Asians spontaneously make V-signs in photos? *Time*. http://time.com/2980357/asia-photos-peace-sign-v-janet-lynn-konica-jun-inoue/.
41. Cosgrove, B. (2014, July 4).V for victory: Celebrating a gesture of solidarity and defiance. *Time*. http://time.com/3880345/v-for-victory-a-gesture-of-solidarity-and-defiance/.
42. Shittu, H., & Query, C. (2006). *Absurdities, scandals & stupidities in politics*. Genix Press.

43. Hung, L. (2015, June 8). Everything I learned about life in Japan, I learned from riding the subway. Matador Network. https://matadornetwork.com/life/everything-learned-life-japan-learned-riding-subway/. Quotes appear in paras. 8, 9, and 10, respectively.
44. Hall, E. (1969). *The hidden dimension*. Anchor Books.
45. Mumm, J., & Mutlu, B. (2011, March). *Human-robot proxemics: Physical and psychological distancing in human-robot interaction*. Proceedings of the Sixth International Conference on Human-Robot Interaction in Lausanne, Switzerland. http://www.cs.cmu.edu/~illah/CLASSDOCS/p331-mumm.pdf.
46. Hill, O. W., Block, R. A., & Buggie, S. E. (2000). Culture and beliefs about time: Comparisons among black Americans, black Africans, and white Americans. *Journal of Psychology, 134,* 443–457.
47. Ballard, D. I., & Seibold, D. R. (2000). Time orientation and temporal variation across work groups: Implications for group and organizational communication. *Western Journal of Communication, 64,* 218–242.
48. Barrett, P., Davies, F., Zhang, Y., & Barrett, L. (2017). The holistic impact of classroom spaces on learning in specific subjects. *Environment & Behavior, 49*(4), 425–451.
49. Horr, Y. A., Arif, M., Kaushik, A., Mazroei, A., Katafygiotou, M., & Elsarrag, E. (2016). Occupant productivity and office indoor environment quality: A review of the literature. *Building and Environment, 105,* 369–389.
50. Baller, E. (2016, April 1). Why all the signals that make you think a woman likes you are wrong. *Elite Daily*. https://www.elitedaily.com/dating/signals-woman-likes-you/1438005. Quote appears in para. 1.
51. Gupta, N. D., Etcoff, N. L., & Jaeger, M. M. (2015, June 14). Beauty in mind: The effects of physical attractiveness on psychological well-being and distress. *Journal of Happiness Studies, 17*(3), 1313–1325.
52. Milazzo, C., & Mattes, K. (2016). Looking good for election day: Does attractiveness predict electoral success in Britain? *British Journal of Politics & International Relations, 18*(1), 161–179.
53. Gunnell, J. J., & Ceci, S. J. (2010). When emotionality trumps reason: A study of individual processing style and juror bias. *Behavioral Sciences & the Law, 28*(6), 850–877.
54. Haas, A., & Gregory, S. W., Jr. (2005). The impact of physical attractiveness on women's social status and interactional power. *Sociological Forum 20*(3), 449–471.
55. Bennett, J. (2010, July 19). The beauty advantage. *Newsweek*. http://www.newsweek.com/2010/07/19/the-beauty-advantage.html.
56. Behrend, T., Toaddy, S., Thompson, L. F., & Sharek, D. J. (2012). The effects of avatar appearance on interviewer ratings in virtual employment interviews. *Computers in Human Behavior 28*(6), 2128–2133.
57. Mobius, M. M., & Rosenblat, T. S. (2005, June 24). Why beauty matters. *American Economic Review, 96*(1), 222–235.
58. Golle, J., Mast, F. W., & Lobmaier, J. S. (2014). Something to smile about: The interrelationship between attractiveness and emotional expression. *Cognition & Emotion, 28*(2), 298–310.
59. Noh, M., Li, M., Martin, K., & Purpura, J. (2015). College men's fashion: Clothing preference, identity, and avoidance. *Fashion and Textiles, 2*(1), 1–12.
60. McCall, T. (2013, August 1.) Why is it so difficult for the average American woman to shop for clothes? Fashionista. https://fashionista.com/2013/08/why-is-it-so-difficult-for-the-average-american-woman-to-shop-for-clothes.
61. Gurung, R. A. R., Brickner, M., Leet, M., & Punke, E. (2018). Dressing "in code": Clothing rules, propriety, and perceptions. *The Journal of Social Psychology, 158*(5), 553–557.
62. Bell, E. (2016, May 13). Wearing heels to work is a game women have been losing for decades. *The Conversation*. https://theconversation.com/wearing-heels-to-work-is-a-game-women-have-been-losing-for-decades-59337.
63. Reddy-Best, K. L., & Pedersen, E. L. (2015, October). Queer women's experiences purchasing clothing and looking for clothing styles. *Clothing & Textiles Research Journal, 33*(4), 265–279.
64. Roberts, S., Owen, R. C., & Havlicek, J. (2010). Distinguishing between perceiver and wearer effects in clothing color-associated attributions. *Evolutionary Psychology, 8*(3), 350–364.
65. Rehman S. U., Nietert P. J., Cope D. W., & Kilpatrick, A. O. (2005). What to wear today? Effect of doctor's attire on the trust and confidence of patients. *The American Journal of Medicine, 118,* 1279–1286.
66. Mercer, M. (2017, June 14). Explosion in tattooing, piercing tests state regulators. Pew Trusts. https://www.pewtrusts.org/en/research-and-analysis/blogs/stateline/2017/06/14/explosion-in-tattooing-piercing-tests-state-regulators.
67. Dickson, L., Dukes, R. L., Smith, H., & Strapko, N. (2015). To ink or not to ink: The meaning of tattoos among college students. *College Student Journal, 49*(1), 106–120.
68. Musambira, G. W., Raymond, L., & Hastings, S. O. (2016). A comparison of college students' perceptions of older and younger tattooed women. *Journal of Women & Aging, 28*(1), 9–23.
69. Galbarczyk, A., & Ziomkiewicz, A. (2017). Tattooed men: Healthy bad boys and good-looking competitors. *Personality and Individual Differences, 106,* 122–125.
70. French, M. T., Maclean, J. C., Robins, P. K., Sayed, B., & Shiferaw, L. (2016). Tattoos, employment, and labor market earnings: Is there a link in the ink? *Southern Economic Journal, 82*(4), 1212–1246.
71. Abdala, K. F., Knapp, M. L., & Theune, K. E. (2002). Interaction appearance theory: Changing perceptions of physical attractiveness through social interaction. *Communication Theory, 12,* 8–40.
72. Agthe, M., Sporrle, M., & Maner, J. K. (2011). Does being attractive always help? Positive and negative effects of attractiveness on social decision making. *Personality and Social Psychology Bulletin, 37,* 1042–1054.
73. Frevert, T. K., & Walker, L. S. (2014). Physical attractiveness and social status. *Sociology Compass, 8,* 313–323.
74. Lausen, A., & Schacht, A. (2018). Gender differences in the recognition of vocal emotions. *Frontiers in Psychology, 9,* nonpaginated. https://www.frontiersin.org/articles/10.3389/fpsyg.2018.00882/full#h6.

75. McDuff, D., Kodra, E., el Kaliouby, R., & LaFrance, M. (2017). A large-scale analysis of sex differences in facial expressions. *PLoS ONE, 12*(4), 1–11.
76. McDuff et al. (2017).
77. Oleszkiewicz, A., Karwowski, M., Pisanski, K., Sorokowski, P., Sobrado, B., & Sorokowska, A. (2017). Who uses emoticons? Data from 86 702 Facebook users. *Personality and Individual Differences, 119*, 289–295.
78. Floyd, K., York, C., & Ray, C. D. (2020). Heritability of affectionate communication: A twins study. *Communication Monographs, 87*(4), 405–424.
79. Kirsch, A. C., & Murnen, S. K. (2015). "Hot" girls and "cool dudes": Examining the prevalence of the heterosexual script in American children's television media. *Psychology of Popular Media Culture, 4*(1), 18–30.
80. Kirsch & Murnen (2015). Quote appears in the title.
81. Stermer, S. P., & Burkley, M. (2012). SeX-Box: Exposure to sexist video games predicts benevolent sexism. *Psychology of Popular Media Culture, 4*(1), 47–55.
82. Matthes, J., Prieler, M., & Adam, K. (2016). Gender-role portrayals in television advertising across the globe. *Sex Roles, 75*(7/8), 314–327.
83. Stermer, S. P., & Burkley, M. (2012). SeX-Box: Exposure to sexist video games predicts benevolent sexism. *Psychology of Popular Media Culture, 4*(1), 47–55.
84. Döring, N., Reif, A., & Poeschl, S. (2016). How gender-stereotypical are selfies? A content analysis and comparison with magazine adverts. *Computers in Human Behavior, 55*(Part B), 955–962.
85. Hall, J. A., Carter, J. D., & Horgan, T. G. (2001). Status roles and recall of nonverbal cues. *Journal of Nonverbal Behavior, 25*, 79–100.
86. Mayo, C., & Henley, N. M. (Eds.). (2012). *Gender and nonverbal behavior*. Springer Science & Business Media.
87. Knöfler, T., & Imhof, M. (2007). Does sexual orientation have an impact on nonverbal behavior in interpersonal communication? *Journal of Nonverbal Behavior, 31*, 189–204.

CHAPTER 7

1. Frei, J. R., & Shaver, P. R. (2002). Respect in close relationships: Prototype, definition, self-report assessment, and initial correlates. *Personal Relationships, 9*, 121–139.
2. Frei, J. R., & Shaver, P. R. (2002). Respect in close relationships: Prototype, definition, self-report assessment, and initial correlates. *Personal Relationships, 9*, 121–139.
3. Marano, H. E., (2014, January 1). Love and power. *Psychology Today*. https://www.psychologytoday.com/articles/201401/love-and-power.
4. See Rossiter, C. M., Jr. (1974). Instruction in metacommunication. *Central States Speech Journal, 25*, 36–42; and Wilmot, W. W. (1980). Metacommunication: A reexamination and extension. In *Communication Yearbook 4*. Transaction Books.
5. Grey, J. (2017, December 29). Don't let the little things turn into big things in your relationship. The Good Men Project. https://goodmenproject.com/sex-relationships/dont-let-little-things-become-big-things-relationship-cmtt/.
6. Stone, D., Patton, B., & Heen, S. (2010). *Difficult conversations: How to discuss what matters most*. Penguin.
7. Tamir, D. I., & Mitchell, J. P. (2012). Disclosing information about the self is intrinsically rewarding. *Proceedings of the National Academy of Science, 109*(21), 8038–8043.
8. Altman, I., & Taylor, D. A. (1973). *Social penetration: The development of interpersonal relationships*. Holt, Rinehart and Winston.
9. Whitbourne, S. K. (2014, April 1). The secret to revealing your secrets. *Psychology Today*. https://www.psychologytoday.com/blog/fulfillment-any-age/201404/the-secret-revealing-your-secrets. Quote appears in para. 2.
10. Luft, J. (1969). *Of human interaction*. National Press.
11. Summarized in Pearson, J. (1989). *Communication in the family*. Harper & Row, pp. 252–257.
12. Chen, Y., & Nakazawa, M. (2009). Influences of culture on self-disclosure as relationally situated in intercultural and interracial friendships from a social penetration perspective. *Journal of Intercultural Communication Research, 38*(2), 77–98.
13. Rosenfeld, L. B., & Gilbert, J. R. (1989). The measurement of cohesion and its relationship to dimensions of self-disclosure in classroom settings. *Small Group Behavior, 20*, 291–301.
14. The friends I've never met. (2014, December 15). *Femsplain*. https://femsplain.com/the-friend-i-ve-never-met-7ae521269047. Quote appears in para and 5. (Maya and Jad are pseudonyms. The post does not include names.)
15. Patton, B. R., & Giffin, K. (1974). *Interpersonal communication: Basic text and readings*. Harper & Row.
16. Ledbetter, A. M. (2014). The past and future of technology in interpersonal communication theory and research. *Communication Studies, 65*(4), 456–459.
17. Lee, S. J. (2009). Online communication and adolescent social ties: Who benefits more from internet use? *Journal of Computer-Mediated Communication, 14*, 509–531.
18. Jin, B., & Peña, J. F. (2010). Mobile communication in romantic relationships: Mobile phone use, relational uncertainty, love, commitment, and attachment styles. *Communication Reports, 23*, 39–51.
19. These are my "real" friends: Removing the stigma of online friendships. (2013, January 29). *Persephone*. http://persephonemagazine.com/2013/01/these-are-my-real-friends-removing-the-stigma-of-online-friendships/. Quote appears in para. 4.
20. Hammick, J. K., & Lee, M. J. (2013). Do shy people feel less communication apprehension online? The effects of virtual reality on the relationship between personality characteristics and communication outcomes. *Computers in Human Behavior, 33*, 302–310.
21. Tannen, D. (1994, May 16). High tech gender gap. *Newsweek*, pp. 52–53.
22. Wright, K. B. (2012). Emotional support and perceived stress among college students using Facebook.com: An exploration of the relationship between source perceptions and emotional support. *Communication Research Reports, 29*, 175–184.

23. Hales, K. D. (2012). *Multimedia use for relational maintenance in romantic couples*. Presented at the annual meeting of the International Communication Association, Phoenix, AZ.
24. The phubbing truth. (2013, October 8). Wordability. http://wordability.net/2013/10/08/the-phubbing-truth/.
25. Przybylski, A. K., & Weinstein, N. (2013). Can you connect with me now? How the presence of mobile communication technology influences face-to-face conversation quality. *Journal of Social and Personal Relationships, 30,* 237–246.
26. Yao, M. Z., & Zhong, Z. (2014). Loneliness, social contacts and Internet addiction: A cross-lagged panel study. *Computers in Human Behavior, 30,* 164–170.
27. Baiocco, R., Laghi, F., Schneider, B. H., Dalessio, M., Amichai-Hamburger, Y., Coplan, R. J., ... Flament, M. (2011). Daily patterns of communication and contact between Italian early adolescents and their friends. *Cyberpsychology, Behavior, and Social Networking, 14* (7–8), 467–471.
28. Turel, O., Brevers, D., & Bechara, A. (2018). Time distortion when users at-risk for social media addiction engage in non-social media tasks. *Journal of Psychiatric Research, 97,* 84–88.
29. Sriwilai, K., & Charoensukmongkol, P. (2016). Face it, don't Facebook it: Impacts of social media addiction on mindfulness, coping strategies and the consequence on emotional exhaustion. *Stress and Health, 4,* 427–434.
30. See Wilmot, W. W. (1987). *Dyadic communication*. Random House, pp. 149–158; and Andersson, L. M., & Pearson, C. M. (1999). Tit for tat? The spiraling effect of incivility in the workplace. *Academy of Management Review, 24,* 452–471. See also Olson, L. N., & Braithwaite, D. O. (2004). "If you hit me again, I'll hit you back": Conflict management strategies of individuals experiencing aggression during conflicts. *Communication Studies, 55,* 271–286.
31. For a discussion of reactions to disconfirming responses, see Vangelisti, A. L., & Crumley, L. P. (1998). Reactions to messages that hurt: The influence of relational contexts. *Communication Monographs, 64,* 173–196. See also Cortina, L. M., Magley, V. J., Williams, J. H., & Langhout, R. D. (2001). Incivility in the workplace: Incidence and impact. *Journal of Occupational Health Psychology, 6,* 64–80.
32. Wilmot, W. W., & Hocker, J. L. (2007). *Interpersonal conflict* (7th ed., pp. 21–22). McGraw-Hill.
33. Wilmot & Hocker (2007), pp. 23–24.
34. Cissna, K. N. L., & Seiburg, E. (1995). Patterns of interactional confirmation and disconfirmation. In M. V. Redmond (Ed.), *Interpersonal communication: Readings in theory and research* (pp. 301–317). Harcourt Brace.
35. Marshall, K. (2014, March 25). 5 truly inspiring love stories from real couples. *Your Tango*. http://www.yourtango.com/2014210193/inspiring-love-stories-about-romance-commitment-relationships. This story appears in "The Package from 1950."
36. Gibb, J. (1961). Defensive communication. *Journal of Communication, 11,* 141–148. See also Eadie, W. F. (1982). Defensive communication revisited: A critical examination of Gibb's theory. *Southern Speech Communication Journal, 47,* 163–177.
37. For a review of research supporting the effectiveness of "I" language, see Proctor, R. F., II, and Wilcox, J. R. (1993). An exploratory analysis of responses to owned messages in interpersonal communication. *Et Cetera: A Review of General Semantics, 50,* 201–220. See also Proctor, R. F., II (1989). Responsibility or egocentrism? The paradox of owned messages. *Speech Association of Minnesota Journal, 16,* 59–60.
38. Grant, E. T. (2018, June 12). 10 ways to de-escalate an argument, if you're a sensitive person. *Bustle*. https://www.bustle.com/p/10-ways-to-de-escalate-argument-if-youre-a-sensitive-person-9360724. Quote appears in topic 10, para. 1.
39. Gottman, J. M., Driver, J., & Tabares, A. (2002). Building the sound marital house: An empirically derived couple therapy. In A. S. Gurman & N. S. Jacobson (Eds.), *Clinical handbook of couple therapy* (3rd ed., pp. 373–400). Guilford Press.

CHAPTER 8

1. Donnelly, M. (2017, May 3). Here's to the best friends who feel like family. *Thought Catalog*. https://thoughtcatalog.com/marisa-donnelly/2017/05/heres-to-the-best-friends-who-feel-like-family/. Quote appears in para. 8.
2. Deci, E., La Guardia, J., Moller, A., Scheiner, M., & Ryan, R. (2006). On the benefits of giving as well as receiving autonomy support: Mutuality in close friendships. *Personality & Social Psychology Bulletin, 32,* 313–327.
3. Demir, M., & Özdemir, M. (2010). Friendship, need satisfaction and happiness. *Journal of Happiness Studies, 11,* 243–259.
4. Buote, V. M., Pancer, S., Pratt, M. W., Adams, G., Birnie-Lefcovitch, S., Polivy, J., & Wintre, M. (2007). The importance of friends: Friendship and adjustment among 1st-year university students. *Journal of Adolescent Research, 22,* 665–689.
5. Demir, M., Özdemir, M., & Marum, K. (2011). Perceived autonomy support, friendship maintenance, and happiness. *Journal of Psychology, 145,* 537–571.
6. Minow, M. (1998). Redefining families: Who's in and who's out? In K. V. Hansen & A. I. Garey (Eds.), *Families in the U.S.: Kinship and domestic policy* (pp. 7–19). Temple University Press. (Originally published in the *University of Colorado Law Review,* 1991, *62,* 269–285.)
7. Galvin, K. M. (2006). Diversity's impact of defining the family: Discourse-dependence and identity. In R. L. West & L. H. Turner (Eds.), *The family communication sourcebook* (pp. 3–20). Sage.
8. Donnelly, M. (2017, May 3). Here's to the best friends who feel like family. *Thought Catalog*. https://thoughtcatalog.com/marisa-donnelly/2017/05/heres-to-the-best-friends-who-feel-like-family/. Quote appears in para. 8.
9. Berglund, J. (n.d.). 22 heartwarming stories of true friendship that will make you want to call your bestie. *Reader's Digest*. http://www.rd.com/advice/relationships/stories-of-friendship/. Quotes appear in para. 6.
10. Hall, J. A. (2019). How many hours does it take to make a friend? *Journal of Social and Personal Relationships, 36,* 1278–1296.
11. Hashim, I. M., Mohd-Zaharim, N., & Khodarahimi, S. (2012). Perceived similarities and satisfaction among friends of the same and different ethnicity and sex at workplace. *Psychology, 3,* 621–625.

12. Nelson, P., Thorne, A., & Shapiro, L. (2001). I'm outgoing and she's reserved: The reciprocal dynamics of personality in close friendships in young adulthood. *Journal of Personality, 79,* 1113–1147.
13. Specher, S. (1998). Insiders' perspectives on reasons for attraction to a close other. *Social Psychology Quarterly, 61,* 287–300.
14. Toma, C., Yzerbyt, V., & Corneille, O. (2012). Reports: Nice or smart? Task relevance of self-characteristics moderates interpersonal projection. *Journal of Experimental Social Psychology, 48,* 335–340.
15. Dindia, K. (2002). Self-disclosure research: Knowledge through meta-analysis. In M. Allen & R. W. Preiss (Eds.), *Interpersonal communication research: Advances through meta-analysis* (pp. 169–185). Erlbaum.
16. Flora, C. (2004, January/February). Close quarters. *Psychology Today, 37,* 15–16.
17. Haythornthwaite, C., Kazmer, M. M., & Robbins, J. (2000). Community development among distance learners: Temporal and technological dimensions. *Journal of Computer-Mediated Communication, 6*(1), Article 2. https://academic.oup.com/jcmc/article/6/1/JCMC615/4584255.
18. Roloff, M. E. (1981). *Interpersonal communication: The social exchange approach.* Sage.
19. Duck, S. W. (2011). Similarity and perceived similarity of personal constructs as influences on friendship choice. *British Journal of Clinical Psychology, 12,* 1–6.
20. Sias, P. M., Drzewiecka, J. A., Meares, M., Bent, R., Konomi, Y., Ortega, M., & White, C. (2008). Intercultural friendship development. *Communication Reports, 21,* 1–13.
21. Hashim, I. M., Mohd-Zaharim, N., & Khodarahimi, S. (2012). Perceived similarities and satisfaction among friends of the same and different ethnicity and sex at workplace. *Psychology, 3,* 621–625.
22. Finkel, E. J., Eastwick, P. W., Karney, B. R., Reis, H. T., & Sprecher, S. (2012). Online dating: A critical analysis from the perspective of psychological science. *Psychological Science in the Public Interest, 13*(1), 3–66.
23. Gold, S. S. (2008, September 10). Do *you* have friends of other races? *Glamour.* https://www.glamour.com/story/do-you-have-friends-of-other-races. Quote appears in para. 5.
24. Allport, G. W. (1954). *The nature of prejudice.* Perseus Books.
25. Abrams, J. R., McGaughey, K. J., & Haghighat, H. (2018). Attitudes toward Muslims: A test of the parasocial contact hypothesis and contact theory. *Journal of Intercultural Communication Research, 47*(4), 276–292.
26. Shook, N. J., Hopkins, P. D., & Koech, J. M. (2016). The effect of intergroup contact on secondary group attitudes and social dominance orientation. *Group Processes & Intergroup Relations, 19*(3), 328–342.
27. Phillips, B. A., Fortney, S., & Swafford, L. (2019). College students' social perceptions toward individuals with intellectual disability. *Journal of Disability Policy Studies, 30*(1), 3–10.
28. Lytle, A., & Levy, S. R. (2019). Reducing ageism: Education about aging and extended contact with older adults. *Gerontologist, 59*(3), 580–588.
29. Pekerti, A. A., van de Vijver, F. J. R., Moeller, M., & Okimoto, T. G. (2020, March). Intercultural contacts and acculturation resources among international students in Australia: A mixed-methods study. *International Journal of Intercultural Relations, 75,* 56–81.
30. Bukhari, S., Mushtaq, H., & Aurangzaib, S. (2016). Attitudes towards transgender: A study of gender and influencing factors. *Journal of Gender & Social Issues, 15*(2), 93–112.
31. Dovidio, J. F., Love, A., Schellhaas, F. M. H., & Hewstone, M. (2017). Reducing intergroup bias through intergroup contact: Twenty years of progress and future directions. *Group Processes & Intergroup Relations, 20*(5), 606–620.
32. Tucker, J. A. (2016, December 28). Actually, friendship is a powerful antidote to racism. Foundation for Economic Education. https://fee.org/articles/actually-friendship-is-a-powerful-antidote-to-racism/.
33. The single best antidote to prejudice and racism? Cross-race friendship. (2010, November 23). The Leadership Conference Education Fund. https://civilrights.org/edfund/resource/the-single-best-antidote-to-prejudice-and-racism-cross-race-friendship/.
34. Davis, D. (n.d.) What do you do when someone just doesn't like you? TEDxCharlottesville. https://www.ted.com/talks/daryl_davis_what_do_you_do_when_someone_just_doesn_t_like_you/transcript?language=en.
35. Mancini, T., & Imperato, C. (2020). Can social networks make us more sensitive to social discrimination? E-contact, identity processes and perception of online sexual discrimination in a sample of Facebook users. *Social Sciences, 9*(4), 1–11.
36. Dahlberg, L. (2015, August 10). 10 great things I learned from my best friend who is quadriplegic. *Life Beyond Numbers.* https://lifebeyondnumbers.com/10-great-things-learned-best-friend/.
37. Wölfer, R., Schmid, K., Hewstone, M., & Zalk, M. (2016). Developmental dynamics of intergroup contact and intergroup attitudes: Long-term effects in adolescence and early adulthood. *Child Development, 87*(5), 1466–1478.
38. McDonnall, M. C., & Antonelli, K. (2020). The impact of a brief meeting on employer attitudes, knowledge, and intent to hire. *Rehabilitation Counseling Bulletin, 63*(3), 131.
39. Quinton, W. J. (2019). Unwelcome on campus? Predictors of prejudice against international students. *Journal of Diversity in Higher Education, 12*(2), 156–169.
40. Tucker, J. A. (2016, December 28). Why do people poke fun at the claim that friendship is evidence of equanimity? Foundation for Economic Education. https://fee.org/articles/actually-friendship-is-a-powerful-antidote-to-racism/. Quote appears in para. 9.
41. Furlan, J. (2019, August 19). Accept the awkward: How to make friends (and keep them). *Life Kit.* National Public Radio. https://www.npr.org/2019/08/15/751479810/make-new-friends-and-keep-the-old. Quote appears in para. 4.
42. Zhang, A. (n.d.) Why intergenerational friendships matter—and how to form them. *The Good Trade.* https://www.thegoodtrade.com/features/intergenerational-friendships. Quote appears in para. 6.

43. Johnson, A., Haigh, M. M., Craig, E. A., & Becker, J. H. (2009). Relational closeness: Comparing undergraduate college students' geographically close and long-distance friendships. *Personal Relationships, 16,* 631–646.
44. Manago, A., Taylor, T., & Greenfield, P. (2012). Me and my 400 friends: The anatomy of college students' Facebook networks, their communication patterns, and well-being: Interactive media and human development. *Developmental Psychology, 48,* 369–380. Quote appears on p. 375.
45. Charleston, A. (2017, January 16). To those who overshare on social media: Don't. *Odyssey*. https://www.theodysseyonline.com/open-letter-those-overshare-social-media.
46. Migliaccio, T. (2009). Men's friendships: Performances of masculinity. *Journal of Men's Studies, 17,* 226–241.
47. Hall, J. A. (2011). Sex differences in friendship expectations: A meta-analysis. *Journal of Social and Personal Relationships, 28,* 723–747.
48. Bello, R. S., Brandau-Brown, F. E., Zhang, S., & Ragsdale, J. (2010). Verbal and nonverbal methods for expressing appreciation in friendships and romantic relationships: A cross-cultural comparison. *International Journal of Intercultural Relations, 34,* 294–302.
49. Guerrero, L. K., Farinelli, L., & McEwan, B. (2009). Attachment and relational satisfaction: The mediating effect of emotional communication. *Communication Monographs, 76,* 487–514.
50. Tabak, B., McCullough, M., Luna, L., Bono, G., & Berry, J. (2012). Conciliatory gestures facilitate forgiveness and feelings of friendship by making transgressors appear more agreeable. *Journal of Personality, 80,* 503–536.
51. Davis, J. R., & Gold, G. J. (2011). An examination of emotional empathy, attributions of stability, and the link between perceived remorse and forgiveness. *Personality & Individual Differences, 50,* 392–397.
52. Bello, R. S., Brandau-Brown, F. E., Zhang, S., & Ragsdale, J. D. (2010). Verbal and nonverbal methods for expressing appreciation in friendships and romantic relationships: A cross-cultural comparison. *International Journal of Intercultural Relations, 34,* 294–302.
53. van der Horst, M., & Coffe, H. (2012). How friendship network characteristics influence subjective well-being. *Social Indicators Research, 107,* 509–529.
54. Rawlins, W. K., & Holl, M. (1987). The communicative achievement of friendship during adolescence: Predicaments of trust and violation. *Western Journal of Speech Communication, 51,* 345–363.
55. Deci, E., La Guardia, J., Moller, A., Scheiner, M., & Ryan, R. (2006). On the benefits of giving as well as receiving autonomy support: Mutuality in close friendships. *Personality & Social Psychology Bulletin, 32,* 313–327.
56. Smith, S. (2016, February 9). An open letter to my guy best friend. Odyssey. https://www.theodysseyonline.com/letter-to-my-guy-bff. Quote appears in para. 4.
57. Hall, J. A. (2011). Sex differences in friendship expectations: A meta-analysis. *Journal of Social and Personal Relationships, 28,* 723–747.
58. Bukowski, W. M., & DeLay, D. (2020). Studying the same-gender preference as a defining feature of cultural contexts. *Frontiers in Psychology, 11,* nonpaginated. https://www.frontiersin.org/articles/10.3389/fpsyg.2020.01863/full.
59. Bleske-Rechek, A., Somers, E., Micke, C., Erickson, L., Matteson, L., Stocco, C., & Ritchie, L. (2012). Benefit or burden? Attraction in cross-sex friendship. *Journal of Social and Personal Relationships, 29,* 569–596.
60. Hart, W., Adams, J., & Tullett, A. (2016). "It's complicated"—sex differences in perceptions of cross-sex friendships. *Journal of Social Psychology, 156*(2), 190–201.
61. Hall, J. A. (2011). Sex differences in friendship expectations: A meta-analysis. *Journal of Social and Personal Relationships, 28,* 723–747.
62. Hall (2011).
63. Hall (2011).
64. Baiocco, R., Laghi, F., Di Pomponio, I., & Nigito, C. S. (2012). Self-disclosure to the best friend: Friendship quality and internalized sexual stigma in Italian lesbian and gay adolescents. *Journal of Adolescence, 35,* 381–387.
65. Barbir, L. A., Vandevender, A. W., & Cohn, T. J. (2017). Friendship, attitudes, and behavioral intentions of cisgender heterosexuals toward transgender individuals. *Journal of Gay & Lesbian Mental Health, 21*(2), 154–170.
66. How can I support my friend who is transgender? (2014, November 11). 7 Cups. https://www.7cups.com/qa-lgbtq--17/how-can-i-support-my-friend-who-is-transgender-410/. Quote appears in post by MonBon.
67. Quinn, B. (2011, May 8). Social network users have twice as many friends online as in real life. *The Guardian*. http://www.theguardian.com/media/2011/may/09/social-network-users-friends-online.
68. Chan, D. K.-S., & Cheng, G. H.-L. (2004). A comparison of offline and online friendship qualities at different stages of relationship development. *Journal of Social and Personal Relationships, 21,* 305–320.
69. Okdie, B. M., Guadagno, R. E., Bernieri, F. J., Geers, A. L., & Mclarney-Vesotski, A. R. (2011). Getting to know you: Face-to-face versus online interactions. *Computers in Human Behavior, 27,* 153–159.
70. Durrotul, M. (2017). The use of social media in intercultural friendship development. *Profetik, 10*(1), 5–20.
71. Ranney, J. D., & Troop-Gordon, W. (2012). Computer-mediated communication with distant friends: Relations with adjustment during students' first semester in college. *Journal of Educational Psychology, 104*(3), 848–861.
72. Hanks, L. (2015, October 19). Why it's okay to stay close with friends from high school while in college. Odyssey. https://www.theodysseyonline.com/stay-close-with-your-friends-from-high-school-while-college. Quote appears in final paragraph.
73. Dunbar, R. M. (2010). *How many friends does one person need? Dunbar's number and other evolutionary quirks.* Faber and Faber.
74. Koerner, A. F., & Fitzpatrick, M. A. (2006). Family communication patterns theory: A social cognitive approach. In

D. O. Braithwaite & L. A. Baxter (Eds.), *Engaging theories in family communication: Multiple perspectives* (pp. 50–65). Sage.

75. Young, S. L. (2009). The function of parental communication patterns: Reflection-enhancing and reflection-discouraging approaches. *Communication Quarterly, 57,* 379–394.
76. Hamon, J. D., & Schrodt, P. (2012). Do parenting styles moderate the association between family conformity orientation and young adults' mental well-being? *Journal of Family Communication, 12,* 151–166.
77. Koerner, A. F., & Fitzpatrick, M. A. (2002). Understanding family communication patterns and family functioning: The roles of conversation orientation and conformity orientation. *Communication Yearbook, 26,* 37–68.
78. For background on this theory, see Baumrind, D. (1991). The influence of parenting styles on adolescent competence and substance use. *The Journal of Early Adolescence, 11,* 56–95.
79. Hamon, J. D., & Schrodt, P. (2012). Do parenting styles moderate the association between family conformity orientation and young adults' mental well-being? *Journal of Family Communication, 12,* 151–166. Quote appears on p. 162.
80. Edwards, R., Hadfield, L., Lucey, H., & Mauthner, M. (2006). *Sibling identity and relationships: Brothers and sisters.* Routledge. Quote appears on p. 4.
81. Epstein, L. (2014, August 4). 16 things that only half-siblings understand. BuzzFeed. https://www.buzzfeed.com/leonoraepstein/things-only-half-siblings-understand. Quote appears in item 7.
82. Stewart, R. B., Kozak, A. L., Tingley, L. M., Goddard, J. M., Blake, E. M., & Cassel, W. A. (2001). Adult sibling relationships: Validation of a typology. *Personal Relationships, 8,* 299–324.
83. Riggio, H. (2006). Structural features of sibling dyads and attitudes toward sibling relationships in young adulthood. *Journal of Family Issues, 27,* 1233–1254.
84. So … my brother just moved out. (2009, January 16). Grasscity. https://forum.grasscity.com/threads/so-my-brother-just-moved-out.322445/. Quote appears in para. 7.
85. Scharf, M., Shulman, S., & Avigad-Spitz, L. (2005). Sibling relationships in emerging adulthood and in adolescence. *Journal of Adolescent Research, 20,* 64–90.
86. Riggio, H. (2006). Structural features of sibling dyads and attitudes toward sibling relationships in young adulthood. *Journal of Family Issues, 27,* 1233–1254.
87. Myers, S. A., & Goodboy, A. K. (2010). Relational maintenance behaviors and communication channel use among adult siblings. *North American Journal of Psychology, 12,* 103–116.
88. Duke, M. P. (2013, March 23). The stories that bind us: What are the twenty questions? *The Blog.* http://www.huffingtonpost.com/marshall-p-duke/the-stories-that-bind-us-_b_2918975.html.
89. Guerrero, L. K., Farinelli, L., & McEwan, B. (2009). Attachment and relational satisfaction: The mediating effect of emotional communication. *Communication Monographs, 76,* 487–514.
90. Young, S. L., The function of parental communication patterns: Reflection-enhancing and reflection-discouraging approaches. *Communication Quarterly, 57,* 379–394.
91. Information in this paragraph is from Petronio, S. (2010). Communication privacy management theory: What do we know about family privacy regulation? *Journal of Family Theory & Review, 2,* 175–196.
92. Baraldi, C., & Iervese, V. (2010). Dialogic mediation in conflict resolution education. *Conflict Resolution Quarterly, 27,* 423–445.
93. Baraldi & Iervese (2010).
94. Strom, R. E., & Boster, F. J. (2011). Dropping out of high school: Assessing the relationship between supportive messages from family and educational attainment. *Communication Reports, 24,* 25–37.
95. Feiler, B. (2013). *The secrets of happy families: Improve your mornings, rethink family dinner, fight smarter, go out and play, and much more.* HarperCollins.

CHAPTER 9

1. Eidell, L. (2020, December 23). *Bachelor* and *Bachelorette* couples still together: The complete list. *Glamour.* https://www.glamour.com/story/bachelor-bachelorette-couples-history.
2. Boardman, M. (2015, February 7). Sean Lowe, Catherine Giudici explain why so few *Bachelor* couples get married. *US Weekly.* http://www.usmagazine.com/entertainment/news/sean-lowe-catherine-giudici-explain-why-so-few-bachelor-couples-wed-201,572. Quote appears in para. 6.
3. Ahmetoglu, G., Swami, V., & Chamorro-Premuzic, T. (2010). The relationship between dimensions of love, personality, and relationship length. *Archives of Sexual Behavior, 34,* 1181–1190.
4. Malouff, J. M., Schutte, N. S., & Thorsteinsson, E. B. (2013). Trait emotional intelligence and romantic relationship satisfaction: A meta-analysis. *American Journal of Family Therapy, 42,* 53–66.
5. Knapp, M. L., & Vangelisti, A. L. (2009). *Interpersonal communication and human relationships* (6th ed.). Allyn & Bacon.
6. Canary, D. J., & Stafford, L. (Eds.). (1994). *Communication and relational maintenance.* Academic Press. See also Lee, J. (1998). Effective maintenance communication in superior-subordinate relationships. *Western Journal of Communication, 62,* 181–208.
7. Quittner, E. (2019, December 9). When the DM slide actually works: 4 couples who met on Instagram. Man Repeller. https://www.manrepeller.com/2019/12/instagram-couples-dms.html.
8. Sprecher, S., & Hampton, A. J. (2017). Liking and other reactions after a get-acquainted interaction: A comparison of continuous face-to-face interaction versus interaction that progresses from text messages to face-to-face. *Communication Quarterly, 65*(3), 333–353.
9. Floyd, K., Hess, J. A., Miczo, L. A., Halone, K. K., Mikkelson, A. C., & Tusing, K. (2005). Human affection exchange: VIII. Further evidence of the benefits of expressed affection. *Communication Quarterly, 53,* 285–303.

10. Wilson, S. R., Kunkel, A. D., Robson, S. J., Olufowote, J. O., & Soliz, J. (2009). Identity implications of relationship (re) definition goals: An analysis of face threats and facework as young adults initiate, intensify, and disengage from romantic relationships. *Journal of Language and Social Psychology, 28,* 32–61.
11. Duran, R. L., & Kelly, L. (2017). Knapp's Model of Relational Development in the digital age. *Iowa Journal of Communication, 49*(1/2), 22–45.
12. Weiner, Z. (2015, July 24). 20 unexpected ways to tell your new relationship is getting serious. Bustle. https://www.bustle.com/articles/99437-20-unexpected-ways-to-tell-your-new-relationship-is-getting-serious.
13. Dunleavy, K., & Booth-Butterfield, M. (2009). Idiomatic communication in the stages of coming together and falling apart. *Communication Quarterly, 57,* 416–432.
14. Knapp, M. L. (1984). *Interpersonal communication and human relationships.* Allyn & Bacon.
15. Battaglia, D. M., Richard, F. D., Datteri, D. L., & Lord, C. G. (1998). Breaking up is (relatively) easy to do: A script for the dissolution of close relationships. *Journal of Social and Personal Relationships, 15*(6), 829–845.
16. Caughlin, J. P., & Sharabi, L. L. (2013). A communicative interdependence perspective of close relationships: The connections between mediated and unmediated interactions matter. *Journal of Communication, 63*(5), 873–893.
17. Flaa, J. (2013, October 29). I met my spouse online: 9 online dating lessons learned the hard way. *The Blog.* http://www.huffingtonpost.com/jennifer-flaa/9-online-dating-lessons_b_4174334.html. Quote appears in para. 13.
18. Aslay, J. (2012, November 3). You lost me at hello, how to get past the awkward first meeting. *Understand Men Now.* http://www.jonathonaslay.com/2012/11/03/you-lost-me-at-hello-how-to-get-past-the-awkward-first-meeting/. Quote appears in para. 11.
19. Flaa, J. (2013, October 29). I met my spouse online: 9 online dating lessons learned the hard way. *The Blog.* http://www.huffingtonpost.com/jennifer-flaa/9-online-dating-lessons_b_4174334.html. Quote appears in para. 13.
20. Meyers, S. (2014, December 23.) 5 ways to put your date at ease (and alleviate awkward tension). *Fox News Magazine.* http://magazine.foxnews.com/love/5-ways-put-your-date-at-ease-and-alleviate-awkward-tension.
21. Meyers (2014). Quote appears in the last paragraph.
22. Moore, L. (2016, February 23). 15 things men don't understand about women. *Cosmopolitan.* https://www.cosmopolitan.com/sex-love/news/a54137/things-men-just-dont-understand-about-women/. Quote is paraphrased from item 2.
23. 50 things men wish women knew. (2013, March 6). *Men's Health.* https://www.menshealth.com/sex-women/men-wish-women-knew. Quote appears in item 17.
24. Kim, I., Feng, B., Wang, B., & Jang, J. (2018). Examining cultural and gender similarities and differences in college students' value of communication skills in romantic relationships. *Chinese Journal of Communication, 11*(4), 437–454.
25. Kim et al. (2018).
26. Ubando, M. (2016). Gender differences in intimacy, emotional expressivity, and relationship satisfaction. *Pepperdine Journal of Communication Research,* 4, Article 13. https://digitalcommons.pepperdine.edu/cgi/viewcontent.cgi?article=1040&context=pjcr.
27. Elliott, S., & Umberson, O. (2008). The performance of desire: Gender and sexual negotiation in long-term marriages. *Journal of Marriage and Family, 70,* 391–406.
28. Harrison, M. A., & Shortall, J. C. (2010, April). Women and men in love: Who really feels it and says it first? *Journal of Social Psychology, 151*(6), 727–736.
29. Zsok, F., Haucke, M., De Wit, C. Y., & Barelds, D. P. H. (2017). What kind of love is love at first sight? An empirical investigation. *Personal Relationships, 24*(4), 869–885.
30. Zsok et al. (2017).
31. Have you experienced love at first sight? (2017). Anonymous post that begins "I was in my class 10th." Quora. https://www.quora.com/Have-you-ever-fallen-in-love-with-someone-at-the-very-first-sight-Do-you-still-love-her. Quote appears in para. 4 of the post.
32. Umberson, D., Thomeer, M. B., & Lodge, A. C. (2015). Intimacy and emotion work in lesbian, gay, and heterosexual relationships. *Journal of Marriage and Family, 77*(2), 542–556.
33. Mackey, R. A., Diemer, M. A., & O'Brien, B. A. (2000). Psychological intimacy in the lasting relationships of heterosexual and same-gender couples. *Sex Roles, 43*(3/4). 201–227.
34. Chapman, G. (2010). *The five love languages: The secret to love that lasts.* Northfield Publishing.
35. Egbert, N., & Polk, D. (2006). Speaking the language of relational maintenance: A validity test of Chapman's (1992) *Five Love Languages. Communication Research Reports, 23*(1), 19–26.
36. Bland, A. M., & McQueen, K. S. (2018). The distribution of Chapman's love languages in couples: An exploratory cluster analysis. *Couple and Family Psychology: Research and Practice, 7*(2), 103–126.
37. Frisby, B. N., & Booth-Butterfield, M. (2012). The "how" and "why" of flirtatious communication between marital partners. *Communication Quarterly, 60,* 465–480.
38. Merolla, A. J. (2010). Relational maintenance during military deployment: Perspectives of wives of deployed US soldiers. *Journal of Applied Communication Research, 38*(1), 4–26.
39. Soin, R. (2011). Romantic gift giving as chore or pleasure: The effects of attachment orientations on gift giving perceptions. *Journal of Business Research, 64,* 113–118.
40. Floyd, K., Boren, J. P., & Hannawa, A. F. (2009). Kissing in marital and cohabitating relationships: Effects of blood lipids, stress, and relationship satisfaction. *Western Journal of Communication, 73,* 113–133.
41. Haas, S. M., & Stafford, L. (2005). Maintenance behaviors in same-sex and marital relationships: A matched sample comparison. *Journal of Family Communication, 5,* 43–60.
42. Haas & Stafford (2005).

43. See, for example, Baxter, L. A., & Montgomery, B. M. (1998). A guide to dialectical approaches to studying personal relationships. In B. M. Montgomery & L. A. Baxter (Eds.), *Dialectical approaches to studying personal relationships* (pp. 1–16). Erlbaum; and Ebert, L. A., & Duck, S. W. (1997). Rethinking satisfaction in personal relationships from a dialectical perspective. In R. J. Sternberg & M. Hojjatr (Eds.), *Satisfaction in close relationships* (pp. 190–216). Guilford.
44. Baxter, L. A. (1994). A dialogic approach to relationship maintenance. In D. J. Canary & L. Stafford (Eds.), *Communication and relational maintenance* (pp. 233–254). Academic Press.
45. Baxter (1994).
46. Morris, D. (1971). *Intimate behavior*. Kodansha Globe, pp. 21–29.
47. Adapted from Baxter, L. A., & Montgomery, B. M. (1998). A guide to dialectical approaches to studying personal relationships. In B. M. Montgomery & L. A. Baxter (Eds.), *Dialectical approaches to studying personal relationships* (pp. 1–16). Erlbaum.
48. Siffert, A., & Schwarz, B. (2011). Spouses' demand and withdrawal during marital conflict in relation to their subjective well-being. *Journal of Social and Personal Relationships, 28,* 262–277.
49. Easterling, B., Kahn, S., Knox, D., & Hall, S. S. (2019). Deception in undergraduate romantic relationships: Who's lying and cheating? *College Student Journal, 53*(3), 277–284.
50. McCornack, S. A., & Levine, T. R. (1990). When lies are uncovered: Emotional and relational outcomes of discovered deception. *Communication Monographs, 57,* 119–138.
51. Kaplar, M. E., & Gordon, A. K. (2004). The enigma of altruistic lying: Perspective differences in what motivates and justifies lie telling within romantic relationships. *Personal Relationships, 11,* 489–507.
52. Markowitz, D. M., & Hancock, J. T. (2018). Deception in mobile dating conversations. *Journal of Communication, 68*(3), 547–569.
53. Inglis-Arkell, E. (2014, October 24). Everyone is lying to you all the time and only butlers know why. *Gizmodo*. https://io9.gizmodo.com/everyone-is-lying-to-you-all-the-time-and-only-butlers-1650198837. Quotes appear in paras. 3, 3, and 5, respectively.
54. Bryant, E. (2008). Real lies, white lies and gray lies: Towards a typology of deception. *Kaleidoscope: A Graduate Journal of Qualitative Communication Research, 7,* 723–748.
55. Kerner, I. (2017, May 16). What counts as "cheating" in the digital age? CNN. https://www.cnn.com/2017/05/16/health/cheating-internet-sex-kerner/index.html.
56. Michele, S. (2015, September 2). I was catfished: This is what I decided to do about it. *HuffPost*. https://www.huffpost.com/entry/i-was-catfished-and-this-_b_8038868.
57. Gunderson, P. R., & Ferrari, J. R. (2008). Forgiveness of sexual cheating in romantic relationships: Effects of discovery method, frequency of offense, and presence of apology. *North American Journal of Psychology, 10,* 1–14.
58. Riter, T., & Riter, S. (2005). Why can't women just come out and say what they mean? *Family Life*. https://www.familylife.com/articles/topics/marriage/staying-married/husbands/why-cant-women-just-come-out-and-say-what-they-mean/. Quotes appear in paras. 6 and 8, respectively.
59. Brandon, J. (n.d.). 37 more quotes on handling workplace conflict. *Inc*. https://www.inc.com/john-brandon/37-more-quotes-on-handling-workplace-conflict.html. Quote appears in item 30. (It must be acknowledged that, although this quote is commonly attributed to Churchill, he may not have actually said it. See https://www.intellectualtakeout.org/blog/5-famous-things-churchill-didnt-actually-say for a rebuttal to that effect.)
60. Zacchilli, T. L., Hendrick, C., & Hendrick, S. S. (2009). The romantic partner conflict scale: A new scale to measure relationship conflict. *Journal of Social and Personal Relationships, 26,* 1073–1096.
61. Bach, G. R., & Goldberg, H. (1974). *Creative aggression*. Doubleday.
62. Bippus, A. M., Boren, J. P., & Worsham, S. (2008). Social exchange orientation and conflict communication in romantic relationships. *Communication Research Reports, 25,* 227–234.
63. Meyer, J. R. (2004). Effect of verbal aggressiveness on the perceived importance of secondary goals in messages. *Communication Studies, 55,* 168–184.
64. The problem. What is battering? (2009). National Coalition Against Domestic Violence. https://www.ozarka.edu/blogs/dojgrant/index.cfm/2009/10/6/The-Problem--What-is-Battering.
65. Are you in a violent relationship? (2013). The Center for Prevention of Abuse. https://web.archive.org/web/20140627172242/http://www.centerforpreventionofabuse.org/violent-relationship.php.
66. Gottman, J. M., & Levenson, R. W. (2002). A two-factor model for predicting when a couple will divorce: Exploratory analyses using 14-year longitudinal data. *Family Process, 41*(1), 83–96; Gottman, J. M., Coan, J., Carrere, S., & Swanson, C. (1998). Predicting marital happiness and stability from newlywed interactions. *Journal of Marriage and the Family, 60*(1), 5–22. http://www.jstor.org/pss/353438; Carrere, S., Buehlman, K. T., Gottman, J. M., Coan, J. A., & Ruckstuhl, L. (2000). Predicting marital stability and divorce in newlywed couples. *Journal of Family Psychology, 14*(1), 42–58; Gottman, J. M. (1991). Predicting the longitudinal course of marriages. *Journal of Marital and Family Therapy, 17*(1), 3–7; Gottman, J. M., & Krokoff, L. J. (1989). The relationship between marital interaction and marital satisfaction: A longitudinal view. *Journal of Consulting and Clinical Psychology, 57,* 47–52; Carrere, S., & Gottman, J. M. (1999). Predicting divorce among newlyweds from the first three minutes of a marital conflict discussion. *Family Process, 38*(3), 293–301.
67. Gottman, J. (1994). *Why marriages succeed or fail: And how you can make yours last*. Simon & Schuster.
68. Gottman, J. M. (2009). *The marriage clinic*. Norton.

CHAPTER 10

1. Employers: Verbal communication most important candidate skill. (2016, February 24). National Association of Colleges and Employers Center for Career Development and Talent Acquisition. http://www.naceweb.org/career-readiness/competencies/employers-verbal-communication-most-important-candidate-skill/.
2. Robert Half. (2017, April 26). The value of teamwork in the workplace. *The Robert Half Blog*. https://web.archive.org/web/20181005154110/https://www.roberthalf.com/blog/management-tips/the-value-of-teamwork-in-the-workplace. Quote is second subtitle.
3. Warrick, D. (2016). What leaders can learn about teamwork and developing high performance teams from organization development practitioners. *Performance Improvement, 3*, 13–21.
4. Improved communication essential to enhance customer satisfaction with after-sale service. (2017, April 27). J.D. Power. http://india.jdpower.com/sites/default/files/2017042in.pdf.
5. Min, H., Lim, Y., & Magnini, V. P. (2015). Factors affecting customer satisfaction in responses to negative online hotel reviews: The impact of empathy, paraphrasing, and speed. *Cornell Hospitality Quarterly, 56*(2), 223–231.
6. Masoud, K., Mohamad Mehdi, M., & Alan, J. D. (2016). Cultural values and consumers' expectations and perceptions of service encounter quality. *International Journal of Pharmaceutical and Healthcare Marketing, 10*(1), 2–26.
7. Myatt, M. (2012, April 4). 10 communication secrets of great leaders. *Forbes*. https://www.forbes.com/sites/mikemyatt/2012/04/04/10-communication-secrets-of-great-leaders/#6cc9808a22fe/. Quote appears in para. 3.
8. Mikkelson, A. C., York, J. A., & Arritola, J. (2015). Communication competence, leadership behaviors, and employee outcomes in supervisor-employee relationships. *Business and Professional Communication Quarterly, 78*(3), 336–354.
9. Dourado, P. (2014, June 5). A leader who inspired me: True story. http://phildourado.com/2014/06/leader-inspired-true-story/. Quotes appear in paras. 13–14 and 16, respectively.
10. Baxter, C. (2012, October 27). She went for broke, and found a job. *New York Times*. http://www.nytimes.com/2012/10/28/jobs/taking-a-chance-and-finding-a-dream-job-in-new-york.html. Quotes appear in para. 1 and 9, respectively.
11. Crispin, G., & Mehler, M. (2010). Impact of the internet on source of hires. *CareerXRoads*. http://www.careerxroads.com/news/impactoftheinternet.doc.
12. Dodds, P. S., Muhamad, R., & Watts, D. J. (2003). An experimental study of search in global social networks. *Science, 301*, 827–829.
13. Brustein, D. (2014, July 22). 17 tips to survive your next networking event. *Forbes*. https://www.forbes.com/sites/yec/2014/07/22/17-tips-to-survive-your-next-networking-event/#59f1c18c7cd4. Quote appears in tip 2.
14. Landsbaum, C. (2015, June 9). "I got a job through social media": 5 Millennials share their stories. *LEVO*. https://web.archive.org/web/20180217194039/https://www.levo.com/posts/i-got-a-job-through-social-media-5-millennials-share-their-stories. Quote appears in para. 2 of Rose McManus post.
15. Salm, L. (2017, June 15). 70% of employers are snooping candidates' social media profiles. *Career Builder*. https://www.careerbuilder.com/advice/social-media-survey-2017#:~:text=According%20to%20a%20new%20CareerBuilder,should%20go%20with%20your%20gut.
16. Lake, L. (2017, June 10). Tips on creating and growing your personal brand. *The Balance*. https://www.thebalance.com/creating-and-growing-personal-brand-2,295,814. Quote appears in tip 5.
17. St. John, A. (2017, August 1). Looking for a job? First, clean up your social media presence. *Consumer Reports*. https://www.consumerreports.org/employment-careers/clean-up-social-media-presence-when-looking-for-a-job/.
18. Hiring managers "spell out" the biggest deal-breakers regarding job candidates' resumes. (2018, February 4). *Talent Inc.* https://www.talentinc.com/press-2018-02-14.
19. Number of employers using social media to screen candidates at all-time high, find latest CareerBuilder study. (2017, June 15). CISION PR Newswire. https://www.prnewswire.com/news-releases/number-of-employers-using-social-media-to-screen-candidates-at-all-time-high-finds-latest-careerbuilder-study-300474228.html.
20. Number of employers (2017).
21. Knight, D. (2017, June 8). 5 social media mistakes most likely to cost you the job. *Yahoo! News*. https://ph.news.yahoo.com/5-social-media-mistakes-most-040200461.html.
22. Poppick, S. (2014, September 5). 10 social media blunders that cost a millennial a job—or worse. *Money*. https://money.com/10-facebook-twitter-mistakes-lost-job-millennials-viral/. Quote appears in para. 2.
23. Kihn, S. (2013). Why it is so important to have a good resume. Career Miner. https://web.archive.org/web/20130314082455/http://careerminer.infomine.com/why-it-is-so-important-to-have-a-good-resume/. Quote appears in para. 1.
24. Tullier, M. (2002). The art and science of writing cover letters: The best way to make a first impression. *Monster.com*. http://resume.monster.com/coverletter/coverletters.
25. 5 popular resume tips you SHOULDN'T follow. (2018, April 12). Jobscan. https://www.jobscan.co/blog/popular-resume-tips-you-shouldnt-follow/.
26. How to make your resume search friendly. (n.d.). ZipRecruiter. https://www.ziprecruiter.com/blog/how-to-make-your-resume-search-friendly/.
27. Graham, A. (2011, January 14). You won't land a job if you can't follow directions. *Forbes*. http://www.forbes.com/sites/work-in-progress/2011/01/14/you-wont-land-a-job-if-you-cant-follow-directions/.
28. Moss, C. (2013, September 28). 14 weird, open-ended job interview questions asked at Apple, Amazon and Google. *Business Insider*. https://www.businessinsider.com/weird-interview-questions-from-apple-google-amazon-2013-9. See also: Top 25 oddball interview questions for 2014. *Glassdoor*. http://www.glassdoor.com/Top-25-Oddball-Interview-Questions-LST_KQ0,34.htm.

29. Smith, A. (n.d.). 5 steps to acing your interview presentation. *The Muse*. https://www.themuse.com/advice/5-steps-to-acing-your-interview-presentation.
30. Do's and don'ts of PowerPoint presentations. (n.d.). TotalJobs. https://www.totaljobs.com/careers-advice/job-interview-advice/powerpoint-pitfalls.
31. Rabin, M., & Schrag, J. L. (1999). First impressions matter: A model of confirmatory bias. *The Quarterly Journal of Economics, 14,* 37–82.
32. Mitchell, N. R. (n.d.). Top 10 interview tips from an etiquette professional. *Experience*. http://www.experience.com/entry-level-jobs/jobs-and-careers/interview-resources/top-10-interview-tips-from-an-etiquette-professional/. Quote appears in para. 7.
33. Kaufman, C. Z. (n.d.). Job interview thank you: Is it better to send a letter or email? Monster.com. https://www.monster.com/career-advice/article/interview-thank-you-email-letter. Quote appears in para. 8.
34. 8 tips for success in a long-distance interview. (2016, May 14). *The Everygirl*. https://web.archive.org/web/20210123145151/http://theeverygirl.com/8-tips-for-success-in-a-long-distance-interview/. Quote appears in tip 2.

CHAPTER 11

1. Goleman, C. (2006). *Social intelligence: The new science of human relationships*. Bantam Dell.
2. Foot-in-mouth stories … post your shame. (2008, August 14). *The Straight Dope Message Board*. https://web.archive.org/web/20180708114322/https://boards.straightdope.com/sdmb/archive/index.php/t-479416.html. Quote appears in the post by Mister Rik.
3. Fleming, P., & Sturdy, A. (2009). "Just be yourself!": Towards neo-normative control in organisations? *Employee Relations, 31,* 569–583.
4. Ragins, B. R. (2008). Disclosure disconnects: Antecedents and consequences of disclosing invisible stigmas across life domains. *Academy of Management Review, 33,* 194–215. See also Ragins, B. R., Singh, R., & Cornwell, J. M. (2007). Making the invisible visible: Fear and disclosure of sexual orientation at work. *Journal of Applied Psychology, 92,* 1103–1118.
5. Rosh, L., & Offermann, L. (2013, October). Be yourself, but carefully. *Harvard Business Review*. http://hbr.org/2013/10/be-yourself-but-carefully/ar/1.
6. Parker, T. (2013, October 25). 30 non-Americans on the American norms they find weird. *Thought Catalogue*. http://thoughtcatalog.com/timmy-parker/2013/10/30-non-americans-on-the-weirdest-things-that-are-norms-to-americans/.
7. Zaslow, J. (2010, January 6). Before you gossip, ask yourself this. … *Moving On*. http://online.wsj.com/article/SB10001424052748704160504574640111681307026.html.
8. Zaslow (2010).
9. "New hires—Stand out at work." (2010, May). OfficePro. http://web.ebscohost.com.libproxy.sbcc.edu:2048/bsi/detail?vid=4&hid=9&sid=079bf30df37c-4ad6-897ec1626aa9b-b49%40sessionmgr14&bdata=JnNpdGU9YnNpLWxpd-mU%3d#db=buh&AN=50544049 (site discontinued).
10. Zimmerman, M. (2010, December 22). Losing your temper at work: How to survive it. CBS News. https://www.cbsnews.com/news/losing-your-temper-at-work-how-to-survive-it/#. Quote appears in para. 5.
11. Chandler, N. (n.d.). 10 tips for managing conflict in the workplace. *HowStuffWorks*. http://money.howstuffworks.com/business/starting-a-job/10-tips-for-managing-conflict-in-the-workplace1.htm#page=1.
12. Leaping lizards! OfficeTeam survey reveals managers' most embarrassing moment at work. (2011, January 18). *OfficeTeam*. http://rh-us.mediaroom.com/2011-01-18-LEAPING-LIZARDS.
13. Simms, A., & Nichols, T. (2014). Social loafing: A review of the literature. *Journal of Management Policy & Practice, 15*(1), 58–67.
14. Wagner, R., & Harter, J. K. (2006). When there's a freeloader on your team. Excerpt from *The elements of great managing*. Washington, DC: Gallup Press. http://www.stybelpeabody.com/newsite/pdf/Freeloader_on_Your_Team.pdf.
15. Paknad, D. (n.d.). The 5 dynamics of low performing teams. Don't let freeloaders or fear undermine your team. *Workboard*. http://www.workboard.com/blog/dynamics-of-low-performing-teams.php.
16. Gallo, A. (2013, May 2). Act like a leader before you are one. *Harvard Business Review*. https://hbr.org/2013/05/act-like-a-leader-before-you-a. Quote appears in para. 1.
17. Prime, J., & Salbi, E. (2014, May 12). The best leaders are humble leaders. *Harvard Business Review Digital Articles,* pp. 2–5.
18. Collins, J. C. (2001). *Good to great: Why some companies make the leap—and others don't*. HarperBusiness.
19. Van Wart, M. (2013). Lessons from leadership theory and the contemporary challenges of leaders. *Public Administration Review, 73*(4), 553–565.
20. Sethuraman, K., & Suresh, J. (2014, August 25). Effective leadership styles. *International Business Research, 7*(9), 165–172.
21. Fiedler, F. E. (1967). *A theory of leadership effectiveness*. New York: McGraw-Hill.
22. Hersey, P., & Blanchard, K. (2001). *Management of organizational behavior: Utilizing human resources* (8th ed.). Prentice Hall.
23. Blake, R., & Mouton, J. (1964). *The Managerial Grid: The key to leadership excellence*. Gulf Publishing Co.
24. Blake, R., & Mouton, J. (1985). *The Managerial Grid III: The key to leadership excellence*. Gulf Publishing Co.
25. Kuhnert, K. W., & Lewis, P. (1987). Transactional and transformational leadership: A constructive/developmental analysis. *Academy of Management Review, 12,* 648–657.
26. Bass, B. M. (1990). From transactional to transformational leadership: Learning to share the vision. *Organizational Dynamics, 3,* 19–31.
27. Pierro, A., Raven, B. H., Amato, C., & Bélanger, J. J. (2013). Bases of social power, leadership styles, and organizational commitment. *International Journal of Psychology, 48*(6), 1122–1134.
28. Van Wart, M. (2013). Lessons from leadership theory and the contemporary challenges of leaders. *Public Administration Review, 73*(4), 553–565.

29. Lapin, R. (2008). *Working with difficult people*. Dorling Kindersley.
30. Claros Group. (2010). Leaving a job professionally: Wrapping up your current position before moving on. http://www.claros-group.com/leavingjob.pdf.
31. Claros Group (2010).
32. The following types of power are based on the categories developed by French, J. R., & Raven, B. (1968). The basis of social power. In D. Cartright & A. Zander (Eds.), *Group dynamics*. Harper & Row, p. 565.
33. Rothwell, J. D. (2013). *In mixed company: Communicating in small groups* (8th ed.). Cengage Learning.
34. For a more detailed discussion of the advantages and disadvantages of working in groups, see Beebe, S. A., & Masterson, J. T. (2003). *Communicating in small groups: Principles and practices* (9th ed.). Allyn & Bacon.
35. Marby, E. A. (1999). The systems metaphor in group communication. In L. R. Frey (Ed.), *Handbook of group communication theory and research* (pp. 71–91). Sage.
36. Rothwell, J. D. (2004). *In mixed company: Small group communication* (5th ed.). Wadsworth, pp. 29–31.
37. Is your team too big? Too small? What's the right number? (2006, June 14). *Knowledge@Wharton*. http://knowledge.wharton.upenn.edu/article.cfm?articleid=1501.
38. Lowry, P., Roberts, T. L., Romano, N. C., Jr., Cheney, P. D., & Hightower, R. T. (2006). The impact of group size and social presence on small-group communication. *Small Group Research, 37,* 631–661.
39. Hackman, J. (1987). The design of work teams. In J. Lorsch (Ed.), *Handbook of organizational behavior* (pp. 315–342). Prentice Hall.
40. Gouran, D. S., Hirokawa, R. Y., Julian, K. M., & Leatham, G. B. (1992). The evolution and current status of the functional perspective on communication in decision-making and problem-solving groups. In S. A. Deetz (Ed.), *Communication yearbook* 16 (pp. 573–600). Sage. See also Wittenbaum, G. M., Hollingshead, A. B., Paulus, P. B., Hirokawa, R. Y., Ancona, D. G., Peterson, R. S., … Yoon, K. (2004). The functional perspective as a lens for understanding groups. *Small Group Research, 35,* 17–43.
41. Mayer, M. E. (1998). Behaviors leading to more effective decisions in small groups embedded in organizations. *Communication Reports, 11,* 123–132.
42. Fisher, B. A. (1970). Decision emergence: Phases in group decision making. *Speech Monographs, 37,* 53–66.
43. This terminology originated with Tuckman, B. W (1965). Developmental sequence in small groups. *Psychological Bulletin, 63*(6), 384–399.
44. Frantz, C. R., & Jin, K. G. (1995). The structure of group conflict in a collaborative work group during information systems development. *Journal of Applied Communication Research, 23,* 108–127.
45. Clark, D. (2012, May 23). How to deal with difficult co-workers. *Forbes*. http://www.forbes.com/sites/dorieclark/2012/05/23/how-to-deal-with-difficult-co-workers/#-6c21476a191d.
46. Dugan, D. (n.d.). Co-workers from hell: Dealing with difficult colleagues. Salary.com. http://www.salary.com/co-workers-from-hell-dealing-with-difficult-colleagues/.
47. See, for example, Pavitt, C. (2003). Do interacting groups perform better than aggregates of individuals? *Human Communication Research, 29,* 592–599; Wittenbaum, G. M. (2004). Putting communication into the study of group memory. *Human Communication Research, 29,* 616–623; and Frank, M. G., Feely, T. H., Paolantonio, N., & Servoss, T. J. (2004). Individual and small group accuracy in judging truthful and deceptive communication. *Group Decision and Negotiation, 13,* 45–54.
48. Rae-Dupree, J. (2008, December 7). Innovation is a team sport. *New York Times*. http://www.nytimes.com/2008/12/07/business/worldbusiness/07iht-innovate.1.18456109.html.
49. Adler, R. B., Elmhorst, J. M., & Lucas, K. (2013). *Communicating at work: Principles and practices for business and the professions* (11th ed.). McGraw-Hill, pp. 215–216.
50. Waller, B. M., Hope, L., Burrowes, M., & Morrison, E. R. (2011). Twelve (not so) angry men: Managing conversational group size increases perceived contribution by decision makers. *Group Processes & Intergroup Relations, 14,* 835–843.
51. Rothwell, J. D. (2013). *In mixed company* (8th ed.). Wadsworth-Cengage, pp. 139–142.
52. Janis, I. (1982). *Groupthink: Psychological studies of policy decisions and fiascoes*. Houghton Mifflin. See also Baron, R. S. (2005). So right it's wrong: Groupthink and the ubiquitous nature of polarized group decision making. In M. P. Zanna (Ed.), *Advances in experimental social psychology* (Vol. 37, pp. 219–253). Elsevier Academic Press.
53. Adapted from Rothwell, J. D. (2013). *In mixed company* (8th ed.). Wadsworth-Cengage, pp. 139–142, note 49.
54. van Knippenberg, D., van Ginkel, W. P., & Homan, A. C. (2013, July). Diversity mindsets and the performance of diverse teams. *Organizational Behavior and Human Decision Processes, 121,* 183–193.
55. Myers, D. (2017, March 1). Research note—86 percent of businesses surveyed to use video conferencing as part of their UC [Unified Communication] Environment by 2018. https://web.archive.org/web/20181220134708/https://technology.ihs.com/589990/research-note-86-percent-of-businesses-surveyed-to-use-video-conferencing-as-part-of-their-uc-environment-by-2018.
56. Brown, N. (2020, April 4). Best practices for video conferencing security. https://blog.paloaltonetworks.com/2020/04/network-video-conferencing-security/.
57. Adams, S. (2020, April 22). Zoom meeting etiquette: 15 tips and best practices for online video conference meetings. *Penn Live*. https://www.pennlive.com/coronavirus/2020/04/zoom-meeting-etiquette-15-tips-and-best-practices-for-online-video-conference-meetings.html. Quote appears in para. 8.
58. Capdeferro, N., & Romero, M. (2012). Are online learners frustrated with collaborative learning experiences? *International Review of Research in Open & Distance Learning, 13,* 26–44.
59. Dewey, J. (1910). *How we think*. Heath.

60. Poole, M. S. (1991). Procedures for managing meetings: Social and technological innovation. In R. A. Swanson & B. O. Knapp (Eds.), *Innovative meeting management* (pp. 53–109). 3M Meeting Management Institute. See also Poole, M. S., & Holmes, M. E. (1995). Decision development in computer-assisted group decision making. *Human Communication Research, 22,* 90–127.
61. Lewin, K. (1951). *Field theory in social science*. Harper & Row, pp. 30–59.
62. Hastle, R. (1983). *Inside the jury*. Harvard University Press.

CHAPTER 12

1. Moore-Berg, S., Hameiri, B., and Bruneau, E., (2020, August) The prime psychological suspects of toxic political polarization. *Current Opinion in Behavioral Sciences*, *34*, 199–204.
2. Mooney, C. (2012, April 12). Liberals and conservatives don't just vote differently. They think differently. *Washington Post*. https://www.washingtonpost.com/opinions/liberals-and-conservatives-dont-just-vote-differently-they-think-differently/2012/04/12/gIQAzb1kDT_story.html.
3. Acho, E. (2020, June 3). Uncomfortable conversations with a Black man. YouTube. https://www.youtube.com/watch?v=h-8jUA7JBkF4. Quote is at the beginning.
4. Haidt, J. (2008, March). The moral roots of liberals and conservatives. TED2008. https://www.ted.com/talks/jonathan_haidt_on_the_moral_mind/transcript.
5. Haidt (2008).
6. For example, see Kopfman, J. E., & Smith, S. (1996, February). Understanding the audiences of a health communication campaign: A discriminant analysis of potential organ donors based on intent to donate. *Journal of Applied Communication Research, 24*, 33–49.
7. Stutman, R. K., & Newell, S. E. (1984, Fall). Beliefs versus values: Silent beliefs in designing a persuasive message. *Western Journal of Speech Communication, 48*(4), 364.
8. Willer, R., & Feinberg, M. (2015, November 13). The key to political persuasion. *New York Times*. Retrieved from https://www.nytimes.com/2015/11/15/opinion/sunday/the-key-to-political-persuasion.html.
9. Willer & Feinberg (2015).
10. Willer & Feinberg (2015).
11. Heshmat, S. (2015, April 23). What is confirmation bias? *Psychology Today*. https://www.psychologytoday.com/us/blog/science-choice/201504/what-is-confirmation-bias.
12. See, e.g., Nichols. T. (2017). *The death of expertise: The campaign against established knowledge and why it matters*. Oxford University Press.
13. See, e.g., Pariser, E. (2012). *The filter bubble: What the internet is hiding from you*. Penguin.
14. AllSides.com provides ratings for Left, Right, and Center bias for news sites: https://www.allsides.com/media-bias/media-bias-ratings.
15. Common Dreams. (2020, June 4). The knee for change. *Radio Free*. https://www.radiofree.org/2020/06/04/the-knee-for-change/.
16. Hardt, M. J. (2019, November). Are we interrupting the kinky sex lives of fish? TEDxMileHigh. https://www.ted.com/talks/marah_j_hardt_the_quirky_sex_lives_of_ocean_creatures.
17. Hardt (2019, November).
18. Abbott, E. (2020). A call for the insurance industry to uphold mental health parity. In *Winning orations, 2020*. Interstate Oratorical Association, p. 10.
19. Roberts, L. (2020). A new battlefield: Veterans' fight to form a family. In *Winning orations, 2020*. Interstate Oratorical Association, p. 22.
20. Pinto, M. (2020). "Underage women" do not exist. In *Winning orations, 2020*. Interstate Oratorical Association, p. 31.
21. Adams, A. (2017). On neurodiversity and race. In *Winning orations, 2017*. Interstate Oratorical Association, p. 55.
22. Malami, S. (2020). Child slavery in the chocolate industry. In *Winning orations, 2019*. Interstate Oratorical Association, n.p.
23. Banks, A (2019). Let's talk about sex: The need to teach consent. In *Winning orations, 2019*. Interstate Oratorical Association, n.p.
24. Elsesser, K. (2010, March 3). And the gender-neutral Oscar goes to ... *New York Times*. Retrieved from https://www.nytimes.com/2010/03/04/opinion/04elsesser.html.
25. Keagan, S. (2019). Recycling contamination. In *Winning orations, 2019*. Interstate Oratorical Association, n.p.
26. Vasquez Rojas, A. (2020). Deconstructing the invisible prison: Providing an equitable educational experience for undocumented students through the UndocuAlly program. In *Winning orations, 2019*. Interstate Oratorical Association, n.p.
27. Perry, A. (2017). Alcoholism: The deadliest disease that doesn't get treated. In *Winning orations, 2017*. Interstate Oratorical Association, p. 109.
28. Perry (2017).

CHAPTER 13

1. Some experts specifically refer to Public Speaking Anxiety, or PSA. See, for example, Bodie, G. D. (2010, January). A racing heart, rattling knees, and ruminative thoughts: Defining, explaining, and treating public speaking anxiety. *Communication Education, 59*(1), 70–105.
2. Ebrahimi, O. V., Pallesen, S., Kenter, R. M. F., & Nordgreen, T. (2019, March). Psychological interventions for the fear of public speaking: A meta-analysis. *Frontiers in Psychology, 10*, 488. https://pubmed.ncbi.nlm.nih.gov/30930813/.
3. See, for example, Borhis, J., & Allen, M. (1992, January). Meta-analysis of the relationship between communication apprehension and cognitive performance. *Communication Education, 41*(1), 68–76.
4. Daly, J. A., Vangelisti, A. L., & Weber, D. J. (1995, December). Speech anxiety affects how people prepare speeches: A protocol analysis of the preparation process of speakers. *Communication Monographs, 62,* 123–134.
5. Researchers generally agree that communication apprehension has three causes: genetics, social learning, and inadequate skills acquisition. See, for example, Finn, A. N. (2009). Public speaking: What causes some to panic? *Communication Currents, 4*(4), 1–2.

6. See, for example, Sawyer, C. R., & Behnke, R. R. (1997, Summer). Communication apprehension and implicit memories of public speaking state anxiety. *Communication Quarterly, 45*(3), 211–222.
7. Adapted from Ellis, A. (1977). *A new guide to rational living.* North Hollywood, CA: Wilshire Books. G. M. Philips listed a different set of beliefs that he believed contributes to reticence: (1) an exaggerated sense of self-importance (reticent people tend to see themselves as more important to others than others see them); (2) effective speakers are born, not made; (3) skillful speaking is manipulative; (4) speaking is not that important; (5) I can speak whenever I want to; I just choose not to; (6) it is better to be quiet and let people think you are a fool than prove it by talking (they assume they will be evaluated negatively); and (7) what is wrong with me requires a (quick) cure. See Keaten, J. A., Kelly, L., & Finch, C. (2000, April). Effectiveness of the Penn State program in changing beliefs associated with reticence. *Communication Education, 49*(2), 134–145.
8. Behnke, R. R., Sawyer, C. R., & King, P. E. (1987, April). The communication of public speaking anxiety. *Communication Education, 36,* 138–141.
9. Honeycutt, J. M., Choi, C. W., & DeBerry, J. R. (2009, July). Communication apprehension and imagined interactions. *Communication Research Reports, 26*(2), 228–236.
10. Behnke, R. R., & Sawyer, C. R. (1999, April). Milestones of anticipatory public speaking anxiety. *Communication Education, 48*(2), 165–172.
11. See, for example, Fearn, N., DeMuro, P., & Turner, B. (2020, November). Best presentation software of 2020: Slides for speeches and talks. *Techradar Pro.* https://www.techradar.com/best/best-presentation-software.
12. Examples of online tutorials include https://www.inc.com/kevin-daum/10-tips-for-giving-great-online-presentations.html, https://www.gsb.stanford.edu/insights/10-tips-giving-effective-virtual-presentations, and https://juliehansen.live/great-online-presentation/. Tutorials covering specific software include https://support.office.com/en-us/article/present-online-using-the-office-presentation-service-c1fd3f16-97c0-4f96-91c3-79e147e7e574 and https://prezi.com/kd5tlxznexpq/prezi-create-online-presentations-for-free/.
13. See, for example, Rosenfeld, L. R., & Civikly, J. M. (1976). *With words unspoken.* New York: Holt, Rinehart and Winston, p. 62. Also see Chaiken, S. (1979). Communicator physical attractiveness and persuasion. *Journal of Personality and Social Psychology, 37,* 1387–1397.
14. Hinton, J. S., & Kramer, M. W. (1998, April). The impact of self-directed videotape feedback on students' self-reported levels of communication competence and apprehension. *Communication Education, 47*(2), 151–161. Significant increases in competency and decreases in apprehension were found using this method.
15. Research has confirmed that speeches practiced in front of other people tend to be more successful. See, for example, Smith, T. E., & Frymier, A. B. (2006, February). Get "real": Does practicing speeches before an audience improve performance? *Communication Quarterly, 54,* 111–125.
16. A study demonstrating this stereotype is Street, R. L., Jr., & Brady, R. M. (1982, December). Speech rate acceptance ranges as a function of evaluative domain, listener speech rate, and communication context. *Speech Monographs, 49,* 290–308.
17. Smith, V., Siltanen, S. A., & Hosman, L. A. (1998, Fall). The effects of powerful and powerless speech styles and speaker expertise on impression formation and attitude change. *Communication Research Reports, 15*(1), 27–35. In this study, a powerful speech style was defined as one without hedges and hesitations such as *uh* and *anda.*
18. Reed, M. (2020, May 13). Should showing faces be mandatory? Confessions of a Community College Dean (blog). *Inside Higher Education.* https://www.insidehighered.com/blogs/confessions-community-college-dean/should-showing-faces-be-mandatory.
19. See, for example, G2. (2020). Zoom competitors and alternatives. https://www.g2.com/products/zoom/competitors/alternatives.

CHAPTER 14

1. Zerback, T., Topfl, F., & Knopfle, M. (2020, March 4). The disconcerting potential of online disinformation: Persuasive effects of astroturfing comments and three strategies for inoculation against them. *New Media & Society.* https://doi.org/10.1177/1461444820908530.
2. Allbright, E. P. (2020) #Childcare4all. In *Winning orations, 2020.* Interstate Oratorical Association, p. 14.
3. Cacioppo, J. T., & Petty, R. E. (1979). Effects of message repetition and position on cognitive response, recall, and persuasion. *Journal of Personality and Social Psychology, 37,* 97–109.
4. For an example of how one politician failed to adapt to his audience's attitudes, see Hostetler, M. J. (1998, Winter). Gov. Al Smith confronts the Catholic question: The rhetorical legacy of the 1928 campaign. *Communication Quarterly, 46*(1), 12–24. Smith was reluctant to discuss religion, attributed bigotry to anyone who brought it up, and was impatient with the whole issue. He lost the election. Many years later, John F. Kennedy dealt with "the Catholic question" more reasonably and won.
5. DeVito, J. A. (1986). *The communication handbook: A dictionary.* New York: Harper & Row, pp. 84–86.
6. González, E. (2018). Speech presented at Ft. Lauderdale Rally for Gun Control, February 17. All quotations in this section come from that speech.
7. Stallings, H. (2009). Prosecution deferred is justice denied. *Winning orations 2009.* Interstate Oratorical Association. Hope was coached by Randy Richardson and Melanie Conrad.
8. Monroe, A. (1935). *Principles and types of speech.* Glenview, IL: Scott, Foresman.
9. Toulmin, S. E. (1964). The uses of argument. New York: Cambridge University Press.
10. Curt Casper presented this speech when he was a student at Hastings College in 2011.

11. There are, of course, other classifications of logical fallacies than those presented here. See, for example, Warnick, B., & Inch, E. (1994). *Critical thinking and communication: The use of reason in argument* (2nd ed.). New York: Macmillan, pp. 137–161.
12. Sprague, J., & Stuart, D. (1992). *The speaker's handbook* (3rd ed.). Fort Worth, TX: Harcourt Brace Jovanovich, 1992, p. 172.

APPENDIX A

1. Future of Fish. (n.d.). Our oceans are in crisis. https://future-offish.org/.
2. Hardt, M. J. (2019, November). Are we interrupting the kinky lives of fish? TEDxMileHigh. https://www.ted.com/talks/marah_j_hardt_are_we_interrupting_the_kinky_sex_lives_of_fish/transcript. Reprinted by permission of the author.
3. Hardt (2019).

APPENDIX B

1. Kraidin, D. (2019, May 9). Saeed Malami '20 wins national forensics championship, first Interstate Oratorical Association Championship. *The Lafayette*. https://www.lafayettestudent-news.com/blog/2019/05/10/draft-saeed-malami-national-champ/.
2. Personal email correspondence with George Rodman, March, 2021.
3. Malami, S. (2019). Child slavery in the chocolate industry. In *Winning orations*, 2019. Interstate Oratorial Association, 2019. Edited for classroom use with visual aids.

Glossary

accent: Pronunciation perceived as different from the local speech style. p. 52

***ad hominem* fallacy:** A fallacious argument that attacks the integrity of a person to weaken their position. p. 228

addition: The articulation error that involves adding extra parts to words. p. 211

adjustment shock: When a person feels confused, disenchanted, lonesome, or homesick in a new cultural environment; another term for culture shock. p. 46

affect blend: The combination of two or more facial expressions, each showing a different emotion. p. 87

affective: Focused on emotions. p. 61

affiliative language: Speech that demonstrates a sense of connection between people. p. 53

affinity: The degree to which one person likes another. p. 99

ally: Someone from a dominant social group (e.g., White, male, cisgender, management) who actively advocates for fair treatment and social justice for others. p. 60

altruistic lie: Deception intended to be harmless or helpful to the person to whom it is told. p. 136

analogies: Extended comparisons that can be used as supporting material in a speech. p. 194

analytical listening: A process in which the receiver's primary goal is to fully comprehend a message. p. 76

androgynous: Combining masculine and feminine traits. p. 21

anecdote: A brief personal story used to illustrate or support a point in a speech. p. 194

apathetic (sibling relationship): A pattern in which siblings only communicate with one another on special occasions. p. 123

***argumentum ad populum* fallacy:** Fallacious reasoning based on the dubious notion that because many people favor an idea, you should, too. p. 228

***argumentum ad verecundiam* fallacy:** Fallacious reasoning that tries to support a belief by relying on the testimony of someone who is not an authority on the issue being argued. p. 228

articulation: The process of pronouncing all the necessary parts of a word. p. 210

assertive communication: A style that directly expresses the sender's needs, thoughts, or feelings in a way that does not attack or demean the receiver. p. 137

attitudes: Predispositions to respond to an idea, person, or thing favorably or unfavorably. p. 184

attribution: The process of attaching meaning to behavior. p. 20

audience analysis: A consideration of characteristics including the type, goals, demographics, beliefs, attitudes, and values of listeners. p. 183

audience involvement: The level of commitment and attention that listeners devote to a speech. p. 219

audience participation: Having your listeners actually do something during your speech. p. 219

authoritarian (parenting): An approach in which parents expect unquestioning obedience. p. 122

authoritative (parenting): An approach in which parents are firm, clear, and strict, but encourage children to communicate openly with them. p. 122

avoidance spiral: A communication pattern in which the parties slowly reduce their dependence on one another, withdraw, and become less invested in the relationship. p. 106

bar chart: Visual aid that compares two or more values by showing them as elongated horizontal rectangles. p. 204

basic speech structure: The division of a speech into introduction, body, and conclusion. p. 188

behavioral interview: A question and answer session that focuses on an applicant's past performance (behavior) as it relates to the job at hand. p. 154

beliefs: Underlying convictions about the truth of an idea, often based on cultural training. p. 184

breadth: The range of topics about which an individual discloses. p. 101

catfishing: Creating a fictional persona to fool people into thinking that they are communicating with a real person. p. 136

channel: The method in which a message passes from sender to receiver. p. 3

chronemics: The study of how humans use and structure time. p. 89

cisgender: Describes a person whose current identity is the same as the sex attributed to them at birth. p. 21

citation: Brief statement of supporting material in a speech. p. 195

claim: One of a series of statements that lead to the conclusion the speaker is trying to establish. p. 225

coculture: A social group that is part of an encompassing culture. p. 33

coercive power: The power to influence others by the threat or imposition of unpleasant consequences. p. 170

cohesiveness: The degree to which group members feel connected with and committed to the group. p. 173

collectivistic culture: A group in which members focus on the welfare of the group as a whole more than on individuals. p. 34

column chart: Visual aid that compares two or more values by showing them as elongated vertical rectangles. p. 204

common ground: Similarities between yourself and your audience members. p. 221

communication: The process of creating meaning through symbolic interaction. p. 2

communication climate: The emotional tone of a relationship, as reflected in the messages that relational partners express. p. 106

communication competence: The ability to maintain a relationship on terms that are acceptable to all parties. p. 10

competitive (sibling relationship): A pattern in which siblings perceive themselves to be rivals. p. 123

complementary: A pattern in which one person's characteristics satisfy the other's needs, as when an introverted and extroverted person inspire each other to try new experiences. p. 113

conclusion (of a speech): The last structural unit of a speech, in which the speaker restates the thesis, reviews the main points, and provides a memorable final remark. p. 192

confirmation bias: Tendency to believe untrue information if it conforms to one's preconceived biases. Also the tendency to reject information that is inconsistent with one's current viewpoint. pp. 57, 187, 222

confirming: A message that conveys that the speaker respects and values the other person. p. 106

conflict spiral: A communication pattern in which a statement perceived as an attack leads to a counterattack and then another, until the communication escalates into a full-fledged argument. p. 106

conflict (storming) stage: A phase in problem-solving groups in which members openly defend their positions and challenge those of others. p. 172

conformity: A family communication pattern in which members are expected to adhere to an established set of rules, beliefs, and values. p. 122

connection power: Influence granted because of a person's ability to develop relationships. p. 170

connotative meanings: Informal, implied interpretations for words and phrases that reflect the people, culture, emotions, and situations involved. p. 50

contempt: Communication behaviors that reflect the speaker's negative attitude or opinion toward another person. p. 139

content message: The dimension of a message that addresses information about the subject being discussed. p. 99

control: The amount of influence exercised by one person over another. p. 99

convergence: Accommodating one's speaking style to another person, usually a person who is appealing or has higher status. p. 53

conversation: A family communication pattern in which members are encouraged to communicate openly about rules and expectations. p. 122

conversational narcissists: People who focus on themselves and their interests instead of listening to and encouraging others. p. 74

credibility: The believability of a speaker or other source of information. p. 221

critical listening: A process in which the receiver's goal is to evaluate the quality or accuracy of a speaker's remarks. p. 76

criticism: All-encompassing and accusatory statements such as "You never do your fair share." p. 139

culture: The language, values, beliefs, traditions, and customs shared by a group of people. p. 33

culture shock: When a person feels confused, disenchanted, lonesome, or homesick in a new cultural environment; also known as adjustment shock. p. 46

debilitative speech anxiety: Intense level of apprehension about speaking before an audience, resulting in poor performance. p. 199

deception bias: A tendency to assume that people are lying. p. 85

decode: To attach meaning to a message. p. 3

defensive listeners: Receivers who perceive a speaker's comments as an attack. p. 73

defensiveness: Striking back when one feels attacked by another. p. 139

deletion: The articulation error that involves leaving off parts of words. p. 211

demographics: Audience characteristics that can be analyzed statistically, such as age, gender, education, and group membership. p. 183

denotative meanings: Formally recognized definitions for words, as found in a dictionary. p. 50

depth: The level of personal information a person reveals on a particular topic. p. 101

developmental model (of relational maintenance): The perspective that relationships develop, maintain stability, and come apart in stages that reflect different levels of intimacy. p. 128

diagram: A line drawing that shows the most important components of an object. p. 204

dialect: A version of the same language that includes substantially different words and meanings. p. 52

digital dirt: Unflattering information (whether true or not) that has been posted about a person online. p. 148

directly aggressive message: Communication in which a sender demeans or insults the other person rather than debating the points they are making. p. 138

disconfirming: A message that expresses a lack of caring or respect for another person. p. 106

disinhibition: The tendency to transmit messages without considering their consequences. p. 9

divergence: A linguistic strategy in which speakers emphasize differences between their communicative style and that of others in order to create distance. p. 53

Dunbar's Number: The average number of friendships an individual can maintain at one time (approximately 150). p. 121

dyadic communication: Communication between two people. p. 5

either–or fallacy: Fallacious reasoning that sets up false alternatives, suggesting that if the inferior one must be rejected, then the other must be accepted. p. 228

emblems: Deliberate nonverbal behaviors with precise meanings, known to virtually all members of a cultural group. p. 84

emergence (norming) stage: A phase in problem-solving groups in which members stop arguing for separate solutions and combine their ideas. p. 173

Emotional intelligence (EI): A person's ability to understand and effectively manage emotions. p. 23

emotive language: Speech that conveys the sender's attitude rather than simply offering an objective description. p. 58

empathy: The willingness and ability to experience things from another person's point of view. p. 23

encode: To put thoughts into symbols (usually words). p. 3

environment: The circumstances in which communication occurs and the perspectives of the parties involved. p. 3

equivocal words: Language with more than one likely interpretation. p. 55

equivocation: A deliberately vague statement that can be interpreted in more than one way. p. 55

ethnicity: A social construct that refers to the degree to which a person identifies with a particular group, usually on the basis of nationality, culture, religion, or some other perspective. p. 38

ethnocentrism: The attitude that one's own culture is superior to that of others. p. 45

ethos: Aristotle's term for the ethical dimension of a persuasive speech. p. 222

euphemism: A pleasant term used in place of a more direct but less pleasant one. p. 56

evaluating: A stage of listening in which a person goes beyond interpreting a message to make a judgment about the message and/or the speaker. p. 70

evasions: Statements that aren't outright mistruths, but are deliberately vague, often to avoid hurting someone's feelings. Also called gray lies. p. 136

evidence: Supporting material used to back up a claim. p. 226

example: A specific case that is used to demonstrate a general idea. p. 193

expectancy violation theory: The idea that when someone's nonverbal communication violates expectations, people may react either positively or negative depending on how extreme the behavior is and how they feel about the rule breaker. p. 83

expert power: The ability to influence others by virtue of one's perceived knowledge about the subject in question. p. 170

extemporaneous speeches: Speeches that are planned in advance but presented in a direct, conversational manner. p. 203

face: A socially approved identity that a communicator tries to present. p. 26

facework: Behavior designed to create and maintain a communicator's face and the face of others; synonymous with identity management. p. 26

facilitative speech anxiety: A moderate level of apprehension about speaking before an audience that helps improve the speaker's performance. p. 199

factual statement: A statement that can be verified as being true or false. p. 57

fallacy: An error in logic. p. 228

fallacy of *ad hominem*: Statement that attacks a person's character rather than debating the issues at hand. p. 58

fallacy of approval: The irrational belief that it is vital to win the approval of virtually every person a communicator deals with. p. 200

fallacy of catastrophic failure: The irrational belief that the worst possible outcome will probably occur. p. 200

fallacy of overgeneralization: Irrational beliefs in which (1) conclusions (usually negative) are based on limited evidence or (2) communicators exaggerate their shortcomings. p. 200

fallacy of perfection: The irrational belief that a worthwhile communicator should be able to handle every situation with complete confidence and skill. p. 200

family: People who share affection and resources as a family and who think of themselves and present themselves as a family, regardless of their genetic commonality. p. 112

feedback: The discernible response of a receiver to a sender's message. p. 4

filter bubble: Online media that enable users to access only that information that conforms with their biases. p. 187

flow chart: A diagram that depicts a process with boxes and arrows that represent the steps in a process. p. 204

formal outline: A consistent format and set of symbols used to identify the structure of ideas. p. 188

formal role: A position and set of behaviors explicitly assigned to a person, such as being a project leader or facilitator. p. 172

frame switching: The ability to adapt one's style to the norms of more than one culture or coculture. p. 42

fundamental attribution error: The tendency to interpret and explain information in a way that casts the perceiver in a favorable way; also called self-serving bias. p. 20

gender: A socially constructed set of expectations about what it means to be "masculine," "feminine," or another gender identity. p. 21

general purposes: Three basic ways a speaker seeks to affect an audience: to entertain, inform, or persuade. p. 186

groupthink: The tendency to go along with a group decision without fully considering the implications or alternatives. p. 175

halo effect: The tendency to assume that a person who impresses one favorably in one way also has other positive qualities. p. 20

haptics: The study of touch. p. 87

hearing: The process wherein sound waves strike the eardrum and cause vibrations that are transmitted to the brain. p. 69

high self-monitors: People who pay close attention to their own behavior and others' reactions, adjusting their communication to create the desired impression. p. 27

high-context culture: A group that relies heavily on subtle, often nonverbal cues to convey meaning and maintain social harmony. p. 35

hostile (sibling relationship): A pattern in which siblings feel jealousy, resentment, and anger toward one another. p. 123

hypothetical (or fictional) examples: Examples that ask an audience to imagine an object or event. p. 193

"I language": Statements such as "When you are late I feel frustrated" that describe a specific behavior by another person and how that behavior affects the speaker. p. 107

identity management: Strategies used by communicators to influence the way others view them; synonymous with facework. p. 26

imaginary audience: A heightened self-consciousness that makes it seem as if people are observing and judging you. p. 40

immediacy: The level of engagement between people in a relationship. p. 99

implicit bias: Prejudices and stereotypes that people harbor without consciously thinking about them. p. 60

impromptu speeches: Speeches given without preparation. p. 203

indirect communication: Hinting at a message instead of expressing thoughts and feelings directly. p. 137

individualistic culture: A group in which members focus on the value and welfare of individual members more than on the group as a whole. p. 34

inferential statement: Conclusion arrived at from an interpretation of evidence. p. 57

informal roles: Behaviors enacted by particular group members although they are not explicitly assigned to do them. For example, some people serve informally as peacekeepers or jokesters. p. 172

informational interview: A meeting in which someone seeks knowledge from another, as when learning information to help with career success. p. 147

informative purpose statement: A sentence that tells what knowledge your audience will gain by listening to your speech. p. 218

informative speaking: Discourse in which the primary purpose is to describe, explain, or instruct. p. 216

in-group: Members of a social group with which one identifies. p. 33

insensitive listeners: Receivers who fail to recognize thoughts or feelings that are not directly expressed by a speaker, and instead accept the speaker's words at face value. p. 73

instrumental use of language: Focused on accomplishing tasks. p. 62

insulated listeners: Receivers who ignore undesirable information. p. 73

intergroup contact hypothesis: A proposition based on evidence that prejudice tends to diminish when people have personal contact with those they might otherwise stereotype. p. 115

interpersonal communication: Interaction between people who are part of a close and irreplaceable relationship in which they treat each other as unique individuals. pp. 5, 98

interpreting: A stage of listening in which a person takes into consideration the situation, the sender's nonverbal behaviors, and other contextual cues. p. 70

intersectionality theory: The idea that people are influenced in unique ways by the complex overlap and interaction of multiple identities. p. 38

intimacy: A state of closeness between people that can be manifested physically, intellectually, emotionally, and via shared activities. p. 128

intrapersonal communication: Occurs within a single person. p. 5

introduction (of a speech): The first structural unit of a speech, in which the speaker captures the audience's attention and previews the main points to be covered. p. 190

irrational thinking: Beliefs that have no basis in reality or logic; one source of debilitative speech anxiety. p. 200

jargon: The specialized vocabulary that is used as a kind of shorthand by people with common backgrounds and experience. p. 56

Johari window: A theoretical model that describes self-disclosure in the context of what individuals know and share about themselves. p. 101

kinesics: The study of nonverbal communication that involves body movement, facial expressions, gestures, and posture. p. 86

language: A collection of symbols, governed by rules and used to convey messages between individuals. p. 50

legitimate power: The ability to influence others based on one's official position in a group or organization. p. 170

line chart: Visual aid consisting of a grid that maps out the direction of a trend by plotting a series of points. p. 204

linear communication model: A characterization of communication as a one-way event in which a message flows from sender to receiver. p. 3

listening: A process in which the brain gives meaning to stimuli in the environment. p. 69

listening fidelity: The degree of congruence between what a listener understands and what a sender is attempting to communicate. p. 70

logos: Aristotle's term for the logical dimension of a persuasive speech. p. 222

longing (sibling relationship): A pattern in which siblings admire and respect one another but interact less frequently and with less depth than they would like. p. 123

low self-monitors: People who express what they are thinking and feeling without much attention to the impression their behavior creates. p. 27

low-context culture: A group in which people use language primarily to express thoughts, feelings, and ideas as directly as possible. p. 35

Managerial Grid: A model that portrays leadership on the basis of low to high emphasis on tasks and low to high emphasis on relationships. p. 165

manipulators: Movements in which a person fidgets with an object, clothing, or part of their body. p. 86

manuscript speeches: Speeches that are read word-for-word from a prepared text. p. 203

mass communication: The transmission of messages to large, usually widespread audiences via broadcast, print, online, and other forms of media, such as recordings and movies. p. 6

memorized speeches: Speeches learned and delivered by rote without a written text. p. 203

metacommunication: Messages that refer to other messages; communication about communication. p. 100

microaggressive language: Involves subtle, everyday messages that (intentionally or not) stereotype or demean people on the basis of sex, race, gender, appearance, or some other factor. p. 59

microresistance: Everyday behaviors that call attention to hurtful language and stereotypes that put some people at a disadvantage. p. 60

mindful listening: Active, high-level information processing. p. 77

model (in speeches and presentations): Replica of an object being discussed. Usually used when it would be difficult or impossible to use the actual object. p. 204

monochronic: A way of using time that emphasizes punctuality, schedules, and completing one task at a time. p. 89

Monroe's Motivated Sequence: A five-step persuasive organizational pattern. p. 224

multimodal: A listening environment that involves a complex array of colors, graphics, images, words, and communication channels. p. 71

narration: Presentation of speech-supporting material as a story with a beginning, middle, and end. p. 194

networking: The strategic process of meeting people and maintaining contacts that results in information and advice. p. 146

noise: External, physiological, and psychological distractions (not just sounds) that interfere with the accurate transmission and reception of a message. p. 3

nominal leaders: People who have been officially designated to be in charge of a group. p. 170

nonassertion: The inability or unwillingness to express one's thoughts or feelings. p. 137

nonverbal communication: A process in which meaning is expressed without using words. p. 82

number chart: Visual aid that lists numbers in tabular form in order to clarify information. p. 204

opinion statement: A statement based on the speaker's beliefs. p. 57

organizational chart: A word chart showing the relationships and hierarchy among various items. p. 204

organizational communication: Occurs within a structured collection of people in order to meet a need or pursue a goal. p. 5

orientation (forming) stage: A phase in problem-solving groups in which members become familiar with one another's ideas and tentatively volunteer their own. p. 172

out-group: People viewed as different from members of a social group with which one identifies. p. 33

paralanguage: Nonlinguistic means of vocal expression such as rate, pitch, and tone. p. 87

paraphrasing: Feedback in which the receiver rewords the speaker's thoughts and feelings. p. 76

passive aggression: An indirect expression of hostility, delivered in a way that allows the sender to maintain a facade of kindness. p. 138

pathos: The use of emotional appeals in a persuasive argument. p. 222

perceived self: The person an individual believes themselves to be in moments of candor. It may be the same or different from the presenting and ideal selves. p. 26

perception checking: A three-part method for verifying the accuracy of interpretations, including a description of what happened, two possible interpretations, and a request for confirmation of the interpretations. p. 24

permissive (parenting): An approach in which parents do not require children to follow many rules. p. 122

personal fable: A belief that one is special and different from everybody else. p. 41

persuasion: The act of motivating a listener, through communication, to change a particular belief, attitude, value, or behavior. p. 216

persuasive speaking: Reason-giving discourse that involves proposing claims and backing up those claims with proof. p. 216

phonological rules: Govern how sounds are combined to form words. p. 51

phubbing: Episodes in which people snub those around them by paying attention to their phones instead. p. 105

pie chart: A visual aid that divides a circle into wedges, representing percentages of the whole. p. 204

pitch: The highness or lowness of one's voice. p. 210

polychronic: A way of using time that emphasizes flexible schedules in which multiple tasks are pursued at the same time. p. 89

positive spirals: A pattern in which one person's confirming message leads to a confirming response from the other person and so on. p. 106

***post hoc* fallacy:** Fallacious reasoning that mistakenly assumes that one event causes another because they occur sequentially. p. 228

power: The ability to influence others' thoughts and/or actions. p. 170

power distance: The degree to which members of a group are willing to accept differences in power and status. p. 35

powerful language: Linguistic patterns considered to be clear, assertive, and direct. p. 53

powerless language: Linguistic patterns that suggest a speaker is uncertain, hesitant, or nonassertive; supposedly "powerless" speech can be effective and goal-oriented at times. p. 53

pragmatic rules: Govern how people use language in everyday interaction. p. 51

prejudice: An unfairly biased and intolerant attitude toward a group of people. p. 45

presenting self: The image a person presents to others. It may be identical to or different from the perceived and ideal selves. See also *face*. p. 26

procedural norms: Shared expectations that influence how a group operates or reaches decisions. p. 171

proof: Explanations of why your claims are true, along with evidence that backs up those claims. p. 223

proxemics: The study of how people use space. p. 89

pseudolistening: Pretending to pay attention without really thinking about what is being heard. p. 73

public communication: Occurs when a group becomes too large for all members to contribute; characterized by an unequal amount of speaking and by limited verbal feedback. p. 6

purpose statement: A complete sentence that describes precisely what a speaker wants to accomplish. p. 186

race: A social construct originally created to explain biological differences among people whose ancestors originated in different regions of the world. p. 38

rate: The speed at which a speaker utters words. p. 210

reasoning: The process of making claims and backing them up, logically and rationally. p. 225

receiver: One who notices and attends to a message. p. 3

***reductio ad absurdum* fallacy:** Fallacious reasoning that unfairly attacks an argument by extending it to such extreme lengths that it looks ridiculous. p. 228

referent power: The ability to influence others because one is liked or respected. p. 170

reflected appraisal: The influence of others on one's self-concept. p. 18

reflective thinking method: A structured problem-solving process for small groups introduced in 1910 by John Dewey and still in use, with some modifications, today. p. 178

reinforcement (performing) stage: A phase in problem-solving groups in which members endorse the decision they have made together. p. 173

relational dialectics: The theory that people in interpersonal relationships must deal with equally important, simultaneous, and opposing forces such as the need for both connection and autonomy, predictability and novelty, and openness and privacy. p. 134

relational listening: A listening style driven primarily by the goal of building emotional closeness with the speaker. p. 75

relational message: An often unstated dimension of a message that reflects how the communicator feels about the other person. p. 99

relational spiral: A communication pattern in which each person's message reinforces the other's so that messages become increasingly positive or negative. p. 106

relative words: Language in which meaning arises from comparisons. p. 55

remembering: The act of recalling previously introduced information. p. 70

residual message: The part of a message the receiver can recall later. p. 70

respect: The degree to which one holds another person in high esteem. p. 99

responding: Providing feedback in reaction to another person's behavior or speech. p. 70

reward power: The ability to influence others by granting or promising desirable consequences. p. 170

roles: Patterns of behavior expected of particular group members. p. 172

rule: An explicit, officially stated guideline that governs group functions and member behavior. p. 171

salience: How much weight people attach to cultural characteristics in a particular situation. p. 33

selection interview: A question and answer session to help a prospective employer evaluate how well a candidate qualifies for a job or other opportunity. p. 150

selective listeners: Receivers who respond only to messages that interest them. p. 73

self-concept: The relatively stable set of perceptions one holds of oneself. p. 17

self-disclosure: Deliberately revealing information about oneself that is significant and that would not normally be known by others. p. 101

self-esteem: The part of the self-concept that involves evaluations of self-worth. p. 17

self-fulfilling prophecy: A prediction or expectation of an event that makes the outcome more likely to occur than would otherwise have been the case. p. 19

self-monitoring: Paying close attention to social cues and to one's own behavior for the purpose of behaving appropriately in a given situation. p. 11

self-serving bias: The tendency to interpret and explain information in a way that casts the perceiver in a favorable way; also called fundamental attribution error. p. 20

self-serving lies: Attempts to manipulate a listener into believing something that is untrue, not primarily to protect the listener, but to advance the deceiver's agenda. p. 136

semantic rules: The rules that govern the meaning of language, as opposed to its structure. p. 51

sender: The originator of a message. p. 3

sex: A biological category such as female or male. p. 21

significant others: People whose opinions are considered important enough to affect one's self-concept strongly. p. 18

signposts: Words or phrases that emphasize the importance of what you are about to say. p. 219

situational leadership: A model that argues that effective leaders adapt their style to suit the circumstances, considering the nature of the challenge and the relationships of people involved. p. 165

slang: Language used by a group of people whose members belong to a similar coculture or other group. p. 56

slide deck: Collection of visual aids presented via presentation software. p. 206

slurring: The articulation error that involves overlapping the end of one word with the beginning of the next. p. 211

small group: A limited number of people (usually between 3 and 20) who interact in an interdependent way with one another over time to reach shared goals. p. 171

small group communication: Occurs within a group of a size that allows every member to participate actively with the other members. p. 5

social exchange theory: A model that suggests that people stay in relationships that offer rewards greater than or equal to the costs of being in the relationship. p. 113

social intelligence: The capacity to effectively negotiate complex social relationships and environments. p. 163

social loafing: Lazy behavior that some people use to avoid doing their share of the work. p. 171

social media: Electronic communication platforms that allow people to post, view, comment on, and share content. p. 6

social media snarks: People who post insulting comments about others. p. 40

social media trolls: People whose goal is to disrupt public discourse by posting false claims and prejudiced remarks, usually anonymously. p. 40

social norms: Shared expectations that influence how group members relate to one another. p. 171

social penetration model: A framework that describes how intimacy can be achieved via the breadth and depth of self-disclosure. p. 101

social roles: Patterns of behavior concerned with maintaining smooth personal relationships among group members. p. 172

specific purpose: The precise effect that the speaker wants to have on an audience. Expressed in the form of a purpose statement. p. 186

speech to change attitudes: Persuasion designed to change the way audiences think about a topic. p. 221

speech to change behavior: Persuasion designed to change audience actions. p. 221

stage hog: Someone who is more concerned with making their own points than with understanding others. p. 74

statistics: Numbers arranged or organized to show how a fact or principle is true for a large percentage of cases. p. 193

stereotyping: The perceptual process of applying exaggerated beliefs associated with a categorizing system. p. 45

stonewalling: A form of avoidance in which one person refuses to engage with the other. p. 139

subclaim: One of a series of statements that support a claim made by a speaker. p. 225

substitution: The articulation error that involves replacing part of a word with an incorrect sound. p. 211

supportive (sibling relationship): A pattern in which siblings talk regularly and consider themselves to be accessible and emotionally close to one another. p. 123

supportive listening: A listening approach meant to offer help or comfort to a speaker. p. 75

symbol: An arbitrary sign used to represent a thing, person, idea, event, or relationship in a way that makes communication possible. p. 50

syntactic rules: The rules that govern the ways that symbols can be arranged (e.g., sentence structure), as opposed to the meanings of those symbols. p. 51

target audience: The subgroup you must persuade to reach a goal. p. 221

task norms: Shared expectations that influence how group members handle the job at hand. p. 171

task roles: Patterns of behavior group members use to help solve a problem. p. 172

task-oriented listening: A listening style guided primarily by the receiver's goal of performing a specific job or task correctly. p. 76

testimony: Supporting material that proves or illustrates a point by citing an authoritative source. p. 194

thesis statement: A complete sentence describing the central idea of a speech. p. 186

Toulmin model: The guideline that reminds us to use evidence to back up a claim, as well as a warrant to tie the evidence and claim together. p. 226

trait theories of leadership: The belief (largely unsupported by research) that leadership ability is innate rather than learned. p. 165

transactional communication model: A characterization of communication as the simultaneous sending and receiving of messages in an ongoing, irreversible process. p. 3

transformational leadership: A model that defines leaders in terms of their devotion to helping a team fulfill an important mission. p. 166

transgender: Describes an individual whose gender is different from the biological sex attributed to them at birth. p. 21

transitions: Phrases that connect ideas in a speech by showing how one relates to the other. p. 192

truth bias: A tendency to assume that people are telling the truth. p. 85

uncertainty avoidance: The cultural tendency to seek stability and honor tradition instead of welcoming risk, uncertainty, and change. p. 35

understanding: The act of interpreting a message; involves syntactic, semantic, and pragmatic rules. p. 70

undifferentiated: A gender identity that involves being neither masculine nor feminine. p. 21

unfair discrimination: Depriving people of opportunities or equal treatment based on prejudice, stereotypes, or irrelevant factors. p. 45

values: Deeply rooted beliefs about a concept's inherent worth. p. 184

visual aids: Graphic devices used in a speech to illustrate or support ideas. p. 204

visual aspects of delivery: The speaker's appearance, movement, posture, facial expression, and eye contact during a speech. p. 208

visualization: A technique for behavioral rehearsal (e.g., for a speech) that involves imagining the successful completion of the task. p. 202

win–win problem solving: A means of resolving conflict in which the goal is a solution that satisfies the needs of everyone involved. p. 140

word chart: Visual depictions of key facts or statistics. p. 204

working outline: Constantly changing organizational aid used in planning a speech. p. 188

"you" language: Statements that contain an accusation, as in, "You are inconsiderate." p. 107

Credits

Photographs

Page ii ©tomwang; **1** © fizkes/Shutterstock; **2** © mangostar; **5** © ferli; **6** © dotshock; **7** © Cathy Yeulet; **8** © Dmytro; **10** © Katarzyna Białasiewicz; **11** © Blend Images; **16** © ljupco; **17** © Metta foto / Alamy Stock Photo; **20** © Nonwarit Pruetisirirot/123RF; **21** © visivasnc/123RF; **22** © StepanPopov/Shutterstock; **23** © milkos/123RF; **26** © Fisher Photostudio/Shutterstock.com; **27** © Fisher Photostudio/Shutterstock.com; **29** © Flamingo Images/Shutterstock; **32** © Michaeljung/Shutterstock; **33** Antonio Diaz/Shutterstock; **34** © Andy Dean/123RF; **35** © Odua Images/Shutterstock; **38** © Igor Kovalchuk/Shutterstock; **39** © V.S.Anandhakrishna/Shutterstock; **41** © iStock/Rawpixel; **43** © iStock/fizkes; **44** © iStock/fizkes; **45** © rawpixel/123RF; **46** © iStock/triloks; **49** © linear_design/Shutterstock; **50** © ljupco/123RF; **52** © iStock/MivPiv; **53** © iStock/sam thomas; **55** © iStock/Nuture; **57** © ImageFlow/Shutterstock; **59** © iStock/metamorworks; **61**© iStock/Dean Mitchell; **62** © Michael Jung/Shutterstock; **66** © Ljupco Smokovski/shutterstock; **67** © milkos/123RF; **69** © Susan Richey-Schmitz/123RF; **70** © Gladskikh Tatiana/Shutterstock.com; **71** © Steven Sallay/Shutterstock.covm; **73** © Marcos Mesa Sam Wordley/Shutterstock; **75** © WAYHOME studio/Shutterstock.com; **76** © Mark Adams/123RF; **81** © Luis Molinero/Shutterstock; **82** © Master1305/Shutterstock; **84** © iStock/g-stockstudio; **85** © ruigsantos/Shuttestock; **86** © iStock/jhorrocks; **87** © iStock/aldomurillo; **89** © Picsfive/Shutterstock; **91** © Mega Pixel/shutterstock; **93** © iStock/Prostock-Studio; **97** © stockphoto mania/shutterstock; **98** © marino bocelli/shutterstock; **99** © pchvector/123RF; **100** © Leo Cullum/Cartoonstock.com; **104** © Kamira/Shutterstock; **105** © ocusfocus/123RF; **106** © 3d_kot/Shutterstock; **111** © Nina Buday/Shutterstock; **112** © Monkey Business Images/Shutterstock; **113** © seventyfour74/123RF; **115** © Rawpixel/Shutterstock; **116** © Rawpixel/Shutterstock; **117** © Tammy Kay Photo/Shutterstock; **120** © Africa Studio/Shutterstock; **121** © Rido/Shutterstock; **122** © Nastyaofly/Shutterstock; **123** © iStock/SolStock; **127** © iStock/4x6; **128** © Olena Ponomarenko/123RF; **131** © iStock/Feedough; **132** © iStock/republica; **132** © Joingate/Shutterstock; **132** © iStock/themacx; **132** © iStock/adempercem; **134** © iStock/santypan; **136** © iStock/innovatedcaptures; **137** © Rido/Shutterstock; **139** © iStock/Neustockimages; **140** © iStock/fizkes; **141** © iStock/fizkes; **144** © zaidi razak/Shutterstock; **145** © fizkes/123RF; **146** © Toncsi/Shutterstock; **148** © iStock/alexmillos; **150** © MetokKarpo / Alamy Stock Vector; **153** © Andriy Popov/123RF; **154** © lightfieldstudios/123RF; **155** © Dragon Images/Shutterstock; **157** © mohd farid/Shutterstock.com; **162** © Kostiantyn Voitenko/Shutterstock; **163** © RomarioIen/shutterstock; **165** © Mr.Whiskey/Shutterstock; **168** © Karsten Schley/Cartoonstock.com; **170** © Marish/shutterstock; **174** © irstone/123RF; **175** © Flamingo Images/Shutterstock; **182** © iStock/damircudic; **183**© iStock/syahrir maulana; **187** © Loren Fishman/Cartoonstock.com; **188** © iStock/Nutthaseth Vanchaichana; **190** © Artur Szczybylo/123RF; **193** Cultura Creative (RF) / Alamy Stock Photo; **198** © Patrick Semansky/UPI/Shutterstock; **199** © iStock/vchal; **203** © iStock/Wavebreakmedia; **206** © iStock/gorodenkoff; **208** © iStock/laflor; **209** © iStock/SDI Productions; **210** © PhotoMediaGroup/Shutterstock.com; **212** © iStock/PixelsEffect; **215** © iStock/recep-bg; **216** © iStock/Andrew Rich; **218** © iStock/MarsYu; **221** © Daniele COSSU/Shutterstock; **222** RHONA WISE/AFP/Getty Images; **225** © Radachynskyi/iStock; **232** Courtesy of Marah J. Hardt; **233** Dr. Dwayne Meadows, NOAA/NMFS/OPR; **233** A. Dona Wiki Commons; **234** Photo by Sebastian Pena Lambarri on Unsplash; **237** Courtesy of Saeed Malami; **238** © Wolper/Warner Bros/Kobal/Shutterstock; **240** © emka74/Shutterstock; **241** Courtesy of Saeed Malami; **241** Courtesy of Saeed Malami

Texts, Tables, and Figures

Page 178 Adapted from Bilhart, J., & Galanes, G. Adapting problem-solving methods. *Effective group discussion* (10th ed.), p. 291. Copyright © 2001 Reprinted by permission of McGraw-Hill Companies, Inc.; **205** Image courtesy of Ben Armson; **220** New York Public Interest Research Group, Brooklyn College chapter. (2004). Voter registration project

Index